D0417839

The Economics of Sport

An International Perspective

Robert Sandy

Chair, Department of Economics, IUPUI
(Indiana University Purdue University of Indianapolis)

Peter J. Sloane

Director, WELMERC (The Welsh Economy Labour Market Evaluation and Research Centre), Department of Economics, University of Wales Swansea

Mark S. Rosentraub

Professor and Dean, Maxine Goodman Levin College of Urban Affairs, Cleveland State University

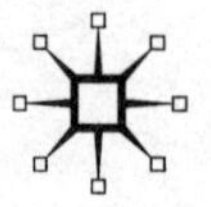

First published 2004 by
PALGRAVE MACMILLAN
Houndmills, Basingstoke, Hampshire RG21 6XS and
175 Fifth Avenue, New York, N.Y. 10010
Companies and representatives throughout the world

PALGRAVE MACMILLAN is the global academic imprint of the Palgrave Macmillan division of St. Martin's Press, LLC and of Palgrave Macmillan Ltd. Macmillan® is a registered trademark in the United States, United Kingdom and other countries. Palgrave is a registered trademark in the European Union and other countries.

ISBN 0–333–79271–8 hardback
ISBN 0–333–79272–6 paperback

This book is printed on paper suitable for recycling and made from fully managed and sustained forest sources.

A catalogue record for this book is available from the British Library.

Library of Congress Cataloging-in-Publication Data
Sandy, Robert
The economics of sport : an international perspective / Robert Sandy, Peter J. Sloane, Mark S. Rosentraub.
p. cm.
Includes bibliographical references and index.
ISBN 0–333–79271–8 (cloth)
1. Sports—Economic aspects. 2. Professional sports—Economic aspects. I. Sandy, Robert. II. Sloane, Peter J. III. Title.
GV716.R65 2004
338.4′7796—dc22 2003063696

10 9 8 7 6 5 4 3 2 1
13 12 11 10 09 08 07 06 05 04

Printed and bound in Great Britain by
Creative Print & Design (Wales), Ebbw Vale

Contents

List of boxes, tables and figures

Boxes

Tables

Figures

Acknowledgements

The authors and publishers are grateful to the Competition Commission for permission to use material contained in Table 6.1; to Kagan World Media for permission to use the data contained in Table 6.3; to Blackwell Publishing for permission to use Tables 8.8 to 8.10 that previously appeared in *Public Administration Review*; and to Ted Bulthraup for permission to reproduce his letter to the editor of the *Indianapolis Star* in Box 9.1. Every effort has been made to contact all the copyright-holders, but if any have been inadvertently omitted the publishers will be pleased to make the necessary arrangement at the earliest opportunity.

Preface

Although the economics of sports is a relatively small field in terms of courses offered, there are now at least three other textbooks on the economics of sports, all published between 2000 and 2003 (Downward and Dawson, 2000; Fort, 2003; Leeds and Von Allmen, 2002). This spurt of new books in a field that until recently had no textbooks raises two questions: why did these books come out at about the same time and why are we offering a competitor? The main reason for these new books is a burgeoning interest in the economics of sports on the part of economists, public officials, lawyers, business leaders and students. The sports pages of newspapers now constantly have articles about public subsidies for new stadiums, labor/management disputes, record-setting payments for players, billion-dollar contracts for broadcast rights, and the merging of sports teams into entertainment businesses. Legal and regulatory decisions and new laws such as the EU Bosman decision, the US Congress Curt Flood Law, and the UK Monopolies and Mergers Commission BSkyB/ Manchester United ruling are reshaping the market for sports. At the same time that news stories brought these issues to students' attention, economists have made rapid progress in analyzing these markets. There is a new *Journal of Sports Economics* and over a thousand articles on the economics of sports.

From a pedagogical perspective, the economics of sports is a wonderful subject. For example, a season ticket is really a complex financial contract with uncertainty over the quality of the team, the value of ticket renewal rights, and the option to purchase post-season tickets. The effects of monopoly power to raise ticket prices, to keep down the number of teams, to force municipalities to subsidize stadiums, and to convince Congress to legislate exemptions from the antitrust laws are all compelling topics. What economists have concluded about the development effects of local professional sports teams and the intangible benefits is largely, if not completely, at variance with public perceptions. What other industry has precise data for measuring worker productivity and assessing all the possible sources of discrimination?

Sports economics provides an excellent framework for discussing standard economic topics such as marginal revenue applied to ticket pricing, capital asset pricing as applied to the selling prices of sports franchises, cartel behavior as applied to the National Collegiate Athletic Association (NCAA) and the major sports leagues of North America. We think the economics of sports will become as popular an upper-level economics course as more traditional subjects such as labor economics or money and banking courses. No economics or public policy instructor who teaches the economics of sports need be embarrassed about teaching a 'lightweight' course. Properly designed, an economics of sports course would be a valuable addition to the undergraduate economics curriculum.

The second question is, why are we offering another book? This book differs in three respects. First, it is intended to be the most comprehensive. Second, it is more rigorous. This textbook builds on a foundation of introductory microeconomics and carries much of its discussion at the level of an intermediate microeconomics textbook. There are some calculus examples and exercises and optional sections where the material suits that treatment. The calculus-based exercises are identified. Third and most distinctively, this book takes a truly comparative approach. The ability to compare different institutional settings illuminates the economic concepts. For example, what are the consequences of the European promotion/relegation system versus the North American system of having teams with permanent major league status? Why does the USA have a gigantic collegiate sports system while the commercial potential of collegiate sports elsewhere remains unexploited? Why are sports broadcast rights in Europe so much lower than in the USA?

Professional sports are undergoing a rapid transformation towards globalization. There may also be a trend toward domination by broadcast/entertainment conglomerates such as Rupert Murdoch's Fox and Sky networks. The pace of fundamental changes will keep professional sports in the daily headlines. New leagues are being formed with different business models such as league-wide ownership of the teams. A 'super league' of top football (soccer) clubs is under discussion in Europe. Soccer is trying again to made headway in the North American market and the National Basketball Association (NBA) and the National Football League (NFL) are marketing their games in Europe. Protracted strikes have cost the players and the team owners billions of dollars in North America. As the total profits from sports broadcasts and team ownership rise, there will be pressure for such strikes to spread to Europe as well. A textbook with an international perspective, focusing primarily on the USA, Canada, Europe and Australia, is the only way to explain these changes in coherent manner and show the common issues across countries.

Note: Words in **bold** in the text can be found in the Glossary at the end of the book.

List of abbreviations

ABA	American Basketball Association
AFL	American Football League
AIAW	Association of Intercollegiate Athletics for Women
AP	Associated Press
BEA	Bureau of Economic Analysis
DGR	defined gross revenue
FA	Football Association
FIFA	La Federation Internationale de Football Associations
IFC	Independent Football Commission
IOC	International Olympics Committee
ITC	Independent Television Commission
IUPUI	Indiana University-Purdue University Indianapolis
LPGA	Ladies Professional Golfers Association
MIT	Massachusetts Institute of Technology
MLB	Major League Baseball
MLS	Major League Soccer
MMC	Monopolies and Mergers Commission
MRP	marginal revenue product
NAIA	National Association of Intercollegiate Athletics
NASCAR	North American Stock Car Racing Association
NBA	National Basketball Association
NCAA	National Collegiate Athletic Association
NFL	National Football League
NIT	National Invitational Tournament
NLSY	National Longitudinal Survey of Youth
OFT	Office of Fair Trading
OPEC	Organization of Petroleum-Exporting Countries
PGA	Professional Golfers Association
PL	Premier League
PPV	pay-per-view
PSL	personal seat license
SAT	Standard Assessment Tests
UEFA	Union of European Football Associations

USFL	United States Football League
WHA	World Hockey Association
WNBA	Women's National Basketball Association
WNSL	Wembley National Stadium Ltd
XFL	World Wrestling Federation's Football League (US)

1 Introduction

Why study the economics of professional sports? Why study the economics of the revenue-generating amateur sports such as the Olympics and intercollegiate sports in the USA? The answer 'Because these sports represent a substantial share of the gross national product' is simply wrong. The spectator sports industry for both professional and amateur sports is a trivial component of all national economies. In the USA its revenues are dwarfed by mundane industries such as meatpacking. The total revenue in professional sports is about 12 per cent of the total revenue in meatpacking. Two correct answers to the question are that the sports industry raises fascinating economic questions and that sports have been a high-profile component of all societies for more than 4,000 years. The Greeks and the Romans made sport a central part of their society. They built their cities with sports facilities as the centerpieces. Mayan civilization in Central America also emphasized sport. The public enthusiasm for spectator sports continues unabated in modern times. There are courses in the economics of sports rather than the economics of meatpacking because sport is a rich area for economic analysis and because societies care a great deal about sports. Beginning in the 1950s, economists have published hundreds of papers on the sports industry. The economics of sport is now a significant branch of economics.

What makes the economics of sports especially intriguing? Professional teams are usually local monopolies which have exemptions from the **antitrust** statutes (competition policies in the UK) that apply to other businesses. One interesting question is how their monopoly status affects their interactions with their players. If the meatpacking companies got together and agreed never to hire a worker who was working for another meatpacker, they would be in serious legal trouble. Until recently athletes were tied to one team that could sell their contracts to another team or keep renewing the contracts indefinitely. This exclusivity was called the **reserve clause** in US baseball. The equivalent restriction on labor mobility in European soccer was called the **retain and transfer system**. In the USA, sports reserve clauses were eliminated through a series of contract negotiations with the players' unions. Management was under pressure because both sides were increasingly convinced that the reserve clause would be ended by court rulings. In Europe the **Bosman** case suddenly ended the retain and transfer system. Some elements of monopoly power over sports labor still remain. All of the US professional leagues have annual drafts of new players (see **player draft**). They agree not to make offers to players drafted by other teams. In Europe there is no parallel to the US draft of what are primarily college athletes.

Teams are also generally monopolies in their product markets. In the USA they have exclusive territorial rights. Teams that are members of the same league cannot enter their market without their approval. The largest cities in the USA have two professional teams in the same sport but beyond those exceptions there is one team per sport per city. The Los Angeles, New York and Chicago metropolitan areas have two baseball teams each. New York and Los Angeles have two basketball teams as well. The New York metropolitan area has three hockey teams. Similarly, London, Birmingham, Liverpool and Manchester have multiple soccer teams in the English Premier League. Although the overall supply of teams in Europe is much greater than in the USA, the common arrangement throughout Europe is one team per city. An interesting economic question is how the monopoly status in the local market affects the actions of the team in setting ticket prices and in negotiating with their host cities.

Another interesting economic and social issue is the apparent public concern with athletes' salaries and their relative indifference to the earnings of movie stars. The public seems to be more bothered by athletes' high salaries than by movie stars' salaries. This difference in indignation is puzzling because both professional athletes and movie stars are performers who are paid for their ability to attract a paying audience. Perhaps the movie star salaries seem less salient because they are not local performers. Perhaps amateur athletes resent the high pay for athletic skills at a level just slightly higher than their own. From an economics perspective the interesting question is what determines the players' salaries? The sports industry is unique in that there are detailed statistics on player performance so that it is possible to estimate the relationship between players' game statistics and their team's revenue. It is one of the few industries in which the **marginal revenue product** generated by each worker can be estimated with a degree of precision. A related question is whether teams exploit their players by paying them less than their marginal revenue product or perhaps teams overbid and pay more than marginal revenue product for players in an attempt to win championships.

There are several other interesting economic questions related to player salaries. Do player salaries drive ticket prices? This is a claim made by many owners. Also, because it is possible to estimate the impact of each player's performance on the team's attendance and its revenues, economists have tried to determine whether there is discrimination in player salaries, e.g., do team owners pay higher salaries to white players than to black players of identical ability?

There are some basic structural issues in the organization and presentation of a professional sport that differentiate it from other industries and that have clear economic implications. The next paragraph has a description of an unnamed sport: try to guess which sport as you read the description. The example will then be used to illustrate the connection between these structural issues and certain economic questions.

> In this unnamed sport individual players sign exclusive contracts with one owner. Ownership in the sport can be a highly profitable investment. The players first go to a school where they learn the basic skills of the sport. The schooling can last up to four years. The sport has huge popularity. The results of games and the merits of individual players are the subject of constant conversation. The sport's symbols and motifs are widely used on cups, lamps, and other household decoration. The games

> are attended by politicians and other public figures. The players get salaries six to ten times as high as other workers, even salaried professionals such as doctors or professors. Players are rated in one of three categories that are ordered in terms of the quality. A last hint – a player who has never been in a professional game is called a 'tyro'. Any ideas?

The games described above are the gladiatorial combats in the ancient Roman Republic and Empire. The schools were called *ludi* and a free person (as opposed to a slave) could sign a contract with a school owner entitling himself to generous room and board and training in return for agreeing to fight in the arena over a fixed period. There was a season each year in which a series of games were held. Most combats were one-on-one affairs. Some of the contestants were free and others were slaves who had no choice about their occupation. Fairly late in the history of the Roman Empire a law was passed forbidding the sale of a slave to a gladiatorial school unless the slave had committed a serious crime and was convicted in a public trial. Gladiatorial games were popular for about 900 years from the earliest times in the Roman republic to the end of the Empire. Recent movies such as Russell Crowe's *Gladiator* show that the sport still has some public interest.

The reason for dredging up this historical example is that it makes clear some of the economic issues inherent in sport. Roman citizens wanted to see close contests and the quality rankings, such as being identified as a 'major league player' as well as the individual gladiator's records, gave them information about how evenly the pairs were matched. They preferred seeing the most skilled players and would pay more to be able to see them. The risks of injury or death for the players were obvious. One estimate is that one in four were killed. The salaries for free men had to be high enough to compensate for these risks. Even for the slaves the school owners had substantial investments in their purchase price and the costs of four years of intense training and room and board. When a promoter hired, say, 10 pairs of gladiators from a particular school, the contract would specify their classifications, the base price, and an additional indemnity to the school owner for each gladiator killed. During the Roman Republic in 27 AD one enterprising promoter built a wooden arena specifically to hold one gladiatorial game. Given his interest in making the largest possible profit, he put up an ultra low-cost arena. However, he went too far in his cost-cutting as the stands collapsed and killed most of the spectators.

Cities all over the empire from Jerusalem to London put on annual municipal games. Citizens were entitled to free tickets to municipal games at the back or top of the arena. They could upgrade their tickets to courtside and also pay extra for seats under awnings. When the municipalities bid against each other for the services of the gladiatorial schools they raised the price of a gladiatorial pair with a given rating. To help these cities out the Roman Senate passed a law fixing the maximum price a city could bid on a gladiatorial pair. Later in the book we will compare this approach to the current bidding by cities for sports franchises.

What is different or missing from this gladiator story that is present in modern professional sports? Team play was unusual because it was expensive. If you had a team of ten gladiators trying to kill or defeat another team of ten gladiators, what would otherwise be an all afternoon show with a series of ten pairs could be over in 15 minutes. Sometimes the emperor or, during the republic, a wealthy politician would pay for a battle in the Coliseum in Rome but the expense was beyond the resources of a promoter or a municipality. Of course, some modern sports are still primarily competitions between two players instead of teams, such as tennis, professional wrestling and kick boxing. The Coliseum was built specifically for gladiatorial games. It held 40–45,000 seated spectators and 5,000 more standing at the back. There were smaller but similarly shaped arenas in every city. Without local teams playing against out-of-town teams, the identification of a team with the municipality, say the Pompeii Slaughterers or the Londinium Britons, is lost. Promoters tried to build up identification by dressing and arming the individual gladiators as Gauls or Thracians, so that the fans could cheer on their favorites. The practice was similar to the personae and costumes adopted by professional wrestlers in the USA. Another way of generating fan interest was to provide novelty. Bill Veeck was copying a Roman emperor's midget gladiators when he had a midget batting for the St. Louis Browns. Another novelty was pairs of female gladiators fighting in leather bikinis. The main point in this gladiator example is that not much of what we think of as the features of modern professional sport was missing in ancient Rome. Admittedly, there were no shoe contracts, no endorsements contracts from McDonalds, and no televised games. The impact of broadcasting on sports is the subject of Chapter 6 below.

What influences do the gladiatorial games have on modern sports? Many modern venues are called the *Coliseum* or the *Arena*. The origin of the word 'arena' is a Latin word for the sand-covered area where the gladiators fought. The sand was raked over the spilled blood. The word 'stadium' has a Greek origin. It refers to a measure of distance, a stadia, or 607 feet, that was used in foot races in the Olympic games. A neophyte in any endeavor is still called a *tyro* (you can look it up), but the word is not common on sports pages which are typically written at the reading level of a 10 year old. The ceremony of lining up the players and singing the national anthem before a game begins mimics the parade of gladiators and the homage to the Emperor before gladiatorial games began. These borrowings from antiquity are often quite deliberate. There are twentieth-century stadiums that look like the Coliseum in Rome.

The gladiator example illustrates the structure of sporting events. *The essential feature of a sporting contest is uncertainty over the outcome.* Some people bet on the games and just care about the point spread, but most spectators want to see a close game in which both sides have a chance to win. Mere athleticism without the uncertainty would draw few fans. For example, male ballet stars can leap as high, jump as far, and turn as sharply as the most accomplished professional athletes. Hardly anyone wins or loses at ballet; as a result it does not draw a mass audience. Similarly, the Harlem Globetrotters as a **barnstorming** team draw much less attention than National Basketball Association (NBA) basketball as the outcomes of the games are well-known, do not count towards a championship, and involve players of very different skill levels.

The central feature of the exemption from the antitrust laws for professional sports teams, that they can agree not to bid against the other teams in a league for player's services, is that sport is unlike any other business in that it requires a competitor. A baker can exist without another baker, and would indeed prefer to have monopoly control, but a team needs another team to attract customers and this gives sport its unique feature which has been recognized by courts and legislatures. This book comes back to this issue to see if the argument is sensible on theoretical grounds and if there is any empirical support. The Bosman case gives us the opportunity to see what happens to competitiveness in a league that shifts from no **free agency** to complete free agency. A *free agent* is player who can sell his services to any team without an obligation on the buying team to pay a transfer fee or any other compensation such as the contracts of other players.

The owners or promoters of a professional league want to convince the public that the league's players are the most talented athletes in the world. They would like to have news stories about the players lauding their skills, prowess, dedication and intensity. In the meantime, they would like to pay them as little as possible. If there was a competitive market for putting on games (i.e., anyone could field a team), promoters would bid up the players' salaries to the point that, adjusted for risk, they would just earn the opportunity cost of the money they invested. Imagine a situation where each city has several municipally owned arenas suitable for basketball which could be rented for a season, and anyone could form a team by hiring players and offering to play other teams. This structure would provide essentially free entry into the basketball market. Free entry means that new firms can enter at the same cost as the existing firms. As you learned in introductory economics, free entry usually implies that profits will be pushed down to a normal rate of return.

What is different here from free entry into the market for producing wheat is that such unstructured competition would generate much less overall revenue than a restricted sports market. You can generate more fan interest if, in addition to skilled players, you have rivalries, league standings and championships. Think of what the National Collegiate Athletic Association (NCAA) tournament in the USA has done to the popularity of college basketball. For a contrary example, think of how having four or five different world champions in professional boxing sanctioned by different organizations has diluted interest in that sport. There are examples of free markets in the beginnings of professional baseball, but for nearly 100 years competitors to an existing league have come into the business as rival leagues. All of these leagues have had some sort of internal agreement in which the member teams do not hire away players from competing teams. *An essential feature of professional sports are structures that determine a league champion.* Some sort of contractual control by team owners over the players is universal in team sports. Individual sports such as tennis and golf do not have owners with contracts for the players' services.

For most cities a professional team is a *natural monopoly.* Once one team is entrenched in the city no other team could hope to make a profit. It is also a *monopoly* in the sense that it sells a service that does not have close substitutes. How many people would switch to seeing an amateur team play or a lower division professional team play in place of a major league team in the same sport if the latter raised its price by 10 per cent? The technical term here is the **cross-price elasticity of demand**. It is near zero. The cross-price elasticity of demand is also low for other sports. For example, how many people would switch their season's ticket from an NBA basketball to a National Football League (NFL) football team in response to a 10 per cent price increase by the NBA team? There might be more of a switch to watching the NBA team in bars or watching a video or a movie. Being a monopoly does not imply a zero cross-elasticity for all other goods. It simply means that there are no goods with high cross-elasticities.

If there is only one arena or stadium suitable for a sport in a city, ownership (or else holding a long-term lease with exclusive rights) is crucial to maintaining the monopoly position. A rival league cannot put a team into a city when there is no place to play. In the USA some stadiums or arenas are privately owned but most are municipally owned and leased to the sports team. The cities view these facilities as an investment that draws tourists, new businesses and favorable publicity. They can cost as much as $400 million. If, as is sometimes done, they are offered rent-free to the team, the stadium can represent a massive public subsidy to the professional team. Think of it this way: in a city of a million people each person, on average, owns a $400 share of the debt used to finance the stadium. Or, conversely, if it was financed by tax revenue, each person paid $400 in taxes to build the stadium. Usually there is a mix of debt and accumulated tax revenue financing. *At what point is a city paying so much in subsidies that it would be better off without the team?* This is the key question facing the mayor in any US city threatened with the loss of a team if it does not build a new stadium or raise its subsidy.

Is this municipal investment in a stadium a new problem? Let us look at another antiquarian example, this time from the Middle Ages: the Cathedral of Chartres. Chartres is a small town about an hour south of Paris. In the Middle Ages it was a pilgrimage town. People went there to see a piece of cloth, the Sancta Camisia, taken from the dress Mary wore when the she gave birth to Jesus. In 1194 the Cathedral housing this relic burned to the ground. The cardinal told the crowd that there had been a miracle; the cloth had survived the fire unharmed. He also said that the Virgin Mary told him that she wanted to have a new cathedral built to house the cloth. Medieval cathedrals were made out of hand-cut stone blocks. So were the Roman arenas, but the difference in wealth was such that most Cathedrals took over

200 years build and the Roman arenas five to ten years. This is a very durable kind of construction. Some small Roman arenas are still being used for bullfights in Spain, while others are still used as outdoor theaters in France.

What is the connection between Chartres and modern sports arenas? What is the modern day counterpart to the pilgrims? Tourists come to mind. Off the main hall in the Cathedral there are private chapels originally owned by various French nobles. When they wanted to pray they closed the door to their chapel and communed with the Virgin in solitude. They had to pay heavily for this privilege. What is the modern day counterpart to these private chapels? Think of sky boxes (also called luxury suites). There are large stained glass windows all over the building. Without artificial light the design was intended to let in as much daylight as possible. The windows at Chartres were mostly donated by local merchants. The windows listed the donors and they were woven into the biblical scenes depicted in the window. For example, the window of Jesus with Mary Magdalene was donated by the prostitutes of Chartres. What is the modern day counterpart to these windows? Think of the signs naming the stadium after a corporation and advertisements along the side of the field. Was the Cathedral of Chartres a good municipal investment? It is usually thought of as an expression of religious fervor rather than commercial interest but it was certainly both. It still draws plenty of tourists. Basketball arenas are thought to have a 25-year life. The stadiums are more durable and are expected to last 30 years before major renovations are required. Many become economically obsolete before they wear out because they lack sky boxes and other amenities. Chartres may have been a better municipal investment.

Another interesting aspect of sports economics is why are there different structures in the USA and Europe. For example, why are collegiate sports in the USA as big financially as the professional leagues while collegiate sports in Europe are financially invisible? Why have unions of professional athletes had such a small effect in Europe compared to unions of professional athletes in the USA? In general, in Europe the legal environment is much more favorable to labor unions and they represent a much higher fraction of the labor force, but US professional athlete unions have forced the removal of reserve clauses, negotiated the fraction of all revenue that must be spent on player salaries, and capped the size of team rosters (see **team roster limits**). There is no counterpart to these salary-raising measures among European professional athletes' unions. The third fundamental difference is that no US league demotes its member teams to a lower division for poor athletic performance. League membership in the US is permanent unless the league buys out the interest of an existing team. All of the European soccer (football in the UK) leagues allow for promotion and relegation. The worst performing teams in the top division are demoted and the best performing teams in the next lower division are promoted. These differences raise two fundamental questions. Why are the USA and Europe so different and what are the consequences of these differences? This book pays great attention to such differences in sport structures. The key is to understand how different economic incentives in each system lead to the current organization. As economists we would hate to rely on history or habit or chance as explanations.

The organization of the book is first to consider whether the owners of professional sports teams are **profit maximizers** and whether the owners' objectives could be different in the USA and Europe. Next the book considers the fundamentals of demand for tickets to sporting events and the complications of season tickets and renewal rights. The fourth chapter is on the labor market for players and the fifth is on discrimination in professional sports. The next chapter is on sponsorship and broadcast revenues. Chapter 7 is on league organization and cartel behavior; it also discusses antitrust policy in the US and competition policy in the UK and the European Union. Chapter 8 seeks to answer whether professional sports help develop local economies by increasing the number of jobs or per capita income. Chapter 9 discusses stadium financing and public subsidies. Chapter 10 is on individual sports such as golf and tennis. Chapter 11 is on intercollegiate sports in the US. The last chapter is on governments' role in sports including international competition, such as the Olympic Games or the World Cup.

2 Club and league objectives: profit versus utility maximization

Chapter goals

This chapter attempts to explain the importance of the objectives of club owners and league organizations. In North America economists generally assumed that both bodies attempt to maximize profit (see **profit maximization**), the normal assumption for other industries. In Europe more stress has been placed on **utility maximization** in which winning games is given pre-eminence. To some extent owners may choose between these objectives because they have a degree of monopoly power.

It is shown that very different predictions follow depending on which assumption of maximizing behavior is made and that the attempt to maximize games won may lead to product market instability. Objectives will also be affected by the extent to which clubs are publicly traded, the extent to which clubs are geographically mobile and the extent to which there is a **principal-agent problem**.

Are the motives of team owners and leagues important?

A first important question in studying the economics of sport is what are the objectives of the team owners and the leagues? The monopoly position of most sports clubs makes the question of motives more important than the objectives of owners in other industries because monopolies have much more discretion over pricing and output levels than do competitive firms. A firm's motives lead to predictions about its behavior on economic decisions such as pricing, hiring labor and location. In professional team sports we have to consider not only the objectives of the club owners but also of the league itself. The question of profit maximization versus utility maximization can be viewed at two levels: do individual team owners try to maximize team profits and do leagues try to maximize joint league profits?

The traditional assumption of profit maximization has been maintained in most analyses of North American professional teams. However, in the theory of the firm alternatives such as sales revenue maximization, growth maximization and utility maximization have been advocated (Baumol, 1959; Marris, 1964; Williamson, 1963). Further, the owners of clubs are frequently wealthy fans who may treat their team not as a business but rather as a consumption activity from which they derive utility. The North American literature has tended to de-emphasize utility maximization on the grounds that there is no evidence that the owners, whether they are sports fans or large publicly-traded corporations, have received less than the market rate of return on their investment. Hardly any North American team in the four major leagues loses money over a series of years. Even on rare occasions when teams have an operating loss over several years the owner can recoup these losses by selling the franchise at a profit or by relocating. In contrast, in Europe hardly any soccer, rugby or cricket club makes consistent profits. They only remain in business through donations from wealthy directors and owners, or donations from supporters' clubs (an organized fan club tied to a particular team). It is of course possible that the objectives of sporting entrepreneurs vary from one country to another. Differing tastes by owners in different countries is an unsatisfactory explanation for differences in behavior. Economists try to explain differences in behavior on the basis of prices and incentive structures. Differences in tastes cannot be tested.

North America versus Europe

There is some indirect evidence suggesting that US owners maximize profits. What, other than profit maximization, could the owners of so many US teams be up to when they move their teams from city to city in response to the increases in stadium subsidies? Al Davis has moved his Raiders football team three times in the last 20 years. Team owners such as Art Modell (formerly of the Cleveland Browns and now of the Baltimore Ravens of the NFL) and the late Jim Irsay (formerly of the Baltimore Colts and now of the Indianapolis Colts) faced death threats from irate fans when they moved their teams. Presumably the extra profits helped pay for their bodyguards. One might argue that these owners relocated because they thought the higher subsidies would help them pay for stronger teams. However, none of these teams has been a consistent powerhouse in its division after its move (or moves). It is very hard to point to any motive other than profit maximization for these relocations.

There is also some indirect evidence that owners do not maximize profits. In the USA a few owners in a few years obviously treated their teams as expensive hobbies. They spent more than could conceivably be justified on the basis of future profits generated by the team. They were more interested in winning than in making a profit. Sports teams that are not publicly traded at least have the possibility of choosing not to maximize profits. Privately held firms do not have to worry about being taken over by a corporate raider. The best example of the 'hobby' owner is probably Freddie Debartelo, who owned the San Francisco Forty-Niners of the NFL. NFL teams are so flush with equally shared television money that it is hard for any team, even in the smallest NFL market, to lose money. However, prior to the NFL salary cap, Debartelo may have spent enough on his players to actually do it.

Forty-five of the owners of 115 major league teams were on the *Forbes* list of the 400 richest people in the USA in 1999 (Siegfried and Peterson, 2000). That means that they each had assets of least $500 million. Obviously, any of those 45 has enough money, provided they are willing to liquidate some of their other business interests and no one else is trying to buy all of the best free agents in their sport in the same year, to put together a championship team. Similarly, the UK has extremely wealthy club owners, including the late

Jack Walker of Blackburn Rovers and Sir Jack Hayward of Wolverhampton Wanderers. These owners could buy championship teams year in and year out. However, the ability of either US or UK owners to spend more on player talent than would maximize profits does not tell us if they actually do it.

Over a 20-year period starting in 1980 there appear to be just three clear exceptions to profit maximization in the USA. In addition to the one described as the best example, Debartelo and the Forty-Niners in the early 1980s, the others are currently the New York Yankees under George Steinbrenner and the Washington Redskins under Daniel Snyder. In terms of team-years there were about 10 clear exceptions to profit maximization in the more than 2,000 team-years over the two decades. If a similar percentage of mid-sized privately held companies were obviously not profit maximizing either by hiring too many workers or selling their products or services at a below profit-maximizing price, very few economists would abandon profit maximization as the basic description of overall industry behavior.

Anecdotes about owners who are colorful characters, such as Debartelo, may be interesting or amusing but an understanding of overall owner behavior requires a more systematic description of the incentives they face and a careful empirical analysis of their behavior. Before considering whether the owners of professional sports teams generally maximize profits, it would help to fit this question into a broader context and to start by discussing whether businesses overall try to maximize profits. Most owners of firms have little choice about whether to try or not try to maximize profits. In a perfectly competitive industry the firm's owner has no discretion over prices and has to worry about being able to cover his or her costs. A *perfectly competitive industry* means that there are so many firms that each one treats the market price as fixed and that there are no barriers to the entry of new firms. In the USA wheat farmers are the standard example of firms in a perfectly competitive industry. Although few industries fit the strict definition of **perfect competition**, many industries are so highly competitive that the owners have almost no discretion when it comes to trying to maximize profits.

Even in industries with few competitors, publicly traded firms have to worry about being taken over if someone thinks that they can make more profits by installing a new management. A corporate raider can make many millions of dollars in a few days by ousting the management of a firm that did not pursue maximum profits and replacing it with a new management that would. The financial sections of newspapers constantly have stories about firms being taken over, unproductive workers being laid off or divisions being sold off, all followed by sharp increases in the value of the firm's stock.

In terms of the incentives for profit maximization, there are two fundamental differences between the major league teams in the USA and the UK. First, professional sports teams in the USA are usually local monopolies with permanent major league status; poor performance on the field does not cause relegation to the next lower level. The second difference is that US leagues will not allow another member of the league to locate within a team's exclusive territory. In the UK additional teams in a city can be promoted into the Premier League. London alone generally has at least five Premier League teams. In comparison, the largest US cities – New York, Los Angeles and Chicago – usually have one major league team in a given sport. The few exceptions (two baseball teams in New York and Chicago, and two football, basketball and hockey teams in the New York area) were either created through a merger with a competing league or play in distant locations such as Long Island and New Jersey.

Within very broad limits, the owners of major league teams in the USA can field as good or as bad a team as they want. The absence of the threat of relegation gives them much more freedom. In the late 1970s Charlie Finley's Oakland Athletics were one of the best teams in baseball. He discovered that Oakland residents cared so little for baseball that he could not make a profit even in a season when his team had won the World Series. He held a 'fire sale' offering the contracts of every good player he had. The league disallowed some of these sales as not in the best interest of baseball. Two decades later, Wayne Huzinga's Miami Marlins were a World Series winning baseball team. Huzinga also held a post-victory fire sale and the team went from finishing in first to finishing in last place. This time around the league did not intervene.

In the UK the case that at least a fraction of the owners do not maximize profits seems more plausible. Many (if not most) UK teams consistently lose money and have their losses covered out of their owners' pockets. Part of the difference between the USA and the UK is that the distinction between major and minor league teams is not as sharp. The big name teams, such as Manchester United and Arsenal in the English Premier League, are always going to be in the majors but teams from cities near the bottom of the Premiership table in terms of population and income can float in and out. The big name teams in the UK face similar incentives and have similar finances when compared to major league teams in the USA. However, the revenues of UK Premier League teams with a tiny population base are more like a single A (fourth division) US baseball team. For example, two teams in the Scottish Premier League are trying to make a living from the 145,000 people in the city of Dundee. A typical single A team baseball team (the lowest division) in the USA has a larger population base than 75,000. With so little money at stake in such a small market, it is more plausible that someone might be willing to treat owning the team as a hobby. But there may be limits on the extent to which individuals are prepared to do this (see Box 2.1).

In the UK 25 professional soccer (football) teams are publicly traded. Very few of these teams ever earn enough of a profit in accounting terms to give their owners a better return than having invested the money in a bank savings account. Indeed, some of these teams have consistent operating losses (see Deloitte Touche's *Annual Survey*). However, many investors in the stocks of the more prominent teams are gambling that cable or entertainment networks will pay large sums to get a controlling interest. A ruling in 1999 by the UK Monopolies and Mergers Commission (MMC) against the take over of

Manchester United by Rupert Murdoch's BSkyB satellite network depressed the stock prices of all 25 traded clubs.

Box 2.1 Money out of the folds of the miser's toga

The 1998/99 season was a mediocre one for the Aberdeen Dons of the Scottish Premier League. Their on-field troubles led to a curious article in the local *Press and Journal*. The head of the Dons supporters' club blamed the poor showing on the miserliness of the team owner. The owner of the Dons, a wealthy builder, was unwilling to open his wallet wide enough to sign some good players that other teams were offering to sell. The talent level of the Dons was clearly slipping further and further behind that of the league's big name teams, Rangers and Celtic, which are both based in the large Glasgow market. The Dons had been losing money for years, unsurprisingly for a team with a population base of just 250,000 competing against teams with much larger population bases. What was curious in the article was the threat by the leader of the Dons supporters' club. He said if the current owner was unwilling to spend more of his own money to sign a reasonable level of football talent, the supporters' club would find another owner for the team who would. Clearly, the expectations on the part of the fans placed on the owners of small-market football clubs in the UK are vastly different from the expectations placed on someone who owns an ordinary business. These expectations seem to be more like the financial obligations placed on elected city magistrates during the Roman Empire. In return for a bit of local glory they were expected to cover, out of their own pockets (or, more likely, out of folds of their own toga), the costs of the annual local gladiatorial games. Is Aberdeen, a city noted *within Scotland* for the frugality of its citizens, an aberration when it comes to financing football in the UK, or are the team owners in the UK really more willing to lose money than those in the USA?

A second example of the difference in expectations regarding owners is the Tottenham Hotspur owner, Sir Alan Sugar, the wealthy founder of Amstrad Computers. The club had done poorly in recent years and a journalist in the *Daily Mail* alleged that the cause was that Sugar was a miser. He accused Sugar of refusing to sign players that the team manager had sought. Sugar sued the paper under the UK's strict libel laws and was awarded damages of £100,000.

What is profit maximization and what is utility maximization?

Profit maximization has direct implications for the firm's behavior in both factor and product markets. On the factor market side a profit-maximizing firm would keep hiring labor or any other factor until the marginal revenue generated by the last unit hired just equaled the marginal cost of the factor. On the product side the firm would produce enough output so that the revenue from the last unit would just equal the marginal cost. Sports teams usually participate in a set number of games but the output they can vary is the number of wins. In principle, empirical evidence on profit maximization could come from either the product or the factor market.

A profit-maximizing approach to the setting of ticket prices will be described in Chapter 3. Here we are mainly concerned with the question of how good a team it will pay an owner to field and what the quality of the team implies about the owner's motives. Since there is a relationship between winning and attendance it might be surmised that the more successful a team is on the field of play the more profitable it would be. That, however, ignores the costs of producing a winning team. In fact, Szymanski and Kuypers (1999) found that there was no strong link between profits and performance for 40 English soccer clubs over the period 1978–97, though 92 per cent of total variation in league positions could be accounted for by wage expenditures. It is, therefore, possible to spend 'too much' on players in search of playing success. A model that illustrates the optimal level of talent can be found in the next section.

As we have stated, it is generally asserted that North American clubs attempt to maximize profit. Yet in Europe, with few notable exceptions, there is nothing more pervasive in the literature on European sports than the idea that teams do not pursue maximum profits (Fort, 2000). The extreme version of the utility maximization hypothesis is the assumption is that the owner's objective is to maximize the number of games won, regardless of financial constraints. A more plausible assumption is the maximization of games won subject to a minimum profits (or maximum loss) constraint, with the prediction that where opportunities for strengthening a team exist only minimum profits will be earned.

What differences are implied by utility versus profit maximization models?

The following six forms of behavior would be consistent with utility maximization but inconsistent with profit maximization. The most decisive example is accepting consistent long-run losses. A profit-maximizing firm would sell out or, failing that, walk away from a line of business that made consistent losses. Some years of losses could be justified on the basis of building up a market in anticipation of future profits. However, many European soccer clubs have lost money every year in the last 20 and no one could argue that Europe is a new market still being developed. Further, there is nothing on their horizon to suggest that these losses will be reversed. Broadcast revenues from cable or satellites have not turned into the bonanza their many investors imagined and clubs have lost the ability to hold promising players to lifetime contracts and earn big transfer fees. The patterns of long-term losses are the single strongest evidence that the owners of many European soccer clubs are not profit maximizers.

A second form of behavior that is inconsistent with profit maximization is paying players more than the value of their marginal product. To measure whether this behavior has occurred, one needs to know the player's salary and his contribution to the team's wins, and how much money those wins add to the team's revenue. Below, we will describe one careful empirical estimate of marginal revenue and salaries in US football.

A third inconsistent behavior pattern is hiring too large a squad. Outside the USA, soccer clubs have no **team roster limits**. Although not all US team sports have roster limits, US baseball and hockey clubs can stack major-league quality players in their farm teams and bring them up as needed. Having too many players either on the roster or under contract in farm teams is defined as paying more in salary to the last player stacked than that player's expected contribution to future team revenue.

The fourth example of behavior that is inconsistent with profit maximization is building a stadium larger than needed, (e.g., the **marginal revenue product** of capital is lower than the cost of capital, or the opportunity cost of funds). This example also applies to the factor market but the factor is capital rather than labor. Since the vast majority of all US teams have subsidized stadiums the issue of too big or too lavish a stadium is difficult to address. The municipalities may only be willing to subsidize the team's stadium rather than simply handing the team cash. The issue here is political. The city 'owns' the stadium, so building a fancier or larger stadium may be more palatable to voters than being taxed to make cash payments to a wealthy sports magnate or wealthy players. Fewer European stadiums are municipally owned. If a club builds a stadium so large that it is rarely filled, the owner either grossly miscalculated or values size more than profits.

The fifth example of behavior inconsistent with profit maximization is charging prices below the marginal cost of providing the product. The product could be ticket prices or some ancillary product such as hot dogs in the stadium. Having a waiting list for new season ticket holders for many years would be strong evidence of behavior inconsistent with profit maximization. The waiting list could be quickly wiped out by raising ticket prices. Another type of evidence of prices that are too low is estimates of the **elasticity of demand** for tickets. Since most of the teams are local monopolies, profit maximization requires that ticket prices be set on the elastic segment of the demand curve. On the inelastic segment a team can raise prices and increase total revenues. The evidence on this issue will be discussed in Chapter 3.

The sixth and last form of behavior is excessive charitable donations. Some charitable donations by a club are consistent with profit maximization because they buy the club some goodwill. This consideration is crucial in cities in which the club is facing a municipal referendum on financing a new stadium. However, if the marginal dollar in contributions buys less of a marginal return than the last dollar spent on labor or other inputs, the charitable contributions would be excessive.

The Scully model of profit maximization

Scully's 1995 analysis of the theoretical relationship between a club's winning percentage, ticket prices, attendance and profits is a useful exposition of the implications of the profit maximization hypothesis. Figure 2.1 is based on the assumption that all teams have identical supply functions for talent: that is, the cost of creating a winning team does not differ across teams. In practice this assumption does not strictly hold. The teams in the largest media markets have the advantage that high-profile players know that they can get more income from commercial endorsements. Nevertheless, the equal cost of hiring a given level of talent is a reasonable starting point. The marginal cost of acquiring player talent, T, is represented in Figure 2.1a by $MC(T)$. Demand for wins by a team depends on a number of factors such as the size of the franchise market and the elasticity of its fans' demand for wins. The elasticity

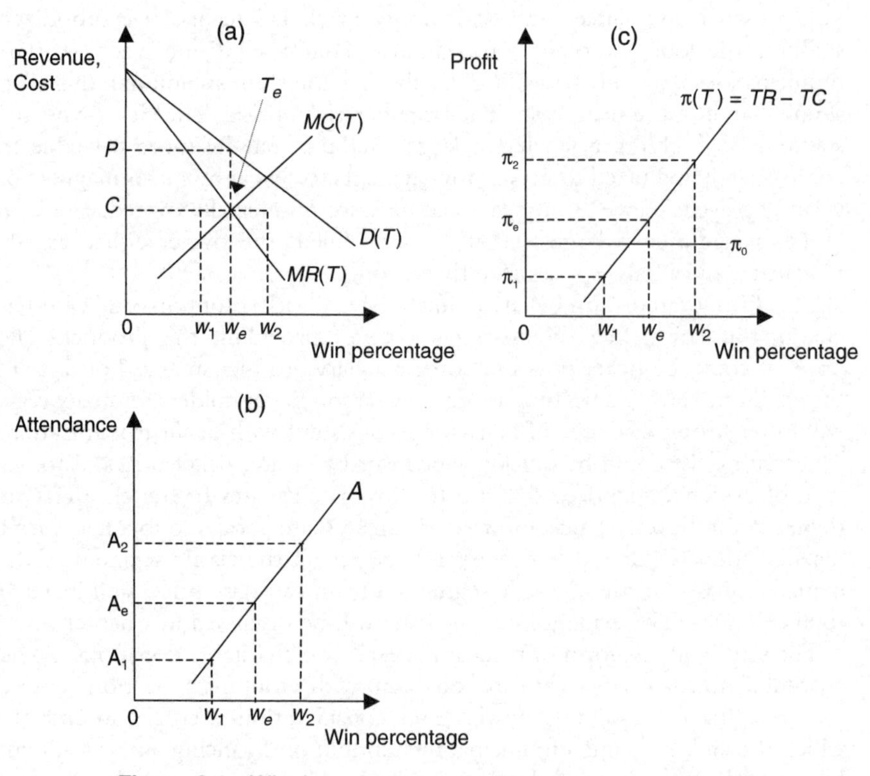

Figure 2.1 Winning, average revenue, attendance and profit

of demand for wins is influenced particularly by real income per capita in the locality and the number of competing sports. Loyal fans show up no matter how the team is doing so a city with many loyal fans would have an inelastic demand for wins. Conversely, fickle fans would have an elastic demand for wins.

In this model the term w_e represents a profit-maximizing winning percentage where $MC(T) = MR(T)$, the marginal revenue derived from a particular level of talent, with T_e, the profit-maximising level of talent required to produce this outcome. However, playing success has a random component due to injuries, mistakes by referees, or a mismatch between the skills of the coach and the types of players on the roster. Thus there is a range of win percentages associated with T_e talent such as $w_1 - w_2$. In turn, this range gives rise to variation in attendance between A_1 and A_2 (see Figure 2.1b).

Since Scully assumes that revenue is proportional to the team's winning percentage as indicted by $\Pi(T)$ in Figure 2.1c, but that costs are fixed for the season, teams will make positive profits for winning percentages above or close to the profit maximizing level w_e, as shown by Π_0.

In Europe, a complicating factor that changes the profit-maximizing level of talent is that soccer clubs compete within a national league and in international club competitions such as the European Cup and the Union of European Football Associations (UEFA) trophy. This extended level of play means that some clubs might acquire more talent than can be justified for domestic competition in order to compete successfully at international level and maximize overall profits. International club competitions are likely to make domestic competitions much less stable if for no other reason than that clubs do not know if they will qualify for the European competitions. The effect of this complicating factor on the optimal level of team talent will be discussed in Chapter 4 on the labor market.

Scully's model focuses on proportion of games won. Fans may be more interested in their team contending for a championship. These are not the same because in an evenly balanced league a team with nearly 50 per cent wins could be in contention while in a highly unbalanced league a team with 60 per cent wins could be out of contention. Whitney (1988) has argued that if fans care primarily about championships, then a shorter season or a smaller league will enhance the role of chance in determining outcomes and increase uncertainty of outcome. Similarly, the elaborate play offs common in many leagues, whereby the top teams play each other for the title or promotion, will help to sustain fan interest.

When teams are located in franchises of widely different population sizes Scully's model implies cross-team variations in the demand for talent. It is profitable for the teams in large cities to win more often than teams in small cities (i.e., the marginal revenue generated by an additional win is higher in a larger city). Strictly following the dictates of profit maximization might cause some small city teams to have no chance of winning a league trophy. Deliberate mediocrity would not, however, be acceptable to most fans, White

Sox fans being an apparent exception. Such a policy can never be openly declared as a team's objective. It also follows that a profit-maximizing league would attempt to ensure that differentials in population sizes were kept to a minimum in terms of awarding franchises or allowing member teams to change their locations. There is evidence supporting this thesis in the pattern of team relocations in North America (e.g., the smaller Canadian cities losing NHL teams to larger US markets).

The Sloane model of utility maximization

The first paper to suggest that team owners may not be profit maximizers was written by one of the authors of this book (Sloane, 1971). In Sloane's model the utility, U, of a hobbyist/owner is a function, u, of playing success defined as the percentage of wins, w: average attendance which adds to the spectacle and atmosphere, a; the competitive balance of the league defined as standard deviation of league-wide winning percentages, x, since having attractive opponents increases the interest in games; and the level of after tax profits π minus the threshold level of profits or losses required to stay in operation, since profits add to the stability of the club and its ability to retain and attract star players. Thus,

$$U = u(w, a, x, \pi)$$

subject to $\pi_r \geq \pi_0 + \text{taxes}$

where π_r equals actual profits and π_o minimum profits

Both π_0 and π_r may in fact be negative, in which case the taxes due would be zero. This is possible where the club has access to external sources of finance, f. Assuming that π_0 is the amount of profits (positive or negative) required to keep a club in existence, the constraint becomes

$$\pi + f \geq \pi_0 + \text{taxes}$$

In this model if the hobbyist/owner puts a high weight on w then he will be prepared to trade off some profit in order to secure additional playing success. A club owned by such a hobbyist would never pursue mediocrity as a deliberate policy. Once the owner's minimum profits constraint has been met most of the additional income will be spent on new players in order to improve playing success.

This spending strategy has a number of implications. Relative to having profit-maximizing owners a league in which most of the owners maximized utility and placed great weight on playing success would have a more unbalanced cross-team athletic performance and great financial instability. This result is illustrated in Figure 2.2 which compares a big city club, L, with a small city club S, competing

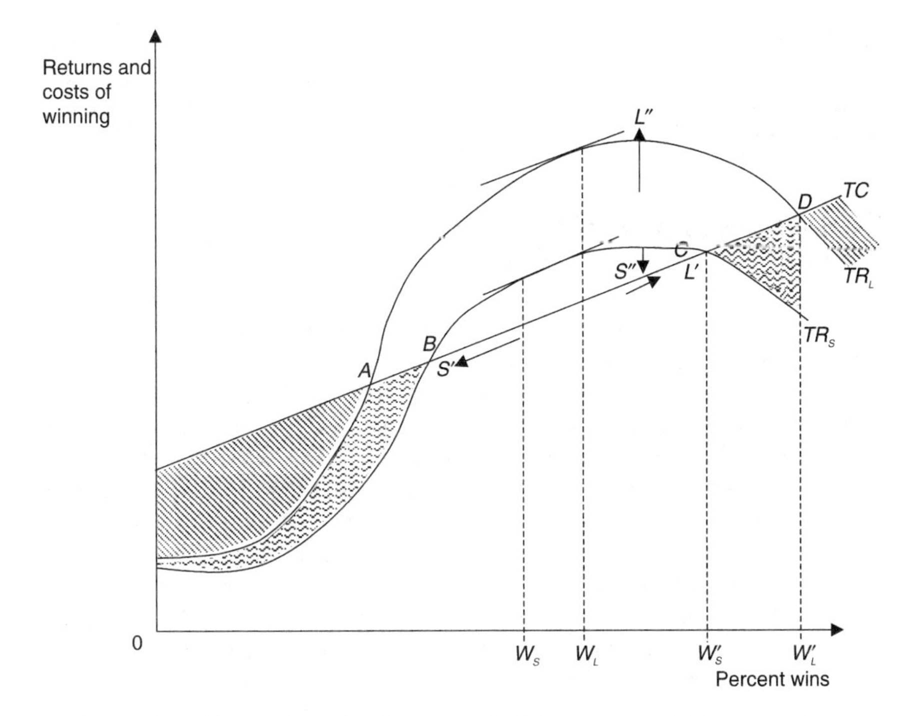

Figure 2.2 Uncertainty of outcome, instability and mutual interdependence

in a two-team league. As with the Scully model, it is assumed that the costs of producing wins rise linearly and are identical for both clubs.[1] Returns to winning rise initially at an increasing rate, but then at a decreasing rate as interest wanes if a team wins too often. The total returns to winning schedule for a large city team TR_L lies above that for a small city team TR_S as the larger population catchment area in the former case means that the large city team will attract more spectators for any given winning percentage. There will be a unique profit-maximizing winning percentage, OW, for each team, but plausibly this will be greater for the large city team OW_L than for the small city team OW_S.[2]

The financial instability arises from the zero sum nature of the wins within the league. If the large city team wins more often, denoted by L', this means that the small city team will win less often, denoted by S'. Thus, the success of one club will drive the other into the shaded area of loss making. A further cause of instability is the fact that the smaller club is more vulnerable than the larger club as it has a smaller range of winning percentages over which it is profitable, namely *BC* as opposed to *AD* in the case of the large city club. Additionally, the pursuit of the maximization of playing success subject to a break even constraint, OW_S' for the small city club and OW_L' for the large city club, will increase the likelihood of financial losses. **Mutual interdependence** is also illustrated by the fact that if the large city population grows as indicated by L'' this may induce a belief on the part of the fans in the rival small city club that future championships are no longer attainable. The small team's total revenue schedule will then shift down as indicated by S''. It is clear that successful leagues need to limit differences in local population catchment area among member clubs.

Constraints on utility maximization: publicly-traded clubs

Many professional sports teams in the USA are publicly held. When a large corporation such as Disney, Time/Warner, Viacom, Fox or Cable Vision Systems owns one or more professional sports team, it faces the same pressures to maximize profits as any other corporation whose stock in not closely held. **Closely held shares** means that just a few people own a controlling fraction of the shares. There are two exceptions to this pressure among the publicly held teams in the USA. The Green Bay Packers in the National Football League (NFL) are widely held but the shares pay no dividends and all of the profits are put back into the team's operation. The restrictions on paying out dividends as well as on the team moving away from Green Bay, and NFL's policy of sharing all television revenue equally, are the reasons that such a small market team can exist and even field winning teams. Green Bay's novel stock ownership provisions go back to the 1920s when professional football was primarily a Midwest game and the city was terrified about losing its beloved Packers. Another exception in the USA to publicly-traded teams being under pressure to maximize profits is the Boston Celtics in the National Basketball Association. A minority of their stock is publicly traded, so it is impossible for someone to buy them out and either change the management or move the team.

In Europe there has been an increasing tendency for clubs to become listed public companies. Szymanski and Hall (2003) examined the performance of 16 English soccer clubs that acquired a Stock Exchange listing in the mid-1990s. They hypothesize that this should have led to a shift towards profit-maximizing behavior at these clubs in order to satisfy shareholders. However, there was no evidence of any such shift in behavior. In fact there was a decline in profitability among those clubs accompanied by an increase in expenditure to improve league performance. There are a number of potential explanations, one of which is that the extent to which financial markets can constrain behavior is not as strong as supposed, and another that investors were largely composed of fans of the individual clubs. Szymanski and Hall suggest one explanation is that the clubs were profit maximizing before they became publicly traded.

Immobility of clubs

Most European football clubs may be not be able to make a profit even in a year with reasonable playing success because there are too many clubs given the overall population. There simply are no large cities without clubs. Because of the absence of profitable new locations and inflexible league rules, European clubs also do not have the ability to relocate. In contrast, in the USA there are many million-plus population cities without a full complement of teams in the four major league sports. The under-provision of teams, and their ability to relocate almost at will, has forced US cities to pay most (and sometimes all) of the costs of the team's arenas, stadiums and practise facilities. These differences in public-sector financial support are one of the main reasons that almost every US major league team makes a profit no matter how it does on the field of play, while most of the European teams lose money. The Americans at least have the opportunity to profit maximize. The Europeans are either minimizing their losses or maximizing their utility.

Principal-agent problems

Much of the industrial economics literature focuses on the divorce between ownership and control, and more recently on the principal-agent problem. In typical principal-agent models the owner is the principal and some employee is the agent. The owner cannot completely observe the actions of the agent and/or does not have all of the information that the agent has. The central issue in principal-agent models is how the principal can create a set of incentives that would cause his agent to act in his interest. Principal-agent problems are particularly relevant to professional team sports where managers are frequently former players who might be expected to give greater attention to playing success, as opposed to the profit maximization that the owner might prefer. Managers tend to concentrate on playing success since they can lose their job when their team does poorly. Conversely, it is difficult to remove a successful manager even when a team loses money because this would create fan discontent. The principal-agent problem requires an **information asymmetry** in which the manager knows more about the amount of talent required for any number of wins than the owner does. The difference in the interests of the owner and the manager might cause the manager to over-state the required talent. As long as the coach or team manager has an information advantage over the owner he is in a position to cause the owner to stock too much talent.

This principal-agent problem does not provide a clear test of profit maximization versus utility maximization. The owner might still be a utility maximizer but he might not place as great a weight on wins as the coach. It is also possible that the owner is a profit maximizer but the coach is able to push him away from the profit maximizing level of talent. Presumably, an owner will eventually figure out that he is spending too much on talent either for utility maximization or for profit maximization. The process can continue for a long time, however, in a dynamic situation in which the talent levels in other teams are changing and new players with uncertain abilities are constantly being added.

One way of making the coach's interest match the interest of the owner is to make the coach a part owner of the team. That is rare in the USA but more common in Europe. Obviously, giving away shares of an enterprise that consistently loses money (i.e., most European soccer clubs) is much less costly than giving away shares of a highly profitable enterprise. Nevertheless, part ownership can give the coach an incentive to try to improve the team's finances. Coaches' salaries and incentives will receive a full discussion in Chapter 5.

Testing the models of individual owner behavior

Atkinson, Stanley and Tschirhart

There has been only one empirical test of Scully's model of profit maximization (Atkinson, Stanley and Tschirhart, 1988). The effort Atkinson, Stanley and Tschirhart had to make may account for this being the only empirical paper on this subject. They estimated the marginal revenue for every US football team in 1980 of winning an additional game and the effect of improving the quality of different units (running backs, quarterbacks, offensive line, etc.) on the probability of winning. These detailed estimates allowed them to calculate the marginal revenue product of each unit: that is, how much the unit added to the team's ticket revenue. Finally, they compared these marginal revenue products to the actual salaries paid to the players in a unit. They found that the teams were generally paying above the marginal revenue product. 'With salaries approximately seven times greater than current marginal revenue products, we fail to accept profit maximization as the sole motivation for owners' behavior' (p. 39).

The first papers on estimating the elasticity of demand for ticket prices also rejected profit maximization because the ticket prices were found to be too low (on the inelastic portion of the demand curve). The more recent papers have accounted for the extra profits made from ancillaries. These papers do not reject profit maximization in ticket pricing (they will be described further in Chapter 3). The same neglect of ancillaries may be part of the explanation of the paradoxical result in the Atkinson, Stanley and Tschirhart paper. They do not consider team revenue from ancillary sales or premium seats. The only factor besides tickets that they consider is broadcast revenue. If the fans of successful teams buy more hats and t-shirts at the stadium or are willing to pay more for the club seats and the premium seats (personal seat licenses did not exist in 1980) then Atkinson, Stanley and Tschirhart may have underestimated the marginal revenue products.

Using early 1990s data Krautmann (1999) has an alternative approach for estimating a player's marginal revenue product. He relies on the information obtained from contracts for free agents. More specifically, he regresses free agent performance in a given year against the salary in that year. Krautmann argues that free agent salaries capture the market value of the player's performance. He then applies these marginal productivity estimates to those baseball players subject to a reserve clause. His results indicate that a typical player is paid his marginal revenue product (MRP). Krautmann criticizes Scully's method and claims that it produces implausibly high MRPs, five to six times larger than the average free agent's salary. Since Atkinson, Stanley and Tschirhart are using Scully's method, the Krautmann paper is, in effect, a critique of their estimates as well. These studies show the difficulty of obtaining accurate estimates of players' marginal revenue products and thereby obtaining a decisive test of profit versus utility maximization.

League motives

There are a few instances, such as US Major League Soccer, in which the league owns all of the teams. When the teams in a league are jointly owned there is no distinction between league motives and team motives. The more common case is team ownership by separate entities. The league might still be a separate financial entity making and retaining its own profits or a simply a service organization that reports to all of the team owners. Motor sports provide several examples in which the league, which is the race sanctioning entity, is a separate for-profit enterprise while the teams and the facilities are owned independently. Thus the North American Stock Car Racing Association (NASCAR) and Formula One Holdings are separate financial entities that either approve races, tracks and teams, or negotiate broadcast rights.

In leagues in which the team owners control the league there are different voting rules depending on the league (and even on the issue) being considered. Some US leagues require unanimity to approve new entrants while others require simple majorities or clear majorities. Clear majorities are also common in European leagues for issues such as increasing the number of teams in the league.

Within the typical team-and-league structure the teams have individual interests (depending on the owner these might lean toward profit maximization or toward win maximization) and the league has a collective interest in overall profit maximization. The league as an entity has no interest in the total number of wins. Every win within the league is also a loss for one of its teams. League-wide profit maximization requires competitive balance. Thus the universal problem in professional sports leagues is to set up and police a structure that maximizes joint profits in spite of the interests of individual owners in either individual profit maximization or in utility maximization.

Regarding the question of profit maximization versus utility maximization, the difficulty in considering the conflicts between team owners and leagues is that it is not clear that a league that was made up entirely of teams whose owners were profit maximizers would behave any differently from a league that was made up entirely of utility maximizers. There are at least three papers that discuss league incentives under different types of owners for baseball, ice hockey and cricket (Davis, 1974; Jones, 1969; Schofield, 1982). They do not provide clear indicators of behavior or conflicts that apply to one type of maximization and not the other.

Conclusions

Utility maximization appears to be the norm throughout Europe. The long-term losses by European teams seem to rule out profit maximization as the primary objective. In contrast, in North America we do not have the data to provide a decisive test between the hypotheses. Although almost all teams make a profit in the USA it may still be the case that their owners are utility maximizers. The financial environment for North American teams may be so favorable that the owners can make a profit while all are pursuing more than the profit maximizing level of playing success. The discussion of Atkinson, Stanley and Tschirhart and the critique by Krautmann point out the technical difficulties in estimating players' marginal revenue products and thereby the difficulty in using these estimates to assess profit and utility maximization.

The trend toward publicly traded teams in Europe may reduce the apparent differences between North America and Europe. The increasing globalization of sports leagues (the NBA and NFL in Europe and FIFA's – La Fédération Internationale de Football Associations – efforts to promote soccer in the USA) will also reduce cross-continent differences in the operation of teams. Throughout most of the remainder of this textbook we will rely on the assumption of profit maximization as the initial description of the market. This is done because profit maximization provides clear predictions and it is simpler. Wherever the assumption of profit maximization seems weakest or leads to obviously counter-factual predictions, we will bring in utility maximization behavior as a possible explanation.

Notes

1. Strictly we require that when one team increases its investment in acquiring a winning team the other team does not react.
2. This will be the case if TR_L exceeds TR_S by a fixed percentage, so that the slope of the former is steeper than that of the latter over the relevant range.

Exercises

1. Why do the motives of team owners and the league management committee matter?
2. Why might such motives differ in North America and Europe?

3. What are the conditions for profit maximization in terms of a club's product market and factor market operations?
4. Is it possible to differentiate between profit-maximizing and utility-maximizing behavior on the part of clubs?
5. Why might leagues with utility-maximizing owners be unstable?
6. What is the principal-agent problem and how is it relevant to the management of clubs?
7. 'Even if individual clubs pursue the objective of maximizing games won subject to some financial constraint it is still reasonable to assume that the objective of the league as a whole is to maximize joint profits.' Discuss.
8. Krautmann argued that free agents' salaries reflected their marginal revenue product. Would this argument hold if owners were utility maximizers?
9. If the marginal cost of talent function in Figure 2.1 shifted up, what effect would this have on prices, attendance, profits? Draw all of the old and new functions.

3 Demand and pricing

Chapter goals

What determines the demand for tickets to a single sporting event? Given that demand, how are ticket prices determined? What determines the gradient in prices as the quality of the seats rises? How does the opportunity to sell ancillary goods at a sporting event – such as food, drinks, parking and souvenirs – affect the prices of tickets? Is an unrestricted market for resale tickets (called scalping in the USA and ticket touting in the UK) beneficial or harmful? How is a season ticket similar to a call option on the stock market? Why would a fan prefer a season ticket to buying tickets to individual games? Why would a team owner prefer selling season tickets to selling individual game tickets? What determines the demand for and pricing of season tickets? Starting with the assumption that the owner's objective is to maximize profits, the main goal of this chapter is to answer these questions with simple microeconomics tools. Whether owners indeed try to maximize profits was discussed in Chapter 2.

The determinants of demand for sporting events

Demand is a function that relates the number of tickets sold to the price. *Increasing the demand* means shifting the demand function to the right so that a greater quantity is demanded at any given price. Both short and long-term factors can shift demand for sporting events. The short-term factors can change in a few days. Increasing demand through the long-term factors might require years (or even decades) of investment by a league and its local teams.

Long-term factors

The long-term factors include the public's familiarity with the rules of the game, the population and per capita incomes in the cities in which the game is played, the reputation for integrity of the referees and administrators, and the public's familiarity with the individual players, especially the stars. Since paid advertisements such as billboard advertisements are relatively expensive, sports teams depend on the free publicity in newspaper, television and radio coverage. It is their central long-term strategy for building up demand. Try to imagine a sport with no news coverage. Only the people attending events would see the big plays or know the team's position in the league. Even people attending the games would know little about the personalities of the players. If the team held a clinic to teach children the sport or sponsored some charity event, who would know? In the USA bowling is an example of a sport with professional players as well as a wide amateur participation but next to no news coverage. The consequence is that currently professional bowling is close to invisible.

Since journalists frequently complain about an individual player's dedication or an individual coach's strategy, the teams and the journalists appear to be adversaries. This appearance of antagonism is deceiving. Going back to the 1880s in the early days of professional cricket in the UK and professional baseball in the USA, sports teams and journalists have had a symbiotic relationship. Sports journalists' incomes depend upon the revenue generated by selling newspapers to sports fans and from the advertisements carried in the sports sections of the paper or the sports segments of broadcast news. In return for the opportunity to earn a living, the journalists provide the teams with constant free publicity about the results of games, prospects in upcoming games, as well as teaching the public the fine points of the game and profiling the personalities of the players. These benefits are why professional teams universally promote journalists' contacts with the coaches and the players through open locker rooms or news conferences that are mandatory for the coaches and players. It is why teams accommodate television crews, employ sports information specialists, and send out highlight tapes to the broadcasters. It is also why general managers call local sports editors to complain about being buried on a back page.

There is a strong tendency for professional sports teams to be located in the largest cities and, other things being equal, in the cities with the highest per capita incomes. Historical accidents or demographic trends can leave teams in the wrong cities. 'Wrong' means a set of locations that does not maximize league revenues. The locations may be just right from the viewpoint of the fans in small media markets. That ice hockey is a Canadian game can be attributed to Canada's long, cold winters. That historical foundation has not prevented the ice from melting out from under the small-market Canadian teams. The five-fold increases in market size were enough to shelter the hockey teams from the abundant sunshine and hockey ignorance of Anaheim, California, and Fort Lauderdale, Florida. In the USA there is also a tendency for major league teams to flow towards the cities willing to provide the greatest subsidies. With a sufficient dose of municipal subsidies along with the National Football League's policy of sharing all television revenues equally, a small market such as Nashville, Tennessee, can draw a National Football League team away from a large market such as Houston, Texas. The subject of local subsidies for professional sports teams will be discussed in Chapter 9.

In soccer (football outside the USA and Canada) the relegation/promotion process serves the same function as the relocation of professional teams in the USA. In both cases the major league status flows towards the cities with the highest population and income. The relegation/promotion process moves the worst performing major league (called Premier League in the UK) teams down to the next lower league (the First Division in the UK is one step below the Premier League) and puts the best performing minor league teams into the majors. If, over time, a city grows or shrinks in terms of population or per capita income, the local team's revenues will change accordingly. An extraordinary string of bad luck or ineptitude might push a large-market team into the minor league but eventually the extra revenue in the large market will be felt in the form of higher-paid talent and enough wins for elevation back to the Premiership. Relegation for a team in an area with declining population and income is likely to be a permanent demotion. For example, when textile production in the UK declined, the Lancashire cities of Burnley and Preston lost their Premiership status.

A sport's reputation for integrity can take years to build and days to destroy. An honest game with each side trying its best to win is the foundation of fan interest. The exceptions to real competition that still draw many paying customers, such as the Harlem Globetrotters traveling basketball team in the USA and World Wrestling Federation matches, are really theatrical performances masquerading as sporting contests. The clowns, buffoons, bad guys and the outrageously blind referees are all part of a scripted show and winning is incidental. An easy way to check whether a sport is a sham or real is to look at the betting. In the US gambling on sports is legal in Las Vegas. If there are posted odds for a sport in the Las Vegas sports' books or in the off-track betting parlors in the UK such as Ladbrokes, then at least the gamblers believe it is an honest competition.

Genuine sports leagues try to keep their play honest. That is why they forbid players, coaches, referees, officials and the team owners from betting on the outcomes of games. No matter how well they can play the game, players who have been caught gambling are banished for life. Choking one's coach, a conviction for rape, sex with a minor, assault, or the possession of a Class I illegal drug or an illegal handgun are all lesser offenses from which a player, after a due respite, can be rehabilitated. A reasonable inference from these relative punishments is that losing the image of integrity and thus real competition through a gambling scandal would cost the league more revenue than losing goodwill by retaining players who had committed a crime.

Short-term factors

What are the short-term demand factors? A game that ought to attract hordes of customers would feature outstanding athletes at the peak of their training engaged in an all-out effort. For sporting events the word *customers* includes the people who buy a ticket or buy the right to watch on **pay-per-view** (ppv) television as well as those who 'pay' to watch regular television broadcasts by being part of the audience for commercials. The key short-term factor in attracting customers is not athletic ability, or training, or skill, or even the intensity of the play; the key to attracting both paying customers and a broadcast audience is uncertainty over the game's outcome. Sports leagues and television networks have access to hundreds of games that have the best athletes in the world playing with ferocious intensity, yet they hardly ever broadcast them. What are these mysteriously uninteresting games? They are the games from the previous season. The ESPN Classics network, which broadcasts only old games, draws a tiny fraction of the audience that ESPN gets for current games. The old games are uninteresting because most viewers know how they turned out. Even for viewers who forgot or who had never heard the score, watching last season's game is a pale pleasure. Viewers know that the winner was decided long ago and the end-of-season trophy has been awarded. It is all a sepia-toned history.

The importance of uncertainty of outcome extends to live games as well. If the outcome of a live game is a foregone conclusion, then it will be terribly dull. No live game can have a perfectly certain outcome, but to make a game boring, perfect certainty is not required. If the imbalance is so great that one team would be expected to win 990 out of 1,000 contests between the two teams, then it will be dull game indeed. The players on the strong team can relax yet the players on the weak team still have next to no hope of winning. *Other things being equal, games with evenly matched teams draw the biggest audiences.*

'Evenly matched' can be defined on a prospective or subjective probability basis: that is, each team is thought to have a 50–50 chance of winning the game. Gambling odds shortly before a game is played provide a measure of these prospective probabilities. 'Evenly matched' can also be defined on a retrospective basis (i.e., purely on past performance). Under a retrospective definition of evenly matched teams with equal winning percentages up to the day of the match would be assumed to have equal chances. A priori, it is not clear whether past performance or gambling odds based on subjective judgments provide a better measure of competitive balance. The gambling odds can reflect up-to-the minute information on the health of the players but often bets are made on an emotional basis, to show support for the team, rather than just to make money. Gambling odds reflect the amount bet on each side. When a team with a huge following (e.g., Notre Dame in US college football) plays a team with a small following, the gambling odds can drift away from the real probabilities. Based on either gambling odds or a win-loss record of the evenness of competition, there is evidence that the more evenly matched games draw better attendances and larger television audiences. The earliest evidence on the issue of the effect of uncertainty of single game outcomes is by Noll (1974c). He found that measures of the closeness of the competition in individual games were important in predicting attendance in baseball and ice hockey. In a given league the other things that have to be held equal in these comparisons are the city size, per-capita income, and the availability of nearby competing games.

For sports with a seasonal championship uncertainty over the outcome extends beyond the predictions about a single game. A team that is out of the race for a play off spot will draw poorly even when the opponent is evenly matched. A team making a run for a playoff spot will draw well even if the opponent has a much better or a much worse record. The topic of demand and pricing of season tickets will be discussed later in this chapter. Most of the published studies on demand for games are done in the context of a season and a league. Some studies are based on prospective estimates of the uncertainty of outcome, or posted gambling odds (Forrest and Simmons, 2002; Peel and Thomas, 1988 and 1992) while others are based on differences in past performance (Borland and Lye, 1992). These studies find that after controlling for the potential impact of the game on post-season prospects, such as making the playoffs or being relegated to a lower division, the uncertainty of outcome for an individual game is a strong determinant of attendance.[1]

Competitive balance can be controlled by a league and can have an immediate pay-off in terms of a higher demand. Thus a league's central problem is promoting and maintaining balance. League rules on the players' salaries, the transfer of players between teams, the signing of new players, the relocation of teams, the relegation/promotion process, and on the sharing of ticket or television revenue all affect the competitive balance. A large part of this book is about how leagues maintain competitive balance.

Setting ticket prices

Let us shift the discussion from the determinants of demand to ticket pricing. How does a team determine ticket prices given its level of demand? The simplest model of pricing involves only ticket revenue rather than broadcast revenue. It is also simpler to start with a one-time event rather than the pricing of tickets for an entire season. Figure 3.1 shows a straight-line demand function for a one-time only sporting event (say, a boxing match). The price is on the vertical or *y*-axis and the quantity of tickets is on the horizontal or *x*-axis. All of the seats are assumed to be of the same quality in this simple example. An increase in demand means that the entire function has shifted to the right and thus more tickets can be sold at any given price. The demand function would be shifted to the right if any of the favorable long-term factors, such as the public's familiarity with the sport or the fame of the

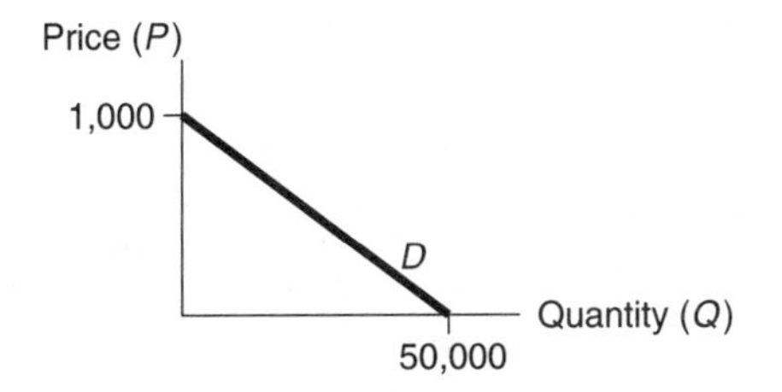

Figure 3.1 Straight-line demand function(D)

athletes, increased or if a short-term factor improved, such as the competitive balance for the event.

The numbers in Figure 3.1 are purely for illustration. The highest price anyone would pay for a ticket is a little below $1,000 (or £1,000). For any price (P) at or above $1,000 the quantity ($Q$) demanded is zero. If the tickets to the event were free then 50,000 people would attend. The demand function (D) is

$$P = 1,000 - 0.02Q$$

With this function, if you substitute zero for P then Q takes the value 50,000.

A sports promoter for a boxing match or the local team owner in a team sport finds the profit-maximizing price by equating marginal revenue (MR) and marginal cost (MC). The ***marginal revenue*** is the addition to total revenue from selling one more unit of a good or service or, in this case, one more ticket. This $MR = MC$ rule is equivalent to setting a lower price to sell more tickets until the marginal revenue of the last ticket sold brings in just enough money to cover the cost of having one more person attend the event. The marginal revenue for a straight-line demand function is also a straight line that is twice as steep as the demand function. The marginal revenue function is shown in Figure 3.2. The marginal revenue function, labeled MR, runs from $1,000 on the price axis to 25,000 tickets on the quantity axis. The marginal revenue function in this example would be $MR = 1,000 - 0.04Q$.

What is missing so far is the ***marginal cost***, which is the cost of having one more person attend the boxing match. For sporting events the marginal cost of an additional person is usually zero. The reason is that all the costs of putting on the boxing match are fixed costs. These costs are: rental cost of the hall, the salaries of the ticket takers and guards, the advertising costs, and the prize money for the boxers. They all have to be paid however many people attend the event. With a zero marginal cost the profit-maximizing quantity is 25,000 tickets. This solution assumes that the capacity of the hall is at least 25,000 seats. The assumption is implicit in the marginal cost function. If the hall had fewer than 25,000 seats the marginal cost of building new seats or enlarging the hall to accommodate more viewers would no longer be zero.

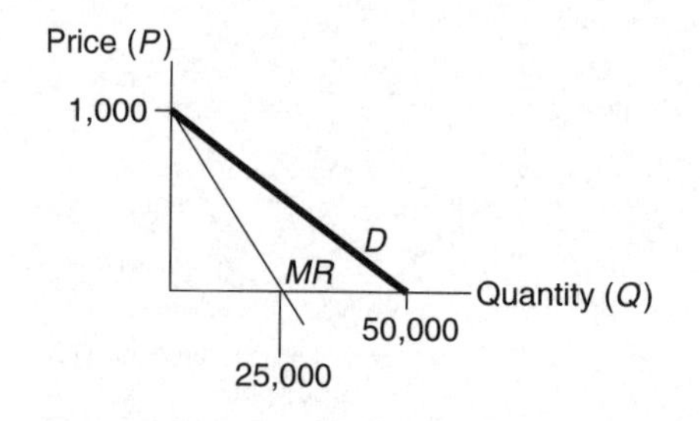

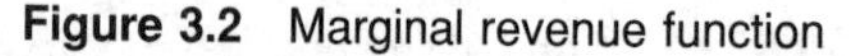
Figure 3.2 Marginal revenue function

$$MC = 0$$
$$MR = 1{,}000 - 0.04Q$$
$$MR = MC$$
$$1{,}000 - 0.04Q = 0$$
$$Q = 25{,}000$$

The profit-maximizing price is $500. This price can be found by substituting the quantity of 25,000 into the demand function. The total revenue is $500 times 25,000, or $12,500,000. If the total costs of putting on the boxing match were $10,000,000 (picking a round number) then the promoter would make a profit of $2,500,000. Although these numbers were made up for the sake of illustration, the ticket prices in this example are not far off the figures in real boxing matches. The average ticket price for Mike Tyson's fight against François Botha (January 1999) was $690. There were 10,221 tickets sold. The *gate*, or the value of the total ticket sales from the live audience, was $7,051,800. The PPV gate was $45 for each of the 750,000 households that viewed the match, or $33,750,000. This fight was not a championship fight and Botha is a relatively obscure boxer. The ticket prices and the total gates in this example are not exceptional.

Readers who have had introductory (first year) economics should find this discussion of profit-maximizing price setting familiar. It is called the ***monopoly model***. As simple as this model might appear, it reveals a fundamental relationship between costs and ticket prices that is often confused by sports fans. Many teams justify increases in the price of their tickets by pointing to increases in the player's salaries. The argument usually goes: 'Our fans want a competitive team and we are determined to remain competitive. The recent increases in players' salaries have forced us to raise ticket prices so that we can continue to afford the best players.'

The problem with this argument is that, as in this boxing example, the wages or the prize money have no effect on the ticket price. Given the demand function, the $500 ticket price generates the highest possible profits. If the salaries and prize money increased the profits would go down, but the ticket price chosen by a profit-maximizing promoter would stay the same. Any increase in ticket prices with the demand fixed would just cost the promoter some of his or her profits. The only possible effect of an increase in fixed costs would be to make the promoter cancel the match. If the fixed costs rose above the total revenue of $12,500,000 then there would be no profits left. In the other direction (i.e., a drop in fixed costs through a reduction in the salaries and the prize money) the profit-maximizing ticket prices would also stay at $500. Again, this result depends on the demand for the event staying the same. Presumably the demand for the boxing match depends on how famous the boxers are and how evenly they are matched rather than how much the ticket takers are being paid or the amount of prize money.

What else might affect the setting of ticket prices for a one-time event? The sports promoter might sell souvenirs, parking, and food to people attending the event. Suppose the promoter expected to make a profit of $5 per customer on all of these ancillary sales. From the promoter's point of view it does not matter whether a customer buys a hat or a beer or parking services as long as the promoter can charge $5 more for what is bought than what it costs to provide. These profits on ancillary sales just reduce the net cost of having one more person attend the event by $5. Now the marginal cost of having one more person attend the event is minus $5. This change increases the profit-maximizing quantity. Equating marginal revenue and marginal cost yields:

$$MC = -5$$
$$MR = 1{,}000 - 0.04Q$$
$$MR = MC$$
$$1{,}000 - 0.04Q = -5$$
$$Q = 25{,}125$$

The corresponding price is $497.50. Total revenue from ticket sales is now 497.50 × 25,125, or $12,499,687.50. The profits on the tickets alone fall with the price cut. The ***profits*** are defined as total revenue minus total cost. The profits from ticket sales, assuming that the $10,000,000 cost of putting on the event stays the same, is now $12,499,687.50 – $10,000,000, or $2,499,687.50. However, there is no reason to worry about a decline in profits for the promoter. He or she also has $5 in ancillary profits for each of the 25,125 customers so the total profits from all sources is $5 × 25,125 + $2,499,687.50 profit on the ticket sales, or $2,625,312.50. Figure 3.3 shows the marginal cost of minus $5 and the profit-maximizing price and quantity.

This example of the effective cross-subsidy between ancillary sales to ticket sales illustrates how a sports promoter might find it profitable to set ticket prices on an inelastic section of the demand function. At the midpoint of a straight-line demand function the elasticity equals 1. **Elasticity of demand** is the percentage change in the quantity divided by the percentage change in the

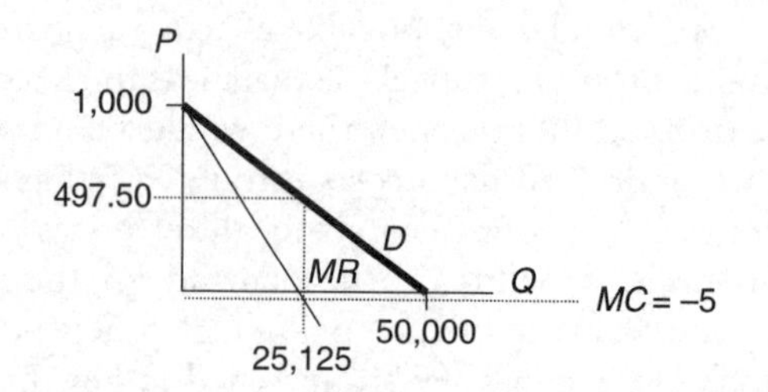

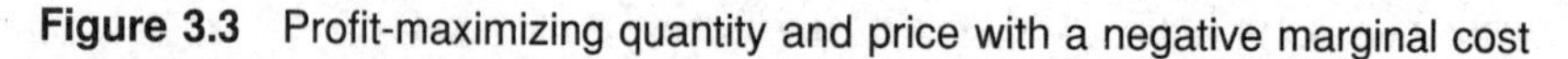
Figure 3.3 Profit-maximizing quantity and price with a negative marginal cost

price. To the right of the midpoint the elasticity of demand is less than 1 or is inelastic. Ordinarily, a monopolist would never set the price below the midpoint of the demand function but here the ancillary sales provide an exception that will be described below.

At first glance, estimating the elasticity of demand for tickets to sporting events ought to be easy. The usual identification problem in demand estimates (figuring out if the supply or the demand is varying) is not present because the supply of tickets can be treated as fixed. In practice the estimation is difficult because there is usually no variation in ticket prices within a season for a particular team. Big city teams are able to sell more tickets even though they have higher prices. Sometimes the reported elasticity estimates are even positive (implying an upward sloping demand curve). There is no easy way to disentangle the effects of population, income and ticket prices because they are highly collinear (they move together). Almost all empirical estimates of the elasticity of demand for ticket prices that do come up with a negative elasticity (implying a downward sloping demand function) have found that prices are set on an inelastic portion of the demand curve. Szymanski and Kuypers provide an extensive review of elasticity estimates in *Winners and Losers: The Business Strategy of Football* (1999). Some of the main papers are: Bird (1982) with an estimate of −0.2, Borland and Lye (1992) with an estimated elasticity of −0.59, and Dobson and Goddard (1994). They do not report elasticity estimates but elasticities calculated from their results would be highly inelastic for all the nine regions in their study. Another recent estimate that was highly inelastic was established by Jaume Garcia and Placido Rodriguez (2002) for Spanish soccer. Robert Simmons (1996) had separate long-run elasticity estimates for 19 different clubs, and 14 of these were inelastic. Andrew M. Welki and Thomas J. Zlatoper (1994) had an elasticity estimate of −0.275 for US football. These results come from studies based on cross-section data, time series data and panel data with many different econometric techniques. They have been applied to different regions and different sports such as US football and baseball, English soccer, Spanish soccer and Australian rules football.

Until a paper by David Forrest, Robert Simmons and Patrick Feehan (2002), the extreme price inelasticity seemed to be a well-established result. The problem with prices being set on an extremely inelastic portion of the demand curve is that a profit-maximizing monopolist would never do that. Many of the clubs in these studies are publicly traded so it seems unlikely that they would be utility maximizers. The profit motive in the UK is a much debated question and some authors even doubt that publicly-traded teams are profit maximizers because their shares may be bought by die-hard fans. Part of the explanation for why so many studies find that the point estimate of demand elasticity is highly inelastic is that none of them include the profits from ancillaries and broadcasts. Having fans in the stands helps the broadcast because of the atmosphere the excited fans create and the aura of importance a full stadium gives to the game. Ancillary sales or broadcast revenues could cause a monopolist to set prices on an elastic section of the demand curve. Even so, the estimates of elasticity with values in the range of –0.2 to –0.5 are implausibly low. The chance to make some money from ancillaries or broadcasts would push the optimal price just a little lower than the monopolist's theoretical optimum of an elasticity of –1.0 in a model with zero marginal costs and no ancillaries.

What Forrest, Simmons and Feehan did differently was to incorporate the information on the costs of traveling to the stadium into their elasticity estimate. That additional variation in how much fans actually paid to see games within a season and within a city allowed them to estimate demand elasticity much more precisely. Their principal finding is that the elasticities overall were just slightly inelastic (slightly above –1.0). They attribute the slightly inelastic result to the effect of ancillary sales on optimal ticket prices. Their method did not work well for the London football clubs because the costs of travel and the substitutes were more difficult to measure for the London area.

The effects of ancillary sales are actually more complicated than this simple model that assumes a flat $5 profit from ancillaries per person attending the event. It is almost always the case that a beer or a hot dog or a team pennant costs a lot more inside the stadium than it does a few blocks away. High prices on ancillary goods and services are really a mechanism by which the promoter can price discriminate. *Price discrimination* means selling the same good or service at different prices according to how much a customer is willing to pay. A promoter could make much more profit from a given demand for a sporting event by charging individual customers more or less according to how much each one was willing to pay. *Perfect price discrimination* is defined as charging each customer his or her *reservation price* or the most that they would pay. It is difficult for a promoter to charge different prices for the same type of seat at a sporting event. Imagine walking up to the ticket office and being told you have to pay $250 because you look rich and the next person in line being able to buy a ticket in the same section for $50 because they looked poor. There would immediately be a market for poor-looking people to buy and resell tickets.

In contrast, airlines are able to divide their customers into people who are willing to pay more for a seat by charging dearly for a little flexibility and convenience while charging a low price to those who would not fly at all unless they were offered a low price. Business customers usually book their flights at short notice, often have to change their plans, and do not want to stay for a Saturday night. For the airlines, restrictions requiring a purchase two weeks in advance and a Saturday night stay effectively excludes those customers willing to pay high prices from any of the discount fares. The sports promoter cannot use the same restrictions because requiring a Saturday night stay makes no sense in selling a local ticket and requiring two weeks' advance purchase for a discount would not exclude the high income sports fans from the discount tickets.

Price discrimination applies to situations in which exactly the same good is being sold at different prices. Technically, the same seat on the same flight is not always the same good because the regular or nondiscount airline tickets have fewer restrictions. Nevertheless, the airlines' restrictions squeeze more money out of high-income buyers while still getting low-income buyers to purchase some of the tickets. The convenience of being able to cancel a reservation or change the tickets does have a real cost for the airlines. If the airlines charge a lot more than their costs of providing the unrestricted service then they are *effectively* price discriminating. Consider these actual fares quoted to one of the authors of this text. A one-way coach ticket from Boston to Indianapolis costs $554 while a round-trip ticket with an advanced purchase and a Saturday night stay costs $178. These differences in the prices appear to far exceed the differences in the costs of providing the two types of service. Thus the airline in question is effectively price discriminating by charging a lot more for services that cost just a little more to provide.

The ancillaries sold at a sporting event serve a purpose similar to the restrictions on low priced airline tickets. The ancillaries are priced so that the higher income customers who value convenience usually buy them and the poorer customers make do with just their ticket. The convenience comes in the form of parking right next to the arena, drinks brought by vendors into the stands, and pennants or hats for sale a step from the entrance.

Instead of being a flat $5 per customer, profits from ancillary sales are highest for those customers who are willing to pay the most for a ticket and lowest for customers who are willing to pay the least for a ticket. In this example there is just one type of ticket because the seats are assumed not to vary in quality (i.e., distance from the event). We will come back to the issue of pricing different quality seats. Continuing with the same boxing match example, let the marginal cost be $MC = -500 + 0.01Q$. This function generates more ancillary profits from the people who are willing to pay the most for their tickets. The straight function for MC is being used for simplicity. What is the new profit-maximizing price and quantity?

$$
\begin{aligned}
MC &= -500 + 0.01Q \\
MR &= 1{,}000 - 0.04Q \\
MR &= MC \\
1{,}000 - 0.04Q &= -500 + 0.01Q \\
0.05Q &= 1{,}500 \\
Q &= 30{,}000
\end{aligned}
$$

The price that corresponds to 30,000 seats is $P = 1{,}000(0.02 \times 30{,}000)$, or $400. Again, the implicit assumption built into the MC function is that there are more than 30,000 seats. The total revenue from ticket sales is now $\$400 \times 30{,}000 = \$12{,}000{,}000$. The profits from ticket sales are $12,000,000 – $10,000,000 in fixed costs, or $2,000,000. The shaded area in Figure 3.4 represents the profits on the ancillary sales. It is the triangle going from the origin to −500 on the price axis and from the origin to 50,000 on the quantity axis minus the unshaded triangle going from 30,000 to 50,000 on the quantity axis and from the zero to −200 on the price axis. The −200 comes from substituting the quantity of 30,000 into the *MC* function:

$$MC = -500 + 0.01Q$$
$$MC = -500 + 0.01(30{,}000)$$
$$MC = -200$$

Recalling that the area of a triangle is half the base times the height, the large and small triangles have areas respectively of $0.5 \times 500 \times 50{,}000 = 12{,}500{,}000$ and $0.5 \times 200 \times 20{,}000 = 2{,}000{,}000$. The shaded area or the profits on the ancillaries is the difference between 12,500,000 and 2,000,000, or 10,500,000. The total profits on tickets and ancillaries are 10,500,000 on ancillaries plus the 2,000,000 on tickets, or 12,500,000.

This numerical example, which has greater profit from ancillaries than from ticket sales, is unrealistic; yet the basic theme of the importance of ancillary sales is accurate. The sale of ancillaries helps sports promoters or franchises effectively price discriminate and make a much higher profit from a given demand for an event. Historically, using teams to sell ancillaries has always been part of the promoter or team owner's strategy. Early on breweries owned some of the major league baseball teams. Team ownership was a means of selling more beer. Now, as a means of signing up more households for their services, cable/satellite companies own prominent sports teams.

The promoter's problem in using ancillaries to price discriminate is to think of enough ancillaries to divide up the customers according to their incomes and interest in the sport. Some of the newer ways of dividing the customers into different groups is to have special sections of seats offering a separate

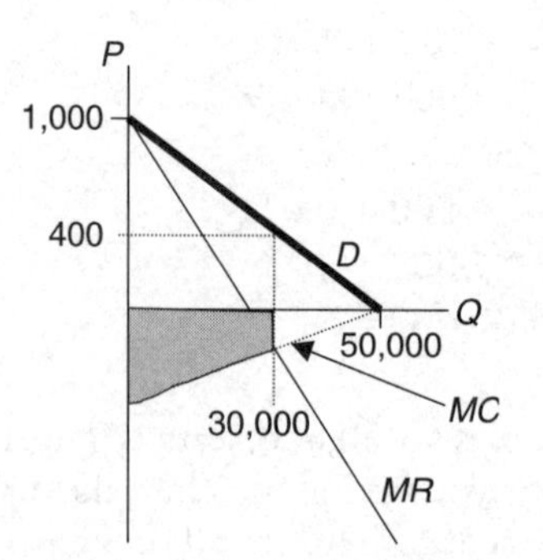

Figure 3.4 Profit-maximizing price and quantity with ancillary sales per customer related to the willingness to pay for tickets

entrance, a behind-the-stands lounge, and at-the-seat cocktail service. For yet higher income fans there are glass-enclosed sky boxes (also called luxury suites) with built-in bars. Because these sky boxes are often far from the playing field they come with closed-circuit televisions to help the occupants see the action.

Price discrimination can only occur when the firm has some monopoly power over the consumers. At airports with excess capacity 'no-frills' airlines, such as Southwest Air, are selling tickets at the same price with or without a weekend stay and with or without an advanced purchase. In these cities the regular airlines have to lower their prices on coach fares to compete with the no-frills carriers. At the busiest airports (such as O'Hare and La Guardia) all the landing slots are held by the major airlines and the no-frills airlines are unable to enter the market. In these cities the major airlines have much more opportunity to price discriminate. Major league professional sports teams in the USA are all monopolies by virtue of their exclusive territorial rights under their league agreements. Suppose the major leagues lost their ability to exclude new entrants. Suppose anyone could form a team and join one of the major leagues by hiring players, renting a stadium and compensating the existing teams for reduction in their national television revenues: the effect on both prices and on price discrimination would be similar to the entry of no-frills carriers into the major airline market. The personal seat licenses (a substantial fee charged for the right to buy season tickets) levied by some teams would disappear, and so would the extraordinary prices for amenities such as club seats and valet parking.

Pricing good and bad seats for a single event

A guess-and-hunt solution

So far we have pretended there is only one quality of seat available. This simplification is obviously unrealistic because some seats provide a better view. How does a promoter set the prices for different types of seat? To simplify the problem we will assume that there are just two types of seat, called *good* and *bad*. For the boxing match these could be seats near the ring and balcony seats far from the boxing ring. The solution to this two-types-of-seat problem can easily be generalized to more gradations in seat quality. Each type of seat has its own demand function. The complication compared to simply finding the profit-maximizing price for each type of seat separately is that the two types of seats are *substitutes*: if the price of one type goes up some customers would switch to the other type of seat. What needs to be maximized is the sum of the profits over the two types of seat. Let the subscript g refer to good seats and the subscript *b* refer to bad seats. Two linear demand functions for these seats could be:

$$P_g = 1{,}000 - 0.02Q_g - 0.01Q_b$$
$$P_b = 500 - 0.01Q_b - 0.001Q_g$$

Figure 3.5 shows the two demand curves drawn under the assumption that no seats of the other type were being sold.

A simple-minded solution to the pricing-two-types-of-ticket problem is to draw two marginal revenue curves under the two demand curves in Figure 3.5, set each marginal cost to zero and set the corresponding prices to \$500 for the good tickets and \$250 for the bad. Can you see the contradiction inherent in this solution? The two demand curves were drawn under the assumption that none of the other type of tickets would be sold. If the promoter increases the number of good seats sold by lowering their price, then the demand for the bad seats will shift to the left as some customers switch from bad to good seats. The opposite happens if the promoter lowers the price on the bad seats.

In the end-of-chapter exercises there are some calculus problems on finding the optimal ticket prices. Often a promoter solves the optimal pricing problem by the guess-and-hunt method. The initial guess is based on experience. The hunt means looking at the turnout for each type of seat and adjusting prices for the next match accordingly. If the good seats are full and the bad seats are mostly empty, the promoter would raise the prices on the good seats a little and cut the prices on the bad seats a little and then check to see if his or her profits went up. The hunt would be over when there was no small price change for either type of seat that would increase profits. The same sort of guess and hunt could be done for more than two types of seats. Promoters who had put on many boxing matches would develop a feel for the profit-maximizing ticket prices.

Note that the types of tickets are not necessarily fixed or strictly determined by the shape of the hall as with the ringside and balcony seats in the boxing example. The 'sections' do not have to correspond to physical partitions. A section simply refers to rows assigned the same price. For popular ('hot') events the hall will be divided into more sections with finer

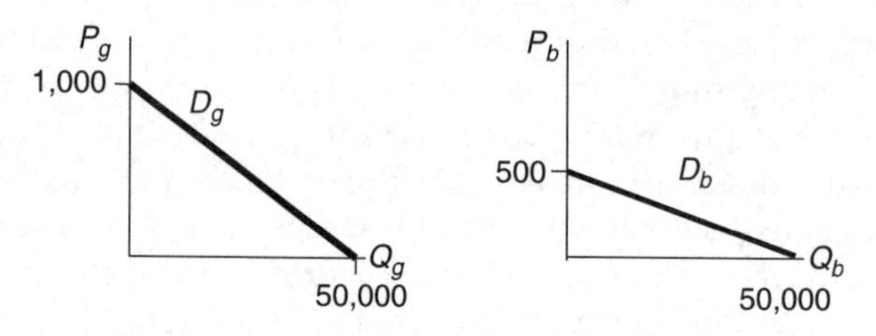

Figure 3.5 Demand for good and bad seats

gradient in prices and a higher top price. The finer gradation in ticket prices is an attempt to capture as much of the *consumer surplus* (the difference between a buyer's reservation price and the actual price) as possible. For a less popular ('cold') event the hall is divided into just a few sections and the top price goes down.

Figure 3.6 shows the consumer surplus for the good and the bad seats, assuming again that none of the other type of seat was sold. The consumer surplus is simply the area under the demand curve and above the selling price. For each customer the height of the demand curve at the price at which they just come into the market represents their maximum willingness to pay. The shaded area just adds consumer surpluses across the individual ticket buyers.

The diagrams of the demand for the two types of tickets are inconsistent because both would shift to the left once the substitute tickets were available. However, for the purposes of illustrating the loss in consumer surplus through price discrimination, this inconsistency is not important. In the upper two panels the price for good tickets is set at \$500 and the price for bad tickets is \$250, and the consumer surplus is represented by the shaded areas in between the selling price and the demand curves. In the lower two panels the promoter has divided the good seats into four price levels. This example is unambiguously one of price discrimination because the quality of all the good seats is assumed to be identical. All the bad seats provide an identical quality, which is lower than the good seats. If the promoter can figure out how to divide the customers so that the richest ones pay the highest price and so on, then he or she can capture most of the consumer surplus. The four small shaded triangles represent the remaining consumer surplus. The same division of customers is going on in the lower right panel but for the bad seats there are only two price levels.

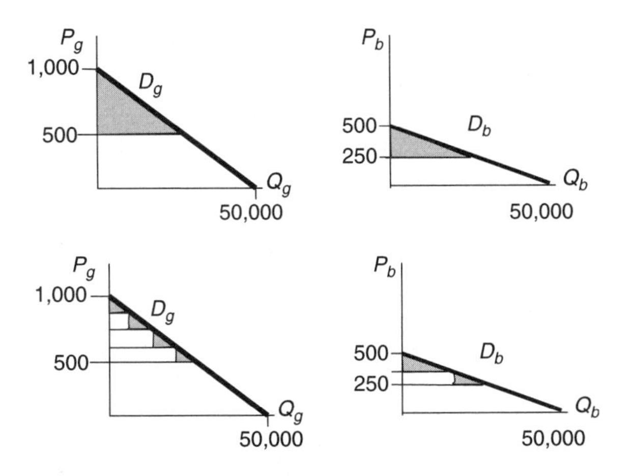

Figure 3.6 Consumer surplus for good and bad tickets before and after price discrimination

The lost consumer surplus (or, equivalently, the gain in the promoter's profit) is greater for the good seats than for the bad seats. The shaded triangle in the upper left panel of Figure 3.6 is larger than the triangle in the panel on the upper right. With the good seats there is more consumer surplus for the promoter to capture. The scaling on the quantity axis is the same. Both the good and bad seats start out at 25,000 tickets before the price discrimination. The difference between the left and right panels is that the demand for the good seats is more inelastic. That is why the pay off to dividing up the customers for the good seats and tracking the demand function as closely as possible is greater with the good than with the bad seats. That is the reason why the good seats are divided into four price levels and the bad seats into two levels. If there was no cost of monitoring the customers or figuring out how to divide them into different groups, then the promoter would be better off having dozens of price levels for both the good and bad seats. However, there are usually some costs to dividing up the higher and lower income customers for each type of ticket.

Charging different prices for seats of identical quality is often done. The promoter can set up separate entrances, give the higher-priced seats a fancy name such as 'patrons' seats' or the 'centurion's section'. All that is required is some ingenuity. Here is an example of a little ingenuity in dividing up the customers. For the exact same movies the Virgin Cinema in Aberdeen charges £6 for seats in its regular halls and £15 for seats in its fancy hall. The fancy hall has a bar service and free popcorn. You would have to eat your weight in free popcorn to justify the extra £9 ($15). However, the fancy hall is a good place to give someone the impression that you have loads of money.

Discounting and scalping (ticket touting)

What happens if the promoter miscalculates and sets the ticket prices above the profit-maximizing level or, for that matter, below it? Even the most experienced and savvy promoter's calculations can be upset by events that occur after the ticket prices were set. The neat fixed lines on the graphs representing demand functions are in reality conditioned on every other element remaining fixed, whereas some of those other elements have a random component. Examples of random changes are another event for the same day being either announced or cancelled, or a riot near the arena discouraging fans from attending. If the prices are too high the promoter can 'paper the house'. This phrase is an old expression used in theaters for selling some of the tickets in a largely empty hall at a discount or even giving them away so that the event will not look like a failure. One way to paper the house is to put a coupon in the local newspaper allowing family groups to come in for half price. Another strategy to draw customers when demand is lower than expected is to give away free baseballs or team hats.

If the promoter errs in the direction of charging too low a price, then he or she has almost no opportunity for recovering the lost profits. Once the tickets have been sold at the low price and there are no more seats in the arena left to sell, how can the damage be undone? The promoter just looks at the queue of customers being turned away from the ticket office and cries. Some lucky people who bought tickets for, say, $50 now discover that they can resell them for $250. If they would rather have $250 than watch the event, they resell the tickets. Selling tickets for more than their face value is called scalping in USA (the UK term is ticket touting). The term scalping, which comes from the American Indian practice of cutting off enemy's scalps, is certainly pejorative. However, ticket scalping causes benefits rather than harm. It simply corrects the promoter's mistake of setting the ticket prices too low and allows the transfer of tickets from people who are less interested in seeing the event to those willing to pay the most. It does not harm a promoter who has no more tickets to sell. It does not harm any of the buyers of the under-priced tickets. Indeed, an unrestricted resale market benefits the final buyers of the tickets. After all, they are all willing participants in the resale market. They would rather pay $250 than not see the game. Nevertheless, scalping is banned in 26 US states, primarily those with major league teams, as well as in all of Europe. A review of US anti-scalping laws can be found in Happel and Jennings (1995).

Why is a scalping ban, enforced with fines and even criminal sanctions, so common? The reason is that there is a widespread, but mistaken, belief that middlemen can drive up ticket prices and make a profit at the expense of the public. Simple supply and demand curves can prove that this belief is mistaken. After the tickets have been sold at too low a price there are a fixed number of tickets in the hands of the public. Each person holding a ticket has a maximum price at which they would hold on to the ticket. The variation in this maximum across ticket holders creates a supply function that must become vertical at the capacity of the arena or stadium. The demand is just the reservation price of every potential ticket buyer. Suppose the equilibrium or market-clearing price was $250. Figure 3.7 shows this supply and demand.

In the diagram the capacity of the arena, which corresponds to the quantity at the vertical segment of the supply function, is set at 40,000 seats. The seats

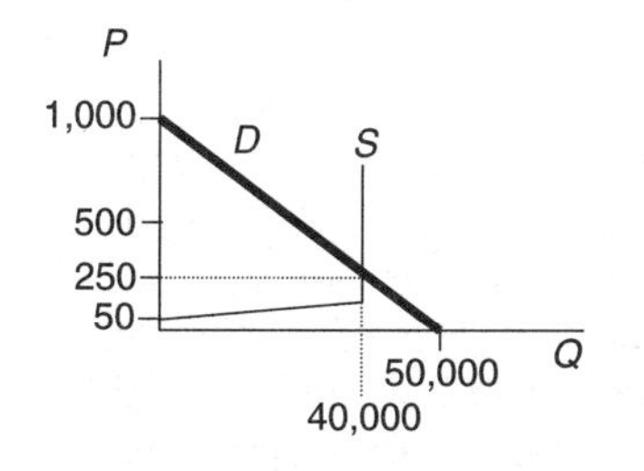

Figure 3.7 Demand and supply for resold tickets

were originally sold for $50 so the supply function starts at $50: that is, each of the original ticket buyers is assumed to prefer seeing the event rather than sell their ticket for less than $50. In an efficient resale market all the ticket-holders who would rather have $250 in cash than keep their ticket would sell their tickets at the market-clearing price of $250. If some people did not want to bother standing at a street corner hawking their tickets and checking on what other people were paying, they could sell them to a scalper (or, if you prefer a less pejorative term, a ticket reseller). If reselling tickets is perfectly legal then everyone has the choice of reselling them on their own or selling them to a ticket reseller. The reseller/scalper would get a little money for saving people the bother of standing around waiting for a good price, say $10 per ticket sold. In this static supply and demand model the lucky buyers of the $50 tickets pocket most of the profits and the promoter is miserable about having let the tickets go so cheaply.

What would happen if the scalpers were the lucky cheap ticket buyers? Suppose the scalpers got in line first and bought up every ticket at $50? The ending price and the ending quantity, $250 and 40,000 tickets, would stay the same. So would the individuals who wound up seeing the event. The same 40,000 people who were willing to pay $250 for a ticket would see the event as would have seen it if the scalpers had just acted as middlemen between the original $50 ticket buyers and the buyers of the resold tickets. Of course, it would now be the scalpers who pocket the profits of 40,000 × $200 (the $200 is the difference between the original and the reselling price).

If may seem unfair that the scalpers are the ones making a profit out of the sports promoter's original mistake, but they would bearing a huge risk if they bought all 40,000 tickets. Maybe the promoter was right or even optimistic about the demand. Then the scalpers would be sitting on 40,000 tickets that they could not unload for more than they had paid. They might even have to sell them for $10 each and 'eat' the balance of $40. Indianapolis is one of the few cities in the USA with major league teams and almost no laws against ticket scalping. In Indianapolis the NCAA Final Four tickets are an exception that will be discussed in Chapter 11. The hundreds of scalpers for all sorts of sporting events provide a highly competitive market for people who want to resell their tickets and for people who want to get into a sold-out game. On a cold rainy day with an uninteresting game on offer the scalpers are lucky to get rid of any tickets they have at half their face value. Either on a good day or a bad day, it is hard to identify anyone who is victimized by this resale market.

Public suspicions about scalpers are so ingrained that the above arguments may not be persuasive. That has been our experience when teaching courses on the economics of sport. At the risk of belaboring the topic, let us try one more example. In this example a Super Scalper buys all 40,000 tickets and then throws away 15,000 of them. With the same demand curve as before, the 25,000 remaining tickets could be sold for $500 each. This is the monopolist profit-maximizing solution in the original example with the same demand function with a zero marginal cost. From the point of view of this Super

Scalper, the $50×40,000 tickets is the fixed cost of cornering the entire market for the tickets and the marginal cost of selling one more ticket is zero. In this example there are identifiable victims. The 15,000 people who were willing to buy the tickets from the original sports promoter at $50 or more and could not because they had been thrown away would clearly be better off in an environment that banned reselling tickets at prices above their face value. Yet even with the Super Scalper these victims are no worse off than if the promoter had set the price at $250 to begin with. The 15,000 who would have bought at $50 might not be in the market at the $250 price. If the promoter had set the price at the profit-maximizing level at the outset, few people would have complained. It must bother people that someone who did nothing to put on the event can make most of the profits. Whether the Super Scalper bore any risk would be immaterial.

The problem with this Super Scalper story is that it is completely unrealistic. Even if a Super Scalper who had enough cash to buy up all of the tickets existed, sports promoters would not sell all their tickets to one buyer. Think about the situation from the sports promoter's viewpoint. Super Scalper comes up to the ticket window with a wheelbarrow full of cash and offers to buy the 40,000 tickets at $50 each. What would the sports promoter immediately think? The answer is that his or her tickets must be been priced too low. Why would any sports promoter give up the opportunity to make more profits? Even if the sports promoter was in a charitable mood (whether owners of professional sports teams profit maximize was the topic of Chapter 2) and wanted to sell the tickets at a lower than market clearing price, why would the promoter feel charitable toward the Super Scalper? Presumably the sports promoter would have his or her own objectives in giving to charity, say, supporting crippled children who would be more deserving than the Super Scalper. The entire scenario of a Super Scalper cornering the ticket market and raising prices is a shibboleth. Promoters universally limit the number of tickets that any one person can buy because they do not want a Super Scalper to hold all or even a substantial fraction of the tickets.

Two other arguments are often raised against the practice of scalping tickets. One is that the scalpers may sell forged or out-of-date tickets. The fraudulent sale argument could apply to almost any product. For example, should only licensed dealers be allowed to sell Levi's ™ jeans? In the European Union (EU) the answer is 'yes'. The fear in the EU is that an unlicensed seller might get away with palming off counterfeit jeans. Currently there is a blanket ban on selling brand name goods without a license from the manufacturer. In the USA the answer is 'no'; anyone can sell Levi's if they can get their hands on them. It is the government's job to police the sale of counterfeits. In terms of the potential for fraud, there is nothing special about the resale of tickets for sporting events. Killing the resale market by making it illegal to sell tickets over their face value seems to be a blunt instrument for preventing fraud.

The second argument against an open resale market is that the ban helps poor sports fans get tickets. If the poor fans were the most willing to stand in line all day when the tickets first go on sale, then a ban on reselling tickets might keep some scalpers out of the queue and give the poor fans a better shot. A ban on reselling would also prevent the poor fans from getting more money out of the tickets they bought, so it would be a mixed blessing. A weakness in the 'poor fan' argument for a ban on scalping is that scalpers would recruit and pay even poorer people to stand in line. In an open market everyone has the same right to get in line. When this chapter was first being drafted there were news stories about queues forming in front of movie theaters in the USA for the first showing of Star Wars Episode I – The Phantom Menace, a full month before it was to be released. Any ticket scalper who hoped to make a profit from waiting in the queue would have an incredibly low opportunity cost for his or her time or find incredibly poor stand-ins. It is hard to make a consistent argument that a ban on the resale of tickets market would help the poor if they both benefit by reselling tickets and they have the lowest opportunity cost of time for standing in line.

Occasionally lotteries rather than a queue are used to ration under-priced tickets to big events. The most famous examples are the World Cup for soccer and the NCAA Final Four Basketball Tournament. In these prestigious events a small proportion of the possible tickets are set aside for the general public at a below-market clearing price while the majority are reserved for the 'fat cats' such as officials of the sport's governing body, corporate sponsors and politicians. The NCAA received 174,000 fully paid applications for the 10,356 tickets it offered to the general public for the March 2000 Final Four in Indianapolis. Only 24 per cent of the seats in the arena were sold to the general public. To simplify computing a probability from these numbers, let us assume that all these tickets were bought as singles. Then everyone who sent in money would have a 10,356/174,000, or roughly 0.06, probability of getting a ticket.

Lotteries change the conclusions on the costs and benefits of antiscalping laws (see Swofford, 1999). Poor fans can no longer use their time as a means of getting a ticket. Now people who have no interest in the game can apply for a ticket just for the chance to resell it. They have to tie up some money until the NCAA refunds their ticket fees but they do not have to spend much time to enter the lottery. This widespread applying-for-tickets-just-to-resell-them behavior increases the number of applications for lottery tickets and reduces the chances of a genuine fan winning a lottery ticket. The fans with the highest reservation prices are willing to use scalpers as an alternative source for a ticket if they do not win one in the lottery. The middle income fans who would never pay the market clearing prices charged by a scalper are unambiguously worse off when legal scalping draws more people into the lottery and their chances of winning a ticket fall. In a lottery situation each individual faces the choices shown in Figure 3.8.

People sort themselves into three categories based on their reservation price. The three categories are scalpers, winners of the lottery who keep their tickets, and customers of the scalpers. The scalpers have the lowest reservation

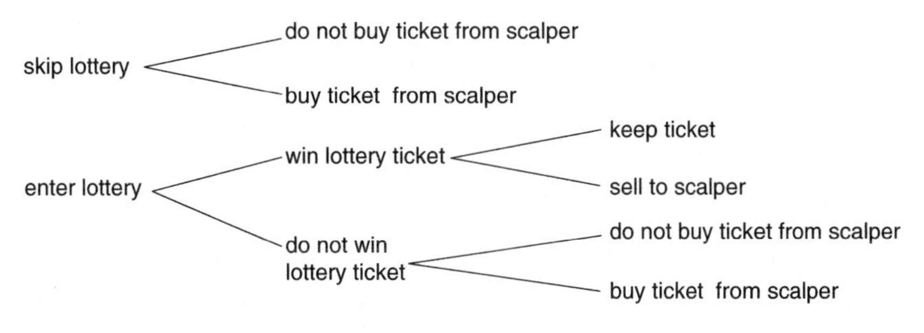

Figure 3.8 Decisions in lottery

prices for a ticket while the customers of the scalpers have the highest reservation prices. The proportions in these three categories depend on the costs of acting as a scalper and of finding a scalper. Scalping has costs such as the expected fine when scalping is illegal and the opportunity cost of the time it takes the scalper to stand on a street corner and sell the ticket. Finding a scalper and negotiating the selling price or comparison shopping to make sure that you are getting the market price are costs for the buyer of the scalped ticket. Figure 3.9 relates the expected benefit of applying for a lottery ticket as a function of the person's reservation price.

The expected net benefit to all of the scalpers is the same. It does not depend on their reservation price (i.e., the most they would pay to see the game themselves). That is why the net benefit is a horizontal segment labeled 'scalpers'. The expected net benefit to the scalper is the sum of two terms. The

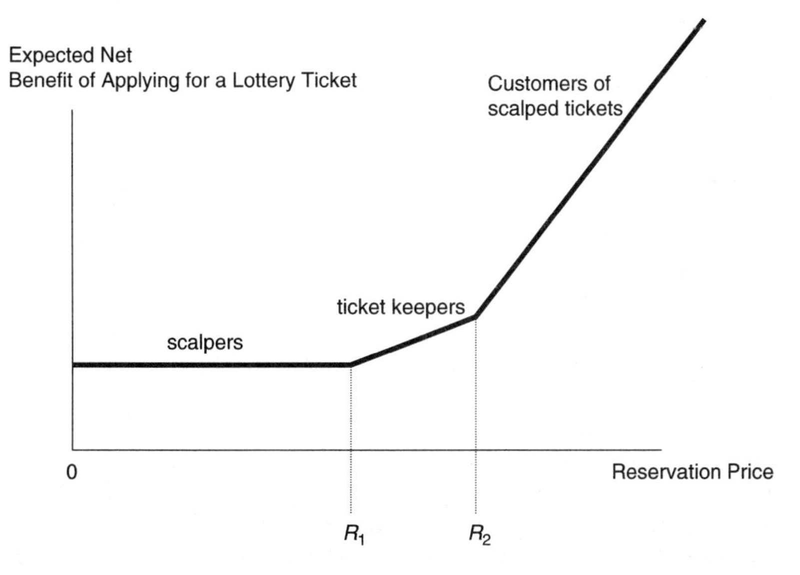

Figure 3.9 The expected net benefit of applying for a lottery ticket

first term is the probability of getting a ticket in the lottery (the 0.06 in the NCAA Indianapolis example) times the price of the ticket in the scalping market (say $500) minus the price of a ticket in the lottery (say $50) minus the direct cost of scalping a ticket (say $25). The second term is the probability of not winning a lottery ticket (0.94 in this example) times the direct cost of entering the lottery such as postage and the lost interest on the money held by the NCAA (say $10). With these figures the expected net benefit to a scalper for entering the lottery would be $0.06 \times (\$500-50-25)+0.96 \times (-10) = \$15.90$. Thus, everyone entering the lottery with the intention of scalping the ticket they might win would have an average benefit of $15.90. The actual benefit would be $425 if they won a ticket and –$10 if they lost. The expected benefit is just these two outcomes weighted by their probabilities.

The expected net benefit to people who keep their tickets does depend on their reservation price. Once a person's reservation price reaches the tipping point, R_1 in Figure 3.9, such that they value their ticket more than the net gain from scalping it, their benefit rises with their reservation price. Again the expected net benefit has two terms. The first is the probability of winning times their reservation price minus the cost of buying the lottery ticket. The second term is the direct cost of applying for the ticket. The expected net benefit for someone who keeps their ticket would be $0.06 \times (R-50)-10$. If someone had a reservation price of $600 their expected benefit from entering the lottery would be $0.06 \times (\$600-50)-10 = \$23$.

The second tipping point, R_2 in Figure 3.9, is when a person's reservation price is high enough to cause them to buy a ticket from a scalper if they do not win the lottery. Here the reservation price has to be higher than the price of a scalped ticket plus the cost of finding and negotiating with a scalper, say $5. The net expected net benefit would be $0.94 \times (R-500-5)+0.06 \times (R-50)-10$. The term $0.06 \times (R-50)-10$ is the probability of winning times the net benefit of winning a lottery ticket minus the postage and lost interest. Suppose the reservation price of someone who would buy a ticket from a scalper was $1,000: the expected net benefit for that reservation price would be $512.30.

It is possible to increase the number of people who keep their ticket and reduce the number who scalp and buy from a scalper by imposing costs on the process of scalping. Fines on scalpers would raise the cost of offering scalped tickets. Restrictions on where people could scalp tickets – such as not allowing scalping within a mile of the stadium – would raise the cost of finding a scalper. These sorts of costs would move the two tipping points but not change the slopes of the expected net benefit function. Figure 3.10 shows what would happen if the scalping market were restricted.

The thin line represents the net benefit of applying for a ticket under the restrictions. There are two new tipping points, labeled R_1' and R_2'. In this environment, a reduction in the number of scalped tickets, the fines and restrictions impose a cost with no benefit to anyone. As long as scalpers can make any money by applying for lottery tickets they will continue to apply for them. Some scalpers who have the highest reservation prices switch from

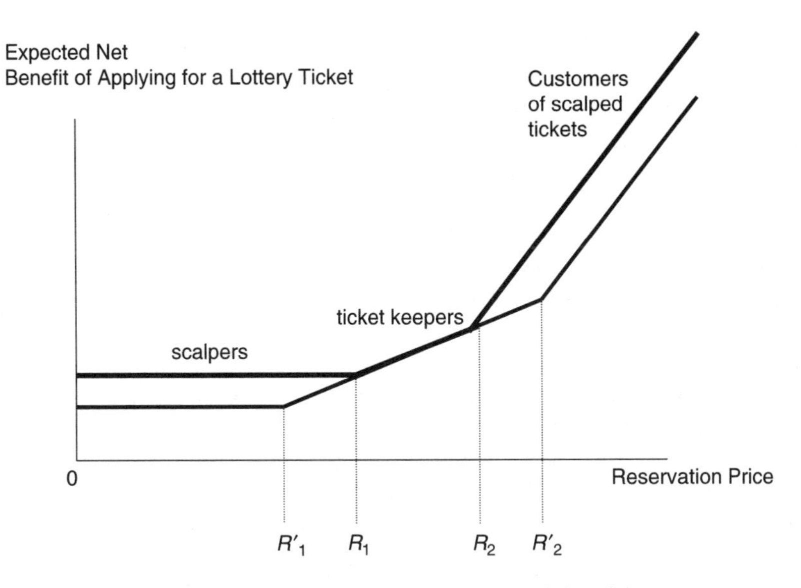

Figure 3.10 Effect of restrictions on scalping tickets

scalping a ticket if they win to seeing the game because the restrictions make them better off as spectators than as scalpers. However, the total number of applicants and thus the probability of winning a ticket stays the same.

It is possible, however, to raise the penalties and restrictions so high that the scalping market disappears: for example, printing the tickets so that they carry the name of the lottery winner and not honoring any ticket unless the holder had sufficient identification to prove that he was the person named on the ticket would effectively kill the resale market. In this situation the net expected benefit line would have no kinks. It would be a straight line starting at the lowest reservation price that would make it worthwhile for someone to entry the lottery in order to get a ticket that they intend to keep. What is interesting about having sufficient restrictions to kill the resale market is that there would now be some people better off. The richest fans would be worse off because they would lose access to the resale market, but some middle income fans would be better off because their chances of winning a lottery ticket would rise once the scalpers stopped applying for tickets.

The result that some people are better off when there are enough restrictions to kill the resale market does not really explain the widespread public support for restrictions on scalping. First, lotteries are relatively rare methods of allocating tickets. Second, restrictions effective enough to kill off the entire resale market are extremely rare. As long as the restrictions merely raise the cost of dealing in scalped tickets, the scalpers will continue to apply for lottery tickets and the scalpers and their customers will just be carrying an extra cost of doing business. The reason for the near universal antipathy to scalping is that the public blames the messenger (scalpers) for the message that tickets are scarce.

Andrew T. Williams (1994) studied the effect of scalping laws on ticket prices in the National Football League. He regressed average ticket prices for the 1992 season on a measure of each winning performance over recent seasons, a club's spending on players for the current season, area population, a dummy variable for competition from a nearby NFL team, average income in the area, stadium capacity, and a dummy variable for the presence of scalping. This dummy variable was a loose measure of toleration of scalping because in some of the ten 'scalping' cities there were no antiscalping laws, and in others there were laws against scalping but these were considered unrestrictive or lightly enforced. Team performance over past seasons was closely related to ticket prices. The *t* score on this variable was highly significant even though there were only 28 observations. The scalping variable was also significant at the 0.05 level but the sign was unexpected. The ability of buyers to easily resell tickets raised the price that the teams charged for the original tickets by 7 per cent. Since most NFL teams sell out most of their games, Williams argued that an open scalping market provided the teams with a better measure of the demand for their tickets. He concluded that: 'In fact, if owners of NFL teams followed their economic self-interest, they would vigorously *oppose* any laws that interfered with the scalping of tickets at prices higher than the face value of the ticket.'

There is an alternative explanation to the higher prices in cities in which scalping is legal or tolerated. A ticket that can be freely resold is more valuable to the fan than a ticket that can only be resold at its face value or, for some events, not resold at all. Any buyer who thinks they might resell the ticket would be willing to pay more for a ticket that can be resold. Although the evidence here is weak because of the poor measure of the degree of restrictions on scalping, it appears that NFL teams are able to capture some of the higher benefit to fans of having a resalable tickets.

Box 3.1 The real costs of antiscalping laws

An additional problem with the laws against ticket scalping is that their enforcement can be completely arbitrary. In 1998 in Maryland undercover policemen posing as ticket buyers arrested two people. The undercover police told the ticket sellers that they did not have the exact change to pay the face price of the tickets. The sellers rounded the ticket up to an even dollar. They were arrested for charging $0.25 cents more than the face price. The charges were later dropped. Another example of enforcement so arbitrary that the *New York Times* called it Kafkaesque occurred in New York City in 1999. The State of New York allows scalpers to sell tickets for $5 more than their face value. A city scalper named Jerry Nahay as well as his wife were arrested, prosecuted and convicted for not paying a sales tax on the difference between resale price of the tickets

Box 3.1 continued

minus the $5 tolerated mark-up over the ticket's face value. The absurdity of this conviction was that services are exempt from sales taxes in New York and no ticket broker pays a sales tax on the tolerated $5 mark-up. The prosecutor simply invented the crime. At the time of the Nahays' conviction the State Legislature in New York had a bill under consideration that would require such a sales tax but it never passed. The sponsor of the bill wrote on the Nahays' behalf arguing that, as the law stood, not collecting this sales tax on resold tickets was not a crime. The *New York Times* accused the prosecutor of attacking a ticket scalper as any easy target just during the prosecutor's re-election campaign (John Tierney, 'The Big City: Need a Re-election Issue? Just Jail a Ticket Scalper', October 29, 1998). Their conviction was overturned by an appeals court. See http://www.steinrisomantel.com/Pages/decisions.html.

On the other hand, if a scalper works out of an office, even in a state with a complete ban on ticket scalping, and sells the tickets as part of a package, it becomes legal. No one can say how much of the package can be attributed to the airfare or the hotel or the dinner built into the package as opposed to the tickets. But a scalper who just stands on a street corner and sells only a ticket is committing a criminal act. So far scalpers working through the Internet by putting up tickets on auction sites such as ebay have been immune from prosecution. That is small comfort to the 242 people who were charged with ticket scalping for the 1998 American League playoff games in New York City. (AP, October 16, 1998)

Pricing season tickets

Demand for season tickets

What is a season ticket? Why would a fan prefer a season ticket to buying tickets to individual games? Why would a team owner prefer selling season tickets to selling individual game tickets? The answers to these questions are prerequisites to a discussion of the demand and the pricing of season tickets.

A season ticket is a complex commodity. The most salient feature of a season ticket is that it entitles the holder to the same seat at every home game over a season. Season ticket holders generally also have the right to renew their tickets and keep their seats for another season. Whether the renewal right has much value to the ticket holder depends on whether the team is expected to field competitive squads in future seasons, how much the ticket prices go up the next season, and on whether the team is expected to stay in town. The rights to buy tickets for famous events such as the Masters' Golf Tournament in Augusta, Georgia, or the main grandstand at the Indianapolis 500 race or

University of Michigan Football home games in Ann Arbor often become family heirlooms that are passed from generation to generation. The value of the renewal rights to these events is enhanced by the events being fixed permanently to one spot.

The renewal rights to most professional sports teams in the USA do not reach such heirloom status because professional sports teams can (and frequently do) move from city to city. Yet many teams that commit to a city with a long-term stadium rental agreement try to capture the renewal value of their season tickets by charging a fee, called the personal seat license (PSL), for the right to buy season tickets. For example, the Houston Astros are selling PSLs for the seats in the front row along the baselines for $10,000. The renewal rights in these PSLs are guaranteed for 30 years. PSLs for baseline seats for the Giants' new stadium in San Francisco sell for $7,500, but the renewal period is a random variable. They are good for the life of the PSL holder. Although they can be sold to another person once per year they lose all value if the current holder dies before he or she can transfer the PSL or neglects to renew the season ticket. Other teams have sold PSLs with 10- and 20-year renewal right guarantees. Some PSLs are good for as long as the team continues to play in the same stadium.

PSLs are common for expansion teams (i.e., new teams admitted when it was decided to increase league size) and for the most desirable seats in a new football or baseball stadium or a hockey arena. When the team stays in the same city PSLs are difficult to impose for ordinary seats in a new stadium or in a renovated old stadium because the existing season ticket holders are used to renewing their tickets without having to buy a special license. The NFL Cincinnati Bengals are the first nonexpansion team to try to sell PSLs for their entire new stadium while staying in the same city. The new stadium opened in 2000. The PSLs were priced at $500 for each of the 50,000 regular seats. They had a difficult time selling them.

Valuing any asset that has been used over a number of years requires discounting the future benefits. Discounting simply reflects the fact that money in hand today can earn interest so it is necessarily more valuable than equal amounts of money available in the future. The present value (PV) of a stream of benefits is:

$$PV = \frac{B_i}{(1+r)^i}$$

where B_i is the benefit in the ith year. (In the context of a PSL the benefit is the difference between the maximum someone is willing to pay for each season and the actual cost of the season ticket through the guarantee period.) The r is the interest rate that reflects the opportunity cost of money, usually taken to be the interest rate on a risk-free asset such as a government bond. For illustration, suppose someone was willing to pay up to $5,000 per year for a season ticket and the actual charge was only $4,000 per year. The benefit per year to the season ticket holder would be the difference of $1,000. If the opportunity cost of money was 5 per cent or 0.05, what is the most that they would pay for a 30-year PSL?

$$
\begin{aligned}
PV &= \frac{B_i}{(1+r)^i} \\
&= \frac{1{,}000}{(1+0.05)^1} + \frac{1{,}000}{(1+0.05)^2} + \cdots + \frac{1{,}000}{(1+0.05)^{30}} \\
&= 15{,}372
\end{aligned}
$$

The season ticket holder might know how much he or she is willing to pay for the season ticket each year but it is harder to know what the price of the tickets will be. Some of the teams selling PSLs are also offering guarantees about how much the price will increase each year. For example, the Cincinnati Bengals will freeze prices in years 1, 2 and 3 and cap increases at 3 per cent in years 4–10 for a 10-year club seat lease.

A PSL is unlikely to fully capture the renewal value of the season ticket. Although the gradient in prices for the most conspicuous seats tends to be quite high, the team is just unable to capture the full consumer surplus of movie stars who want stay in the public eye. Season tickets that do not require a PSL also have a substantial renewal value. The main point about PSLs is that they demonstrate the importance of the renewal rights that are inherent in a season ticket package. The PSLs represent an attempt by teams to capture some of that renewal value whenever a team has made a long-term commitment to a city.

The effect of post-season tickets on the pricing of season tickets

In all professional team sports season ticket holders also have the right to buy post-season tickets, provided their team reaches the play offs. The season ticket holder's right to buy play off tickets is irrelevant for any team that is expected to finish in last place. For a team expected to contend for the league championship, the right to buy post-season tickets is a major consideration. Prospective season ticket buyers factor the option of buying post-season tickets into their calculations of the value of a set of regular season tickets.

The option to buy play-off tickets has features similar to a call option contract in the stock market (i.e., the right to buy a fixed number of shares of a stock up to a specified date). The value of the option depends on the expected price of the post-season tickets. If the play-off ticket prices were set so high that you would not want to see any of the play-off games and you also could not sell the play-off tickets at a profit then the option would be worthless. Professional teams usually do not announce their post-season ticket prices until just before these tickets go on sale. In contrast, stock options have pre-set buying prices. The buyer of a regular season ticket literally has an option to buy post-season tickets at a yet-to-be-determined price. Experience with previous prices for post-season tickets is all the information available to guide the regular season ticket buyer. If the post-season tickets usually sell for 25 per cent more than the regular season tickets then the team would lose the goodwill of its regular season ticket holders if it raised the post-season ticket prices to way above the regular season tickets. The team might be able to fool its fans once or twice into buying season tickets on the basis of fans expecting a relatively low price on play-off tickets but being charged a high price, but the team cannot do that again and again.

The fact that regular season tickets are a combination of both tickets to the regular season and the right to buy tickets for post-season games immediately explains the apparent anomaly of below market-clearing prices charged by teams for such games. At the end of the season when everyone knows that the local team has made it to the play-offs and knows who the opponent will be there is little risk to the ticket buyer and a play-off ticket sold on its own could command a price of, say, $250. Yet, in the same city before the season started, the regular season ticket buyer could only be convinced to buy regular-season tickets under an implicit promise to be sold play-off tickets, provided the team makes it that far, for (say) only $50. *Ex post* or after-the-fact it looks like the team is making a huge blunder by selling post-season tickets for $50 when it could sell the entire arena or stadium out at $250 a seat. Rather than making a huge mistake by under-pricing the post-season tickets, the team owner is maximizing his or her profits for the regular and the post season on an *ex ante* or expected basis.

This *ex ante* profit maximization is the main reason for the existence of active markets for reselling tickets in post-season play. In the lucky cities whose teams make it to the championship round there are hordes of fans eager to see the big games. Many of the regular season ticket holders would rather pocket a high figure (such as $250 per ticket) than see the game in person. Thus the high price scalpers can charge for tickets to the championship game are not at all a sign that the team made a mistake when it set the prices for post-season tickets.

Season tickets as an implicit contract

Not only do the season ticket buyers take it on faith that the mark-up over regular-season tickets for the post-season tickets will be close to what they have experienced in previous years, but they also have to trust the team owners to field a competitive team. For a single game the ticket buyer knows the quality of the local team. The purchase of season tickets, often six months in advance of the start of the season, is done with much less information. The team owner could sell off the contracts of his or her best players and replace them with much less expensive over-the-hill veterans and rookies. Again, the season ticket buyer has to take promises about the overall quality of the team on faith. The same argument about taking the expected prices of post-season tickets on faith applies to the expected team quality. Team owners can fool their season ticket holders once by promising a contender and then having a fire sale of their most talented players, but they cannot fool their season ticket holders more than once. A 'bait-and-switch' strategy on the part of the team owner would hurt long-term profits.

What are the advantages to the ticket buyer, beyond the right to buy post-season tickets and to renew the season ticket, of a season ticket for the current season? Season ticket holders have the first choice of seat location within a price range. Having the same seat year-after-year surrounded by the same people can make attending a game more of a social event. Also, a season ticket guarantees the holder that he or she can attend the most sought-after games of the season. The tickets to the games with the least desirable opponents can be sold or given to friends or business associates. The disadvantages are: having to pay up front for the tickets, having to dispose of tickets for any games that look uninteresting or will be played when the holder will be out of town, and having to bear the risk that the team will do poorly relative to its expectations. A string of injuries can hobble an otherwise competitive team and make the season much less interesting.

Why would a team prefer to sell a season ticket to selling its seats on an individual game basis? Some of the disadvantages for the ticket buyer are advantages for the team. The team would much prefer to get its ticket money six months before the season begins. The team would prefer to have the seats to less attractive games sold in advance. It would prefer the fans to bear most of the financial risk of injuries causing the team to become uncompetitive. Most importantly, the team would prefer to have a pool of season ticket buyers who automatically renew their season tickets to having to market the seats again and again. A team with a solid base of season ticket holders has a secure source of revenue. A team without a base of season ticket holders can rapidly lose ticket revenue if it falters on field. If season ticket holders purchased every seat and there was a waiting list to buy season tickets, then the team could forgo the expense of advertising. It could even forgo the expense of running a ticket office on game days. The ticket office would be replaced by a neatly printed sign, 'This Game is Sold Out'. From the point of view of the team the pool of season ticket holders is a capital asset. A team that has a high fraction of its seats sold to season ticket holders can command a much higher price in the market for professional teams than a team without a strong season ticket base.

It is interesting that in spite of the substantial advantage to the team of having a strong season ticket holder base that teams almost always sell season tickets for the same price per ticket as the individual tickets. Rather than 'discount' the season tickets they alter some of the minor terms of the 'implicit contract' with the season ticket holders to try to attract more season ticket holders. Some examples are a card given to season ticket holders that provides a 10 per cent discount on any souvenirs bought at the team's gift shop, or coupons good for a dollar off the price of stadium parking, or free tickets to the pre-season exhibition games. The implicit contract offered by the owner is that he will consistently field a competitive team, hold the post-season ticket prices to a constant multiple of the regular-season ticket prices, and hold the increase in the price of next season's tickets to close to the rate of inflation.

Auction markets for tickets

In US professional sports, until the 2002 season most of the games in the season had the same face value tickets. If a team did not sell season tickets then it would be free to charge a low price for the least desirable home game and a high price for the most desirable. The only constraint would be the team's uncertainty over which games would be the hot tickets and which the cold. But if the team is juggling the prices of individual games it takes away part of the reason for a fan to buy a season ticket. The season ticket holder is presumably among those most interested in seeing the top games during the regular season and typically wealthier than the average fan. If the season ticket holders can buy tickets for the best games on an individual basis because the team has raised their prices above the amount most ordinary fans would pay, why would season ticket holders bother to renew? The season ticket requires either attending or getting rid of the tickets to any 'dud' games.

A mathematical solution to the owner's **profit-maximization** problem for pricing regular season tickets and post-season tickets is beyond the scope of this text. It requires formulas for discounting the future stream of profits from the renewal of season tickets in subsequent years, the expected profits based on the probability of entering post-season play, and the optimum team quality, regular season ticket prices and the markup for post-season games. The relationship between spending on player quality and the probability of reaching the play offs is nonlinear: expenditures increase faster than the increase in the probability. Even the simplest possible version of this problem would be difficult to solve without a computer program for solving simultaneous equations (such as Mathematica or Maple).

Many of the common practices for selling individual tickets and season tickets are due to the technical constraints of having to print tickets and sell them well in advance of the season. Juggling prices for individual games is difficult with preprinted tickets that were prepared before the owner knew which opponents would be hot and which cold. Selling tickets via the Internet would eliminate these constraints. Teams could **auction** off both season tickets and individual tickets. They could unbundle renewal rights from the sale of season tickets by auctioning tickets with and without a renewal right. They could vary the renewal terms with different guarantees for future price increases and years of renewal rights. Tickets to team sports would be handled more like the sale of airline tickets. Airlines use computer programs to adjust the number offered at discount fares and economy coach fares as the orders arrive. This practice is called yield management. The teams are being pushed in this direction because active auction markets already exist for tickets on the Internet. All this may sound very strange to a fan who has been buying tickets at the box office for decades but it is no stranger than asking a fan who has been buying the same seats with season tickets for decades to now hand over $10,000 for the right to continue to buy season tickets. Variable pricing of tickets by the attractiveness of the opponents has been common in European soccer for some time, probably because of the greater disparities in team quality. It has also been common in intercollegiate sports in the USA to charge a higher price for football and basketball games against traditional rivals. In both European soccer and college sports the fans and management have a good idea of which opponent will be the hot draw. Variable pricing is just beginning in US professional sports. For example, for the 2002 season the Colorado Rockies divided their home games into four different 'tiers' with different prices. Happel and Jennings (2002) discuss the prospects for the differential pricing and auctions for tickets. They have an excellent discussion of the entire ticket market.

Conclusions

Conceptually, ticket demand and pricing are complex topics because of the uncertainty over the quality of the good being sold. The game could be a close contest with implications for the team's promotion or relegation or its play off prospects, or a listless affair with the star players on both sides absent and no implications for the team's standings. The uncertainty grows exponentially when the object being sold is a season ticket. Then the uncertainty expands to the post-season prospects and the value of any bundled renewal rights. Empirically, the topic is difficult as well because of the collinearity problems in estimating the elasticity of demand. Almost all of the point estimates have been extremely inelastic, which would make no sense for a profit-maximizing monopolist. The estimated values would not even make sense for a utility-maximizing team owner who enjoyed full stands and successful teams. The estimates are so low that the prices could be raised, the extra revenue applied to hiring better players, and the stands would still be close to full. Including the cost of travel has provided a solution to the technical problems in estimating demand elasticity for sports tickets. The last point is that the market for tickets is changing rapidly as technology allows firms to unbundle the components of the tickets and vary their prices depending on the attractiveness of the game. The scalping laws may become irrelevant once teams figure out how to capture the entire consumer surplus in their tickets.

Note

1. Forrest and Simmons (2002) examined attendance demand and uncertainty of outcome in the English Football League in 1997–8. They used

betting odds data for individual games, finding that the football betting market is broadly efficient, but – more importantly for our argument – that attendance demand does, indeed, respond positively to the outcome uncertainty measure devised from betting odds data. However, interventionist strategies to equalize team strengths will not necessarily succeed, since such devices ignore the important property of home advantages in team sports. Thus almost 50 per cent of league games in English football are won by the home team (note there are three possible outcomes: home win, away win and draw). An equal contest is actually a home team placed twelfth, say, facing an away team placed fourth rather than twelfth versus eleventh. Forrest and Simmons argue that outcome uncertainty and competitive balance are quite distinct concepts.

Exercises

1. The quote below is from a ticket scalper who blames the high prices of the scalpers for tickets to Michael Jordan's final basketball game on the season ticket holders who asked the scalpers for so much money when they sold them. Is this argument credible? Who would gain if season ticket holders had no information about the resale price of the tickets for this game? Use supply and demand curves in your answer and show the situation with and without ticket scalpers. Assume that the season ticket holders have all the tickets to start with and that the resale market is perfectly legal.

   If the price is right . . .
   Game 5 ticket prices skyrocketing with championship hopes
   Posted: Thursday June 11, 1998 09:37 PM
   CHICAGO (AP)

   Fans should know that it's the season ticket-holders who are driving prices so high, said Lars Geary, a manager with Gold Coast Tickets who won't talk about prices. Season ticket-holders see one high price on the news and it ruins it for everybody. We're buying their tickets at high prices and then we're forced to sell them at high prices.

2. (a) A promoter has booked a rock group for an outdoor arena. The seating is first come-first served (also called festival seating in the USA). The demand for these tickets is $P=50-0.005Q$. The fixed cost of putting on the concert is \$100,000. What is the profit-maximizing price level? What are the promoter's profits?

   (b) If the promoter could make a profit of \$10 by selling a t-shirt to everyone attending the concert, what would be the profit-maximizing price level and what are the promoter's profits?

3. A golf tournament has the following demand for tickets, $P=200-0.002Q$. The golf tournament can make a profit from parking, food and souvenirs which varies inversely with the reservation price of the customer. These ancillary profits make the marginal cost of letting in a customer negative. The marginal cost function is $MC=-100+0.001Q$. What are the profit-maximizing ticket price and quantity of tickets? If the fixed cost of putting on the tournament is 2,000,000, what are the tournament's profits?
4. A tennis promoter has rented tennis stadium with 2,000 seats. The demand function for the tennis match is $P=50-0.01Q$. If the promoter could perfectly price discriminate and the fixed costs of putting on the tennis match were $25,000, what would be the promoter's profits? If the promoter could only divide his or her customers into four price bands, what would be the profits?
5. The Indianapolis Colts of the National Football League hire guards to stand at the entrances to the RCA Dome to inspect the fans coming into the games. The inspections are intended to intercept any food or drink that a fan might try to carry into the game. Not even water can be carried into a game. Presumably any fan who would prefer to bring in their own food or drink would be willing to pay more for a ticket that allowed them to do so than for a ticket to an identical game with a restriction on carrying in food or beverages. The team cannot justify the restriction on safety grounds because fans can drink as much beer and alcohol as they want if they buy it within the stadium. Also, these restrictions were in place long before anyone was concerned about terrorists bringing a bomb into a stadium in a cooler. Why do the Colts find it more profitable to maintain this restriction?
6. (calculus) A stadium has two types of seats, the good and the bad (with the respective subscripts g and b). The respective demands are:

$$P_g = 1{,}000 - 0.02Q_g - 0.01Q_b$$
$$P_b = 500 - 0.01Q_b - 0.001Q_g$$

   Assuming a zero marginal cost, what are the profit-maximizing ticket prices?
7. (calculus) A stadium has two types of seats, the good and the bad (with the respective subscripts g and b). The respective demands are:

$$P_g = 1{,}000 - 0.01Q_g - 0.001Q_b$$
$$P_b = 250 - 0.05Q_b - 0.01Q_g$$

   Assuming a zero marginal cost, what are the profit-maximizing ticket prices?
8. Suppose the World Cup in soccer required ticket buyers to send in a photocopy of their passport with their ticket order. The ticket holders would have their passport inspected as they entered the stadium to make sure that they were the original buyers of the ticket. This mechanism would completely kill the resale market.

(a) If the World Cup tickets were sold on a lottery basis, who would gain and who would lose from eliminating the resale market for tickets?
(b) What would this passport checking regime do to the demand for World Cup tickets?

9. (calculus). Suppose a team's total revenue as a function of its proportion of wins was: $TR = w + w^2 - 3w^3$ where w is the proportion of wins and TR is total revenue.

   $0 \leq w \leq 1$

   Suppose further that the total cost function is:

   $TC = w^2$

   (a) Plot the TR and TC functions. Why should the total cost function be modeled as nonlinear in the proportion of wins? Why should the total revenue function be modeled with a cubic and a quadratic term?
   (b) What is the optimal proportion of wins for a profit-maximizing owner?
   (c) What proportion of wins would a utility-maximizing owner have with the constraint that the team break even?

10. (a) The demand for tickets at a rock concert is $P = 100 - 0.01Q$. The marginal cost of providing an additional ticket is zero. What is the profit-maximizing price and quantity?
    (b) If the profits from the rock concert were zero, what must be the fixed costs of putting on the concert?
    (c) Suppose the promoters of the rock concert sold t-shirts to every ticket buyer at $20 each. The t-shirts cost $5 to produce and sell. What would happen to the number of tickets sold, the ticket price, and to overall profits?
    (d) The assumption in question (c), that everyone buys a t-shirt, is not realistic, otherwise the promoter could just charge one price for the combination of the ticket and the t-shirt and save the money used to hire t-shirt sellers. Assuming that not everyone buys a t-shirt, why is it in promoter's interest to set a high price on the t-shirts while just covering his fixed costs with the price set on the tickets?

11. In Indianapolis the Comcast digital cable system offers different types of pay-per-view shows at different prices. The categories and prices are:

    old movies for $3.95
    recent movies for $5.95
    'adult' movies for $11.95
    live English Premier League Football games for $16.95

    (a) Assuming that the marginal cost of providing a show to one more viewer is zero and that Comcast was effectively a monopoly to its subscribers, what can you infer about the demand for English Premier League Football relative to the other types of show?

(b) Suppose the owners of the different types of shows charged Comcast a fixed fee per viewer. Would this change your conclusions in part (a)?

12. (a) Why are the prices of the tickets for post season games, such as the NBA finals, set far below the market clearing price at the time the team reaches the post-season?
    (b) Why do teams prefer selling a personal seat license over simply raising the price of season tickets?
    (c) After he or she has bought a personal seat license, why would anyone trust a team to spend enough on players to be competitive in the future?
13. If a perfect price discriminator had the demand for a sporting event of $P = 500 - 0.1Q$, a marginal cost of zero, and a fixed cost of $1 million, what would be the level of profits?
14. A season ticket buyer's reservation price for one set of season tickets is $2,000. The price of a set of season tickets is at $1,000. What is the most that the ticket buyer would pay for a personal seat license if he or she thought that they would continue to buy the tickets for 30 years and that the margin between their reservation price and the selling price would be constant? Assume that a ticket buyer discounts future benefits at 5 per cent per year.
15. Use supply and demand curves to illustrate the effect of scalping tickets for a sporting event in which every seat in the stadium has been sold at a price lower than the market-clearing price. Who gains and who (if anyone) loses through the introduction of a market for reselling tickets?
16. What are the effects of a ticket lottery for a sporting event combined with penalties for selling tickets above their face value? Use a diagram to illustrate these effects. How would the diagram change if the penalties were so severe that no one sold tickets over their face value?
17. The term 'rational behavior' in economics means that an individual uses the available information to make the 'best' or utility-maximizing choice given his or her preferences. In what ways do fans of professional sports teams behave rationally?
18. Once in a while Martin would like to see a hot game (say, once a year), but he is not interested in buying season tickets. He would like to go to a game and just pay the face value for the best seats. To his chagrin the best seats are always sold out when he tries to buy them on game day. He thinks the local teams are making a big mistake by not raising ticket prices on the best seats enough so that they will not always sell out first. Can you explain the logic of the team's pricing policy to Martin?
19. Are professional sports teams monopolies? Are they natural monopolies? Explain.
20. Why do most Major League baseball teams not sell out most of their games while in the NFL around 90 per cent of the games sell out?

4 The labor market for players

Chapter goals

Labor markets are central to the understanding of sporting activity. It is product demand that determines the demand for labor. The chapter begins by outlining the perfectly competitive model of the demand for labor, but emphasizes the fact that the market for athletes is more complex than this model implies. Contracts need to be specified in such a way that they induce maximum effort from the players with elements of both bonuses and long-term contracts. The market for sports stars is then monopsonistic, given a shortage of players with star quality and restrictions on mobility of players. Conditions of **bilateral monopoly** may apply with the probability of the wage diverging from the **marginal revenue product**. The reader should by the end of the chapter have some understanding of the nature of the player contract and how to ascertain the economic value of individual performance, which may be influenced in team sports by the dispersion of pay within a team. Historically, the **reserve clause** in North America and the **retain and transfer system** in Europe were the main mechanisms for achieving an acceptable degree of competitive balance, but have been weakened through key legal judgments such as in the **Bosman case**. Some economists have argued that they were in fact bound to fail, through the implications of the **invariance thesis** of the **Coase theorem**, and the actual impact of such restrictions is a matter of some debate. Other controversial issues are whether more equal **gate-sharing** will increase competitive balance and what are the likely results of the implementation of **salary caps**. Reference back to Chapter 2 suggests that these policies will be influenced by the goals of the club owners.

Introduction

Derived demand

The demand for labor is called a **derived demand** because it depends on (or is derived from) the demand for the final product or service that the labor produces. The analysis of the labor market for athletes is central to our understanding of the economics of sports because at sporting events spectators are paying to observe part of the production process itself. In a real sense the product the industry is selling is its athletes.

In this chapter we first examine the nature of supply and demand for professional athletes, comparing and contrasting these functions with the supply and demand for labor in more conventional industries. We then examine the ways in which leagues in team sports in North America, Europe and elsewhere have imposed restrictions on the free mobility of professional athletes. Such restrictions may increase the uncertainty of outcome, which sustains fan interest, and it definitely reduces overall labor costs. These restrictions have led to conflicts with players' unions and with the US and EU **antitrust** (competition) laws.

The supply of and the demand for professional athletes

The Law of Diminishing Returns

Before analyzing the labor market in professional sports it is useful to review the supply of and the demand for labor in the conventional model of a firm that is a perfect competitor in both the product and the labor market. The marginal productivity theory that is the basis of this model relies on the assumption of **profit maximization**. Firms maximize profits when labor is employed up to the point that the last unit of labor adds as much to the firm's revenue as it adds to its cost. That is, the *marginal revenue product of labor* (MRP_L) must equal the *marginal cost of labor* (MC_L). The logic of this rule is that if the last unit of labor hired brought in more revenue than it cost, the firm could increase its profits by adding additional units of labor. Conversely, if the last unit of labor hired cost more than the revenue generated from its output, the firm could increase its profits by reducing the amount of labor. When the marginal revenue product and marginal cost of labor just balance, any increase or reduction in the amount of labor reduces profits. Hence the rule that is familiar to students who have taken introductory microeconomics: profits are maximized when marginal revenue equals marginal cost. For a factor of production such as labor the rule can be restated as profits are maximized when the marginal revenue product of the factor equals the marginal cost of the factor.

Marginal revenue product is a function of the amount of output produced by a unit of labor (MPP_L, the *marginal physical product of labor*) and the price at which this output is sold (i.e., $MPP_L \times MR = MRP_L$), where MR is *marginal revenue*. In a perfectly competitive firm the marginal revenue is a constant equal to the per unit selling price of the product. The MPP_L is the change in physical output for a one-unit increase in labor. In calculus terms it is the derivative of total output with respect to labor. As the amount of labor used by the firm increases MRP_L may initially rise, but as more labor is added to a fixed amount of capital the MRP_L will eventually decline. This relationship is known as the **law of diminishing returns**. It is illustrated in Figure 4.1.

The average revenue product (ARP_L) is defined as the total revenue at given level of labor input divided by the amount of labor. The MRP_L intersects the ARP_L at its highest point. Where the average revenue is not increasing or decreasing it must by definition be equal to the marginal revenue. To determine the profit-maximizing level of employment the firm must equate the MRP_L with the marginal cost of labor. If the supply curve of labor is perfectly elastic (horizontal), the marginal cost of labor equals the going wage rate. For example, if a firm can hire all of the labor it wants at $10 per hour then the marginal cost of any hour of labor is the wage rate of $10

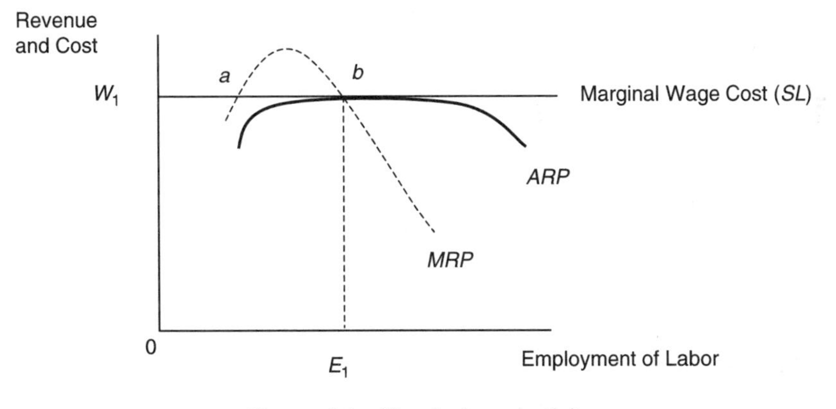

Figure 4.1 Marginal productivity

per hour. For one firm in a large labor market the assumption of a perfectly elastic supply of labor is reasonably accurate. In Figure 4.1 MC_L equals MRP_L at two points, *a* and *b*. However, only point *b* maximizes profits. Formally, the calculus second-order condition for profit maximization requires that the MRP_L curve cut the MC_L curve from above. The firm gives up profits if it operates at *a* because adding units of labor beyond *a* adds more to revenue than it adds to costs. Once the firm reaches point *b*, adding more labor would result in the costs of each unit being higher than the revenue that unit generates. In long-run equilibrium in a perfectly competitive industry only normal profits are earned. At that situation employment would be at OE_1, and the wage at OW_1, since $ARP_L = MC_L$. If above normal profits were being earned by the firms in a perfectly competitive industry average revenue product would be forced down by the entry of new firms.

The market for professional athletes is more complicated than the **perfect competition** model of a firm's hiring decisions. In the perfect competition model the quality of the labor is assumed to be known to the firm. Sports teams have uncertainty over the eventual quality of a rookie they hire. At the start of a season firms have substantial uncertainty about the full-season performance of even a veteran athlete. Also, teams have to make hiring decisions over a much longer horizon than a season. They often sign seven- or ten-year contracts with athletes who are in their twenties. No one knows how much the athlete's skills will deteriorate or improve over that period. In contrast, in the perfect competition model the firm is assumed to be able to observe the worker's current and future quality and his level of effort. Observing and controlling the level of effort is much more difficult in sport. For example, maximum performance from athletes requires a weight training regimen, a careful diet, hours of daily study of game films, and training and exercise sessions in the off season. It also requires that the athletes avoid recreational drugs and all-night parties that could harm their health. Teams cannot watch an athlete around the clock. Instead they structure the athlete's contracts to encourage the forms of behavior that raise performance and discourage behavior that reduces performance. These contracts often forbid certain risky activities (e.g., banning play in pick up (casual) basketball games is standard in NBA contracts) or provide bonuses for desired outcomes (e.g., reporting to training camp under a specified weight). All of these issues are absent in the perfect competition model.

Another dimension of professional sport that is outside the competitive model is teamwork. Players have to learn the weaknesses and strengths of their teammates and to coordinate their strategies. A group of players who have been together for years will be much more effective than a group of equally talented individuals who have just been assembled into a team. In the perfect competition model labor is hired in a *spot market*, (i.e., day by day). There is nothing for the workers to learn so there is no reason for the firms to tie them to long-term contracts. Most real labor markets, as opposed to the idealized perfect competition model, require some worker training, have some monitoring of effort costs, and have some pay off for teamwork. Also, poor health habits will eventually affect a worker's productivity in even the most sedentary of jobs. Yet very few firms outside sport have the degree of uncertainty over future productivity, the high training and monitoring costs and the extreme sensitivity of productivity to teamwork found in professional sports.

Monopsony

Perfect competition does not prevail in professional sports in the product market since each club typically has a local monopoly. The league itself can be regarded as a monopoly except in the rare situations that there is a competing league in the same sport.

Squad sizes or team rosters are usually fixed. Thus it is more sensible to consider the supply of labor in teams in units of quality rather than in the number of players. Even if rosters were not fixed (as is the case in soccer outside the USA), if a club already has 50 players it may not be sensible to add another player of average quality. The marginal revenue product of the fifty-first player may be zero because he would never play in a regular game and he would contribute little to the team's practise sessions. However, the team's profits may increase if it hired a star player. The idea of adding a unit of player quality is more abstract than the concept of adding the services of one more person. A unit of quality could be defined as enough additional talent to win one more game per season, holding the talent in the other teams in the league constant. The talent could be embodied in one star player or spread over several players who are each slightly better than the players on the current roster.

Since star players by definition are extremely scarce, the supply of labor measured in quality units is not perfectly elastic. To add a unit of player quality the team has to pay a higher price than it paid for its last unit of quality.

A labor market in which one firm bids up the price of labor as it hires more units is called *monopsonistic*. **Monopsony** is the factor market counterpart to having a monopoly or a single seller in the product market. Literally, monopsony means a factor market in which there is just one buyer. More generally, the term 'monopsonistic market' refers to a factor market with few buyers, rather than just one buyer. The key idea is that there are so few buyers that each one bids up the price of the factor if it tries to hire more.

There are labor markets in which the firm is a monopsonist in the labor market and a perfect competitor in the product market. The only firm in an isolated area could be a monopsonist, (e.g., a coal mining company in a remote part of Wyoming). To attract additional miners the firm has to pay enough to convince some miners to relocate. This pay would be much higher than it had been paying to local miners. In contrast, the firm's product, coal, is sold in a perfectly competitive worldwide market. It is also possible for the firm to be a monopsonist in the labor market and a monopolist in the product market. The only hospital in an isolated area would have to pay enough to convince any additional nurses that it hired that it was worthwhile to relocate. The hospital's product market is serving the local customers. In this example the single hospital has a monopoly. The restrictions on player mobility make the sports labor market more like the one-hospital-in-the-town example, with monopoly in the product market and monopsony in the labor market.

Bilateral monopoly

If there was only one nurse who had the skills the hospital required then the example would be even more complicated. In this situation the hospital is the sole buyer and the nurse with the unique skills is the sole seller. One seller facing one potential buyer is a bilateral monopoly. Often the bilateral monopoly model fits the sports labor market. A team that has drafted a player out of college is the only buyer that player faces. If only one player available in the draft pool has the skills the team needs (say a center in basketball or a quarterback in football), then the team is facing a single seller. In bilateral monopolies the equilibrium wage is indeterminate. There is a range of wages high enough to convince the player to sign rather than sit out the season and low enough to convince the team to sign rather than give up the player's services.

If there was a union representing all players, the union could keep the team from exploiting its monopsony power. Figure 4.2 shows the intervention of a union in a market in which one employer faced a rising supply curve of labor, AWC. In this situation the final outcome will be determined by the skill in negotiations of the individual club owner or the representative of the owners group and the players' union.

A club or the owner's association maximizes its profit by setting the MRP_L equal to the MWC_L (the marginal wage cost of labor). This would produce the

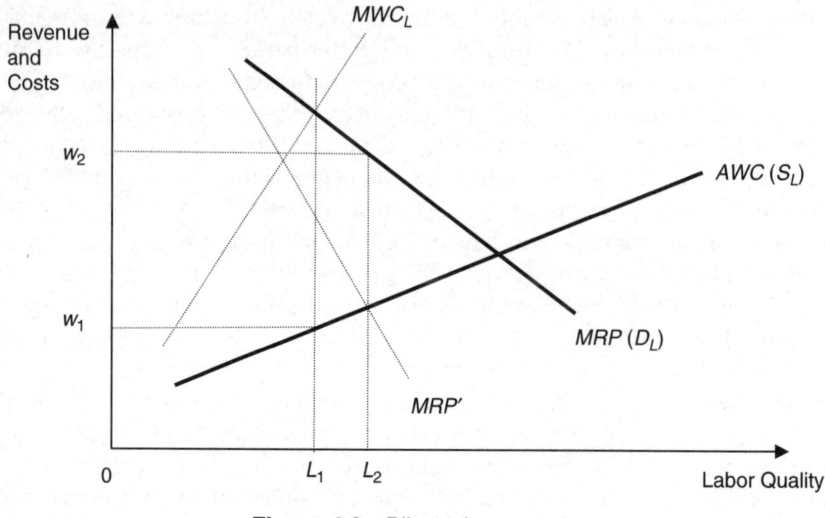

Figure 4.2 Bilateral monopoly

outcome given by L_1 labor quality and a wage w_1. The players' union would wish to maximize the economic rent going to the players by setting S_L equal to MRP', producing a wage w_2 and labor quality at L_2 (i.e. maximizing the size of the total wage bill given the labor supply constraint). This defines the limits within which wages and employment will settle with a wage somewhere between w_1 and w_2 and labor quality somewhere between L_1 and L_2.

Measuring productivity

In most industries outsiders do not have access to data that identifies the marginal product of each worker. There are a few exceptions to this statement. Industries that pay piece rates have data on individual productivity. Two interesting examples are the automobile window repairers studied by Lazear and stadium vendors studied by Oettinger. In sports, however, it is possible to obtain more precise estimates of each player's marginal revenue product and determine whether salaries match this figure. If players are paid less than the value of their *MRP* they are, by definition, being **exploited**. This term has a narrower meaning in economics than in everyday language. An athlete being paid a vast amount of money, say $10 million per year, could still be exploited if he was adding $20 million a year to the team's revenue. Conversely, someone being paid a lower than subsistence wage, say $1 an hour, would not be exploited if his marginal revenue product was $1 an hour or less. In a monopsonistic labor market with profit-maximizing employers the expected result is that the workers are exploited: that is, a monopsony pays its workers a wage less than the MRP of the last worker.

It is also possible that a monopoly could pay a worker more than his marginal revenue product. Monopolies do not have to worry about maximizing profits since they will not go bankrupt if they fail to maximize profits. In competitive industries firms have no discretion about whether they maximize profits. Again, the detailed data available on the productivity of individual athletes makes it possible to test for such behavior.

The first direct approach to measuring players' MRPs was that of Gerry Scully (1974a) using data from major league baseball. Marginal productivity is derived from a three equation model. First, he estimates the impact of various team performance measures on a team's playing success:

$$PERF_j = F(PERF_{ij}, Z_j)\text{for all } i \text{ on team } j \tag{4.1}$$

where PER_j is the j team's performance measured as a function, F, of player $PERF$ and Z

$PERF_{ij}$ is the ith rostered player's performance in the jth team

Z_j is a vector of the other inputs which determine a team's performance, such as quality of management or training facilities.

Second he estimates the effect of these performance measures on a team's playing success:

$$WPCT_j = \alpha_o + \alpha_2 PERF_j \tag{4.2}$$

where $WPCT_j$ is the jth team's winning percentage. Finally, we estimate the effect of a team's winning percentage on its total revenue:

$$TR_j = \beta_o + \beta_1 X_j + \beta_2 WPCT_j \tag{4.3}$$

where TR_j is the jth team's total revenues and X is a vector of other variables influencing TR. Using this approach on data for 1967–8 Scully estimated a player's salary function which related salaries to such performance measures and compared those with marginal revenue products, yielding an estimate of the extent of exploitation. Dividing players into mediocre, average and star players he found substantial exploitation in relation to the last two of these categories. 'Considered over career length, average players receive salaries equal to about 11% of their gross and about 20% of their net (after the deduction of training and other expenses) marginal revenue products. Star players receive about 15% of their net marginal revenue products' (Scully, 1974, p. 929).

A number of further papers showed that exploitation was a common phenomenon. Thus, Porter and Scully (1982) extended the analysis to baseball managers, concluding that there was substantial exploitation of the most skilled managers. At 1982 prices the MRP of baseball's top manager from 1969 to 1980 was estimated to be in excess of $1 million. Porter and Scully claimed that actual salaries were a small fraction of this sum. Further evidence of player exploitation was detected by Medoff (1976a) using data over the period 1972 to 1974 in baseball. Adopting different performance variables from those of Scully and a changed estimating procedure for the revenue equation, this study found a generally lower but still substantial degree of exploitation, with players paid between 30 and 50 per cent of their MRPs. In contrast, Zimbalist (1992), whose study occurred after the introduction of **free agency**, reported that the average free agent received 23 per cent in excess of his MRP. His approach was rather different from that of Scully in that his estimates are based on the difference in a team's performance with and without a particular player on its roster. Finally, McDonald and Reynolds (1994) directly seek to answer the question of whether the new institutions of free agency have brought baseball salaries into line with MRPs. They find that the answer is basically positive. For hitters the coefficient on performance is not significantly different from one, indicating that hitters are paid according to their marginal productivity, but for pitchers the coefficient is 1.26, indicating that pitchers are overpaid at the margin and implying that in this case it is the team owners who are exploited.

One problem in all the above estimates, however, is that they ignore **cross-player complementarities** (the teamwork discussed above) as well as factors such as managerial quality: that is, equation 4.1 above is assumed to be separable (Krautmann, 1999). Using data on baseball players eligible for free agency over the period 1990 to 1993 Krautmann estimates the competitive return to performance and uses these estimates to impute the value of a young player restricted by the reserve clause. He obtains much higher estimates than are provided by the Scully method, with the average player receiving about 85 per cent of his estimated MRP. Other studies have attempted to measure such features directly. Thus, Kahn (1993) attempted to investigate the impact of managerial quality on team and individual player performance in baseball. In effect, he finds that high quality managers get more victories out of a given runs-scored: runs-allowed ratio than do low quality managers. However, better managers may also get higher values of scoring to defence ratios for given offensive and defensive inputs (i.e., player performance relative to player ability). Thus it may pay players to accept a lower initial salary to play for a better manager.

A failure to include a quality of management variable in the above studies means that they are likely to be subject to omitted variable bias. In theory such bias could go in two directions. If inputs are substitutes, individual player attributes may be rewarded at a lower rate when other players have higher values of this attribute. Alternatively if players are complements, individual attributes will be rewarded more highly in teams which also have other players with higher values of this attribute. Idson and Kahane (2000) have tested this omitted variable bias hypothesis for ice hockey, a sport which has the advantage of not having a salary cap, which may distort the relationship between salary and productivity. They find that team attributes have both direct and indirect effects on player salaries in a positive direction. Thus estimates of the effects of individual attributes on salaries are upwardly biased when team effects are not taken into account in standard salary regressions.

Pay dispersion

Performance may also be affected by the dispersion of pay within teams. For example, there are many cases in European soccer of clubs refusing to sign star players because this would upset the established wage structure with the implication that if star players were paid much more than existing players this would affect the degree of teamwork. The implication of this is that star players may be paid 'too little' relative to their ability. Such a model, though not applied to sport, is contained in Levine (1991). He distinguishes two types of labor, high skill and low skill. Then team productivity can be written as:

$$Q = C(W_L/W_H)F(L_L, L_H) \tag{4.4}$$

where Q represents team output, $C(-)$represents a measure of team cohesiveness, (W_L/W_H) is the ratio of low to high skill salaries, and $F(L_L, L_H)$ is a production function characterized by some level of labor complementarity.

If $C > 0$ less salary disparity will result in greater team cohesiveness and thus more efficient team production. Adopting such a model Depken (2000) finds support for this using a panel approach to explain win percentages in terms of total salary, salary dispersion and a time trend for baseball data from 1985 to 1998.[1]

We must also consider the possibility that there are positive **externalities** in the sense that a team which hires a superstar may raise the revenues of other teams in the league. Thus Hausman and Leonard (1997) find that the presence of a superstar such as Michael Jordan can have a substantial effect on the number of viewers watching NBA basketball games and increase other teams' revenue as well as his own. Using a fixed effects model for 1989–90 they find that Magic Johnson increased ratings by 31 per cent, Michael Jordan by 28 per cent and Larry Bird by 27 per cent. There is also a superstar effect on paid attendance. Hausman and Leonard estimate Michael Jordan's total value to other NBA teams to be over $50 million, or roughly $2 million per team. The implication of their model is that with an externality of this type small teams will tend to free ride on large teams, leading to a distribution of talent which is too heavily weighted towards large teams relative to the efficient (league revenue maximizing) talent distribution.[2]

The reserve clause in North American team sports and the retain and transfer system in soccer implicitly recognize that existence of externalities. In the latter case transfer fees are payable to the previous employer for the loss of a worker's services, as explained in Box 4.1. Lucifora and Simmons (2003) have tested for superstar effects in Italian soccer and found that earnings were strongly influenced by two goalscoring performance measures after controlling for personal characteristics and team effects. The implied earnings ratio for the median superstar was over four times that of the median ordinary

Box 4.1 Transfer fees and the price of footballers

Prior to the Bosman ruling, football clubs in European soccer were entitled to compensation for the loss of players to other clubs even when out of contract. Transfer fees are also evident in Rugby League and more recently in Rugby Union following its change from an amateur to a professional sport. In scale and size these are much more modest than in soccer where transfer fees have rocketed to over $50 million for the top players. What determines who gets transferred, and the size of the transfer fee?

During the 1993/94 season English Premier and Football League clubs spent £92 million on player transfers within these leagues at a time when their total revenues were only £387 million. Out of 240 transfers 42 took place without a fee being involved, but in other cases fees reached over £3 million for individual players. The number of players transferred in that season represented over 12 per cent of the total player population.

Carmichael, Forrest and Simmons (1999) note that in the transfer market the sample of players is self selected since players are only transferred when the fee offered is higher than, or equal to, the reservation fee of the selling club. Transfers are not random. The probability of a transfer is highest for more experienced players who can score goals. Correcting for sample selection bias they find that the sort of variables suggested by the standard human capital model are capable of explaining the size of transfer fees. Transfer fees increase with age, but at a decreasing rate, peaking at the age of 23. Players with more playing experience, *ceteris paribus*, are worth more. Being an English international player increases the size of fee by nearly half a million pounds. Each goal scored adds over £20,000 to the fee of a forward and over £30,000 to the fee of a defender. These variables reflect the expected contribution to the new team's output, which is usually measured in terms of success on the playing field and is also related to the player's marginal productivity.

player. Further, a player located at the ninety-ninth percentile of the distribution earned more than ten times as much as players located at the median and forty-five times as much as players located at the tenth percentile of the distribution. Only nine players in the Series A of the Italian League scored at a rate of once every two games or more and the rewards for these leading goal scorers were much greater than for those who contributed the final pass which created a goal. It is goal scoring which denotes star status in the eyes of the consumer. There is also the question of the most appropriate incentive system to elicit maximum performance, and this applies as much to individual sports as to team sports (see Chapter 10).

Collective bargaining in professional sports

Player unions

Unlike most other unions, sports unions both in North America and Europe do not negotiate salaries for individual members. These are left to the player, who usually hires an agent to negotiate on his or her behalf. The absence of common pay scales (such as a schedule that determines pay by position and years of experience) is explained by the ability of sports teams and the athletes to directly monitor performance, and the understanding by both parties of the importance of providing individuals with incentives to improve their performance. However, sports unions do bargain collectively over such matters as working conditions, insurance against injury, pension arrangements, grievance procedures and the sharing of television income.[3] Another major difference from conventional industry arrangements in the USA is that in sport collective bargaining agreements provide a shield against the antitrust laws, except in the case of baseball which has a blanket exemption following a controversial Supreme Court decision in 1922. The **player draft**, which originated in football in the 1930s, is essentially an agreement not to compete in hiring a particular player, which itself would violate the antitrust laws if it were not incorporated into the collective bargaining agreement. The salary cap and many other league rules that limit how much teams can pay or whom they can hire have the same tenuous legal standing. Thus sports are fairly unique in limiting an individual enterprise's hiring choices (since the closed shop was outlawed by the Taft–Hartley Act in 1947) and in placing a cap on salaries.

In North America unions have generally opposed plans by the owners to cap salaries. However, this did not prevent the NBA from instituting a payroll cap beginning in the 1983/4 season. Similar arrangements were agreed in the NFL in 1993. In baseball the attempt to enforce a cap eventually led to the 1994/5 players' strike[4] and ended with a compromise solution: a luxury tax on payrolls that exceeded pre-determined levels. There has also been general opposition on the part of the unions to increased revenue sharing as this is felt to decrease the value of players and hence salaries through the alleged reduced incentive to win.

An important feature of sporting labor markets is the short duration of careers for the average athlete. This is estimated to be no more than four years in US football and seven years in soccer. This arises not only through physical decline with the ageing process, but also because of injury. It is not surprising, therefore, that players' unions should focus on health and safety risks, though we would expect through the theory of compensating differences that sports and positions within particular sports with the higher risks of injury would have higher salaries, *ceteris paribus.* Another issue under the labor market effect of injury risks is how contracts (either explicit or implicit) are structured to provide players with appropriate incentives. Teams would presumably prefer that players play with abandon and disdain the threat of injury if this leads to greater playing success. In contrast, the players have a natural concern over the potential loss of future earnings due to temporary or career-threatening injuries. North American teams have designated universal policies to mitigate these concerns. Thus they continue to pay players over the remainder of a season who have been injured even where such payments are not part of an explicit individual contract or part of a collective bargaining agreement. Indeed, this practise antedates all the collective bargaining agreements. Furthermore, teams guarantee injured starters the opportunity to return to their starter position no matter how well a reserve does during their absence. Again, this practise serves to reduce the financial risk for a player caused by injury.

Arbitration

Another key aspect of industrial relations in sport, both in North America and Europe, is the use of arbitration as a means of resolving disputes. In conventional arbitration a neutral third party makes a binding decision, which may or may not coincide with either party's claim or offer. Under **final offer arbitration** the third party must select the last offer made by management or union. This provides bargainers with an incentive to reach agreements bilaterally and also distributes bargaining power in a manner similar to what would be the case with the right to strike. This procedure has, for example, been used in the resolution of salary disputes in major league baseball beginning in 1974. According to Chelius and Dworkin (1980), this procedure changed the distribution of wealth in favor of the players without resort to the strike weapon. Conventional arbitration is the preferred form of resolution to deal with disputed transfer fees between clubs in the English

Football League through the Football League Appeals Committee (FLAC) with representatives of the employers, the players' union, the Executive Staff Association and an independent chairman forming the arbitration panel. Speight and Thomas (1997b) find that the value of a player's human capital affects the arbitrated settlement rather than the disputants' final offers influencing the arbitration panel's decision.

Trade unions in professional team sports face a dilemma in so far as the more unequal are salaries through the scarcity of star players, the more likely are the majority of their members to face declining employment opportunities. The trade-off between higher payment and lower employment is particularly marked in this industry.

Competitive restrictions in sporting labor markets

The reserve clause and free agency

One of the most marked features of labor market restrictions in professional team sports has been their worldwide parallel development across different sports. A general pattern has been evident beginning with the development of controls, the response of players through unionization and, subsequently, increasing irresistible public pressures to remove or modify controls.

Taking first the example of baseball where changes have been most marked and the literature on the issue most extensive, controls on the ability of players to transfer at will from club to club in search of higher earnings first appeared in the professional game in 1879. National League clubs imposed unilaterally and in secret a 'reserve rule' which gave clubs exclusive rights to the services of up to five of their players for the following season (Gregory, 1956; Sobel, 1977). This informal arrangement was formalized in 1884 with the National Agreement between the National League and its hitherto rival in bidding for player talent, the American Association. This agreement contained a provision, the 'reserve clause', which gave club owners an exclusive option to renew the annual contracts of initially 11 (and subsequently all) players under contract to them. A series of annual renewals could, therefore, tie a player to a club for the duration of his career. By 1887 the reserve clause was inserted into standard player contracts despite the opposition of the newly formed players' union. It remained essentially intact until 1976, surviving a series of antitrust actions partly as a result of a controversial 1922 US Supreme Court judgment that baseball was exempt from antitrust laws as it was not engaged in interstate commerce.

In 1965 the monopsony power of organized baseball was extended via the introduction of the 'free agent draft'. The draft system gave the major league clubs, in reverse order of their previous season's league finishing position, a choice among all new players available to the professional game. Once a player was drafted only the drafting team could negotiate a contract with that player. The reverse order rule was ostensibly an attempt to equalize playing performances among clubs. Eliminating competitive bidding and high 'signing' fees may have been the real reason.

Over time the reserve system became an increasing source of grievance between players, their union and Major League Baseball (MLB). Matters came to a head in 1975 when two players, Andy Messersmith of the Los Angeles Dodgers and Dave McNally of the Montreal Expos, failed to reach agreement with their clubs at the end of their contracts. Being reserved both players sat out the 1975 season without a signed contract and, having played out the club's option, declared themselves free agents. Their interpretation of the contracts was contested by the owners who claimed that the two players were still bound by the provisions of the reserve clause in the prior year's contract. The dispute was referred to an arbitrator, who concluded that the players were free agents. The arbitrator's ruling became the basis for a new national collective bargaining agreement in 1976 that included free agency. Players had the option of becoming free agents after the completion of six years in the major leagues. The reserve system was severely restricted but not totally abolished. Free agents could bargain with up to 14 of 26 professional clubs then in existence with the clubs' right to bargain being allocated in a 're-entry draft', again prioritized in reverse order of league standings. Finally, under the agreement a club losing a player to free agency was compensated by the signing club giving the club that lost the player one of the signing club's selection rights in the following year's amateur draft.

This 'compensation' was regarded as insufficient by the owners who attempted to introduce increased compensation in the 1980 National Agreement, but backed off following strike threats. In 1981 the compensation issue re-emerged. Player objections to the cross-club compensation scheme led to strike action, lasting over 700 games, from mid-June to the first week of August, ending with a concession by the owners. They agreed to a considerably smaller compensation for losing a player to free agency. Further strikes interrupting the regular season occurred in 1985 and 1990. Under the present system the restrictions placed upon the bargaining power of the player diminish as he accumulates years of experience. Players with less than three years' experience (ineligibles) are bound to a single team, and hence negotiate with a true monopsony. Players with between three and six years' experience are similarly bound to one team, but may opt for final offer arbitration to reach a settlement as outlined above. Those with six years or more experience (free agent eligibles) may negotiate freely with other teams. The development of restrictive controls in the other major North American team sports – basketball, football and ice hockey – has followed similar paths and, as it is well documented elsewhere, is not discussed here for reasons of space. (For basketball, football and hockey see Staudohar, 1996.)

The retain and transfer system

The European equivalent to the reserve clause is the retain and transfer system in the professional soccer and rugby leagues which originated in Britain late in the nineteenth century. In England, for example, the rules specified that at the end of each season a club was forced to place any player on either the transfer list or the retained list on whatever terms it wished, provided that these terms were no lower than the league-wide agreed minimum. Even where players were placed on the transfer list a player could only be transferred provided another club was prepared to offer a transfer fee acceptable to the player's current club. There was also a league-wide maximum wage with financial sanctions against any club paying more, which was first introduced in 1905 at £4 per week (Sloane, 1969).

These restrictive conditions came under increasing attack after the World War II. In 1960–1 the maximum wage was abolished and in 1963–7, following the Eastham case, the retain and transfer system was changed in favor of the players. Then in 1977–8 partial freedom of contract was granted, in so far as players could negotiate a move to a new club when their contract expired. The clubs were still required to agree a transfer fee. If the two clubs could not agree on a fee it was to be determined by independent arbitration. Following the landmark **Bosman case** in 1995 (see Box 4.2) the European Court of Justice ruled that requiring a transfer fee at the end of a contract was unlawful within the European Union. In 2000 the European Commission requested further changes to eliminate transfer fees even within the duration of a multi-year contract.

The development of strikingly similar labor market controls in a different sports and different countries suggests that sports leagues have a common reason for instituting these restrictions. The standard defense of the mobility restrictions is based on the special characteristics of professional team sports as outlined earlier in this text. The argument is that without such controls the wealthiest clubs would acquire so much player talent that they would consolidate their dominance and kill spectator interest in the league as a whole.

Box 4.2 The Bosman case

Jean Marc Bosman, a Belgian footballer, was offered a new contract with the Belgian club, RFC Liège, on inferior terms to his previous expired contract. RFC Liège refused permission for him to join a French club, US Dunkerque, whereupon the player sued RFC Liège on the grounds of restraint of trade, with the case eventually reaching the European Court of Justice.

cont. overleaf

Box 4.2 continued

At the European Court of Justice in December of 1995, the Advocate-General, Heinz Otto Lenz, ruled that the UEFA restriction on out-of-contract players moving between clubs in different EU countries was incompatible with Article 48 of Treaty of Rome. UEFA allowed transfers only when a transfer fee was agreed between the clubs, whereas the Treaty of Rome requires free mobility of labor. Restrictions on the number of foreign players permitted in a team were also found to be incompatible with the Treaty.

The need to preserve uncertainty of outcome was accepted by the Advocate-General as necessary to maintain interest in the sport, and he also recognized that smaller clubs often covered their financial losses by selling some of their players. However, he came to the view that these factors could not in themselves justify the transfer rules because other means were available to achieve those objectives without impinging on freedom of movement. Further, it appeared from the literature on the economics of sport that there was some doubt about whether transfer rules were capable of achieving competitive balance. He also noted that transfers of players from smaller to larger clubs would actually increase the degree of sporting imbalance, and that transfer fees on the basis of salary imply that smaller clubs will be unable to buy the best players. In the case of transfers to clubs abroad, there can be no contribution to competitive balance at home. Therefore, he proposed two alternatives: a collective wage agreement, specifying limits on player salaries (i.e., a salary cap) and a more equal sharing of gate receipts and television income (his preferred option).

His ruling did not, however, mean that transfer fees would be unlawful under all circumstances. They might be justified if they were limited to the amount expended by the previous club on the player's training and development and to the first change of clubs where the previous club had borne the costs of the player's development. Lenz also recognized that abandonment of the existing arrangements would lead to some loss of asset value where clubs had recently invested in players. It would also cause a general increase in player salaries and disrupt to some degree the worldwide organization of football, since any ruling of the court would not apply beyond the confines of the European Union.

The Coase theorem and the invariance thesis

The argument that the reserve clause enhances competitive balance or reduces **market dominance** has been challenged by some economists, most notably by Rottenberg (1956). His counter-argument is essentially a restatement of the Coase theorem. The Coase theorem consists of two propositions. First, in the absence of transaction costs, the parties to any contract will settle on an efficient outcome. Second, the same outcome will be achieved regardless of the distribution of property rights (the invariance thesis). An illustration of the Coase theorem is the use of a trademark or brand name. Often more than one company would like to use the same name: for instance, there is a St. Louis-based brewery named Budweiser and a Prague brewery named Budweiser. The efficient solution to the use of the name is whichever allocation generates the most income across the two breweries. If consumers were not confused both of them could use the same name without hurting overall sales. If consumers were confused then both using the name could hurt the sales of one of the breweries more than it might help the sales of the other. Then the efficient solution would be sole use of the name by whichever brewery would gain the most. As long as the costs of meeting and coming to an agreement were small relative to the losses caused by the dual use of the name, the parties should be able to come to an agreement giving the use of the name to the brewery that would gain the greatest benefit. The second proposition, the invariance thesis, implies that the result of the negotiations over the name do not depend on who has the legal ownership of the name. If the Prague Budweiser legally owned the name because it was older than the St. Louis Budweiser but the latter could make much more money through exclusive use of the name, then Prague would sell the rights to St. Louis. If St. Louis had the legal right to the name and made more money from the exclusive use then it would not sell the right to the name and Prague would not be able pay for it anyway. The only difference the legal ownership status makes is in the direction in which any payment may flow.

The implication of the Coase theorem for sport is that the distribution of talent would be identical under either the reserve clause or free agency, the only difference being in the distribution of rent arising from the ability of players. Rottenberg argued that in the market for baseball players as elsewhere, the law of diminishing returns applies. At some stage the addition of an extra star player to a team will add a diminishing number of extra spectators to the team's games. At some point returns may be actually negative where additional dominance begins to reduce uncertainty of outcome and kill spectator interest, although this will occur for the league as a whole before affecting the dominant team. Clubs will not be prepared to offer players more than their MRPs and therefore 'At some point ... a first star player is worth more to poor Team B than, say, a third star player to rich Team A. At this point B is in a position to bid players away from A' (Rottenberg, 1956, p. 255). In other words, if transaction costs among teams are small a free market for players would be self-regulating in the sense that it is in each team's own interest to ensure that it does not become too strong relative to all others, and hence labor market restrictions are unnecessary. If transactions costs are zero the distribution of player talent would the same under free agency as under the reserve clause.

The Yankee Paradox

Sloane (1969, 1971 and 1976b) questioned Rottenberg's contention that, given profit maximization, a free market is sufficient to limit the appearance of sporting inequalities so severe that they reduced league-wide revenue. Sloane's challenge is based on the argument that the attendance-depressing effects of domination by a single team are largely external. Team A's attendance will be a function of, amongst other things, both uncertainty of outcome and Team A's current performances. Continuing winning performances by Team A will have two effects tending to work in opposing directions, one acting to increase attendance and the other to decrease them. For other teams in the league, however, the effect is unambiguously one of depressing attendance. In a two-team league this externality could be internalized as described by Rottenberg (e.g., by negotiation between the teams on trading players), but in a many-team league this is less obviously the case. In terms of Rottenberg's example teams C, D, E, F and so on may all enjoy benefits from the close competition engendered by B bidding for A's star player, but the market will fail to take those benefits into account. Vrooman (1996) refers to this undue dominance arising from the interdependence of clubs as the **Yankee paradox**. This phrase refers to more than the success of that team. Vrooman notes that empirical evidence for the Yankee paradox is mixed. Demmert (1973) could find no evidence that returns to narrow victories were larger than those to easy victories, while Hunt and Lewis (1976) found that league revenue was maximized when large city teams won 43 per cent of the time, while an individual club would maximize revenues when it won 80 per cent of the time. Demmert suggests that these results imply that competitive balance may be inconsistent with league-wide joint profit maximization.

The irreversibility proposition and the winner's curse

A player's talent may be team-specific (or what Vrooman refers to as the **irreversibility proposition**). Thus it may be reasonable to assume that the club for which a player has performed for some time will have more information about that player's future potential than other clubs (e.g., whether the player has health problems). If such **information asymmetry** exists then the expected performance of free agents will be lower than the performance of eligible players who do not become free agents. Thus, a **lemons model** may apply to the free agent market. This derives from Akerlof's example of the economics of **adverse selection** in relation to second-hand cars (1970). Assume there are two types of car, good cars and bad cars (lemons), and that the seller is able to categorize each type while potential buyers cannot. If buyers fix their offer price on the expected value of the two types of cars, then good cars would never actually be sold, as the offer price will never reach the seller's reservation price. The only cars available will be lemons. Low quality cars will drive good quality cars out of the market. Applying this to the transfer market for athletes it would appear that only poor quality players would be traded. In practice we do observe on occasion that star players are traded. Here, the information asymmetries may be less, because there is more evidence revealed about the player's true qualities. However, for average players the lemon phenomenon may well apply.

A related feature is the **winner's curse**. Cassing and Douglas (1980) argue that with free agency there will be a tendency to acquire a biased set of players: those for which the bidder has overpaid. Because of information asymmetries and uncertainty, bids by potential owners will not always mirror the true worth of a player, but the team that values correctly has a poor chance of signing a player compared to a team that over-estimates the player's value.

A further source of market failure may arise when a high final league position is necessary to qualify for an additional source of revenues. This is quite common: for instance, in the various European-wide club soccer tournaments, baseball's World Series, and ice hockey's Stanley Cup. In these cases it may pay to be much stronger than rivals in one's own league or division.

Finally there is the issue of club objectives. Where clubs are prepared to sacrifice profits for playing success, wealthy clubs in areas of large population may continue to bid for superior players without taking account of the effect this may have on their own profits, let alone the rest of the league. This implies that, contrary to Rottenberg's assumption, clubs may well be prepared to pay players in excess of their MRPs. The proposition that a free labor market brings about 'reasonably' close competition is, therefore, subject to some dispute.

However, one must also ask the question whether a highly-restricted labor market is capable of yielding close competition. This also appears to be in some doubt once the possibility of interclub sales of players is allowed for. El-Hodiri and Quirk (1971) demonstrated that, given profit-maximizing teams, a regime of restrictive controls would still yield unequal playing strengths as long as players could be sold from team to team and, crucially, teams were located in cities of such different population sizes as to provide widely different revenue streams. For this reason they advocated the abolition of the sales of players' contracts among teams in order to remove the owners' profit motive in these dealings.

Measuring the impact of restrictions

There are now a number of studies which have attempted to measure the impact of restrictions or changes in the rules on the closeness of competition. Here we limit ourselves to one or two examples to illustrate the fact that there is little consensus. Hunt and Lewis (1976) examine just one element of competitive performance: the extent to which a large city team tends to dominate the championship over a period of years. They estimate how dominant team and all other division revenues vary with the extent of dominance of the large city team, where dominance is defined as the probability of winning the division. They estimate that the profit-maximizing level of dominance for a large city team roughly approximates to the level observed over a long period in North American baseball. This implies that the transfer market in player registration operating during the reserve clause period corresponds roughly to the situation of a perfectly competitive labor market. However, Hunt and Lewis's method involves defining marginal cost of increasing dominance by the large city team as the revenue lost from increased dominance to *all* other teams in the division. This implies, of course that the external effect of dominance is, through some mechanism, perfectly internalized: a plausible result in the case of a two-team league but rather less so in other circumstances.

A more comprehensive attempt to test the effect of restrictive controls was made by Daly and Moore (1981). They examine the influence of player drafting and the modifications to the reserve clause made in baseball in 1976, arguing that player sales provide the mechanism through which the case is made for the ineffectiveness of restrictive controls. However, they also note the 'tradition among team owners of not selling first-line players for cash' (Daly and Moore, 1981, p. 84). Baseball, they suggest, is in a prime position to enforce an internalization of the dominant externality given relatively small numbers, a coordinating league not subject to antitrust laws and a high degree of visibility making violations of collective agreements among the owners easily detected.

In contrast to some earlier work, Daly and Moore find evidence that the restrictive controls operative in the period 1965 to 1976 in baseball *did* produce a greater degree of competitive equality and a lower correlation between city size and winning performances. They find no evidence that player transfers for cash increased after the draft, although this may have been expected if the Coase theorem held, such that the eventual distribution of resources was independent of the initial allocation of property rights. However, they found some evidence that the 1976 reserve clause modifications did lead to significantly larger movements of 'star' free agents (with salaries of $150,000 per annum and above) from smaller to larger population base clubs than vice versa. This implies that the reserve clause was successful in preventing the shift of star players from poorer to wealthier clubs.

A more recent study is that of Hylan, Lage and Treglia (1996) who have data on over 2,400 pitchers in MLB with 16 years' pre- and 16 years' post the implementation of free agency experience. The results lead to the rejection of the invariance thesis of the Coase theorem. Their empirical analysis shows that after the introduction of free agency pitchers with more major league experience were less likely to move relative to their mobility in the pre-free agency period. Their results also suggest that in general better pitchers are less likely to move and that pitchers playing in teams with higher winning percentages or in large market cities are less likely to move. They speculate that utility-maximizing players may prefer to play for a championship team or a team nearer their home, and since players will be wealthier after free agency they can afford to indulge their tastes. Similar results were obtained by Krautmann and Oppenheimer (1994). They go on to argue that it is the player draft that is the single most important factor affecting competitive balance in the major leagues.

The baseball draft was established in 1964 with the objective of substantially reducing competition between clubs for amateur prospects and reducing inequality in the distribution of talent across clubs. The rules of the draft (which also applies in the cases of football and basketball) is that major league clubs make their selections in reverse order of their record of wins and losses in the previous season.[5] Daly and Moore (1981) also found the introduction of the draft had a significant impact on subsequent team standings and the closeness of competition in MLB. Further, they found that the rank correlation between population size and team winning percentages declined with the introduction of the draft, implying that it had a significant impact on the competitiveness of such teams.

Scully's model of salary determination for starters and backups

The original tournament models to explain the determinants of pay are due to Sherwin Rosen and Edward Lazear. The subject is reviewed in Lazear and Rosen (1995). In these models small differences in worker ability make big differences to firms' earnings because the firm is engaged in a winner-take-all competition. For example, in a court case, having a slightly better lawyer than the opposition can be the difference between winning and losing. Other occupations in which such winner-take-all considerations apply are movie stars, Chief Executive Officers and opera singers. For example, the best tenor in the world will sell vastly more recordings than the second best tenor. Another common aspect is that many people train for the high paying positions but just a few make it to the top of the ladder. Sport is a natural application for tournament models. Scully extended these models to explain how teams set the salaries of starters and backups for the same position (Scully, 1995). His model requires using some calculus but, in return for the effort, it provides powerful insights into how athletes' salaries are determined.

Scully begins his model by with equations that describe the team revenues:

j indicates the jth club in the league
Q_j is club performance level
N positions on a roster counted from $i = 1$ to N
t_i is talent of the ith player

Talent in this model is one-dimensional and simply additive. In reality there are different types of talent such as pitching and hitting, and they might combine in nonlinear fashion. These assumptions are for simplification:

T_j is the total team talent
ε_j is the luck of the jth team, assumed to be drawn from the standard normal distribution

Total talent on a team is a function of the individual talent:

$$T_j = T(t_{ji})$$

The club's performance level depends on its total talent and its luck in a particular game:

$$Q_j = T_j + \varepsilon_j$$

The probability that the jth club will defeat the kth club in one game is w_{jk}. This probability depends on their differences in their total talent. If the lower talent team has enough luck it can beat the higher talent team:

$$w_{jk} = \text{prob}(Q_j > Q_k) = \text{prob}(T_j - T_k > \varepsilon_k - \varepsilon_j)$$

The total broadcast revenue for the league is a positive function $B(\Sigma T_j)$ of the talent summed across all of the teams in the league. The symbol Σ is the summation operator. More talent in the league adds to overall broadcast revenues because more people are willing to watch better athletes. Obviously, if all of the talent was concentrated in one team which won every game it played, adding more talent to that team would not add to the league's broadcast revenues. Again, the talent-to-broadcast-revenue function is a simplification. The simplication is not a concern because leagues try to spread the talent over the teams.

The broadcast revenues per club are a simple average of the total. This relationship implies equal sharing of broadcast revenues as in the NFL:

$$\overline{B}_j = \frac{B(\Sigma T_j)}{J}$$

Local revenues, which are primarily tickets, depend on expected team performance, $L_j(W_{jk})$.

The expected overall revenue, R, is

$$ER_j = \overline{B}_j + L(W_{jk})$$

The E is the expectation operator. The model allows uncertainty because of the luck term at the team level.

After laying out the framework for team expected revenues Scully considers individual player's pay. The pay level at a position is related to how much a marginal improvement in talent at that position would contribute to the team's win ratio. The idea is whether from the team's point of view spending enough to get a better, say, center in basketball, will add more to the team's wins and profits. The value, V_n, of the *n*th position is the following expression:

$$V_n = \int_0^{t_n^*} \left[\overline{B}_j' + L_j' f(T_j - T_k)\right](\partial T/\partial t_n)dt_n$$

In words, the value to the club of the *n*th position is how much that position adds to national broadcast revenue plus how much it adds to local revenue through more wins. The $\overline{B}_j'$ is the derivative of average league-wide broadcast revenues with respect to increasing talent at position *n* at team *j*. The term L_j' is the derivative of local revenues with respect to changes in the talent level of the team. The local ticket revenues depend on the local team's win probability, which in turn depends on the difference between its total talent and its opponent's total talent. That is the term $f(T_j - T_k)$. The partial derivative of total talent to talent at position *n* is $\partial T/\partial t_n$. Extra talent at a position feeds into extra total talent via this term. The value of the *n*th position to team *j* is the integral of changes in its team share of the league-wide broadcast revenue and its changes in local revenue as more talent at that position changes its win probabilities swept over the range of talents from 0 to t_n^*, which is the optimal level of talent at the position.

This math is preliminary to determining individual salaries at a position. This is where the rank-order tournament comes in. Each position has two players who compete for the starting slot such as the starting center in basketball. The model could be extended to having a third player competing for the back-up's spot but no insights would be gained by adding to the number of players competing at a particular position. S_1 is the salary for the starter at a particular position, while S_2 is the salary for the back-up. Scully assumes that the starter salary exceeds the back-up salary, and *q* is individual player's performance level. The starter and the back-up are usually close in ability and there is some chance that the back-up will perform better during pre-season trials and wrest away the starter slot.

P_{ab} is the probability that player *a* beats player *b* for the starter position, so

$$p_{ab} = \text{prob}(q_a > q_b) = \text{prob}(t_a - t_b > e_b - e_a) \equiv D(t_a - t_b)$$

where *t* is an individual's talent level, *e* represents an individual's luck and D is the cumulative density function. The expression is similar to the team expression for the probability of winning a game. The expected salary for player a depends on the two salaries, and the probability that player a beats b in the tournament which could be trials in the pre-season training camp:

$$ES_a = p_{ab}S_1 + (1 - p_{ab})S_2$$
$$ES_b = (1 - p_{ab})S_1 + p_{ab}S_2$$

Scully's crucial idea is that players control, at least partially, their own talent level. They can train harder, watch their weight, study game films, hire a personal coach, and so on.

C_i is the cost of raising talent for ith player. This cost has positive first and second derivatives, meaning that more training has more personal cost to the players and that that cost increases at an increasing rate. Players maximize expected net income, $EY_i = ES_i - C_i(t_i)$. Their only choice variable is their effort and time in raising their talent. They will expend more effort in training until the last bit of effort pays back as much as it costs: that is, until marginal costs equal marginal benefits:

$$\frac{\partial EY_i}{\partial t_i} = (S_1 - S_2)d(t_1 - t_2) - C_i'(t_1) = 0$$

where d is the probability density function of $e_b - e_a$, i.e., D'. The two individual luck terms are normal random variables so the difference would be a normal random variable. Figure 4.3 shows a stable equilibrium between two rivals for a starting position in which one has more innate talent and therefore a lower cost of raising his talent. The shapes of the individual cost of training curves reflect the rising costs of training that rise at an increasing rate. There is an

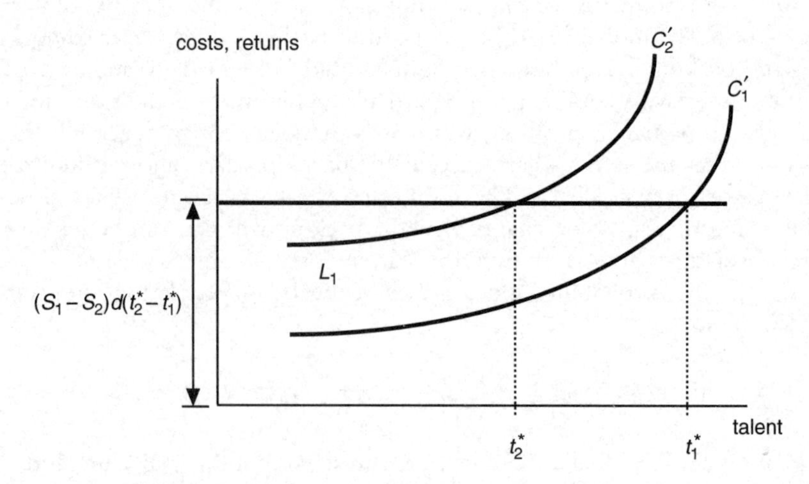

Figure 4.3 Equilibrium talent levels for a starter and a back-up in a rank order tournament

optimum talent level for each player, respectively, t_a^* and t_b^* such that $t_a^* > t_b^*$. This means that the optimal level of the starter's talent is above that of the back-up. This assumes that the starter has more natural ability or more experience.

The value of all starter versus back-up tournaments to the club across all of the positions is

$$V = \Sigma_n V_n$$

There are simple bounds on the maximum for the starter and the minimum for the back-up salaries. These are the profit constraint, since no team will offer so high an S_1 that it loses money and no back-up will accept less than his opportunity cost (this opportunity cost is $\overline{C}$). The expected salary has to cover the effort of the back-up player as well so the expected salary of the back-up has a minimum of

$$ES_b = C_b(t_b^*) + \overline{C}$$

To narrow these bounds, Scully introduces a competiveness parameter in player salary markets, c, with values in the range 0 and 1. The lower bound cannot be reached. Perfect competition is when $c = 1$.

In perfect competition

$$S_1 + S_2 = V_n$$

That is, the players capture all of the value to the team of their position. With monopsony power (i.e., the reserve clause), $S_1 + S_2 < V_n$: that is, the team retains some of the value of the position. The less competitive the market for players is the more the team retains. Scully then gets a unique values for S_1 and S_2 based on the value of the competitiveness coefficient:

$$S_1 = cV_n\left[\frac{p_{12}}{2p_{12} - 1}\right] - \left[\frac{C_2(t_2^*) + \overline{C}}{2p_{12} - 1}\right]$$

$$S_2 = \left[\frac{C_2(t_2^*) + \overline{C}}{2p_{12} - 1}\right] - cV_n\left[\frac{p_{12}}{2p_{12} - 1}\right]$$

Here is a derivation of this expression: starting with the profit constraint, $V_n = S_1 + S_2$, the opportunity cost constraint set to zero

$$EY_2 = \overline{C} = 0 = (1 - p_{12})S_1 + p_{12}S_2 - C_2(t_2^*)$$

and no monopsony power (i.e., lower case $c = 0$)

$$
\begin{aligned}
0 &= (1 - p_{12})S_1 + p_{12}(V_n - S_1) - C_2(t_2^*) \\
0 &= (1 - p_{12})S_1 + p_{12}V_n - p_{12}S_1 - C_2(t_2^*) \\
0 &= S_1 - p_{12}S_1 + p_{12}V_n - p_{12}S_1 - C_2(t_2^*) \\
0 &= S_1 - 2p_{12}S_1 + p_{12}V_n - C_2(t_2^*) \\
2p_{12}S_1 - S_1 &= p_{12}V_n - C_2(t_2^*) \\
(2p_{12} - 1)S_1 &= p_{12}V_n - C_2(t_2^*) \\
S_1 &= \frac{p_{12}}{(2p_{12} - 1)}V_n - \frac{C_2(t_2^*)}{(2p_{12} - 1)}
\end{aligned}
$$

the derivation of the second equation is similar.

Under perfect competition the value of the contest is entirely exhausted (i.e., paid out in the two salaries). The higher the effort cost for the second player, the lower the first player's salary. Fixing the effort costs and raising the probability of the starter (1) beating the back-up (2) lowers the starter's salary. Even under a strict reserve clause there is an incentive to pay the starter more than his opportunity cost so that there is a contest in which both the starter and the back-up are putting out extra effort to raise their talent levels. The players in the old reserve clause days got far more than their opportunity cost. They were being paid to do something they enjoyed doing at multiples of 10 to 20 times the average wage for manual labor, which was often their effective opportunity cost.

Scully's model addresses the puzzle of why under a strict reserve clause regime the owners found it profitable to pay starters so much more than their opportunity cost. The reserve clause is like slavery. The player is bound to one team for life unless the owner wants to sell the player. When there was real slavery in ancient Rome or in the pre-Civil War USA some owners found it profitable to give slaves a cash payment because the payments elicited more effort than they cost. The pay occurred in situations were the slave could not be easily supervised and where judgment and initiative were important. The difference in the Scully model compared to the slave story is the complication of a **rank order tournament**. The team owner is trying to get the profit-maximizing amount of total talent, from the starter and back-up, at each position. As monopsony power rises in this model, the team owner absorbs an increasing fraction of the monetary value generated by each position. Greater monopsony power reduces the incentives of the players to improve their talent levels. They are much more likely to be idle over the off season and show up in training camp overweight. In theory careers would be shorter and age: earnings profiles flatter under the reserve clause. In addition, under monopsony power the starter's salary is pushed down faster than the back-up's salary.

The Scully model offers deep insights into the within-team structure of pay. The starter and the back-up are playing a game against each other. The team wants the back-up to train as hard as possible so that he pressures the starter into training harder out of a fear of losing the starter slot. Since the team cannot control the actions of the players directly (e.g., how much and what they eat, if they sleep enough, if they exercise during the off season), the team uses the contest between the starter and the back-up to encourage this training. Armchair empiricism supports the conclusion of the Scully model that these training incentives have become stronger under free agency. Players with potbellies and reputations for all-night carousing used to be common in baseball when there was a reserve clause. These players relied on their natural talent. Now the players are stronger and train year round.

Revenue sharing and salary caps as mechanisms for achieving uncertainty of outcome

Gate-sharing arrangements and competitive balance

The effect of free agency and the abolition of the retain and transfer system has led not only to an escalation of player salaries[6] but a widening in the earnings distribution. This poses a threat to the smaller clubs and has led to calls for greater income sharing and the introduction of salary caps, particularly in North America.

The extent to which **gate-sharing** takes place varies across team sports with clubs keeping 100 per cent of the home gate in basketball, ice hockey and European soccer, while more equal gate-sharing occurs in baseball and particularly football, where until 2002 it was 60:40. Following Fort and Quirk (1995) and Vrooman (1995) one can model the effects of more equal gate-sharing by using a simple example of a two-team league, with team A being a strong drawing team and team B a weak drawing team. The model yields the same results with an *n* team league where *n* is an arbitrary but finite number of teams. The assumption of two teams is convenient for exposition. It is assumed that each club is a profit maximizer and that it initially retains all of its home gate receipts. Given uncertainty of outcome helps to draw fans, there will be diminishing returns to winning. This means that as the winning percentage of either team increases total revenue will continue to rise, but at a decreasing rate, so that the marginal returns to winning schedule will be downward sloping when the winning percentage is measured on the horizontal axis from left to right. This is a consequence of the fact that though it is true that spectators obtain satisfaction from seeing their own team win, they also obtain satisfaction from a close competition between two equally matched teams. If, in contrast, winning percentages diverge the league competition will be decided earlier in the season, leaving a higher proportion of games where there is nothing at stake. The zero-sum nature of the league requires that

$$\sum_{i=1}^{n} w_i = n/2 = 1.0$$

where w_i equals the winning percentage of the ith team.

In Figure 4.4 the winning percentage for team A reads from left to right and that for team B from right to left. Market cost per unit of playing strength is assumed to be equal for both teams at C_1 and invariant to winning percentage. The implicit assumption behind the horizontal cost function is that enough additional athletic talent can be purchased to increase the win percentage by one point at a constant marginal cost over the entire range of win percentages. This assumption is equivalent to treating the two teams as small relative to the world market for athletic talent. The assumption is reasonable for soccer, which has a worldwide market for athletic talent. It is less accurate

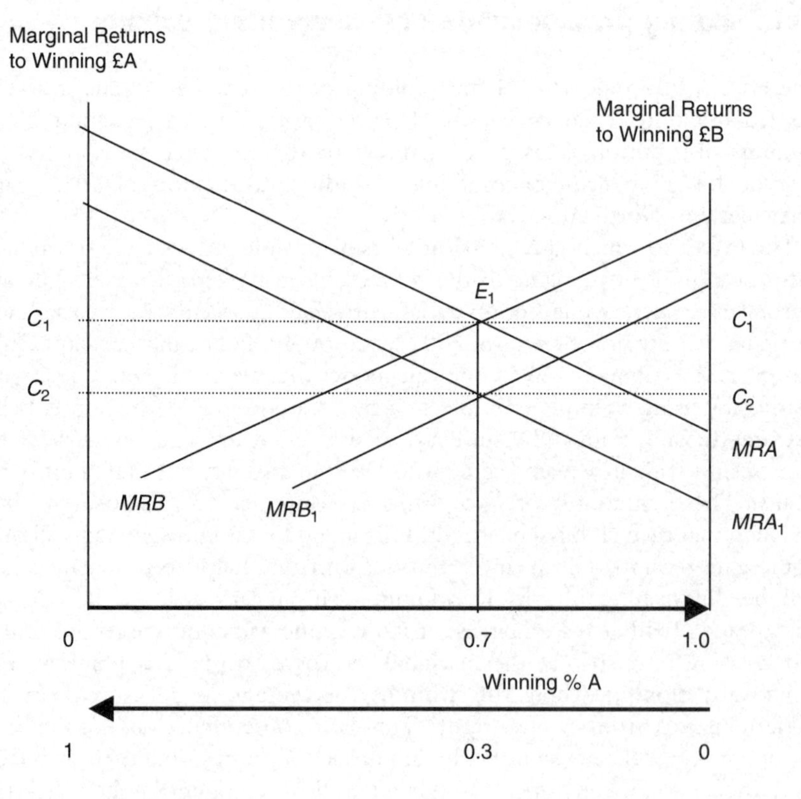

Figure 4.4 Effect of gate-sharing in a two-team league

for the US leagues with 30 or so teams. However, the constant marginal cost assumption would not change the basic conclusions. Under these assumptions about marginal cost and marginal revenue the equilibrium occurs at E_1 where each team equates MC with marginal returns to winning (MR) and the strong drawing team, A, wins more games (70 per cent) than the weak drawing team (30 per cent). The model has no uncertainty in the sense that a given distribution of talent results in a given ratio of wins. Also, there is no home field advantage in the model. Team A would win 70 per cent of its home and its away games.

Now let us introduce gate-sharing arrangements in which the home team receives a percentage of gate revenue and the away team $(1 - a)$ per cent, where a is a number between 0.5 and 1.0. Gate-sharing above 50 per cent of local gate receipts would make the wins of other teams in their home stadiums more valuable to a team than its home wins and thus destroys the incentive to field winning teams. No gate-sharing schemes have gone beyond sharing 50 per cent of the local gate revenue. Total revenue R^* for teams A and B will be as below:

$$R^*(A) = aR(A) + (1 - a)R(B)$$
$$R^*(B) = aR(B) + (1 - a)R(A)$$

Thus the intersection point will occur directly below the original point as both MR curves are shifted down by the same amount. The introduction of gate-sharing has no effect on competitive balance. Further, the fact that a given winning percentage will have less effect on revenues than previously implies that gate-sharing will tend to reduce player salaries, so that costs will be forced down, say to C_2, so that in equilibrium $MR_{A1} = MR_{B1} = C_2$. The teams in the league collectively bid up the marginal cost of athletic talent to the point where it is equal to marginal revenue of enough additional talent to generate a percentage point of wins. If the wins are worth less revenue the teams will bid less. That is why the players' union opposes revenue sharing.

Fort and Quirk acknowledge that there may be an indirect effect on competitive balance if the reduced player costs enable weak drawing franchises, which would otherwise be loss making, to become profitable. Gate-sharing allows some small market teams to exist. Vrooman also points out that competitive balance might increase if the revenue that is transferred from large to small drawing teams is revenue inelastic, in the sense that revenue rises less than proportionately as the percentage of games won rises. This restriction is necessary because of the negative interdependence between the teams' MR and MC functions implied by the zero sum nature of the league. That is, when a team shares revenue, the away team's share depends directly on the demand of the opponents' fans for winning, which varies inversely with its own ability to win away. If the elasticity of revenue to changes in the win proportion is greater than 1 and teams are subject to the same sharing formula, there will be no effect on competitive balance to changes in a in the range of 0.5 to 1.0.

However, implicit in this model is the assumption that marginal returns to winning are unrelated to away game attendance, an assumption that is less tenable in Europe, given the fact that away support is not unsubstantial. Further, the above result no longer holds if clubs are win maximizers (Késenne, 1999).

Salary caps

Basketball was the first team sport to introduce a league-wide salary cap in 1984 when a guaranteed 53 per cent of NBA designated gross revenues was designated to players. In the NFL a salary cap of 64 per cent of league-wide assigned revenues was introduced in 1994. Similar caps were opposed in baseball and ice hockey, leading to a strike in the former and a lock-out in the latter in 1994. In the event luxury taxes on payrolls were introduced in baseball when a certain figure was exceeded and ice hockey now has a salary cap for rookies. For the operation of the salary cap in the NFL see Box 4.3. In England both rugby league and rugby union have introduced salary caps. Fort and Quirk argue that such caps can lead to competitive balance. Assume in Figure 4.5 that C_1 equals costs under free agency and C_2 equals costs under a salary cap on the supposition that owners will only introduce a cap which lowers the salary bill. If all clubs end up spending the same amount on players and have equally capable managers, teams would have roughly the same playing strength and would end up at 50 per cent wins. However, in this situation Team A would not be maximizing its profits, since additional wins would bring in more marginal revenue than their marginal cost, and neither would Team B, which has wins that have a higher marginal cost than they generate in marginal revenue. Thus, a salary minimum is required as well as a salary maximum.

Box 4.3 Salary caps in the NFL

A series of court rulings in 1993 re-established the principle of free agency and the NFL moved quickly to re-negotiate a new collective bargaining agreement (CBA) with the players' union (the NFLPA) which phased in free agency but also established salary caps. The new CBA made a distinction between the payment of established players (veterans)

Box 4.3 continued

and the payment of newly drafted players (rookies). The CBA defines the 'entering player pool' as a league wide limit on the total salary payments which each club may contract for in signing rookies (NFLPA, 1993, p. 48). This amounts to a league-wide rookie salary cap, and in each year this is the greater of:

(a) $2 million multiplied by the number of teams at the time of the draft, or
(b) 3.5 per cent of projected defined gross revenue (DGR), which includes gate receipts net of taxes and broadcasting income.

Out of this each team's allocation for rookies is proportional to its share of the entering players' pool, which is estimated on the basis of each team's position in relation to draft selection. For the 1993 season the total rookie salary cap was $56 million, or roughly $2 million per club based on the above criteria. If a team exceeded its rookie salary cap in that year it was required to pay an equivalent sum to its veteran players. In addition it was stipulated that the salary of any rookie could not be raised by more than 25 per cent of the first-year base salary.

Further, the new CBA established a total team salary cap for every team in the league. In 1994 this amounted to 63 per cent of the projected DGR minus certain league-wide projected benefits divided by the number of teams. This permitted each team to spend roughly $35 million on player salaries. As well as the cap there was provision for minimum salary levels depending on length of service. This was set at $100,000 for players with less than one year of service in 1993, $125,000 for one year's service and $150,000 for two or more years' service. The CBA stipulates also that these minima should increase in line with the DGR on an annual basis.

A **Lorenz curve** analysis, a standard measure of inequality, shows that salaries became more unequally distributed following the introduction of the salary cap. In 1992, prior to its introduction, the Gini coefficient derived from the Lorenz curve was 0.393 and in 1994 after its introduction it was 0.479, an increase in inequality of almost 22 per cent. Thus those players paid less lost out, while the superstars gained substantial salary increases.

(Kowaleski and Leeds, 1994.)

There is an enforcement problem in ensuring that teams do not renege on such arrangements. The forgone profits provide a strong incentive to cheat on the salary cap. In 2001 The Minnesota Timberwolves of the NBA exceeded the salary cap with a secret agreement with one player. When the NBA discovered the cheating it imposed huge penalties on the player, the team's general manager and owner, and the player's agent. The team forfeited first-round picks in 2001, 2002 and 2004, and paid a $3.5 million fine. The owner was

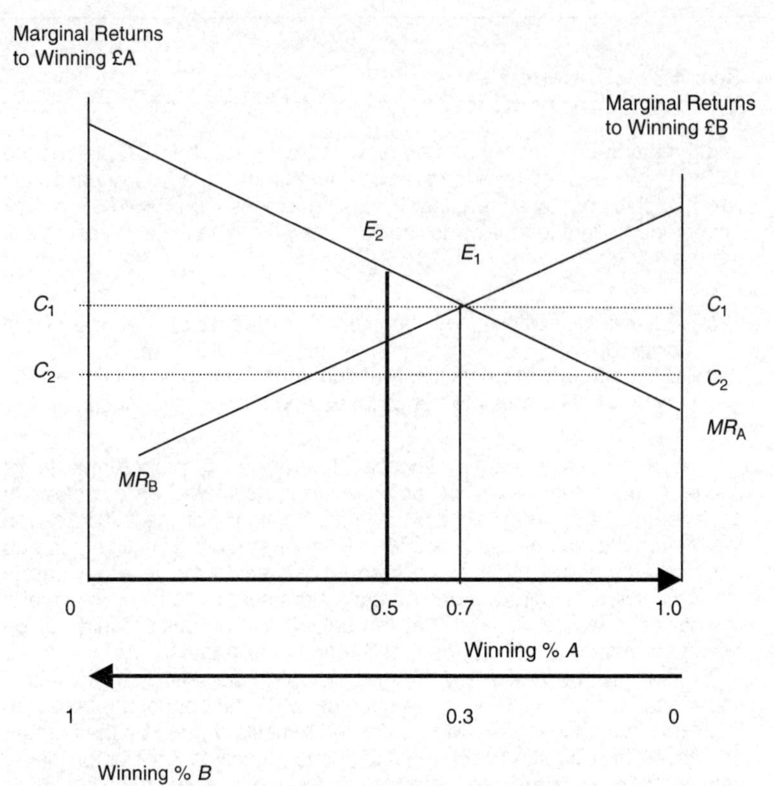

Figure 4.5 Effect of an equal salary cap in a two-team league

suspended and the general manager had a forced 'leave of absence' without pay. The player involved had his contract voided and he spent the next season with another team. The agent who represented the player when he signed the secret contract was the first agent to be fined by the National Basketball Players' Association. The agent agreed to accept a $57,000 fine and a six-month suspension. The point of detailing these punishments is to show that cheating on the salary cap is viewed as so corrosive to the league's efforts to promote competitive balance the penalties were set at a level that would make it unprofitable for anyone contemplating cheating. The chance of catching cheaters is low so the penalty has to be set high enough to make the crime unprofitable on an expected value basis: that is, the expected gain from cheating and not being caught minus the expected loss from cheating and being caught has to be a negative number. This is sometimes called the 'boil them in hot oil' theory of punishment.

Vrooman denies that equal spending on teams under a salary cap necessarily implies equal playing success, because the distribution of talent will still depend on the revenue characteristics of teams (e.g., whether revenue is winning elastic or inelastic and the market size revenue effect) as well as the costs of each team. In European soccer salary caps would need to be agreed across national boundaries if they were to be effective and the international nature of soccer perhaps explains their absence in this sport.

The luxury tax which has been instituted in baseball also effects competitive balance. In Figure 4.6 the large market team is subject to the tax, which is a fixed percentage of the payroll over some threshold. The small market team's payroll is too low to trigger the tax. The tax causes a kink in *A*'s marginal revenue of wins function and reduces its proportion of wins from w to w^*. More generally, every change that affects the two clubs differently will affect competitive balance. The invariance results in the Quirk and Fort model for gate-sharing or for broadcast revenue-sharing are due to their symmetrical effects. The gate-sharing lowers both teams' marginal revenue functions by the same amount. Broadcast revenue-sharing does not change the marginal revenue of local wins function if the broadcast revenue comes from a national contract.

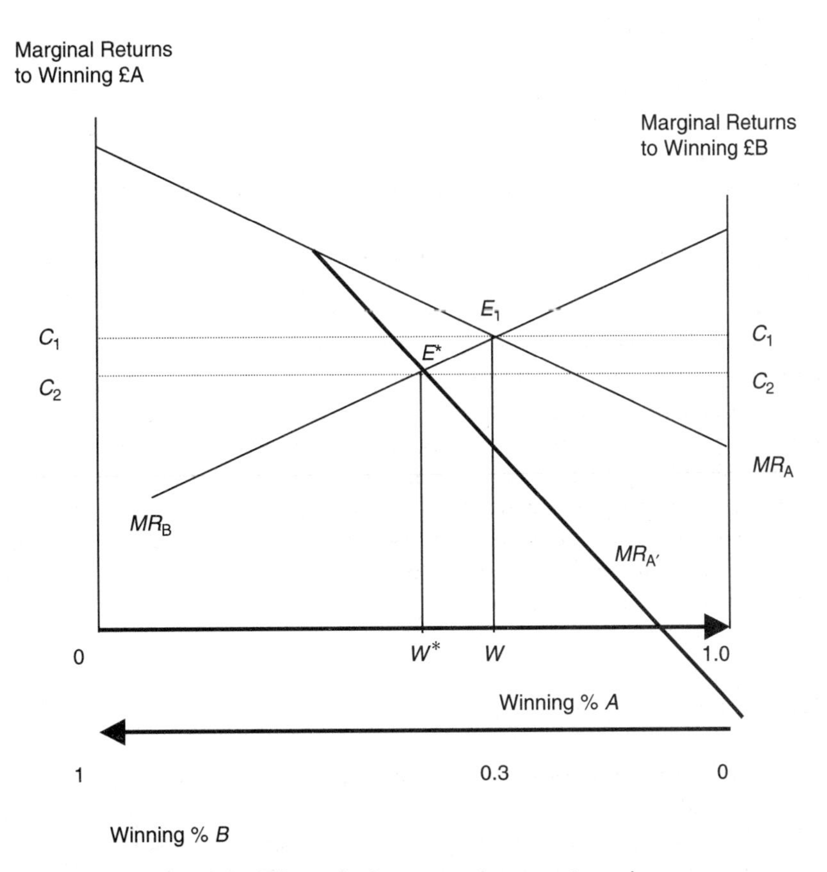

Figure 4.6 Effect of a luxury tax in a two-team league

Another way to break the symmetry is to add a new source of revenue tied to wins such as play off revenue in US leagues or European level competition for clubs in national leagues in Europe. If the chance to be in the limelight of post-season play was more valuable to the fans in the small market team because it was less common for them, introducing the post-season play offs to the model would overturn the invariance result: that is, it would change the competitive balance. The model with post-season play is more complicated to diagram because it requires a discontinuity (i.e., a jump in the marginal revenue function due to reaching the threshold of wins for post-season play). To be realistic, the model would have to include uncertainty because the threshold would depend on the win percentages of many other teams. The Quirk and Fort model with two teams in a large and a small market is a good starting point for analyzing competitive balance issues but it does not capture all essential features of the incentives for competitive balance.

Conclusions

The labor market holds a key position in the analysis of the economics of sport and of professional team sports in particular, as a consequence of the close relationship between product and labor markets. The impact of restrictive labor market controls has been a major research issue, but one in which considerable controversy abounds.

That restrictive controls have not equalized playing performances is neither in doubt nor unexpected given the disparate size of populations served by competing clubs, especially in Europe. In part these disagreements follow from the different assumptions made about club objectives. Do clubs maximize profits or some more general utility function such as win maximization? Do controls lead to more equal performance than some hypothetical 'free' market in player talent? Do controls lead to a 'sufficient' degree of competitive balance or do controls lead to an optimal degree of competitive balance and, if so, optimality in terms of which objectives? These uncertainties have been compounded by the inadequate formulation of the uncertainty of outcome variable and lack of a clear distinction between short-run and long-run uncertainty of outcome. It is likely that the sports labor markets will remain an area of great interest.

Notes

1. For a further study of baseball, but with weaker results, see Richards and Guell (1998).
2. This is one argument for imposing a salary cap, discussed below, though Hausman and Leonard prefer the option of a flat tax on team payrolls.

3. Thus in 2002 the English Professional Footballers' Association threatened to strike over the Premier League's refusal to increase sufficiently its share of the new television contract. In the event the Premier League agreed to guarantee the Association a sum of £175 million over ten years with the money to be spent on player welfare, particularly those who have to retire from the sport because of injury.
4. Player strikes are much more common in North America than in Europe. Strikes also took place in the NFL in 1987 and in 1998–9 in basketball. In ice hockey there was a lock-out by the owners of the NHL in 1994.
5. For a study of the baseball draft in practice see Spurr (2000).
6. Sanderson and Siegfried (1997) report that following the introduction of free agency the average nominal salary for veteran baseball players rose from $46,700 in 1975 to $371,200 in 1985; in basketball the average salary of NBA players rose from $20,000 in 1967–8 to $143,000 in 1977–8; in football the average salary increased less rapidly from $25,000 in 1967 to $55,000 in 1977; likewise in ice hockey, salaries increased from $96,000 in 1977 to $176,000 in 1987.

Exercises

1. Can marginal productivity theory explain the payment of sports stars? Are there substantial differences that distinguish the labor market for sports stars from that of labor markets in general?
2. In what sense may star players be paid too much and what sense too little?
3. Why might pay dispersion within teams be important in the context of professional team sports?
4. What is the rank order tournament model? How might it affect athletic performance?
5. Why have team sports chosen to restrict the mobility of players and what is the likely outcome of such restrictions?
6. Compare and contrast the player draft, the reserve clause, revenue sharing and salary caps as mechanisms for achieving competitive balance.
7. What is the Coase theorem and what is its relevance to professional team sports?
8. To what extent is market failure likely to occur in professional sport and what form is this failure likely to take?
9. 'We cannot understand the significance of restrictions on competition in the labor market, unless we know what is the primary objective of the clubs.' Discuss.
10. A league wants to increase the number of games in the regular season from 82 to 100. Holding the level of pay constant, the players would prefer

a shorter season. Assume that the extra revenue to the league for the longer season is $250 million. Assume that the players would be indifferent between playing the extra games along with $200 million in extra salary or keeping the 82-game season and having no extra salary.

(a) Suppose the union-league contract gave the league the right to increase the number of games in the season at any time during the five-year life of the contract. What would happen to the length of the season and the payments to the players? Explain your reasoning.

(b) Suppose the union–league contract gave the union the right to veto any change in the number of games in the season during the five-year life of the contract. What would happen to the length of the season and the payments to the players? Explain your reasoning.

(c) Five years pass by, the contract has expired, and the league and the union are negotiating over whether the season will be 82 or 100 games. What will be the length of the season? What determines how much more or less the players will be paid for an increase or a reduction in the length of the season?

11. There is a paradox that unions are much stronger in the USA in professional team sports than in Europe but in general unions are much stronger in Europe than in the USA. Why are the US players' unions stronger than their European counterparts?

12. In Europe there are no roster limits, no league minimums for player salaries, and no age restrictions when signing professional contracts. Why don't the richest teams, such as Manchester United, sign long-term contracts with hundreds of promising teenagers at modest salaries? This strategy might prevent those teenagers who mature into major league-quality players from being available to other teams. Given how little teenagers usually earn, the required salaries would be modest. Still, the richest teams seem to be content to have just 70 to 80 players, including their teenagers, under contract. How can you explain this?

13. (calculus) A sports team has the following relationship between total talent, T, and the number of wins (W) over a 1,000 game season, $0 \leq W \leq 1{,}000$.

$$W = 20T - 0.25T^2$$

The marginal revenue (MR) of an additional win is $1,000,000. (A constant MR is not realistic but it is being assumed to simplify the problem). If all units of talent cost $2,000,000 what is the quantity of talent the team will demand and how many wins will it have?

14. Why are the stadium beer vendors paid according to their daily output (a fixed amount per tray of beer they sell) and professional athletes are signed to long-term contracts?

15. Many people think professional athletes are overpaid. They tend to think of the salaries in moral terms: 'Doctors provide a more important service than athletes and have much longer and more expensive training, so why should athletes earn more than doctors?'

    (a) Explain why in economic terms athletes are not overpaid.
    (b) What advantage do athletes have over other workers that raises their pay?

16. The Women's National Basketball Association (WNBA) is closing two franchises. Also, all of the teams are losing money. The league owns the players' contracts and charges the individual salary costs to the teams. Use these facts to draw the total cost and total revenue functions for a typical WNBA team.

17. A league has two teams, A and B, that each play 100 home games. The marginal revenue for team A is $MR_A = 500 - 5Q_A$ and the marginal revenue for team B is $MR_B = 250 - 2.5Q_B$ where Q_A and Q_B are the number of home wins for each team. Assume that the expected number of home and away wins for each team is the same.

    (a) What ratio of wins would maximize league-wide revenue?
    (b) What is the league-wide revenue under this ratio of wins?
    (c) What would happen to the revenue maximizing ratio of wins if the players owned the league?

18. A league consists of two teams, A and B. Each team plays 100 home games. Each team is expected to win the same number of games at home and away. The marginal revenue for an additional expected home win for team A is $MR_A = 100 - Q_A$. The marginal revenue for an additional home win for team B is $MR_B = 25 - 5Q_B$.

    (a) What split of the wins for A and B would maximize league revenues? What is the maximum level of league revenue?
    (b) If revenue was shared 60 per cent to the home team and 40 per cent to the visiting team, show that the ratio of wins for A to B would be unaffected.
    (c) Suppose the two teams agreed to a salary cap that limited them to the same level of spending and thus the same level of player quality. What would happen to the number of wins for each team and what would be the new level of overall league revenues?

19. If salary caps reduce overall league revenue why are they so common in professional sports leagues?

20. What effect would a salary cap for the players have on coaches' salaries? Explain.

21. Suppose the league described in question 18 started with free agency for the players. What would happen to the ratio of wins if the two teams merged into one corporation and simply assigned players to either team A or team B? Assume that there is no other competing league in this sport. What would happen to league profits as opposed to league revenue?

22. In an efficiently run sports league no trade of players exists that will raise overall league revenues; in other words, all beneficial trades have been exhausted. Under what systems for organizing a league, sharing its revenues or paying its players' salaries will this efficiency be achieved? What could prevent this efficient outcome?
23. (optional section) Define each term in the following equations and describe the effect of an increase in the level of each term on the starter and back-up salaries.

$$S_1 = cV_n\left[\frac{p_{12}}{2p_{12}-1}\right] - \left[\frac{C_2(t_2^*)+\overline{C}}{2p_{12}-1}\right]$$

$$S_2 = \left[\frac{C_2(t_2^*)+\overline{C}}{2p_{12}-1}\right] - cV_n\left[\frac{p_{12}}{2p_{12}-1}\right]$$

24. (optional section) Explain the concept of a Nash equilibrium and apply this concept to the following diagram from the lectures:

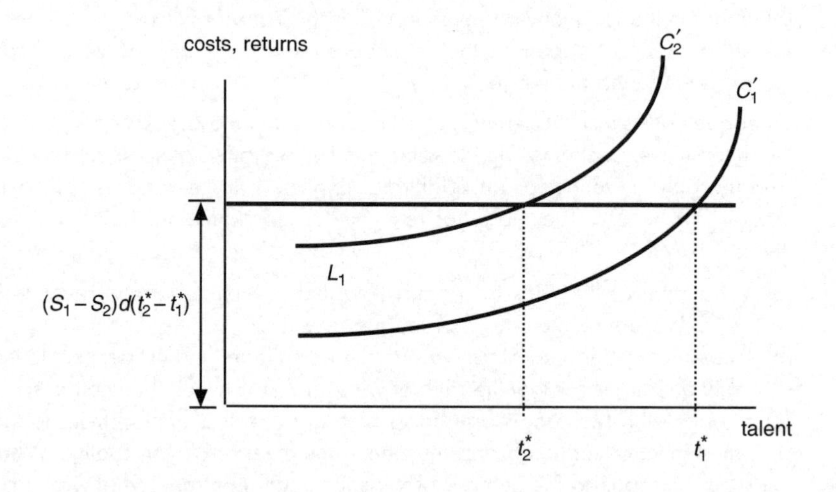

25. (optional section) What determines the relative salaries of starters and backups in professional sports teams?
26. (optional section)

$$S_1 = cV_n\left[\frac{p_{12}}{2p_{12}-1}\right] - \left[\frac{C_2(t_2^*)+\overline{C}}{2p_{12}-1}\right]$$

$$S_2 = \left[\frac{C_2(t_2^*)+\overline{C}}{2p_{12}-1}\right] - cV_n\left[\frac{p_{12}}{2p_{12}-1}\right]$$

Derive the above equations for salaries from the profit constraint, $V_n = S_1 + S_2$ and the opportunity cost constraint, $EY_2 = \overline{C} = 0 = (1 - p_{12})S_1 + p_{12}S_2 - C_2(t_2^*)$.

27. Suppose the estimated relationship between a player's salary and his years of playing in a league was

$$\text{Salary} - 450{,}000 + 150{,}000 \text{ years} - 5{,}000 \text{ years}^2$$

At what number of years would a player's salary peak?

28. (optional section) The switch from a regime of reserve clauses to free agency has had an obvious effect in raising the salaries of players. What more subtle effects on the players' labor market has free agency had?

29. Rank the four professional league sports in the USA in terms of their equality of distribution of player salaries and explain why these differences in equality of salary distribution exist.

30. What effects will the elimination of transfer fees have on European soccer?

5 Discrimination in professional sports

Chapter goals

This chapter examines the possibility that in sports, despite being over-represented relative to their population share, members of minority groups may still be discriminated against. The chapter defines what is meant by discrimination and considers how it may be measured, noting that it is easier to measure player productivity in sport than is generally the case for workers in other industries. Further, it is necessary to consider which sources of discrimination are likely to be of significance in sports – employer, co-worker or customer – and what forms it may take (hiring, salaries, or position in the team). The role of antidiscrimination legislation is considered in relation to college sports where gender participation rates have been a matter of particular concern in the USA.

Introduction

In most countries, discrimination against at least some minority groups is an active public policy issue. Labor market discrimination has been a growing area of study for many economists, often prompted by national equal pay and/or equal opportunities legislation. Similar studies have appeared in the case of sport but, although numerous (see Table 5.2) these are largely confined to North America. Sport has been held up as 'a laboratory' for testing for the presence of discrimination (Pascal, 1972). Studying discrimination in sports may provide insights into discrimination in the rest of the economy. In sports we have good data on individual player performance as the production process is directly observable (in baseball we can observe batting and pitching performance, and in cricket batting and bowling performances). While in other team sports such as football or rugby the importance of teamwork makes it more difficult to measure the true marginal product of any individual, there are still better measures of individual performance than in any other industry. That is why sports are a laboratory for measuring with precision labor market discrimination.

Black players' participation rates in major sports

Professional sport has often been held up as an area of wide-open opportunity where members of minority groups excluded from many high-paying occupations may gain entry and earn substantial incomes. It is true that in the past blacks, for example, were excluded from many of the major North American team sports but today, with the exception of ice hockey, black participation rates exceed the black population share. In baseball, for example, over the period 1898 to 1946 blacks were banned from the Majors by an unwritten rule. They were confined to their own leagues (the Negro Leagues). It was only with the signing of Jackie Robinson by the Brooklyn Dodgers in 1947 that the racial barrier was broken (Hanssen, 1998; Scully, 1974(b)). Yet by 1975 the percentage of blacks in professional baseball had reached 27 per cent and has roughly remained at this level since that time. Similarly in football the figure, which had been zero in 1950, reached 42 per cent in 1975 and 56 per cent by 1988. In basketball the figure rose from zero in 1948 to 63 per cent in 1975 and 74 per cent in 1985/86 (Kahn, 1991).[1] Claims of discrimination against French-speaking Canadians in ice hockey have also occasionally come to the fore. According to Jones, Nadeau and Walsh (1999), historically 95 per cent of players have been English-speaking Canadians, but following league expansion the number of ethnic minority players grew and, in 1990, 7.9 per cent were French-speaking Canadians by birth. A study of discrimination in English soccer (Szymanski, 2000) found that 8.4 per cent of players in 1993 were black, or about five times their share in the total population. Over-representation of minority groups appears to be universal in team sports and the same appears to be true in some nonteam sports such as boxing and athletics, though not obviously so in other sports such as golf and horse-racing.

Earnings by race

Further, it appears that the mean earnings of black players in the major team sports often exceed those of whites. Thus, Kahn (1991) reports that in the NBA four out of five players earning salaries of at least $3 million in 1988/9 were black; in MLB four out of twelve players making at least $2 million per year were black; and in the NFL roughly half of the 30 players making at least $1 million in 1988 were black. While recognizing that blacks are rarely found in managerial or executive posts and may be under-represented in certain key playing positions such as quarterback in football and pitcher in baseball, the above facts stand in stark contrast to those pertaining to other areas of economic life. In spite of the higher participation rates and the apparently higher salaries, allegations of discrimination against black players continue to surface. Racially charged statements by whites still make the headlines. For example, John Rocker of the Atlanta Braves National Baseball League team lashed out against homosexuals, minorities and teammates amongst others in the *Sports Illustrated* of December 1999 and was subsequently forced to apologize. Ron Noades, at the time chairman of Crystal Palace Football Club in London, alleged that black players lacked determination (see Szymanski, 2000).

What is discrimination?

Before we come on to consider the relationship between sport and discrimination it is necessary to define what we mean by the term discrimination.

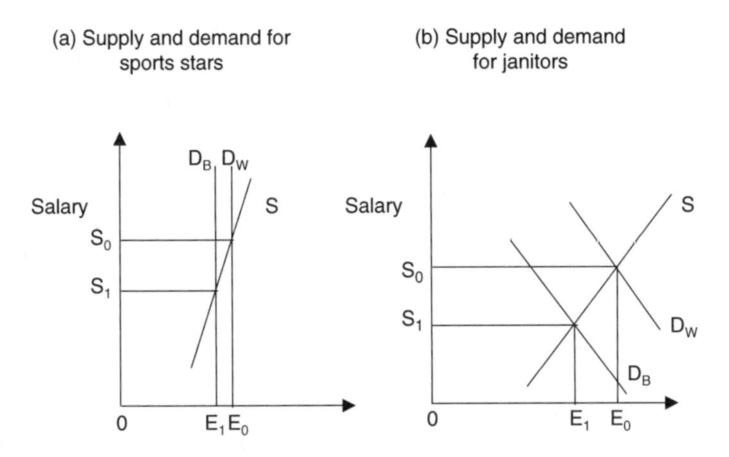

Figure 5.1 Supply and demand for sports stars and janitors

Following Becker (1971) it is premised that certain groups, such as whites, have a **'taste for discrimination'** based on some sort of aversion to other groups, such as blacks, for which they are prepared to pay a price, as for any other commodity. The effect of such behavior will be to shift to the left the labor demand curve for the group against which discrimination is practised, as in Figure 5.1.

Here we assume that D_w represents the demand for white labor and D_b the demand for black labor. The result of the discrimination is that black labor will suffer lower employment and lower wages. Depending on the elasticity of the supply curve, most of the impact could fall on the wage or on the level of employment. In the case of sport the labor supply curve will be relatively inelastic as these abilities are rare and based on genetic endowments. Demand in most sports will be highly inelastic because of **team roster limits**. NBA basketball clubs are allowed a maximum of 15 players plus three on the injured list. MLB teams have rosters of 25, but some players may also be farmed out to the minor leagues. In football, the roster is 65. In other occupations (e.g., janitors in Figure 5.1b) both supply and demand will tend to be much more elastic, so that discrimination has a relatively larger effect on employment than on salaries. In sports in contrast, we might expect to find that the major difference between whites and blacks will be in salary rather than in employment to the extent that discrimination is present. The figures also assume that labor supply is more elastic in the case of whites than for blacks as alternative employment opportunities are greater.

Types of discrimination

Discrimination can be derived from a number of sources including employers, co-workers or consumers. In the employer case Becker assumes that an individual employer forfeits profits by refusing to hire members of minority groups even when the marginal value product of the minority workers exceeds the marginal cost of hiring them. Thus, where the wage required to hire such workers is w, the employer behaves as though this is $w\ (1 + d)$ where d represents the **employer's discrimination** coefficient. Becker suggests (in line with the argument above) that such discriminatory behavior by employers is likely to be eliminated in the long run through the operation of competitive forces, since discrimination implies higher costs. Discriminators would be unable to survive if nondiscriminatory competitors had lower costs. However, since sports clubs are often local monopolies to some degree they do not have to worry about local competitors operating at a lower cost. We cannot rule out the possibility that discriminating employers could survive indefinitely. On the other hand, sports are subject to more scrutiny than other industries. Sports were integrated well before other high paying occupations, such as investment banking, became integrated.

The relative wage demand curve

A convenient way to represent employer discrimination is to utilize a **relative wage demand curve** which represents the supply of and demand for majority and minority groups in terms of their relative wage rates (Hoffman, 1986). In Figure 5.2, W_w represents the wage of white players and W_b the wage of black players. The demand curve for black labor is initially horizontal, reflecting the fact that some club owners are nondiscriminatory, but then slopes down from left to right, indicating increasing levels of discrimination on the part of individual clubs.

With relative wages set at $(W_b/W_w)_0$, b_0 black players will be employed with supply given as S_1. If, however, supply had been limited to S_h there would have been no discrimination and no difference in wages between white and black players. As the number of black players increases, according to this model blacks would have to accept lower wages relative to white players. Given supply

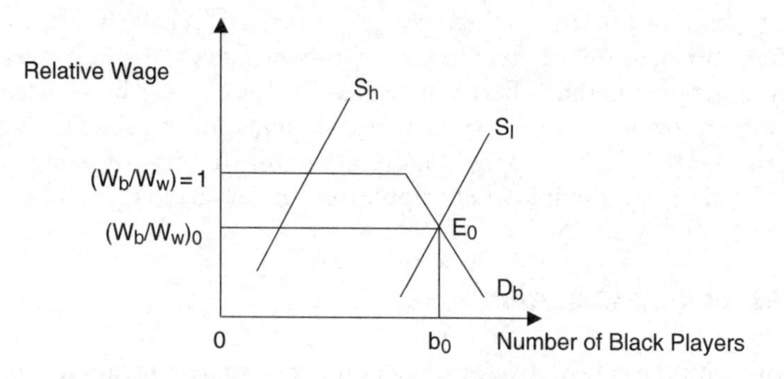

Figure 5.2 Discrimination and the relative demand curve

curve S_1 and a relative wage $(W_b/W_w)_0$ clubs represented on the demand curve above E_0 will hire only black players and clubs represented on the demand curve below E_0 will hire only white players, since the wage differential in existence is not sufficient to offset their prejudice against black players. Assuming that black and white players are equally productive, those clubs unwilling to hire black players will have higher costs and lower profits.

The importance of free entry

The entry of new clubs, in so far as league rules permit it, will tend to drive out discrimination, particularly if new clubs are less discriminatory than existing members of the league. This is shown in Figure 5.3 where the effect of new entry is to shift the relative demand curve to the right, thereby raising the relative wage of black players.

Profit maximization in a competitive market with free entry should, therefore, eliminate discrimination. There is some evidence for this in basketball. Bodvarsson and Brastow (1999) suggest that the entry of four new teams into the NBA increased player mobility and enhanced the degree of labor market competition to such an extent that the wage gap between white and black players vanished between the 1985–6 and 1990–1 seasons.

Some economists believe, however, that **co-worker discrimination** is more plausible than discrimination by employers, as it is co-workers that have the most direct contact with members of minority groups. If whites have an aversion to working or playing with blacks, they may be prepared to sacrifice salary income in order to exclude minorities. Then employers who attempted to integrate their workforces would be faced with rising wage bills.

There is, however, a third possibility, largely ignored in the general discrimination literature, but which might be particularly important in the case of sport, namely **customer discrimination**. Professional sport represents an unusual situation in so far as customers pay to observe the process of

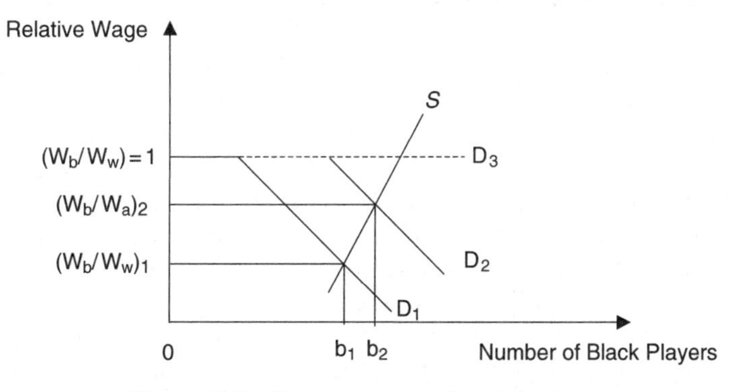

Figure 5.3 New entry and discrimination

production, whereas most other goods are not produced with customer contact. Furthermore, customer discrimination may be a more plausible source of any racial wage gap than either employer or employee discrimination as it will not be eliminated through competitive forces because it results in lower productivity for the discriminated-against group in terms of the ability to generate revenue (see Nardinelli and Simon, 1990).

We must also allow for the nature of bargaining in professional team sports. We may view salary negotiations as involving elements of **bilateral monopoly**. This was particularly so before the emergence of **free agency**, but may still apply today to the extent that players negotiate with clubs on an individual basis and to the extent that salary caps are imposed. One approach is the **Nash bargaining** framework under which in equilibrium neither party has an incentive to change their strategy given the strategy of the other party.[2] Adopting an approach consistent with this, Kahn (1992) points out that racial salary differences may emerge which do not necessarily reflect discrimination, at least on the part of the club owners. For example, blacks may have fewer opportunities than whites in alternative occupations or smaller income from sources such as player endorsements which may weaken the bargaining power of black players relative to white players.[3] Further, customers (or fans) may have preferences for players of their own race which affect potential revenues from playing in particular locations. Thus in US football, Kahn notes that nonwhites represent only 16 per cent of the average market, but 60 per cent of the players. In that case replacing nonwhite players by whites in the typical team will increase revenue if fans are prejudiced. This effect may be moderated to the extent that national television revenues are shared or games are sold out. But even in such cases there may be a positive association between fan support and revenue, because of the ability to increase ticket prices, raise concession income and add to local broadcasting revenues.

Measuring discrimination

The Mincer human capital model

As mentioned in the introduction, there is another reason, however, for economists' interest in analysing the presence of discrimination in professional team sports, given the preoccupation with statistics and the laboratory nature of the industry. In conventional industries the degree of discrimination is normally tested using Mincer-type human capital earnings functions, which in their basic form explain the log of earnings in terms of years of education and experience, and by applying decomposition techniques to infer if there are statistically significant differences in rewards between the different races. This procedure assumes that the productivity of each race is identical. That is a convenient starting point but it would be much better to have a direct measure. Here we are defining discrimination as 'unequal pay for equal, measurable and objectively evaluated work, or its variant, equal pay despite unequal productivity' (Mogull, 1979).

Mincer's basic human capital model provides the following estimating equation:

$$\text{Log}\, W_t = a + b_1 S + b_2 EXP + b_3 EXP^2 + e \tag{5.1}$$

where
W_t = earnings at age t
S = years of schooling
EXP = years of experience
a = intercept
b_s = coefficients
e = stochastic error

Decomposition techniques

Normally in the discrimination literature separate equations of the above type are estimated for whites and blacks. Earnings are then decomposed into differences resulting from varying endowments and coefficients, and the unexplained differential arising in the constant terms. Thus taking as an example whites (w) and blacks (b), the crude mean wage differential (R) can be decomposed as follows:

$$E_w - E_b = (a_w - a_b) + (X_w - X_b)b_w + X_b(b_w - b_b) \tag{5.2}$$
$$(R) = (U) + (E) + (C)$$

where
X = mean characteristics
(U) = the proportion explained by differences in the intercepts
(E) = the proportion due to differing personal characteristics
(C) = the proportion due to differing coefficients

Discrimination (D), a residual, is normally taken to equal $C + U$, which implies that no part of C is nondiscriminatory. In sports, however, certain aspects of performance can be directly measured, while education is unlikely to play a major role in determining productive ability. This makes the estimation of discrimination much more straightforward than is normally the case.

Measuring productivity

In professional team sports there is a range of possible measures of player productivity and some examples of measures used are summarized in Table 5.1.

In baseball, for example, player performance indices have been developed as part of the arbitration process. It has been found that three productivity

Table 5.1 Productivity variables in professional team sports

Baseball	*Basketball*	*Football*	*Hockey*	*Cricket*	*Rugby League*	*Soccer*
Hitting	Field goals	Rushing yardage	Career goals plus assists	Run average	Tries	Shots at goal
Pitching	Free throws	Passing	Average goals covered	Wicket average	Goals	Passes
Experience	Offensive rebounds	Interceptions	Career penalty minutes played	Catches	Drop kicks	Tackles and clearances
Superstar status	Defensive rebounds	Quarterback sacks	Physique	Run-outs	Player fitness and form	Dribbles and runs with ball
	Assists	Field goals and attempts			Experience	Fouls and free kicks awarded
	Personal fouls	Pass interceptions			Ability	Goal-keeping aspects
	Steals	Punting yardage			Team organization	Yellow and red cards
	Turnovers	Yardage given up by defence			Coaching skills	
	Blocked shots					

measures have a major role in salary determination: hitting or pitching performance as measured by the lifetime slugging average for outfielders, the lifetime slugging average for infielders, or lifetime power pitching for pitchers; years of experience in the majors; and superstar status or otherwise (Scully, 1974a). In basketball games played during the season, total minutes played, two-point field goals made, free throws made, rebounds, total points per season, average points per game and previous years of professional experience have been found to influence salary (Mogull, 1974).

In football, in contrast, early work suggests that standardizing for playing performance is only feasible for quarterbacks and ball carriers because these are the only positions for which reliable performance statistics are maintained (Mogull, 1973). Generally, statistics of football have therefore relied on variables that are indirectly related to player performance rather than actual performance statistics. These include longevity variables such as playing experience, including games played and games started, together with draft status, and additional measures of players' ability such as injury frequency, total duration of injuries and number of times selected to play in the Pro Bowl, together with position dummy variables (Kahn, 1992).

Similarly, in (ice) hockey a single variable is unlikely to capture the skills required in all positions. Thus, the ability of skaters has been proxied by career goals plus assists and the skills of goaltenders by the average number of goals per game scored against the goaltender in his career. Defensive play is captured by career penalty minutes per game. Also height and weight variables are included on the grounds that certain physical attributes such as reach and strength can assist performance (Jones and Walsh, 1988).

Recently, the so-called **Opta index** has been created in English Premier Soccer with six categories of information including shots at goal, passes, tackles and clearances, dribbles and runs with ball, fouls and free-kicks awarded, and aspects of goal-keeping (Carmichael, Thomas and Ward, 2000). Clearly, however, it is more difficult to measure performance in hockey and football than it is in baseball and basketball and this is reflected in the number of studies undertaken in each of these sports and summarized in Table 5.2.

Evidence of discrimination in professional team sports

As implied in Table 5.1 discrimination can take a number of forms including **hiring discrimination**, **salary discrimination**, **positional segregation** and **customer discrimination**; it is necessary to examine each of these in turn. Each study focuses on the position of racial minorities relative to whites in sports other than (ice) hockey. The situation in hockey is more complicated since

Table 5.2 Count of studies of discrimination in professional team sports, 1968–2000

	Hiring discrimination	*Salary discrimination*	*Positional segregation*	*Customer discrimination*	*Total*
Baseball	8	12	5	10	35
Basketball	5	10	1	13	29
Football (US)	1	4	3	1	9
Hockey	3	6	3	–	12
Soccer	2	–	–	–	2
Total	19	32	12	24	87

Source: Derived from Kahn (1991) and own estimates.

production frictions could arise from language differences between French-speaking Canadians and English-speaking Canadians. Unlike discrimination studies for the general labor market, gender discrimination studies are rare as men and women do not generally compete against one another in sport. However, that has not prevented some issues about gender differences in rewards emerging (see Box 5.1).

Box 5.1 Tennis and gender discrimination

Men and women both participate in Grand Slam tournaments and these events, though separate, are organized by a single employer. It has been customary for prize money in the male events to exceed those for females and this led to threatened boycotts by leading female professionals. After such action prize money in the US Open was equalized for men and women in 1973. The Australian Open has rough equality and in the French Open equality was attained by 1988. Yet a pay gap of about 11 per cent remains at Wimbledon. The question is whether these differences in prize money amount to unequal pay for work of equal value under the law. One way round the dilemma would be to abandon separate competitions for each gender and make them play against each other. However, it is difficult to see how women could compete on equal terms given the greater strength of men. Men also play up to five sets compared to a maximum of only three for women. Against this Kahn (1992) notes that there is some (partial) evidence that the women's tennis events attract larger television audiences than those of men. That might imply that revenues for women more than match those of men and could justify larger prize money for women than for men. But there are other considerations too. High prize money for men may be necessary to ensure that all the best (male) players compete in the Grand Slam tournaments. If star tennis players stayed away the whole tournament may be devalued. Perhaps this effect is stronger for men than for women. (See Kahn, 1992.)

In basketball Humphreys (2000) has examined whether there is discrimination in relation to basketball coaches in women's basketball in NCAA Division 1. These female head coaches earned more than male head coaches of women's teams in 1990–1, though for both groups salaries were much lower than in the male basketball equivalent. Combining the two wage equations the parameter on female was positive but insignificant, so that there was no evidence of discrimination causing this outcome. Humphreys suggests also that the gap in coaches' salaries between women's and men's basketball could be due to the greater prestige associated with men's basketball, with consumer discrimination or with the monopoly rents arising from the fact that NCAA rules prohibit salary payments to student athletes.

Golf has also given rise to two studies, one dealing with discrimination by gender and the other with discrimination by age. Shmanske (2000) noted that in US professional golf prizes were substantially greater on the male Professional Golfers Association (PGA) tour than on the Ladies Professional Golfers Association (LPGA) tour. In 1998 the male leading money earner (David Duval) earned nearly $2.6 million compared to nearly $1.1 million for the leader on the women's tour (Annika Sorenstam). We must take into account, however, that men play more rounds of golf over longer courses. Using earnings per tournament as the dependant variable in a regression equation it appears that men's and women's earnings are influenced by levels of skill in different ways. Further, in the combined regression the female dummy variable is positive rather than negative and of borderline significance. The fact that women appear not to be discriminated against is confirmed by the **Oaxaca decomposition** results. It is also instructive to know that the PGA has a non-discrimination clause in its constitution which forbids discrimination based on race, religion, national origin or sex. Thus if a woman applied who qualified for a PGA event she could compete against the men and in 2003 Annika Sorenstam played in a PGA event, but Failed to qualify for the final two rounds. It is in fact the LPGA that discriminates by not allowing men to compete in its tour.

There are also two distinct tours for men: the main tour, and the Seniors tour limited to those aged 50 or over. In 1999 the average PGA golfer earned over $900,000 or $36,000 per event, while the average Senior golfer earned over $566,000 or nearly $20,000 per event. Rishe (2001) has estimated an earnings equation including a vector of performance statistics as explanatory variables. The *F* statistic suggests the PGA and Senior coefficients are not jointly equal: that is, the underlying structural model determining salary is different on each tour. Furthermore the dummy variable for Seniors in the combined equation is negative and statistically significant and the Oaxaca decomposition shows that only 18 per cent of the earnings gap can be explained by differences in average skill levels. Discrimination cannot be ruled out in this case, but we need to take into account the fact that television audiences are higher for the PGA tour.

Hiring discrimination

Hiring discrimination has been found to be a common phenomenon in labor markets in general. As far as professional team sports are concerned, Pascal and Rapping (1972) found such evidence in baseball. In relation to black nonpitchers this was inferred from the fact that position-by-position the arithmetic mean of black lifetime batting averages significantly exceeded that by whites. For pitchers, ability was proxied by games won by major league season. Again, blacks performed significantly better than whites. If we assume that the ability distributions for blacks and whites are identical we can infer that an average black player must be better than a white player to have an equal chance of moving from the minor leagues to the majors. Similar results were obtained by Medoff (1975a).

Scully (1974) also notes that blacks tend to be excluded from managerial and coaching positions in baseball, despite the fact that their performance in general is superior to that of whites. As far as other sports are concerned evidence of hiring discrimination against French-speaking Canadians has been detected in (ice) hockey. For example, Lavoie, Grenier and Coulombe (1992) found that in the same draft position French-speaking Canadians significantly outperformed English-speaking Canadians in the NHL over the 1982–4 seasons. This result suggests that French-speaking Canadians needed to be better qualified than English-speaking Canadians in order to be selected as early in the draft. In basketball, however, Kahn and Sherer (1988) found, using 1985/6 data, that there were no significant differences in the order in which NBA players were drafted, controlling for college performance. Indeed, if anything, black players tended to be drafted earlier than whites.

A degree of caution is, however, required in interpreting the results of tests for hiring discrimination as the assumption of identical ability distributions for blacks and whites may not hold. Both Pascal and Rapping and Scully note that it is possible that the mean of the black ability distribution and its variance may be greater than that of whites. Three arguments have been put forward in favor of this proposition. First, it has been held that blacks have a genetic advantage in athletics. For instance, shorter distance running events in the Olympics have been dominated by black athletes, though white athletes may have a comparative advantage over blacks in certain sporting activities, such as running over longer distances.[4] Second, black athletes may be more highly motivated to acquire athletic skills than whites because they face a more restricted range of employment opportunities. Third, wage discrimination in other occupations may influence occupational choice in favor of sports by blacks, leading to a systematic difference in ability distributions between blacks and whites. Scully (1973), however, notes that since the earnings differential between sports and other occupations widens as ability increases, the differential will be so substantial for star players that stars of both races would be in totally inelastic supply relative to salary. Thus, we would expect to find the number of stars of each race to be proportional to the population numbers for each race, which does not appear to be the case.

While the precise effect of entry barriers has been disputed there is no doubt that they have been eroded over time. Both Pascal and Rapping and Gwartney and Haworth (1974) are inclined to explain this erosion in baseball in terms of the operation of the profit motive, though its timing would seem to require further explanation. Gwartney and Haworth's estimates suggest that a low discriminator prepared to employ as few as four black players in the 1950s could have increased revenue by more than $200,000 per year, while at the same time reducing the cost of hiring major league players. At that time Pascal and Rapping suggest that bonus payments to black players were lower than for white because of information imperfections, but as black scouting systems were developed and information spread, competition had all but eliminated the differential by the second half of the 1960s. They conclude: 'the original racial differentials in the receipt of bonus payments can reasonably be interpreted as stemming from a combination of information lag and monopolistic practice rather than bigotry per se'. As Hanssen (1998) points out, the most interesting aspect of the integration process was the fact that the National and American baseball leagues proceeded at substantially different speeds, with the American League specializing in white line-ups and the National League in higher quality play. This is puzzling given that the association between black players and winning was almost identical across the leagues. He concludes that the most likely explanation lies in differences in racial fan preferences across the leagues, considered further below in relation to customer discrimination.

Salary discrimination

If employer discrimination were pervasive we would expect to find evidence of salary differences for given levels of productivity: that is, blacks would have to be prepared to work for lower wages than whites in order to persuade white team owners to hire them. However, evidence of salary differences would not itself be conclusive. Differences in pay between black and white players may owe as much to differences in the degree of monopsonistic exploitation[5] (a function of supply side imperfections) as to discrimination (a function of demand side influences). In both cases players would receive a salary lower than the value of their marginal revenue product.

In Figure 5.4, white players have a more elastic supply curve than black players because of greater alternative employment opportunities. A profit-maximizing employer will hire each group up to the point where marginal wage cost (either MWC_w or MWC_b) equals **marginal revenue product** (MRP).

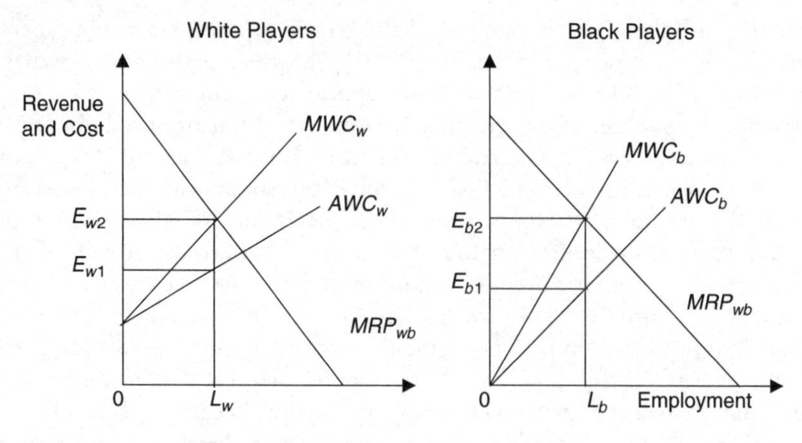

Figure 5.4 Monopsonistic exploitation

The wage is, however, determined by the supply curve at that point. Hence, we have a higher wage (E_{w1}) for whites than for blacks (E_{b1}). Given bilateral monopoly the wage may, however, be set in the range $E_{w2} - E_{w1}$ for whites and $E_{b2} - E_{b1}$ for blacks.

As far as baseball is concerned little evidence of salary discrimination has been found. Pascal and Rapping (1972) examined a sample of 148 baseball players in 1968 and ran separated regressions for nonpitchers and pitchers. In the former case the estimated race coefficient was insignificant, so that there was no evidence of salary discrimination in favor of whites. In the latter case there was a *negative* race coefficient, significant at the 10 per cent level, indicating that on average blacks obtained *higher* salaries than did whites (though this was highly sensitive to the actual specification of the model). Five further studies report similar results (Medoff, 1975a and 1975b; Mogull, 1975, 1979 and 1981).

There have been relatively few studies which attempt to estimate whether or not there is discrimination against blacks in US football. Kahn (1992), using data on 1,363 NFL players for the 1989 season, finds only a 4 per cent salary difference favoring whites when controlling for performance and other variables, and in most cases the difference is insignificant. More crucially, however, Kahn finds that white–nonwhite compensation differences varied according to the area in which a team was located, such that whites earned more in metropolitan areas with a higher proportion of whites in the population, and similarly nonwhites earned more in metropolitan areas with a higher proportion of nonwhites in the population. These results are therefore consistent with the existence of customer discrimination. Yet the results are quantitatively small, so that they do not lead to large overall white–nonwhite salary differences. Gius and Johnson (2000), using a more recent data set for 938 NFL players in the 1996 season, found that white players earned 10 per cent less than blacks and suggest that their results are consistent with reverse discrimination based on race.

In the case of English soccer Syzmanski (2000) has implemented a market test for discrimination by estimating the relationship between the relative proportion of black player appearances for each club and league position, controlling for the wage bill. He assumes that clubs attempt to maximize playing success subject to a budget constraint and finds that those clubs with an above average proportion of black players systematically perform better than the size of the aggregate wage bill would predict. The results, using data for 39 English League clubs over the period 1978 to 1993, support the evidence for discrimination in that black players appear to receive lower pay than white players for a given level of performance. The model suggests that a club with twice the average number of black appearances would save £358,000 compared to a club which hired no black players. Syzmanski suggests that the source of the prejudice is club owners rather than fans or white players, based on the reported statements of one team official. An alternative test of discrimination is to test whether nonwhite players trade at prices below their white counterparts in the transfer market,[6] given productivity characteristics. Reilly and Witt (1993) examined 202 player transfers, including 31 black players, in the 1991–2 season. The estimated coefficient on the race variable (black equals 1) is negative with a point estimate indicating that black players transfer at prices nearly 9 per cent lower than whites, but the *t* statistic is 0.75, so that one cannot reject the null hypothesis that there is no discrimination.

Research into professional basketball players' salaries indicated significant black salary shortfalls in the 1980s amounting to some 20 per cent (see Kahn, 1991; Kahn and Sherer, 1988). Hamilton (1997) examines whether these differences have persisted into the 1990s, when the NBA has been increasingly dominated by black stars such as Michael Jordan, Shaquille O'Neal and Tim Duncan. His regression for the 1994/5 season suggests that there is no difference between white and black salaries controlling for player and team characteristics. However, there are salary differences at certain points in the salary distribution. Whites earn less than blacks at the lower end of the distribution, though the difference is statistically insignificant and varies with minutes played. At the upper end of the distribution, however, whites receive a significant premium of 18 per cent, consistent with a form of customer discrimination in which fans prefer to see white star players, *ceteris paribus.*

Positional segregation

Segregation may take different forms. There have been 'whites only' leagues, all-white teams in leagues with some blacks and individual playing positions that were exclusively held by white players in teams and leagues that were otherwise integrated. We have already seen examples of league-wide segregation in the American and National Leagues. In relation to positional segregation Scully (1973) found that while 53 per cent of baseball outfielders were black, only 9 per cent of pitchers were. In football the positional dispersion was even greater with two-thirds of defensive backs being black in 1971 at a time when only 37 per cent of all players were black. By 1989 Kahn (1992) observed that predominantly nonwhite positions included defensive back, running back and wide receiver, while whites were disproportionately represented at quarterback, offensive line, punter and kicker, with the remaining positions being integrated. This segregation appeared to have salary consequences with whites being found in better paid positions relative to blacks, although it was not clear whether this stemmed from discrimination by teams, access to training opportunities or simply skill differences. In (ice) hockey, French Canadians were under-represented in defence and over-represented in goal during the 1970s and 1980s (Kahn, 1992).

There are competing explanations for this '**stacking**' phenomenon. First, there are a group of largely sociological explanations, some of which were advanced by Loy and McElvogue (1970). One argument is that such segregation results from the prejudice of managers, who believe that blacks are not capable of playing in positions which call for a high degree of responsibility, decision making or leadership. Alternatively, it has been suggested that blacks find certain positions more attractive than others, or tend to model themselves on previous black players who are themselves self-selected into certain positions. Medoff (1977) has in contrast put forward an economic explanation for the phenomenon, namely that it is more costly for blacks to acquire certain skills which require more coaching than others. The economic hypothesis implies that as black incomes rise in real terms blacks should enter the central positions is greater numbers, and this indeed appears to have happened during the 1960s when black family incomes increased significantly relative to whites. Since sociological and psychological factors would be expected to be relatively stable he finds the economic hypothesis to be more persuasive.

Customer discrimination

We have already observed a number of examples of customer discrimination. In his early work, Scully (1974b) proposed a simple test for this phenomenon in baseball. Pitchers are rotated on a regular basis and the planned starting pitchers are announced in the press prior to each game, so that discriminating fans can choose to attend games or otherwise on the basis of the race of the pitcher. Consequently he estimated the average home attendance of 57 National League starting pitchers over the 1967 season, holding constant opposing team and time of game and including a dummy variable for race. It was found that on average 1,969 fewer fans attended games pitched by blacks than those pitched by whites, with the coefficient on the race variable significant at the 5 per cent level. An alternative test was put forward by Gwartney and

Haworth (1974). They found that the number of black players employed by baseball teams had a significantly positive effect on playing success. For example, the five teams with the most blacks won 58 per cent of their games over the period 1952–6, while the other teams only won 46 per cent. If consumer discrimination was important we might find despite this increase in wins that revenues suffered for those teams employing larger numbers of black athletes. In sharp contrast to Scully's findings this hypothesis was strongly contradicted, however, by the regression results, which revealed a highly significant positive relationship between team attendance and number of black players at this time, even holding past and present playing success constant. Gwartney and Haworth offer two possible explanations for these findings. The first relates to the impact of black superstars over this period. The second is an increase in black fans which was more than sufficient to offset any decline in attendance by whites.

In later work in basketball, Kahn and Sherer (1988) and Burdekin and Idson (1991) provide strong evidence of the importance of consumer preferences in shaping the racial composition of NBA teams. The former found that, *ceteris paribus*, replacing one black player with an identical white player would raise attendance by 8,000 to 13,000 fans per season. The latter found that there is a strong relationship between the racial compositions of NBA teams over the 1980–1 to 1985–6 seasons and the racial composition of the local market population. More specifically, the more closely the ethnic mix of the team reflects that prevailing among the team's fans the higher the average attendance. They refer to this as a textbook case of the theory of consumer-based discrimination. A similar result was obtained by Hamilton (1997). He regressed home attendance of each NBA team for the 1993–4 season on the team's winning percentage that year, population, average income, the fraction of the population which was black in the standard metropolitan statistical area (SMSA) in which the team was located and the number of white players in the team. His estimates imply that adding a white player to an NBA team will increase attendance by 3.9 per cent.

An even more convincing test of the presence of customer discrimination is found in the market for sports memorabilia. This has the advantage over the examination of salary or employment differences that data are readily accessible and easily measurable, and it provides direct evidence, because there is no scope for either owner (employer) or co-worker discrimination (Nardinelli and Simon, 1990).

Evidence for the presence of customer discrimination in the market for baseball cards is presented in Box 5.2. This result was confirmed by Anderson and La Croix (1991) for their 1977 sample, but not for an earlier 1960–1 sample, and by Gabriel, Johnson and Stanton (1995). The latter suggest that there are important differences between players who are still active and those who are retired. More particularly, race and ethnicity have no significant effects on card prices at the start of a player's career, but by the time a player retires the cards of nonwhite players decline in value relative to those of white players.[7] In basketball, however, Stone and Warren (1999) were unable to detect any racial differences in the effect of career performance level on the prices of trading cards. Yet there was some evidence that the effect of career length on trading card prices was lower for whites than for blacks and that the card price premium for players who subsequently coached in the NBA was lower for blacks than for whites.

Box 5.2 Customer discrimination and the market for memorabilia

There is a widespread market for cards of sportsmen. Production is limited in any year, as is the case with coins and stamps. It is also the case that older cards are more valuable than newer ones. Determinants of a card's price also include the star quality of the player and the presence of discrimination by race. Further, collectors of cards include individuals from all age groups and socio-demographic backgrounds. The market for most professional sports cards is national in scope and the industry is substantial in terms of revenue. The question to be asked, therefore, is whether the race of a player displayed on a card directly affects the price consumers are prepared to pay.

In their study of the baseball card market Nardinelli and Simon (1990) found that prices ranged up to $6,000 for old cards with scarcity value and that value was determined by career performance of the player, the age of the card and the number printed. The market for the cards for the average player determines the minimum price for cards and to this is added various performance characteristics. A distinction is made between pitchers and hitters, and race variables are added to their estimating equations. Their results indicate that customer discrimination is present in the market for baseball cards. Among hitters, cards of nonwhites sell for about 10 per cent less than cards of white players of comparable ability. In the case of pitchers there is a discount of 13 per cent on the cards of nonwhites compared to comparable whites.

None of the above studies, or indeed other studies relating to discrimination elsewhere, have considered all three main types of discrimination in a single wage model. However, Bodvarrson and Partridge (2001) have done precisely this in relation to professional basketball in the USA. Using a quadratic production function with diminishing returns to both nonwhite and white players they assume that white fans are prejudiced against nonwhite players and nonwhite fans are prejudiced against white players. Employer prejudice is allowed for by assuming nonwhite players impose a cost on the employer (all owners being white at the time). Finally co-worker discrimination is captured by the premium in pay that a player must receive for working with players of the opposite skin colour, this premium being a function of the team's racial mix. Their results indicate that equally qualified black players earned 19 per cent less than corresponding white players in 1985/6 and 9 per cent in 1990/1. The manager race coefficient was insignificant, suggesting an absence of employer discrimination. The team racial composition coefficient is positive and statistically significant for white players, consistent with co-worker discrimination. However, this variable is insignificant for black players. Finally, in relation to customer discrimination the number of black fans interacted with team racial composition is positive and significant for black players. Thus, these results are consistent with black fans reacting positively as the proportion of blacks in the team grows.

Public responses to discrimination: Title IX antidiscrimination legislation in the USA

US college sports

According to Putnam (1999), the primary force behind the growth in women's sports has been **Title IX** which was passed by Congress in 1972, despite the initial opposition of the NCAA. Title IX states that 'no person in the US shall, on the basis of sex, be excluded from participation in, be denied the benefit of, or be subjected to discrimination under any education program or activity receiving federal financial assistance'. It is doubtful that intercollegiate athletics are educational programs, particularly given the graduation rate of football and basketball players in Division I. However, advocates of women's sports are willing to pretend that they are educational programs. The law applies to schools as well as colleges and universities and has considerable significance given the resources devoted to these activities. As Sack and Staurowsky (1998) point out, over recent years college sport has grown into a multi-million dollar industry. The four-year television contract signed between the NCAA and ABC in 1997 was alone worth $30 million per year. The economic costs of enticing college students to engage in sports in terms of free board and tuition are substantial; according to one estimate reported by Sack and Staurowsky, universities pay out over $500 million per annum in athletic scholarships to Division I athletes alone. The implementation of this legislation has caused considerable controversy. **Contract compliance** is the responsibility of the Office of Civil Rights within the US Department of Education, which relies on the answers to three questions in determining whether an institution is acting within the law. First, does an institution's sports program meet the test of substantial proportionality in the sense that female representation in sports matches their proportion in the institution's student population? Second, can the institution show that it has expanded its sports programs for women over a period of time? Third, can the institution show that it is providing for the demand for sport by women in ways other than equal participation? Though negative answers to those three questions lay an institution open to the removal of federal funding in all programs, this has never so far occurred. This is despite the fact that there is a considerable disparity in the proportion of either sex engaged in collegiate sporting activity. Thus, according to Putnam, a 1997 survey found that only 28 out of 303 institutions in Division I of the NCAA had achieved substantial proportionality in the 1995–6 academic year, defined as having a number of female athletes no more than 5 per cent under the percentage of female enrollments.

Critics argue, however, that women's tastes and abilities in sport may differ from those of men. Proponents use a version of **Say's Law** in suggesting that supply creates its own demand, so that as more sport is offered to women the take up will increase and the ability of women in these sports will grow also. Female participation, though well below that of males, has in fact increased substantially. According to a 1994–5 NCAA participation study the percentage of women among all student athletes rose from 30.8 per cent in 1982–3 to 36.9 per cent in 1994–5, and the 1999 figure is 41 per cent. A further criticism is that Title IX has been damaging to male sporting activity. There is some evidence that men's sporting programs in colleges and universities in sports other than football or basketball have been discontinued as this is one means by which institutions can reach the proportionality targets. Thus, McBride, Worcester and Tennyson (1999) find that between 1978 and 1996 men's relative access to sports programs actually decreased in net terms.

Another issue has been the disparity in pay between male and female coaches. A 1997 NCAA Gender Equality Study found that the average salary for a male basketball coach was just under $100,000 in the 300 largest universities, while the corresponding figure for female basketball coaches was just over $60,000. Zimbalist (1999) points out that college athletics programs are not subject to normal market pressures as, for one thing, the players are not paid a salary. Further, some gender difference in coaches' pay may be justified by the fact that women's basketball generates less than one-quarter of the revenues of men's basketball. Clearly, US college athletics is likely to remain an area of considerable controversy, and one which does not have parallels in other countries.

Conclusions

Despite the fact that nonwhites are now over-represented in professional team sports and are now amongst the highest earners in a very well remunerated profession, there has (at least in the past) been evidence of labor market discrimination against nonwhites. The primary source of this discrimination appears to be the fans rather than club owners or white players. As far as salary difference is concerned, the most recent evidence suggests that this form of racial discrimination has largely been eliminated in most sports.

What does stand out, however, is the dramatic change in the representation of nonwhites among these high paying occupations once entry barriers were overcome in the early post-war period. Certain authors have suggested that nonprofit considerations play a major part in professional team sports (see Chapter 2). If that is the case we might expect tastes for discrimination to be particularly marked in this area of employment as there are no obvious ways of eliminating it, and that makes the dramatic improvement in the employment position of nonwhites even more remarkable.

The finding that customer discrimination is a significant phenomenon in sport may have implications for other sectors of the economy. Two-thirds of employees are now found in service occupations, though service sector employees will not have direct contact with the public in all cases. Sports are highly visible, so that the setting of high standards in terms of equality of opportunity is important as a benchmark for other sectors.

Notes

1. We normally assume that the group against which discrimination is directed is in the minority. As a group increases its share of employment, eventually reaching a majority, there may be a tipping phenomenon in which discrimination disappears. However, it is possible that marginal players who are members of the minorities may continue to be discriminated against and members of such groups may continue to be excluded from managerial posts.
2. In the theory of games, a dominant strategy requires that there is one optimal choice of strategy for each player no matter what the other player does. However, this is very demanding in terms of the information required. An alternative is to require that one player's strategy is optimal given the optimal choice of the other player. Thus, a pair of strategies is said to be a Nash equilibrium if A's choice is optimal, given B's choice, and B's choice is optimal, given A's choice. Such a Nash equilibrium can be interpreted as a pair of expectations about each player's choice such that, when the other player's choice is revealed, neither player will want to change his or her behavior.
3. However, some endorsement agreements may include work stoppage clauses which reduce the attractiveness of this alternative.
4. One author (Taboo, 2000) has gone so far as to suggest that 'there is a new racial barrier in sports. Positions that require speed and jumping ability are almost exclusively black' (p. 20). He also notes that African Americans hold 95 per cent of the top times in sprinting: Kenyans contribute to more than one-third of the top times in middle and long distance races; North Africans excel at the middle distances, particularly the 1,500 metres; and Mexicans are strongest at the longer races.
5. If there is a single employer facing an upward sloping supply curve of labor then in order to maximize profits the monopsonistic employer will equate marginal wage costs with marginal revenue product. As marginal wage

costs exceed average wage costs, employees' wages will lie below the value of the marginal revenue product.

6. In the English soccer leagues, players are free agents when their contract with the existing club has expired. However, during the period of the contract, the club is entitled to a transfer fee as compensation for the loss of a player to another club.
7. Fort and Gill (2000) suggest that race and ethnicity perceptions are likely to be based on a bundle of individual characteristics, suggesting a continuous rather than a binary measure. Further it is the perception of the buyers, not the researcher, that matters. Appropriate corrections in their analysis of the baseball card market only served, however, to confirm discrimination against blacks and Hispanics.

Exercises

1. How can racial discrimination occur in professional team sports when black players are so well paid and over-represented in terms of numbers?
2. Why is it easier to measure discrimination in professional team sports than in other industries?
3. Why might we expect customer discrimination to be particularly important in sport, and what forms might it take?
4. If employers (club owners) practise discrimination is this likely to increase or decrease their profits?
5. How can we explain positional segregation – the fact that racial minorities are under-represented in some positions and over-represented in others?
6. Why is the market for memorabilia a particularly appropriate one for testing for the presence or otherwise of discrimination?
7. Might discrimination take different forms in different sports?
8. It is alleged that Title IX harms men's sport in US colleges and universities by shifting resources from them and into women's sports programs. Is this a valid criticism and does it imply that Title IX should be repealed?
9. Does equal opportunity necessarily imply that the gender mix should be equal across all sports?
10. Explain why customer discrimination against black athletes has different and longer-lasting effects than employer discrimination or employee discrimination.
11. Over the last century boxers from different ethnic groups have been dominant. At various times the leading boxers were Irish, Jews, Italians and African-Americans. Is there an economic explanation?

6 The economic implications of sports broadcasting

Chapter goals

The issue of access to broadcasts of major sporting events is a major policy concern. In Europe concern over access has led to a prohibition on any single broadcaster having a monopoly on the broadcasting of key sporting events. Both in North America and Europe the income from broadcasting has grown dramatically and is now as significant as gate revenue in the total income of major clubs. However, over-exposure of games on television may reduce paid attendance. There is considerable controversy over whether television has overall positive or negative effects on revenue across all clubs as opposed to the leading clubs in a sport. A related concern is broadcasters changing the nature of the game to make it more attractive to their viewers to the detriment of the live spectators. In addition there is a danger of competitive imbalance if individual clubs are allowed to negotiate their own television deals rather than have the league negotiate on behalf of all the members' clubs. This has led to clashes with the competition authorities, particularly in Europe where there is no protection offered by an equivalent of the 1961 US Sports Broadcasting Act. There have been a number of high profile cases such as the Monopolies and Mergers Commission's blocking of BSkyB's attempt to take over Manchester United and the Restrictive Practices Court's decision to allow the collective selling of television rights by the English Premier League.

Introduction

The economics of sports broadcasting

There are two key elements in the economics of sports broadcasting. One is that once a sports program has been produced the marginal cost of making it available to additional viewers is approximately zero. Thus, except for **pay-per-view** (hereafter PPV) broadcasts in which the technology lets the broadcaster exclude some viewers, sports broadcasting fits the two requirements in the economist's definition of a **public good**: nonrivalry (zero marginal cost) and **nonexcludability**. The second key aspect is that the content of sports broadcasting is protected by intellectual property rights laws. US viewers will recognize the message below. It is a legalistic incantation read before all over-the-air (in the UK the term is 'terrestrial') broadcasts: 'The following broadcast is intended solely for the personal use of this audience. It cannot be rebroadcast or retransmitted in any form without the express written consent of the National Basketball Association.' The ability of the league or team to sell advertising time on over-the-air or on cable broadcasts depends on the enforcement of this restriction.

Entry barriers in sports broadcasting have been due to the scarcity of broadcast channels. However, the landscape of broadcasting is rapidly changing. Technical change in the form of cable and satellite television has reduced entry barriers and increased the number of channels available in each country, leading to more vigorous competition for key broadcasting rights. Real time broadcast quality videos on the Internet will provide new ways of marketing sports. Cowie and Williams (1997) note that the take-up of paid television has ranged from 5 per cent in Germany to 20 per cent of viewers in France. Digital television has also led to a substantial increase in the effective spectrum. As a consequence of these developments, the distribution of economic rents has shifted from the television station owners to those owning property rights over content.

The historical scarcity of broadcast outlets was due to both physical shortage in the spectrum of possible over-the-air channels and government restrictions on entry. In the UK just one state-funded and two advertising-funded service providers still dominate the over-the-air (terrestrial) television broadcast industry. When the number of possible channels is severely limited by technological constraints, letting the few possible channels be owned by the highest bidders will not ensure that some public policy objectives, such as high quality programming and diversity of viewpoints, are met. Regulations, including licensing standards for content and limits on the types and duration of advertisements, are intended to foster these public policy objectives. Another way to raise program quality and perhaps offer more viewpoints is public funding of broadcasts. In the UK the revenues for public television broadcasts come from a license on home viewing. At home television viewing of any terrestrial channel, public or private, without a paid-up license is subject to a substantial fine. Special trucks roam the streets in the UK ready to detect any television that has been turned on. They pounce on homes watching television without the required license. The license fee is set so low that almost every household can afford one. The public channels in the UK broadcast major sporting events while in the USA public television more or less avoids professional sports broadcasts. Public broadcasts in the UK and many other countries in Europe were the main source of television broadcasts in the early years. They were set up to have a mass appeal. Public television broadcasting in the USA came later and was aimed at market segments that the commercial broadcasters had not served, such as educational programs for preschoolers (*Sesame Street*) and classical music. Public television in the USA raised much less opposition from commercial broadcasters by sticking to what commercial broadcasters ignored.

The issue of television rights for major sporting events has become a major issue worldwide. The problem is that sport is a perishable good, for which competition at any particular point in time comprises only other sporting events taking place at the same time which are regarded by consumers as reasonable substitutes.

In the UK the 1996 Broadcasting Act requires the Independent Television Commission (ITC) to draw up and review periodically a code on sports and other events listed by the Secretary of State for Culture, Media and Sport. The Act restricts the acquisition by television program providers of exclusive rights to the whole or any part of live television coverage of listed events (as defined in Appendix 6.1) and the broadcasting of such events on an exclusive basis without the previous consent of the ITC. Such permission will only be given if the price paid for such rights is regarded as fair, reasonable and non-discriminatory as between over-the-air (terrestrial as defined in Appendix 6.2) and other providers. Similar provisions apply in Germany, Italy and Denmark (see Appendix 6.3). The effect of these provisions is to distort the market for the purchase and sale of sports broadcast rights. The prohibition against exclusivity affects the bidding process and the value of the broadcast rights in favor of the purchaser. The originators of protected (listed) events will receive a lower price than an unregulated market would provide.

It should, however, also be recognized that live sporting events are in relatively inelastic demand, so that exclusivity will tend to lead to a substantially lower output and higher prices. A possible exception to the lower output is when price discrimination allows the supplier to convert **consumer surplus** into producer surplus. Price discrimination may be possible with PPV. In Figure 6.1 the shaded triangle represents consumer surplus for market price, P, and paid output of hours of sport, Q_{PC}, which would be provided if the supply of hours of sports broadcasts were perfectly elastic at the indicated marginal cost, MC. A supply equal to the marginal cost would be applicable if the broadcast and sports industries were perfectly competitive. If, however,

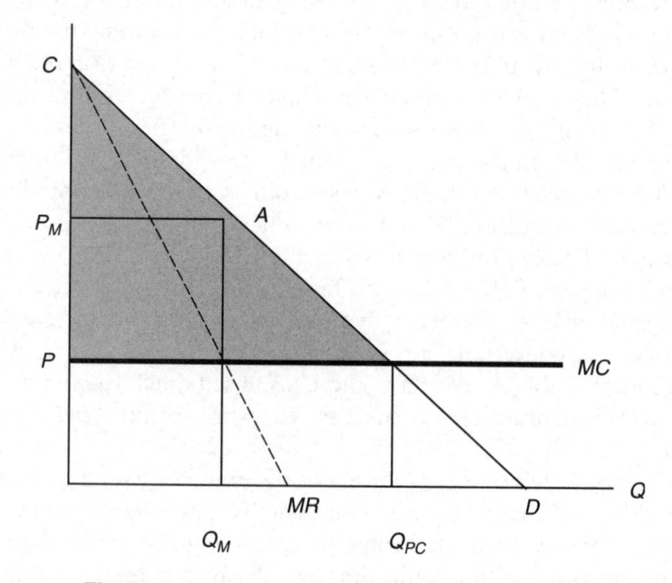

Figure 6.1 Consumer surplus with pay-per-view

a monopoly controlled the broadcasts, the profits would be maximized where $MR = MC$ at Q_M with the monopoly price set at P_M. The consumer surplus is reduced to the triangle $A - P_M - C$. If the monopoly was a perfect price discriminator (i.e., a mind reader), and it could charge every viewer their reservation price, the profit-maximizing output would be the same as with perfect competition, Q_{PC}, but the entire original consumer surplus triangle would be transferred to the monopolist. There are barriers to realizing this perfect price discrimination. One is that technology is making the PPV sports industry more competitive. Satellite and cable companies in the USA compete in most markets while Internet providers, such as local phone companies, are poised to offer PPV as the speed of the Internet increases. The practical drawback is that PPV providers do not know which consumers have the highest reservation prices. The best they can do is charge a higher price to bars and restaurants that have public viewing.

Sport leagues and international federations try to get the highest price for the broadcast rights to their games by selling exclusive rights to the highest bidder for a flat fee. For example, FIFA sold the exclusive rights to the 2002 and 2006 World Cup competitions for $2.5 billion to a German company, Kirch, which then proceeded to segment the market in the basis of individual countries. This led to a prolonged dispute with the BBC and ITV, who refused to pay the amounts demanded by Kirch, citing the UK's listed sporting events requirement. Eventually, the two over-the-air broadcasters agreed to pay £160 million for the right to broadcast the two events, a sum smaller than the original sum demanded, but considerably greater than their original offer.

Kirch essentially provided a marketing service to FIFA. It saved FIFA the effort of negotiating broadcast rights with dozens of individual broadcasters around the world. The other service Kirch provided was risk bearing. Kirch's payment was fixed in advance of the World Cup. If the broadcasts generated less advertising revenue than anticipated, Kirsch would lose money rather than FIFA. Open bidding for a contract such as the one awarded to Kirch allows the originator of the sports broadcast to extract more of the producer surplus from the broadcast. Kirsch declared bankruptcy in 2002. It had over-estimated the willingness of soccer fans to pay for soccer on a PPV basis and over-estimated the value of broadcast rights to the World Cup.

If there is just one potential bidder the situation is called a **bilateral monopoly**. In this situation the split of the producer surplus between the program originator and the broadcast marketer is indeterminate. The high bidder for the broadcast rights faces some risk that the final consumer demand will be less than anticipated. A war or a scandal could reduce interest in the World Cup. Since the most optimistic among the potential bidders makes the winning bid, there is a good chance that the actual revenues from marketing the broadcast rights will be less than that bidder anticipated. In auction theory this result is called the **winner's curse**. The same phenomenon applied to the bidding in **free agents** by teams. This was clearly seen in the deal struck between the English Nationwide League and ITV Digital. The latter attempted to renege on the deal as it was making such heavy losses. It offered to pay only £50 million out of the £180 million owed on the remainder of the contract. This was refused and the company was placed in administration (bankruptcy in the USA) in March 2002.

The growth of sports broadcasting

Shares of total revenue in North America and Europe

National broadcasts of sports leagues in the USA were relatively limited prior to 1962. Cave and Crandall (2001) note that only major league baseball had a national contract with ABC over the period 1960–5. The 1961 Sports Broadcasting Act, however, allowed league-wide sales of national broadcast rights for football and other sports and resulted in a dramatic increase in the value of national network television sports rights throughout the 1960s. Further, as Zimbalist (1992) points out, since network broadcast income grew faster than local broadcast income, the share in broadcast incomes from national as opposed local contracts increased from 25 per cent in 1960 to 49 per cent in 1990. This growth is important for competitive balance, since the national broadcast revenue is divided equally among franchises, while the local broadcast revenue is not. In fact, the disparity among franchises in local media income was growing. Thus the rates of broadcasting income of the top relative to the bottom franchise rose from over 5 to 1 in 1964 to over 18 to 1 in 1990. These disparities were only mitigated to a minor degree by the revenue-sharing of some local television income beginning in 1982. By 1997 sports broadcasting rights' share of total revenue had reached 56 per cent in professional football, 39 per cent in professional basketball, 32 per cent in major league baseball and a much more modest 9 per cent in ice hockey. In dollar terms the growth in revenue has been dramatic. When the National Football League signed its first television contract in 1962 this was worth $4.7 million per annum, but by 1998 this figure had risen to no less than $2.2 billion per annum. Even after being adjusted for inflation, this represents a 29 per cent annual rate of growth. Similar increases were recorded for baseball, but even these were surpassed by those in basketball, which overtook baseball in dollar terms in 1995.

This growth should be put in the context of the arrangements for broadcasting adopted by some of the major US team sports, which include the following:

1. '**Blackouts**': that is, the prevention of live television coverage of a game in the geographical area in which the game is being played unless the game is sold out in advance. Blackouts are most common in the NFL.
2. '**Cartel bargaining**': that is, bargaining by representative of the league as a whole with television authorities for national broadcasting rights.

As referred to above, such arrangements came into conflict with US **antitrust** legislation, and this resulted in 1961 in the granting by Congress of a special dispensation from antitrust laws for the four major professional team sports in relation to broadcasting. This was justified on the grounds of the interests of viewers and spectators, competitive balance and league health.

In addition, teams have generally reserved the right to market local broadcasts of games. The exception is the NFL which markets the broadcasts of every game in a national contract. Local broadcasts have been sold by clubs in a variety of ways: direct sales to a television station, direct sales of broadcasting rights to a sponsor or advertiser, or the purchase by the club itself of television time and then direct contracting with sponsors.

There has been similar growth of broadcasting revenue in Europe, where soccer has remained very much the dominant sport. Live television broadcasts of English league football began in 1983. As shown in Table 6.1, the annual rights fees for the first three television contracts were broadly constant at about £3 million. Substantial increases occurred when BSkyB entered into competitive bidding in 1992. British broadcasters together spent over £2.1 billion to buy the rights to English football for just three years from June 2001 to May 2004. BSkyB has the first pick of premiership matches and must show at least three matches per club per season. NTL has a second choice of the games and cannot show more than eight matches from one club per season. The dominant role of soccer rights in the UK is illustrated by the fact that they account for more than three-quarters of BSkyB's annual expenditure on sports rights and by the fact that of the most watched 100 over-the-air sports broadcasts in 1998, 77 were of soccer (Cave and Crandall, 2001). Table 6.2 provides some further indication of this dominance. A similar situation exists in the rest of Europe. Hoehn and Szymanski (1999) report

Table 6.1 The cost of television rights to live league matches from the premiership in England, 1983–2001

	Start year of contract						
	1983	*1985*	*1986*	*1988*	*1992*	*1997*	*2001*
Length of contract (teams)	2	0.5	2	4	5	4	3
Broadcaster	BBC/ITV	BBC	BBC/ITV	ITV	BSkyB	BSkyB	BSkyB*
Rights fee (£m)	5.2	1.3	6.2	44	191.5	670	1,150
Annual rights fee (£m)	2.6	2.6	3.1	11	38.3	167.5	550
Number of live matches per season	10	6	14	18	60	60	66
Fees per live match (£m)	0.26	0.43	0.22	0.61	0.64	2.79	8.33

* In addition 40 live games were available on a PPV basis. Additional agreements were made with NTL for 40 PPV games (£180 m), with ITV for highlight packages (£183 m), with BBC and BSkyB jointly for FA Cup and Internationals (£400 m) and with ITV Sport for 88 live games from the Nationwide Football League divisions one, two and three, plus the Worthington Cup (£315 m).

Source: MMC (1999) from data supplied by Manchester United and the Premier League for the period up to 1997.

Table 6.2 Value of live sports rights in the UK, 1999

Sport	*Competition*	*Broadcaster(s) (F = Free, P = Pay)*	*Duration (years)*	*Annual charge (£m)*
Cricket	Domestic Tests	BSkyB (P) C4 (F)	4	26
Motor Sport	Formula One	ITV (F)	5	12
Rugby League	Super League	BSkyB (P)	5	11
Rugby Union	England Internationals	BSkyB (P) live	5	18
Snooker	Embassy World Championships	BBC (F)	4	10
Soccer	Premier League	BSkyB (P)	4	167
Soccer	Champions League	On Digital (P) ITV (F)	3	87
Tennis	Wimbledon Championships	BBC	4	7

Source: Television sports markets, reported in Cave and Crandall (2001).

that in 1997 the value of league soccer television contracts in the UK, France, Italy, Spain and Germany combined (i.e., all of the major European markets) were in the region of $1 billion. However, the significance of television incomes should not be over-stated. At that time Manchester United, for example, generated only 15 per cent of its total income from television contracts, far less than from attendances and other commercial activities. It is the growth in the size of television income that is more significant.

Furthermore, the scale of broadcasting contracts is much smaller in Europe than in North America. In 1998 the national broadcast contracts in the latter were $2.2 billion in football, $0.53 billion in the NBA and $0.6 billion in baseball, totaling together $3.5 billion. The major European markets combined are less than one-third of the North American total. The explanation cannot be found in population differences, since the combined population of the UK, France, Italy, Spain and Germany is about 300 million compared to 280 million in the USA.

There are a number of possible explanations. First, legal restrictions in Europe on broadcasting reduce the value of broadcast rights. Second, the lower levels of income in Europe are a factor: viewers with lower incomes are less valuable to advertisers. Average per capita gross domestic product (GDP) in 2002 for the UK, France, Italy, Spain and Germany weighted by population and based on purchasing power parities was $24,400 compared to $36,300 in the USA. But even allowing for a high income elasticity for viewing sports, this difference in incomes does not seem likely to account for the vast difference in the value of broadcast rights. Third, the greater supply of teams in Europe relative to North America may reduce their scarcity value or spread talent too thinly. Fourth, the value of US media contracts is a function of their worth to advertisers trying to put their message across to 'guaranteed' audiences. US television developed with a tradition of advertising, whereas in Europe advertising did not support or sustain television to the same degree.

Even today companies must be careful how advertisements are presented during sports broadcasts so that consumers are not offended by interruption to the flow of play. In the USA, leagues organize the games to facilitate advertising. They create breaks to ensure that there is time for commercials. In baseball there is no problem because of the natural breaks between half innings. Other US sports have created television time outs and/or forced teams to take a minimum number of time outs. European soccer never made such a compromise and neither did other European sports such as cricket and rugby. The traditions and the expectations of consumers are different between the two continents and the value of advertising higher in North America for this reason.

An interesting contrast between Europe and the USA is advertising in movie theaters. Until recently there was no advertising during previews at US movies and but there was a lot in Europe. The advertisements in the USA were limited to trailers for forthcoming movies. Why? Advertisers in Europe were largely locked out of television in countries where the main broadcasters were publicly owned. In the US consumers were loath to pay to see movies and then have to sit through the same commercials they saw on television at home. Since the same consumers were accessible to US advertisers through television, the additional value of advertising in movie theaters was lower in the US than in Europe. In the last few years the stark differential between the USA and Europe has broken down. Advertisements for general consumer products such as soft drinks and cars are creeping into US movie theaters. The theater owners could not resist the extra income. The fracturing of the US television audience across hundreds of cable channels and devices that allow television viewers to skip commercials made the movie audience more valuable to advertisers. The implication for sports broadcasting in Europe of this change in theaters in the US is that there may soon be commercial breaks in soccer. Soccer has natural breaks after goals or injuries so the technical adjustments would be minor. As the fraction of viewers who are watching broadcasts compared to watching live increases in Europe the financial pressure to have commercial breaks will be inexorable. European soccer fans view the idea of commercial breaks as sacrilegious. To paraphrase a common expression, sacrilege happens. Even the Catholic Church switched from its Latin liturgy to the vernacular when it faced declining attendance. When the commercial breaks become common in European soccer the value of broadcasts rights in Europe will be similar to the value of US rights.

The effects of sports broadcasting on live attendance

The most important justification claimed by the sports authorities for restricting the broadcasts of live games is the alleged effect on live attendance. It became virtually an article of faith that televised and live games were in direct competition. There were few formal attempts to model this in the USA, but Hochberg and Horowitz (1973) discussed the relationship between declining college football attendances and the spread of television in the USA during the 1950s. Horowitz (1974) argued that there was no statistical relationship between the number of telecasts and baseball attendances. However, the negative effects of television could be more marked in the case of football and basketball than baseball because these are fall/winter sports in which driving may be more difficult and sitting outdoors more uncomfortable. Also, in these sports attention tends to be concentrated on the ball holder who is more easily seen on television.

It is possible, however, that television might, in fact, have a positive effect on attendances by stimulating spectator interest. There are broader considerations than just whether paid attendance may be lower. The sports promoter has to consider three aspects: the direct financial income from the sale of broadcasting rights, stadium attendance revenue and the within-stadium advertising and sponsorship revenue. While the stadium attendance may be adversely affected if a game is shown live on television, the stadium advertising and sponsorship may be increased by such exposure. Relevant factors are the price differential between ticket prices and viewing costs, the quality of television coverage relative to the atmosphere at the game and weather conditions. A further consideration is the impact on competition. As Cowie and Williams (1997) note, while a sports club acting in isolation simply trades off extra broadcasting revenue against reduced stadium revenue, a rival sports club will ignore the effect of televising its own games on its rivals' gate revenues (unless there is **gate-sharing**). As the market for match attendance is geographically narrow while the market for television viewing is potentially wide geographically, a move towards more extensive television broadcasts of live games is likely to intensify competition, being moderated only by local fan loyalty or identification.

Despite the potential benefits of live television described above, the NFL was convinced of the depressing effect of broadcasting on attendances to the extent of arranging television blackouts even of games which were already sold out. Blackouts of sold-out games were sought for a number of reasons. The NFL argued that although gate receipts would be unaffected, the effect of television exposure would be to increase the number of ticket holders failing to turn up at games, preferring to view at home. This would not only result in a loss of parking and other sales revenue, but also detract from the atmosphere of packed stands. Ultimately, there would be a declining demand for tickets as fans got used to watching local games on television.

However, in 1973, and despite the opposition of the NFL, legislation was introduced to ban blackouts in the home areas of clubs in cases where all tickets offered for sale were sold out 72 hours before the time of the game. Siegfried and Hinshaw (1979) attempted to test the effect of lifting these blackouts on the number of ticket holders failing to turn up for a game. They found that adverse weather and the quality of the teams influenced the attendance of ticket holders but that there was no evidence that live broadcasting had a significant impact. There was no support for the NFL's assertions that the league would be harmed financially by the introduction of the antiblackout law.

Empirical evidence

There have been a number of studies, however, that have found a negative relationship between television exposure and live attendance in general. These include Thomas and Jolsen (1979) in relation to baseball, Fizel and Bennett (1989) for college football attendances, and Zhang and Smith (1997) for basketball. There are relatively few similar studies in other countries. Baimbridge, Cameron and Dawson (1996) found that during the 1993/4 season, satellite television had a significant negative effect on English Premier League soccer attendance (though this was more than compensated for by television income received). With respect to the two live matches per week covered by BSkyB and the recorded highlights on BBC then available, only the scheduling and corresponding live transmissions of matches on Monday evenings led to a *ceteris paribus* reduction in attendance (amounting to some 15–16 per cent). In an earlier study (1995) they also found that live transmission of English rugby league games reduced attendance by 25 per cent. Clearly, there is enough evidence available to lead the leagues to be cautious about the extent and timing of televised live games.

Sports broadcasting and competitive balance

Revenue-sharing arrangements in North America and Europe

As broadcasting revenues have become more crucial to the viability of clubs, their impact on competitive balance has become even more significant. Fort and Quirk (1995) note that in the USA, national television contracts uniformly involve equal sharing of revenues by all league teams (with negotiated temporary exclusions for expansion franchises). They argue that under the conditions of a one-team one-vote environment, equal sharing is more or less assured because the national contract requires consensus for approval. Otherwise, weak drawing teams would block unequal sharing by refusing the live showing on television of their own games with strong drawing teams. In their model, television revenue-sharing has no impact on competitive balance because payments to teams are independent of each team's win percentage. But given that television audiences and advertising revenues are higher when big city teams are involved in the play offs, it will pay a league to adopt some policies favorable to large market teams. The issue for a league is always figuring out the right balance. It was a recognition of the redistributive function of revenues from national broadcast contracts that persuaded Congress to exempt the collective selling of broadcasting rights from the antitrust laws by passing the Sports Broadcasting Act of 1961.

In addition to national broadcasting arrangements North American teams have generally reserved the right to market the broadcasts of games outside the national contract (except the NFL where the national contract covers all games). Local broadcasts are an important source of revenue. Some teams are owned by national cable networks (e.g. the Atlanta Braves), and all of their home and away games are available on that network. Zimbalist (1992) notes that in order to preserve the value of their national package deals, sports leagues have found it necessary to restrict the number of local broadcasts. For example, the NBA restricts these to 41 per year per team, of which a maximum of 25 can be carried by a major station as defined in the NBA rules. MLB has an arrangement whereby each team, in exchange for its share of the major league central fund revenues from the package deals, agrees not to permit television transmission outside its designated geographical area.

Fort and Quirk report that total local television revenues are more responsive to the popularity of teams than is attendance. Attendance is capped by the size of the team's stadium and the number of home games. In most sports the league determines the number of home games. Gate revenue depends on both attendance and ticket prices, so an increase in a team's popularity could raise gate revenue even if the team sells out all of its games. Nevertheless, the potential gains in local television revenue are much higher than the potential gains in ticket revenue when a team starts to draw a high ratings share of the local television audience.

Without local television revenue-sharing the wide disparities between the potential television markets among small and large cities would lead to a concentration of playing talent in big clubs that would be even more extreme than the concentration caused by potential differences in gate revenue. The resulting concentration of playing talent would not maximize total league revenue. Furthermore, if gate-sharing were to be increased without a comparable increase in local television revenue, this would have the effect of increasing the importance of local television in the overall differentiation of the resources of small and large market teams as it would add to the problem. It appears that the rational choice for a league as a whole is to have the same rules for gate and local television revenue-sharing, since this is likely to lead to a distribution of playing strengths that maximizes league-wide revenues in the absence of a **salary cap**. The difficulty leagues have in setting up a local television revenue-sharing is that the richest teams (e.g., the New York Yankees) want to hang on to their local television revenues. It is very difficult under the common unanimity-voting rules for a league to institute a local television revenue-sharing regime. To the Yankees the increase in league-wide revenues from more competitive balance is uncertain but the loss of their local television revenues is certain.

There is also a nontrivial problem in measuring local television revenues. Television stations that are owned by the team can set a below-market price for the broadcast rights and effectively hide some of their local television revenue. Even if the prices for local broadcast rights are at market value, the league may not have access to the books of the privately-owned teams. It is easier for leagues to monitor spending on player salaries, especially when these payments are under a union contract. Taxes on a team's total expenditures on players' salaries beyond some threshold, often called a *luxury tax*, are administratively easier than local television revenue-sharing but serve the same function of promoting competitive balance.

In contrast to the USA, television sports income in Europe was relatively small until the 1990s. In Europe broadcasting agreements typically include a performance-related element and a fixed component. The English Premier Soccer League contract, for example, shares half of the contract value equally among the clubs, 25 per cent on the basis of league performance and 25 per cent on the basis of number of games televised. The only performance element in national US broadcast contracts is extra money for making the play-offs. Hoehn and Szymanski (1999) report that in Italy, income from over-the-air broadcasts is shared equally among clubs and PPV income is distributed on the basis of performance. In Germany clubs receive a fixed share plus a fixed amount for every home game and a smaller sum for every away game televised.

While it often thought that the English Premier League television revenue sharing arrangements are income-equalizing, the result of its distribution method is that the top club receives about double the amount received by the bottom club. This does not look particularly equalizing. Hamil, Michie and Oughton (1999) report that in the 1997–8 season the top five clubs out of the 20 in the league appeared in 60 per cent of matches shown and these accounted for over 70 per cent of total viewers, but these clubs only received 35.62 per cent of total television revenue. However, these same clubs accounted for no less than 68.4 per cent of the total operating profits in the Premier League in 1996. An alternative would be to reward clubs inversely in relation to league position along the lines of the North American player draft system. The advent of PPV is a major threat to competitive balance, where clubs in Europe are free to negotiate their own contracts and have widely differing revenue potentials. One possibility here would be for the Premier League to impose a tax on this revenue for redistribution purposes. Another solution is to adopt the NFL system of league-wide marketing and equal sharing of all broadcast revenue.

Public policy and sports broadcasting

There are two related antitrust (competition) issues for sports broadcasts. First, can an exclusive broadcast agreement between a league and one broadcaster improve competitive balance in the league? This question assumes that having competitive balance in the league serves a public purpose. The implicit argument is that the public benefits if championships are spread over more cities and more people enjoy at least the prospect of having a winning home team. Certainly, if each team negotiated it own broadcast contracts there would be no sharing of broadcast revenues and thus less competitive balance. The converse, that a league-wide broadcast agreement will enhance competitive balance, is not certain. The contract could split all broadcast revenues equally, as in the NFL contracts with three over-the-air networks, or it could reflect existing differences in team popularity, as in the UK Premier League broadcast contracts.

The second antitrust question is whether a broadcaster can gain monopoly power through exclusive agreements with a sports league? Being the sole broadcaster for a sports league gives the broadcaster an advantage with advertisers. No one else may be able to offer the same audience pool (e.g., young males). At the center of the debate over whether an exclusive broadcasting contract harms the public interest is the question of the appropriate definition of the market. A narrow definition of the market will make the exclusive broadcast contract look like a monopoly. A wide definition will make it look benign. Thus, in 1999 the UK Monopolies and Mergers Commission (hereafter the MMC) concluded that the relevant market for soccer in the UK was no wider than the matches of the Premier League clubs and that over-the-air television and PPV were separate markets. A broader definition would be the supply of football matches in total or, even wider still, the total supply of sporting events. The MMC took the view that the definition of the market should be determined primarily by substitutability: that is, if services are readily substitutable for each other from the perspective of consumers or suppliers, then they belong to the same market. Their position was that games in the lower divisions were a poor substitute for Premier League matches. A hypothetical market test for monopoly power would be a situation in which a supplier with a contract to provide 100 per cent of a particular service was able to maintain prices at 5 per cent to 10 per cent above competitive levels. Unfortunately, the competitive price has little meaning in relation to contracts for sports broadcasts because there is not free entry into the market for selling sporting contests at the major league level.

North America

The US broadcast market is more competitive simply because there are four major league sports with substantial followings and collegiate sports programs with as much interest as the professional sports. Even Major League Soccer (MLS) is beginning to establish a national following. There are also many more over-the-air and cable networks. Thus, the public harm caused by the Congressional exemption from the antitrust laws for the MLB, NFL, NHL and NBA is much smaller than the harm that could be caused by an exclusive broadcast contract for the Premier League in the UK. Advertisers that are unhappy with the prices being charged by the owners of national broadcast rights for the NBA (currently the NBC over-the-air network and the TNT cable network) can buy advertising time that delivers viewers with the same demographic profiles from many other broadcasters.

Cowie and Williams (1997) have suggested that sports rights should be sold in units at the lowest practical level. For team sports this is the individual match, for individual sports an individual match within a tournament and in races an individual race. However, they recognize that there are transaction costs to disaggregating broadcast rights. These include the managerial time for negotiating many contracts. Broadcasters prefer having continuity because it builds up the audience and gives the broadcaster a reputation for carrying a given sport. These costs and benefits suggest that the socially optimal arrangement for a contract might be at least a season for the league as a whole. Further reasons for allowing an annual league-wide contract are that the broadcaster wants to show the best games and this cannot be firmly established until the season is under way and the performance level of different clubs is known. The league also has an interest in the timing of broadcasts, given potential detrimental effects on live attendances, a feature which is not relevant in other markets.

The 1961 Sports Broadcasting Act and antitrust exemptions

While as a consequence of the Sports Broadcasting Act 1961 the US antitrust regime might be regarded as permissive with respect to exclusive broadcast contracts, the exemption is not a blanket one. It applies only to 'sponsored' telecasts (i.e., over-the-air broadcasters who generate income from advertising revenue). Without this exemption the structure of US sports broadcasting would be entirely different. For example, in the 1984 NCAA case, in which the governing body of college sport attempted to restrict the right of colleges to market their games on television, the court rejected the NCAA's defense on the grounds that the restrictions violated the US antitrust laws. The NCAA was not part of the 1961 Sports Broadcasting Act. A major effect of this Act has been to create a very strong barrier to entry for any potential rival league. Thus, part of the explanation for the failure of the new United States Football League (USFL) was the inability of this body to obtain significantly lucrative broadcasting rights to enable it to compete effectively with the NFL. More recently, the World Wrestling Federation's Football League (XFL), which had a national broadcast contract with the NBC network, failed in its first season. The NFL had locked up much of the over-the-air broadcast spectrum with contracts that forbade broadcasts of any other professional football league games.

As we have seen above, one of the most contentious aspects of the 1961 law has been the blackout provisions. A shown in Box 6.1, it appears that the gain in team revenue may be small in comparison to the loss of viewership rights. If this conclusion is correct then a policy change might yield a Pareto superior outcome. Pareto superior means that the winners from the change in policy gain more than enough to pay off the losers.

Box 6.1 Should NFL blackouts be banned?

In its defense of the 72-hour blackout rule passed under the 1973 Congress Amendment to the 1961 Sports Broadcasting Act the NFL argued that this agreement was necessary to maintain the long-run economic viability of professional football, based on the argument that '**no-shows**' would result in lost parking and concession revenues and reduced revenues from local radio broadcasts. However, today the revenue from game-day concessions and related income is dwarfed by television income, so that the rationale for the imposition of local blackouts appears to be much weakened.

Game day attendance revenue is comprised of season ticket sales determined prior to the start of the season, and game day tickets determined by the quality of the match and the number of no-shows; and each of these must be included in regressions attempting to explain game day attendance. Using data for the 1996–7 season, Putsis and Sen estimated a profit equation to assess the probability of blackout and used the estimated probability as an instrument in the individual game–ticket demand equation. Their results suggest that both season and individual game ticket sales are highly price inelastic, partly reflecting stadium capacity constraints on demand. The decision not to show up is heavily dependent on game and weather conditions. Surprisingly, there appears to be a negative relationship between the imposition of a local blackout and individual game ticket sales. The reason for this is that the blackout variable not only captures the marginal impact of blackout imposition, but also serves as a proxy for the lower level of interest inherent in games which are blacked out. Holding the overall interest level constant, they estimate the revenue implications of blackouts for each of the eight venues and find that the maximum average increase in total game day revenue for NFL games equaled US$414,396 per team. They then calculate a 'cost per viewer' revenue by dividing the maximum gain in game revenue due to local blackout by the average number of viewers for games that are broadcast in a specific market, allowing one to work out how much one would have to compensate the NFL for broadcasting non-sold-out games, while at the same time improving both viewing welfare

Box 6.1 continued

and total NFL revenue. Overall the cost per viewer is small (for all but two teams less than US$1.00), and this seems to be much less than the value of an individual's time and the likely value of viewing a game on television.

There are at least three potential policy alternatives. First, one could simply legislate against local blackouts. Second, one could use tax revenue to compensate NFL teams. Third, one could create a public mechanisms for viewer charges or PPV. The last of these, if technologically available, would produce a Pareto superior outcome.

Often there is a simple market solution to threatened blackouts. If the game is a few thousand seats short of a sellout, the local broadcaster buys the unsold seats and donates them to charity. The broadcaster gets a little public goodwill from having, say, crippled children attend the game and more than makes up the cost of the tickets by selling local advertising.

Source: Putsis Jr and Sen (2000).

Europe

Collective selling

In Europe the two dominant issues have been the listing of sporting events which forces nonexclusive broadcasts and the collective sale of sports rights, already referred to above. European Union competition law is paramount over national competition policies. In general the European Commission, while recognizing the special nature of sports, has been opposed to long-term exclusive broadcasting contracts because of their perceived negative effects on broadcasting competition and innovation. It has also become more critical over time about collective selling and announced in October 2001 that it was launching a preliminary investigation into the English Premier League/BSkyB three-year deal, as well as deals involving UEFA and the German Football Association. At national level there have been a number of challenges to existing arrangements in soccer. In Germany, the antitrust authorities successfully challenged the centralized sale of broadcasting rights for domestic games in European club competitions. Subsequently, the Bundesliga petitioned for (and obtained) an antitrust exemption from the German Parliament. In the Netherlands Feyenoord Football Club attempted to negotiate its own television contract following the collective sale of rights by the Dutch Football Association to a PPV channel. Feynoord's case was upheld by the court, affirming that the collective selling of rights was in breach of competition law. In Italy the government introduced legislation to prevent any broadcaster controlling more than 70 per cent of the total rights. In the

UK the Office of Fair Trading challenged the agreement between the English Premier League and BSkyB before the Restrictive Practices Court on the grounds that consumer choice was restricted to 60 games a season out of the 380 available. This artificial scarcity was alleged to raise prices. Furthermore, the agreement not only required that BSkyB had exclusive rights to particular live matches (**narrow exclusivity**), but also required that no other matches should be broadcast live (**broad exclusivity**). The court concluded that collective selling did in fact operate in the public interest on the grounds that the public benefited compared to a system in which no restrictions at all applied (see Box 6.2). It should be noted that this decision was made prior to the implementation of the 1998 Competition Act and the Court did not base its decision on EU competition law. In negotiating a revised deal to operate from season 2001 to 2002 the Premier League published an official tender document and introduced a sealed bid process to satisfy the competition authorities. The Premier League also introduced an unbundling of categories of games to be sold and shortened contract duration to three years.

Box 6.2 The Restrictive Practices Court investigation into collective selling of television rights by the English Premier League

In 1999 the Office of Fair Trading (OFT) challenged the exclusive right of the Premier League (PL) to negotiate on behalf of all its members and the exclusive right of BSkyB to show live matches up to the end of the 2000–1 season on the grounds that this was a restrictive practice against the public interest. In particular, the OFT highlighted rule D7.3 of the PL which states 'no league matches shall be televised or recorded or transmitted by satellite or cable or any similar method without the written consent of the Board, save in the case of closed circuit television within the ground of the club where the league match is being played'.

The OFT claimed that this broad exclusivity restricted consumer choice by limiting access to broadcast matches, increased the prices paid by consumers because of the restriction of supply and limited the development of the broadcasting market by restricting access to premium content. In defense the PL claimed that the funds available for investment in players and facilities would be smaller without collective selling. Furthermore, collective selling assisted in the maintenance of competitive balance, because of the relative equal sharing of broadcasting income, the parachute arrangements of relegated clubs (whereby financial protection was offered for a limited period) and substantial payments to the Nationwide Football League to assist with ground improvements.

The Restrictive Practices Court accepted the argument that the PL acted as a **cartel** and that the restrictions came within the scope of the legislation. While, however, the OFT had argued that the relevant market

Box 6.2 continued

was the market for television rights for the PL matches, the Court accepted a much wider definition, stating that the relevant market was on the one hand the television rights relating to sporting events, and, on the other hand, the supply of broadcasting services in general. The court identified five specific and substantial benefits consequent upon the agreements. These were the ability to market the championship as a whole, rather than just parts of it; the provision of extra income to spend on players and stadium improvements; the ability to share television income fairly; the ability to subsidize non-PL income; and the maintenance of competition in broadcasting. It also noted that the main product of 380 PL games per season was not in any way reduced by the exclusivity restrictions. The arrangements did not represent a straightforward example of restriction of output to raise price and a factor which weighed heavily with the court was the fact that PL clubs on the whole did not make large profits. It also accepted the evidence that competitive balance was promoted by the financial equality engendered by collective selling.

The Court found that although the agreement did impose restrictions on the broadcasting of Premier League matches, its disadvantages were outweighed by the benefits and consequently the agreement was not against the public interest.

Source: Restrictive Practices Court (1999).

Vertical integration between broadcasters and sports clubs

In Europe concern has been expressed at the increased tendency for media companies to buy shares in sports clubs, and particularly soccer clubs. The only constraint is that the ruling bodies may pass rules prohibiting a single firm from having a controlling interest in more than one club competing in the same competition. It is felt that allowing this may reduce public confidence in the honesty of the competition. In 1999 ENIC, a publicly quoted UK company with multiple investments in soccer clubs across Europe, challenged UEFA rules prohibiting clubs owned by the same company from competing in the same competition. The Court of Arbitration for Sport ruled in favor of UEFA, finding that the rule was 'necessary and proportionate'. It defined control as a share of 51 per cent or more.

There are also a number of reasons why **vertical integration** by media companies and sports clubs may serve to reduce competition in the market for sports broadcasting rights. **Auction** theory predicts that when a bidder in an auction has an ownership stake in an asset being sold, or a toehold, it is more likely to win the auction than competitors without the toehold (see **toehold effect**).

This occurs for two reasons. First, part of the value of any bid will return to the bidder with the toehold, enabling a higher bid to be put in. Second the winner's curse may operate given the uncertainty of the value of the asset and the probability of others over-bidding given their awareness that the bidder with the toehold can afford to bid more. It is suggested that the winner's curse is likely to operate more strongly in an ascending price (English) auction, where each bidder can observe the behavior of rivals in the bidding process. Its effect is likely to be much less where sealed bid tendering is the norm.

Regarding the USA, Cave and Crandall (2001) suggest that media ownership of sports teams is so limited that the effect of vertical integration on the supply of games broadcast is simply not a policy issue. They do, however, provide a table of media company ownership of US sports clubs (reproduced here as Table 6.3). In the summer of 2003 there were news stories that a substantial share of the current broadcasters who own teams in the USA were offering to sell their teams, specifically Disney and Fox's News Corp. At this point it is not known who will buy their teams but these impending sales will likely reverse the nascent trend in the USA toward media ownership. The NFL has a rule against any corporate ownership of teams, which has limited the penetration of broadcast ownership in the USA.

In Europe this issue is much more critical than in the USA. In particular the attempted takeover of the largest soccer club in the world, Manchester United, by BSkyB (then the only supplier of premier sports programs) was blocked by the MMC in 1999, just before the Restrictive Practices Court decision in relation to collective selling (see Box 6.3). Following this decision, a number of broadcasters purchased minority shares in soccer clubs (see Appendix 6.5) within the limit set by the FA of 10 per cent of the assets. As a consequence, media companies held shares in eleven English clubs and one Scottish club. Thus the market now looks rather different from the one

Table 6.3 Media ownership of US sports clubs, 1999

Media company	*Sport*		
	Basketball	*Baseball*	*Ice hockey*
Comcast Corp.	Philadelphia 76ers (NBA)	–	Philadelphia Flyers (NHL)
News Corp. (Fox)	Los Angeles Lakers (NBA)	Los Angeles Dodgers (MBL)	Los Angeles Kings (NHL) New York Rangers (NHL)
Walt Disney Co.	–	Anaheim Angels (MLB)	Mighty Ducks of Anaheim (NHL)
Cable Vision Systems	New York Knicks (NBA)	–	New York Rangers (NHL)
Time Warner, Inc	Atlanta Hawks (NHB)	Atlanta Braves (MLB)	Atlanta Thrashers (NHL)

Note: In most cases the above represents a share of the total holding rather than total control.

Source: Compiled From Kagan World Media data published in *Media Sports Business Databook* 1998. Used with permission.

Box 6.3 The Monopolies and Mergers Commission investigation into BSkyB's attempted take-over of Manchester United

One important development in professional soccer in Europe is the increasing tendency for clubs to become public companies listed on the stock market (see Appendix 6.4). This has left clubs open to the possibility of takeover. The attempt by BSkyB, a vertically integrated satellite broadcaster, to take over the Manchester United soccer club led to considerable public debate. The parties to the debate were various fan groups and ultimately the MMC. The proposed merger qualified for investigation under the 1973 Fair Trading Act, as the value of the assets taken over exceeded the qualifying limit of £70 million. In fact, only Manchester United was large enough at that time among Premier League clubs to meet this requirement. It should also be noted that while the merger would have represented a change in ownership there would have been no reduction in the number of providers. Unlike the Restrictive Practices Court the MMC used a narrow definition of the market (the matches of the Premier League clubs rather than the soccer market as a whole), while the broadcasting market was similarly narrowly defined as sports premium pay television channels. This was done on the basis of perceived substitutability, though no attempt was made to calculate **cross-price elasticity of demand**. The test used to consider whether this market was competitive or not was one commonly used by competition authorities, namely whether a supplier serving 100 per cent of the market could maintain prices 5–10 per cent above the competitive level. Despite the fact that football clubs are local monopolies, so that a competitive price has no meaning, the MMC concluded that this was, indeed, the case. It is also difficult to see why profit-maximizing prices should be affected by a mere change of ownership. More crucial is the question of stadium capacity constraints. It will almost always pay to price in such a way that the ground is filled, given the existence of substantial ancillary sales and sponsorship. In fact, Manchester United was in the process of expanding its ground capacity to make it the largest of any club in the UK.

On the question of the broadcasting market the MMC was concerned that the toehold effect would provide BSkyB with an advantage over potential rivals. It did not, however, consider making a sealed bid option a requirement of merger or accept the argument of the defense that it was possible for other broadcasters to obtain a toehold in the market by investing in other clubs. Rather it concluded that the proposed merger was against the public interest on the grounds that it would reinforce the tendency towards greater imbalance among clubs in financial resources and provide BSkyB with greater power to influence decisions relating to the organization of football, to the detriment of fans.

Source: Monopolies and Mergers Commission (1999).

investigated by the MMC. Indeed, from the point of view of competition policy a situation in which a single broadcaster holds a minority interest in several clubs may be more problematical than one in which a single broadcaster owns 100 per cent of a single club. In the latter case, the interest of the owner will be to win games whereas in the former case there may be an incentive to manipulate results to ensure boosted ratings.

Media investment and the conduct of sporting activity

One concern expressed in both the Restrictive Practices Court and MMC investigations was of broadcasters attempting to change the rules of games to satisfy the interests of advertisers or their own schedules. An example of such a rule change would be soccer games being stopped to allow more commercials. Similarly, it may be in the interests of the clubs concerned, wishing to maximize their broadcasting income, to modify the organization of the league itself so as to increase the value of broadcasting sales, but in ways that are not necessarily in the interest of fans. This is most clearly seen in the re-arrangements of the timing of fixtures to suit television producers rather than the interests of fans. Thus, games shown on a Monday evening make it difficult for away fans to attend. Where clubs are utility maximizers more concerned with winning games (as has been claimed for Britain and Australia), it is to be expected that there will be less accommodation to the requirements of television than with profit-maximizing clubs.

Arguably the most significant impact made by television on the organization of professional sport came in the late 1970s with the refusal of the Australian Cricket Board to sell exclusive rights to the televising of test cricket to Kerry Packer's Channel Nine Television network. The 'Packer Affair', discussed by Sloane (1980), resulted in a challenge to the **utility-maximizing** cricket authorities by a **profit-maximizing** television entrepreneur. The introduction by Packer in his alternative 'Super-Test' series of a number of innovations (colored uniforms, night games, fielding restrictions and so on) designed to improve the presentation of cricket on television is clear evidence of an unwillingness by the established cricket authorities to maximize their revenues from broadcasting but also indicates a reluctance to change the established traditions (as already noted above).

In contrast, North American sports have been considerably more aware of the demands of television presentation. Horowitz (1974, pp. 298–9) discusses a number of examples of the size of potential broadcasting audiences being a key determinant of decisions to relocate both baseball and football franchises. He further argues that broadcasting potential has been an important influence on decisions to expand the number of clubs in major league baseball. Similarly, Jones (1969) argues that the decision of the Canadian National Hockey League to grant six franchises to cities in the USA, while

Vancouver and Quebec City remained without franchises, can be explained by the importance of obtaining an American television contract.

However, perhaps the best example of accommodating the interests of television is found in Hochberg and Horowitz's (1973) analysis of broadcasting arrangements for American college football. Under the 1966 agreement between the NCAA and ABC television: 'ABC was permitted eighteen one-minute commercial spots – during time outs, after a score, and so on – but teams and referees were encouraged to "look busy" on the field so as to keep the crowd entertained while the television audience was viewing commercials' (Hochberg and Horowitz, 1973, p. 117). The 18 minutes of within-game commercials is a high fraction of the 60 minutes of actual game time.

To forestall the impression that North American Leagues have sold their sporting souls to broadcasters while the Europeans remained pure, consider the direct sponsorship of clubs and competitions in Europe. The Yankees are still the New York Yankees rather than the IBM Yankees. A European example of direct sponsorship is shirt sponsorship under which the name of the team sponsor appears on the front of the players' shirts. Often the team name does not even appear on the shirt. Shirt sponsorship is almost universal in European soccer. In 2000 Manchester United signed a record £30 million four-year deal with Vodafone, allowing the company's name to appear on the club's shirts. There are similar deals elsewhere in Europe, including Juventus and Tele +/D+ (£6 million per annum), Bayern Munich and Opel (£4.7 million), Ajax and AB/Amro (£2.5 million), Stade Rennais and Pinault (£1.9 million) and Real Madrid and Teka (£1.3 million). While revenue from sponsorship of competitions has generally been pooled in soccer and cricket, direct sponsorship of clubs has gone uncontrolled by the leagues. While the possibly disadvantageous effects of these types of arrangement for competitive balance have been briefly raised by Sloane (1980) and Jennett and Sloane (1985), the determinants of sponsorship revenues and the full implications of their retention by clubs are important issues which have been largely ignored in the literature.

Conclusions

The increasing proportion of television income in the total revenues of clubs raises a wide range of public policy issues. While professional sports have seen large increases in revenues there are strains in terms of how this wealth should be shared with players, how it should be divided up among the clubs and how far leagues should compromise in the organization of their sport in order to suit the interests of television broadcasters. The attitude of the antitrust authorities to the development of the broadcasting market has been ambivalent. In the UK the decisions of the Restrictive Practices Court in relation to collective selling of television rights and the MMC in the attempted takeover of Manchester United by BSkyB are difficult to reconcile. The antitrust exemption under the 1961 Sports Broadcasting Act in the USA sits uneasily with the general implementation of antitrust laws. The European Commission has yet to develop a coherent policy despite its acknowledgement that sport is a special case.

Exercises

1. Is live televising of games likely to increase or reduce attendances in the long run?
2. What is an optimal division of broadcasting revenue among the member clubs of a league?
3. Should the equivalent of the 1961 US Sports Broadcasting Act be introduced in Europe?
4. Can the ITC Code on Listed Sporting Events be justified from an economics perspective?
5. Why should the UK Restrictive Practices Court and the Monopolies and Mergers Commission have defined the market for broadcasting in such different ways?
6. Should collective selling of broadcasting rights be banned?
7. Should media companies be allowed to own sports teams? Does it matter if ownership is limited to one club or extends over a number of clubs?
8. Should television dictate the conduct of individual games or the organization of a league?
9. The NFL bans corporate ownership. Presumably having more potential bidders for a team would raise its sale price. Why would the current owners adopt a rule that might reduce the resale values of their franchises?
10. Internet-based broadcasts of sports events are just starting. For example, the NCAA is planning to have live Internet broadcasts of the NCAA basketball tournament.
    (a) Would an Internet broadcast fit the definition of a pure public good?
    (b) Does an over-the-air broadcast fit the definition of a pure public good?
    (c) Suppose the cross-elasticity of demand for NCAA internet and over-the-air broadcasts was zero. That means changes in the price of one good do not affect the quantity demanded of the other. The demand function for the NCAA Internet broadcasts is $P = 100 - 0.01Q$. The marginal cost is zero. There are no ancillaries to sell to the Internet audience but the NCAA gets \$5 in advertising revenue for the Internet broadcasts per customer. What is the optimal quantity and price?
11. How has television altered the economics of professional sports since the 1950s? Address its affects on player salaries, the creation of rival leagues, and competitive balance across different sports.

Appendix 6.1: Listed UK sporting events

Group A

The Olympic Games
The FIFA World Cup Finals Tournament
The FA Cup Final
The Scottish FA Cup Final (in Scotland)
The Grand National
The Derby
The Wimbledon Tennis Finals
The European Football Championship Finals Tournament
The Rugby League Challenge Cup Final*
The Rugby World Cup Final*

Group B

Cricket test matches played in England
Non-finals played in the Wimbledon Tournament
All other matches in the Rugby World Cup Finals Tournament*
Five Nations rugby tournament matches involving home countries*
The Commonwealth Games*
The World Athletics Championship*
The Cricket World Cup: the final, semi-finals and matches involving home nations' teams*
The Ryder Cup*
The Open Golf Championship*

Notes:

Group A is designed to ensure that no broadcaster has exclusive rights to the live broadcasts of the events listed.
Group B requires that if one category (either free-to-air or pay television plus Channel 5) has coverage there should be adequate and timely secondary coverage by a broadcaster in the other category.
Restrictions apply to rights acquired after 1 October 1996 except for those events marked by an asterisk(*) where the relevant date is 25 November 1997.

Appendix 6.2: List of services meeting the 'qualifying conditions' as set out in the television regulations, 2000

Channel 3 (ITV)
Channel 4
BBC 1
BBC 2

Appendix 6.3: Events designated in other EU states under Article 3a of the Broadcasting Directive

Germany

The summer and winter Olympic Games.
All European Championship and World Cup matches involving the German national football team, as well as the opening match, the semi-finals and final, irrespective of whether the German team is involved.
The semi-finals and final of the German FA Cup.
The German national football team's home and away matches.
The final of any European club competition (Champions League, Cup Winners' Cup, UEFA Cup) involving a German club.

Italy

The summer and winter Olympic Games.
The football World Cup final and all matches involving the Italian national team.
The European football Championship final and all matches involving the Italian national team.
All matches involving the Italian national football team, at home and away, in official competitions.
The final and the semi-finals of the Champions League and the UEFA Cup where an Italian team is involved.
The Tour of Italy (Giro d'Italia) cycling competition.
The Formula One Italian Grand Prix.
The San Remo Italian music festival.

Denmark

Olympic, summer and winter, Games; the games in their entirety.

World and European football championships (men); all matches with Danish participation together with semi-finals and finals.
World and European handball championships (men and women); all matches with Danish participation together with semi-finals and finals.
Denmark's world and European championship qualifying matches in football (men).
Denmark's world and European championship qualifying matches in handball (women).

Note:

This information is correct as at 1 January 2000. Germany, Italy and Denmark are at present the only countries to have drawn up lists of designated events which have been accepted by the European Commission.

Appendix 6.4: Listed British soccer clubs 1999/2000

London Stock Exchange

Premier League	Aston Villa
	Leeds United (Leeds Sporting)
	Leicester City
	Manchester United
	Newcastle United
	Southampton
	Sunderland
	Tottenham Hotspur
Nationwide I	Bolton Wanderers (Burnden Leisure)
	Sheffield United
Nationwide II	Millwall
Scottish Premier	Celtic

The Alternative Investment Market (AIM)

Premier League	Charlton Athletic
	Chelsea Village
Nationwide I	Birmingham City
	Preston North End
	Queens Park Rangers (Loftus Road)
	Nottingham Forest
	West Bromwich Albion

OFEX

Premier League	Arsenal
	Bradford City
	Manchester City
Scottish Premier	Aberdeen
	Hearts
	Rangers

Appendix 6.5: Media interests in British soccer clubs (1999/2000)

	Club	*Media company*	*Share*
Premier League	Arsenal	Granada	5 % (with further 4.9 % if planning permission for new ground)
	Aston Villa	NTL	9.9 % (five year convertible loan certificate)
	Chelsea	BSkyB	9.9 %
	Leeds United	BSkyB	9.1 % of Leeds Sporting
	Leicester City	NTL	9.9 % (five year convertible loan certificate)
	Liverpool	Granada	9.9 %
	Manchester City*	BSkyB	9.9 %
	Manchester United	BSkyB	9.9 % (originally 11 %)
	Middlesborough	NTL	5.5 %
	Newcastle United	NTL	9.8 %
	Sunderland	BSkyB	6.5 %
Scottish	Hearts	SMG	37.4 %

BSkyB also has an agreement with Tottenham Hotspur as an Internet-only partner.
* In Nationwide Division 1, 2001–2.

7 Sports teams and leagues: from a business necessity to dominating cartels

Chapter goals

Sporting events are profitable if total revenue exceeds total cost. Total revenue includes income from advertising, parking, concessions, the sale of luxury seating, the sale of tickets, broadcasting revenue, and public subsidies. As discussed in Chapter 3, competitive or exciting events attract more fans. The pay off from having competitors of similar strength differentiates sports from all other businesses.

This chapter looks at the economic reasons for the creation of leagues. Six questions are addressed in this chapter. *First,* what is the economic rationale for a league structure? *Second,* how can the league's authority over rules and schedules create a cartel? *Third,* what are the costs and benefits of the cartel structure of sports? *Fourth,* if leagues are both necessary and inevitably create cartels, how can governments protect the public interest? *Fifth,* since cities vary in wealth and size, how do income differentials among teams affect competitiveness? *Sixth,* does balanced financial success undermine competitiveness and the popularity of a league? The goals of this chapter are to understand why leagues are needed, how their initial authority can be translated into market power, how this power influences outcomes and affects the public sector, and how leagues share revenues to influence competitive balance and popularity.

Introduction

When sports leagues were initially formed, few would have imagined the market power these organizations would have in the twenty-first century. In North America, the four major sports leagues have unfettered control over the supply of teams and the location of these franchises. These powers, coupled with successful management strategies, have raised the value of some franchises to more than $500 million (3 teams in the NFL). Fifty-two teams are worth in excess of $200 million (Gruen *et al.*, 2000). The success of leagues in enhancing the value of teams is not limited to North America: the two most valuable sports franchises in the world are Manchester United and Arsenal. Each of these clubs, which are members of the English Premiership, is worth at least $800 million. The escalating growth in the value of these two teams is associated with the formation of the Premiership in 1992 (Findlay, Holahan and Oughton, 1999). The twenty-team Premiership emerged from the Football League, which had 92 clubs divided into four divisions.

Leagues and teams that once struggled to break even now negotiate multi-billion dollar contracts for broadcast rights, and individual teams receive tens of millions of dollars from advertising, the sale of souvenirs, and the use of the Internet for the transmission of games and the sale of merchandise. Part of this increased value is a direct result of the quality of entertainment provided and an increasing demand for sports by populations with more disposable income and leisure time. The combination of the supply and location of teams in North America by leagues and rising demand for sports increased the levels of profits.

This chapter focuses on the need for leagues to manage sports and attract spectators to matches, and then moves on to look at the emergence of the four major professional team leagues in the USA and Canada and the powers they possess, as well as the emergence and development of leagues in the UK and their abilities to control the market for soccer. The last sections of the chapter focus on the issues associated with the sharing of revenues between teams in a league. As cities vary in size and wealth, some teams (such as Manchester United, the New York Yankees, FC Barcelona and the Los Angeles Lakers) earn far more money than teams that play in smaller and less prosperous markets. These extra resources in turn give those teams the ability to attract and retain the best players, further enhancing their ability to win games and attract more revenue.

Why are leagues, associations and organizing committees needed?

Teams, owners and athletes as competitors

While sport shares some similarities with other businesses – the ability to charge a fee for services provided and to prohibit those who do not pay from watching the event – there is one critical difference: teams or athletes require other teams and athletes to stage matches (Fort and Quirk, 1992; Neale, 1964). In contrast, both Ford and Microsoft can sell their products even if no other car manufacturers or computer software firms exist. Indeed, both the Ford Motor Company and Microsoft would probably prefer not to have competitors so they could completely dominate the market for their products. Individual sports teams cannot produce entertainment without competitors. A team needs several other competing teams to maintain fans' interest. The existence of many different teams increases the sense of competition and uncertainty and hence raises the entertainment value. It has been argued in Chapter 3 that the more unpredictable the outcomes with regard to who wins and loses, and the greater the number of teams that have a chance to win a championship, the more suspense that is generated and hence the higher the entertainment value. As entertainment value increases, more people will be attracted to games or watch matches that are televised.

Every team in a league both competes with other teams and cooperates to produce games. In addition to the link between demand and competitive balance, sport differs from other businesses because it requires joint production. To win, teams will compete to attract the best players. In some instances the only constraint on spending for players is the total amount of money available to a team's owner. As was discussed in Chapter 2, some owners will spend wealth earned from other businesses to attract the best athletes. There have also been examples when players accepted lower salaries to permit an owner to hire an additional or very talented player in an effort to win a championship.

Teams, owners and athletes as partners in joint-production efforts

The joint-production element is a result of the cooperation needed between teams or athletes to produce matches or games. This cooperation ranges from the setting of a schedule of games to the establishment of common rules. However, there is an inherent conflict between the interests of the league in having most teams win half of their games to maximize competitiveness and those of the individual team owner who maximizes income through winning as many games as possible. Owners know they must have teams capable of competing to attract fans (Scully, 1995), but with income correlated with winning percentages, each owner wants to win more than he or she wants to see league revenues maximized. As Gratton (2000) has noted, individual teams may behave as profit maximizers seeking to win games at the expense of their competitors and the league. If the league seeks to maximize league-wide revenues it would seek to have all teams maximize the uncertainty of outcome. The resolution of this conflict between the league and individual team owners will be discussed later in this chapter.

***Conjoint* production** occurs when independent firms cooperate to produce a good. With conjoint production the two firms provide the same inputs, so not all cooperation among firms in production is conjoint production. For example, a car could be produced by an integrated manufacturer of engines and car bodies or by a cooperative enterprise of an engine maker and a car body maker. Neither of these examples represents conjoint production. Forms of organization other than independent teams and under the umbrella of a league have been tried in sports, but most have failed. For example, in the early years of professional baseball in the USA there were teams of professional athletes that traveled to different cities to play pick-up teams of local athletes. This method of presentation of games is called **barnstorming**, drawing its name from the fact that some games were played against barns where people sat and stood. The athletes on these barnstorming teams were professionals in that they played games for money, but their games did not attract the attention or crowds that became common in the 1880s and early 1900s after the formation of leagues which offered regularized competition.

The first league in North America, founded in 1871, was formed by players but collapsed after a season. A league requires a level of organization and coordination that the players did not have and they failed to hire people who had the necessary management skills. The players also have a shorter time horizon than a team owner because players think in terms of their playing careers. Players would be reluctant to accept a low salary to finance long-term investments such as stadiums that would mainly benefit future players. The forerunner of the modern sports league in North America was the National League of Baseball Associations. 'To induce a degree of financial stability, membership was restricted to eight clubs, and franchises were awarded only to well-financed investors in cities with a minimum population of 75,000' (Scully, 1995, p. 7). In this manner it was hoped teams would eventually operate in about 24 different markets. Implicit within this design of a league was the premise that teams needed a wide range of competitors to maintain fan interest. A pool of 24 teams would permit the creation of two leagues, each with a champion, who could then play each other for an overall championship. There would then be several different levels of competition and uncertainty. The original plan for professional baseball envisioned two leagues and an eventual championship series by the two leading teams. However, the National League never created a second league.

The original league in baseball with independent owners, the National League, survives to this day and is referred to as the 'Senior Circuit' of Major League Baseball. The National League did not end the life of barnstorming teams. Today, a handful of barnstorming teams remain, with the Harlem Globetrotters being the most successful. This basketball team, however, is appreciated more for its artistry and comic abilities than for its athletic prowess. Other barnstorming teams include a men's softball team and a women's baseball team that attempts to schedule games with (men's) minor league baseball teams. While these teams include some extremely gifted athletes and remain popular attractions at a variety of community fairs and other exhibitions, these franchises are not serious competitors to the four major leagues.

The importance of a league structure for economic success in baseball has encouraged other professional sports to develop similarly even beyond team sports. For example, while automobile racing does not require a league structure, race sanctioning bodies have found that the awarding of points and the creation of season-long competition for a racing championship has increased fan interest. Professional skiing has adopted a similar format, and the rankings issued for tennis players allow fans to cheer for the season-long performance of their favorite player.

Rules and regularized play

Leagues do more than create fan interest through a championship; they also guarantee and enforce the rules of play. For example, a soccer league ensures that no team may have more than 11 players on the pitch at the same time.

A baseball league ensures that four balls are a walk and that three strikes are an out. Individual fields in baseball might have some peculiar dimensions or 'ground rules' reflecting the circumstances of a particular ballpark. However, these local peculiarities – part of the game's charm and attraction – do not diminish the point that basic rules of the sport are agreed to by teams before a season begins and the agreed rules are both followed and enforced by impartial referees or umpires. Luck aside, the team that wins is the one that plays best under a common set of rules.

To assure fans and players that impartial decisions are made with regard to the outcome of plays or the interpretation of rules, each league is also responsible for the hiring of officials. Home teams do not hire the referees or umpires.

From stability to market control

Every league, in its formative years, focused on the establishment of a set of rules, regularized schedules and protected market areas for each team. In North America the standard practice was for leagues, through a vote of a specified number of member teams, to control the supply of franchises and the catchment areas of each team. There is only one metropolitan area in North America with three major league teams from one professional league, and that is the three NHL hockey teams in the greater New York metropolitan area. Even this large urban area has only two major league basketball, baseball and football teams. This situation sharply contrasts with the distribution of franchises in Europe, for example, where there have been as many as eight premiership football teams in the London area. In North America there has been virtually no formal role for the public sector in determining the number of teams; the only role for the public sector has been to lobby (through subsidies and other means) to gain or retain local franchises. Relationships between the professional leagues and members of Congress established through campaign contributions have worked against the passage of any law that would change the distribution of teams or the number of teams. How did the four US leagues gain such control?

Leagues: the early years and fight for survival

Prior to World War II, and in the immediate post-war years, it was not uncommon for major league professional football, basketball or hockey teams in North America to declare bankruptcy or relocate to avoid bankruptcy. For example, in 1949 the NBA was created from competing leagues. The NBA began with 17 teams, but only nine teams were left by the end of the 1954–5 season. The NHL was formed with four teams in 1917, and prior to World War II the league had only six members, including just two of the original four franchises. Expansion in hockey would not occur until the 1980s with the formation of the World Hockey League and its eventual merger with the NHL.

The early years of the National Football League (NFL) were also precarious. The precursor to the NFL, the American Professional Football Association, was founded in 1920 and just three of its teams survived to become members of the NFL. From 1926 to 1949 four other professional football leagues would emerge and compete to be the leading organization for American football. Only one team from these fledgeling organizations would survive to join the NFL (the New York Giants). Challenges to the supremacy of the NFL would continue into more recent times with the formation of the American Football League in 1960. Each of the original teams in this league would eventually join the NFL when the two leagues merged in 1966. In the 1980s the World Football League attempted to compete with the NFL, but it went bankrupt and none of its teams survived to become a member of the NFL. Recently a new professional football league, the XFL, tried to develop a fan base through media exposure and live games, but this league collapsed at the end of one season of play.

By comparison, MLB had a far more stable early history. The National League was founded in 1876. Four of the eight teams in this initial league would fail, but the eight teams that existed in 1892 are still members of MLB. The American League was created in 1901, and each of its original eight teams is still part of MLB.

Summarizing, the early history of the four major North American sports leagues was characterized by teams and leagues struggling to survive. Many teams in three of the leagues were forced to declare bankruptcy, and often entire leagues ceased operation. Baseball had the lowest failure rate, but some teams did declare bankruptcy and several of the original franchises moved to find more profitable venues. The failure rates in terms of teams and leagues may have not been larger than what is common for new business ventures. Professional team sports did not emerge as a business until the 1870s (for baseball). The other leagues were created in the twentieth century. Failures and instability are characteristics of new industries. Scully (1989) noted that from 1876 until 1900 approximately one team per year failed. This yields a 3 per cent business failure rate (given the number of teams in the leagues at the time) and such a rate is comparable to the rates in other sectors of the economy.

Each league attempted to ensure financial stability and profitability through the establishment of territorial rights. These 'rights' were designed to provide each team with a sufficient market of fans. Further, league members agreed not to move into the market area of another team and not to play matches or games with nonleague teams. This exclusive within-league play rule is crucial to league organization. It ensures that the power of a league to draw fans to games is restricted to member teams. By not sharing the attractiveness of its team with nonleague members, leagues have been able to command extraordinary entrance fees from investors wanting to be part of a league.

Recently one investor paid $700 million to secure the right to have an NFL team in Houston. This fee represents the owner's view of the value of all shared revenues and the potential for future income for the new investor as a result of being a member of the league.

The establishment of four cartels

The roots of what would become a powerful **cartel** system that dominates the supply and location of professional team sports in North America lie in a 1922 US Supreme Court ruling that pertains solely to baseball. Other actions by the US Congress and other federal courts would secure the cartel power of the other sports leagues.

As noted, MLB had its beginnings with the National League in 1876. For the 1901 season the National League left Cleveland without a team. Cleveland was then America's seventh largest city with 381,768 residents and the size of the market attracted the interest of a then minor league, the Western League. Franchise owners of Western League teams wanted to create a second major league to compete with the National League. The opportunity to place a team in Cleveland gave the upstart league a powerful position from which to launch its new initiative. Other teams in major cities were soon added and the league changed its name to the American League to compete with the National League. Franchise owners in the American League packaged their teams to appeal to North America's immigrant population (using members of large local immigrant groups as players and serving locally popular foods and beer) and soon were attracting sufficient fans and revenues that they were able to recruit players from the more established National League. The upstart American league was so successful that in less than two years team owners from the 'Senior Circuit' were willing to accept a merger in an effort to control labor costs. In 1903 Major League Baseball was formed through a merger of the National and American Leagues.

In 1913, a different set of investors formed the Federal League, and in 1914 a new 8-team league emerged as a competitor for MLB. Its popularity by 1915 permitted teams located in Newark, Brooklyn, Baltimore, Buffalo, Chicago, Kansas City, Pittsburgh and St. Louis to compete for players employed by MLB teams. Just as player salaries had increased when the American League challenged the National League, the Federal League increased the costs of fielding a winning a team for franchise owners in MLB. Conflicts over players and other issues between the two leagues eventually led to lawsuits. At the urging of a federal court judge, an out-of-court settlement was reached. The owners of the Chicago and St. Louis franchises in the Federal League were permitted to buy franchises in MLB (the Cubs and Browns, respectively) and the owners of the other Federal League teams received money in exchange for the sale of their franchises to MLB. Each of the teams sold to MLB was dissolved and the players dispersed among MLB franchises. Most of the owners of the dissolved Federal League teams were pleased with the proposed settlement. The exception was owner of the Baltimore franchise in the Federal League. He sued MLB, arguing that the forced buyout represented an abusive trade practise by a monopoly. In 1922, the US Supreme Court ruled that MLB was exempt from US **antitrust** laws under the simply bizarre reasoning that baseball teams were not engaged in interstate commerce. The court reached this decision by noting that a college professor or lawyer, who gave a lecture or argued a single case in another state, was not engaged in commerce but producing a service from a base in a single state. Baseball was also seen as entertainment rather than commerce.

The effect of the 1922 decision was to establish MLB as a monopoly with unfettered control of the supply of franchises and the location of teams. The 16 teams that existed in 1922 would be the same franchises that would play until the 1960s when MLB would finally expand rather than face the possibility of the creation of another baseball league. Teams would continue to move, but until the City of New York threatened to anchor the Continental League in 1960 in response to the movement of the Brooklyn Dodgers to Los Angeles and the New York Giants to San Francisco, MLB was content to fix the number of teams despite the growth of the US population. In 1922, a population of approximately 110 million Americans supported 16 MLB baseball teams. However, since there were no teams west of St. Louis, the 16 teams in MLB in 1922 actually had a fan base of just 63.7 million, with the balance of the nation living to the west of any of MLB's teams. The smallest city with a team in 1922, Cincinnati, had a population of 402,000. By 1960 the population of the USA had increased to 179.3 million, and Kansas City (with a population of 475,539) was the smallest with a major league team. In 1960 there were 11 cities with populations larger than Kansas City's that did not have a team. Placing a team in some of those other cities was not a priority in the 1950s and 1960s.

Subsequent Supreme Court and federal court cases dealing with professional sports have recognized that the logic used to grant MLB an exemption from antitrust laws was misguided (Rosentraub, 1999). However, rather than reversing itself, the Supreme Court argued that it was the Congress's responsibility to amend the antitrust laws to include baseball. The Supreme Court has continued to give MLB limited protection from the antitrust laws, interpreting a lack of action by the Congress as a decision to support the Court's initial, albeit irrational, decision. The Supreme Court was unwilling to compound its error in baseball by extending the exemption to the other sports leagues. When other sports leagues wanted to restrain expansion and expand their control of the supply of teams they needed Congressional action. The requests by leagues to Congress for protection from antitrust laws have rarely been denied.

For example, in 1966, the NFL and the American Football League (AFL), founded in 1960, sought permission to merge. As a result of its success in markets without an NFL team, the AFL was able to offer players lucrative contracts to join the new league. Just as the American League had challenged the National League in MLB and raised the cost of operating a team, the new football league was making it increasingly expensive for NFL team owners to retain and attract the best players. Players' salaries continued to rise as the AFL secured itself in several key markets and by the 1960s owners in both leagues wanted a merger. Eliminating the competition for players between the established NFL and the AFL could have been interpreted as the establishment of a monopoly and thus a violation of US antitrust laws. In addition, the presence of one instead of two leagues would also reduce the opportunity of other cities to acquire a team. To ensure that no legal challenges could be filed the two leagues sought Congressional exemption of their proposed merger from the antitrust laws.

During the Congressional hearings held to discuss an antitrust exemption for a merged football league, questions were raised over the implications for cities if one league had complete control over the supply of professional football franchises. Representatives of the NFL and AFL made two commitments: first, the leagues pledged to add several teams over the next few years; second, owners from both leagues pledged to keep all teams in their existing markets. Some members of Congress were concerned that without the existence of a competing league a community that lost a team would have no option but to steal a team from another city. The owners flatly assured Congress that they would not move their teams. Bob Dole, a future senator and candidate for the presidency, was a member of the House of Representatives and a co-author of the proposed antitrust-exemption legislation. He reported that he too had received a guarantee that the existing teams would stay in their present locations. 'According to their testimony, professional football operations will be preserved in the 23 cities and 25 stadiums where such operations are presently conducted' (US House of Representatives, 1966, p. 106).

The NFL added just one team from 1967 to 1976. From 1976 to 2000 the NFL would add just five more teams and a sixth team began to play in 2002. While the NFL was able to avoid making a specific commitment to add an agreed number of teams, there was a clear expectation that more teams would be created (US House of Representatives, 1966). The NFL also did not honor its commitment not to move teams. Since 1967 five teams have moved to other cities, and two of these teams moved twice, yielding a total of 7 franchise relocations since Congress agreed to permit the NFL and AFL to merge.

The NBA and the competing American Basketball Association (ABA) also received permission from a federal court to merge. Fearing that a merger between two competing leagues would lead to lower player salaries, several athletes sued in an effort to use antitrust laws to block a merger. Eventually the players and the league's owners compromised on a compensation plan and the court permitted the NBA and ABA to merge. However, the interests of cities were not protected and one community, Louisville, lost its team. Louisville,

Kentucky, has tried several times to secure another professional basketball team but each time its request has been rejected. Similar logic was used to authorize the merger of the NHL and its competitor, the World Hockey Association (WHA).

None of the cities that lost teams as the result of the merger of the NBA and ABA or the NHL and the WHA elected to sue the leagues. Some cities that have lost baseball teams or had proposed relocations threatened by MLB, such as Seattle and Baltimore, have pressed legal claims against the league and received franchises. Some public officials may have believed that initiating legal actions would work against their community receiving a team.

The impact of cartels

At the conclusion of the mergers each of the four major team sports were organized into cartels that controlled the supply and location of teams. How have these cartel leagues performed? Do they include the interests of all of the **stakeholders**? If the interests of stakeholders are not represented, then the behavior of the cartels may simply be aimed at generating higher profits. Who are the stakeholders with interests in the structure of team sports, and who stands to benefit or lose from alternative organizational frameworks? In any sport the stakeholders consist of owners, players, fans, community leaders and taxpayers. Players generally seek to earn as much as possible, but they may seek to maximize their welfare through playing for a championship team. Fans want at least one team in their city and as many competitive games as possible with inexpensive tickets. Community leaders want a local team for the publicity and the civic identity. However, one city's gain in publicity and civic identity by adding an expansion franchise comes at the expense of the cities with teams. Prestige is a relative concept. If every city is 'major league' then being a major league city does not mean much. In leagues with substantial shared broadcast revenue, such as the NFL, an expansion team dilutes each existing owner's share of the broadcast pot. This is why new owners pay a high entrance fee and why cities provide subsidies to overcome the reluctance of existing owners and teams to create a new franchise. In the case of the Houston Texans, that owner had to provide a particularly high entrance fee to ensure that the NFL would accept his bid over an alternative from Los Angeles. Los Angeles would have been a more profitable location for the league as a result of the higher television ratings expected in a market so much larger than Houston. In North America, to ensure that owners can provide sufficiently high bids for teams, state and local governments have repeatedly provided extraordinary subsidies to attract and retain teams (Cagan and deMause, 1998; Noll and Zimbalist, 1997; Weiner, 2000).

How have the four North American leagues or cartels performed relative to the interests of stakeholders? With regard to owners, the available evidence would suggest their interests are paramount. Across the last decade, when teams have been placed on the market for sale, there has been no shortage of bidders, and the prices paid escalated through 2002. Four NFL franchises have been sold between 1998 and 2001, and each cost in excess of $500 million. The new Houston franchise cost its owner $700 million, and the New York Jets were sold in 1999 for $635 million despite the handicap that the team must play in an older facility for several more years. Across the last few years two MLB teams have been sold for more than $250 million each, and the Boston Red Sox cost their new owners in excess of $650 million. In mid-2003 the Anaheim Angels sold for approximately $180 million, but the new owner accepted the existing debt of the team, placing the total cost for the investment in the $250 million range. In early 2000 the New York Islanders of the NHL were sold for $190 million despite a rather poor lease that binds the team to an antiquated arena for several additional seasons.

These data clearly indicate that the leagues have protected the owners' interests as the demand for franchises continues to support extremely high rates of growth in franchise profits. Indeed, in almost all the US major league sports, recent rates of return to owning a franchise has exceeded those available in the stock market (Phillips and Much, 2000). The value of franchises has soared because the leagues have restrained the supply of these valuable assets. Further, while player salaries have risen, in the NFL, and for many franchises in other sports leagues, the costs of ownership have not risen to the point where expected economic returns, however measured by those desiring to buy teams, have deteriorated. There is some evidence at least for the recession years of 2002 and 2003 that some teams in MLB and some in the NHL are not profitable in their current locations. However, where unprofitable teams exist it is often a result of the failure of the leagues to share revenues or gross local mismanagement.

The existing system has also provided important benefits for players as their salaries have continued to rise. In MLB, for example, the total amount of money paid to players has more than tripled in a decade (see Table 7.1).

Table 7.1 Team payrolls, 1990–2001

Season	*Team payrolls in millions of dollars*				*Annual change (%)*
	Average	*Total*	*Lowest*	*Highest*	
1990	17.3	450.2	8.1	23.6	–
1991	26.2	680.9	12.1	39.2	51.2
1992	35.2	915.9	10.1	59.3	34.5
1993	35.8	1,003.2	12.2	56.2	9.5
1994	29.9	836.2	11.1	47.3	−16.6
1995	31.2	872.2	12.1	50.5	4.3
1996	35.4	992.2	17.5	63.0	13.8
1997	37.6	1,053.3	11.6	65.5	6.2
1998	41.1	1,232.4	8.3	71.9	17.0
1999	48.6	1,456.5	14.7	92.0	18.2
2000	59.3	1,780.1	15.7	114.4	22.2
2001	65.5	1,964.8	33.8	112.3	10.4

Superstars' earnings have grown faster than those of journeymen. The median salary has actually declined over the last few years (Costas, 2000): the proportion of players earning in excess of $4 million increased from to 10.7 to 13.9 per cent in just two seasons while the proportion of players earning between $300,001 and $500,000 also increased from 7.6 to 10.5 per cent. There were also increases in the percentage of MLB players earning in excess of $1 million (see Table 7.2).

Players and owners in the NBA recently agreed to a new six-year contract that places a cap on the money any one player can earn ($14 million per season after 10 years of service). However, the players were guaranteed that not less than 48 per cent of agreed components of gross revenues would be dedicated to player salaries. This established $34 million as the cap for each team for the 1999–2000 season. With between 12 and 15 players on each team, the potential exists for every key player to earn in excess of $3 million every season. This guarantee was given to the players in exchange for a **salary cap** on the money earned by the sports' leading celebrities. The NBA players' association saw this concession as meeting the interests of their members.

Players in the NFL have had a similar contract with team owners guaranteeing that each club would receive in collective salaries an amount equal to 63 per cent of all broadcast revenues and income from ticket sales. This was expanded to 64 per cent in 2002 and further to include some revenue from club seats and luxury suites, the extra fees being added on to ticket prices. The net effect was to further enhance the total pool of funds available for player salaries. In addition there is also a salary floor that dictates a minimum overall salary level for each team. In this way the players are guaranteed that they will receive a substantial pool of revenue for salaries and that no owner can attempt to pay less than the 'floor' level. In the NHL only the salaries of rookies are capped in exchange for a restrictive free agency policy that permits smaller market teams to retain their stars for several seasons. The players have accepted this provision and their collective bargaining agreement extends through the 2003–4 season. There is little doubt that the cartel system adequately protects the interests of players, although a strong possibility looms for a labor–management battle in MLB and in the NHL.

Table 7.2 MLB salaries in 1998 and 1999: a rising tide carrying all ships

Salary level	*Percentage of all MLB players by salary level*	
	1998 season	*1999 season*
$200,000 or less	28.1	11.4
$200,001 to $300,000	17.3	26.0
$300,001 to $500,000	7.6	10.5
$500,001 to $1,000,000	11.7	12.3
$1,000,001 to $2,000,000	11.7	11.6
$2,000,001 to $4,000,000	13.0	14.2
More than $4,000,000	10.7	13.9

The objectives of fans, community leaders and taxpayers can be grouped together as their interests involve (1) the existence of an adequate supply of teams able to effectively compete for championships; (2) the lowest possible ticket prices for competitive games; (3) the absence of subsidies from the public sector; and (4) the presence of a team in each community that wants one to maintain its civic identity. This last goal includes the benefits stemming from the prestige associated with hosting a major league team, the intangible benefits generated by a team's presence, and the small (or perhaps nonexistent) economic benefits from a team's presence (Swindell and Rosentraub, 1998). The issues that must be addressed, then, are to what extent have the cartels (1) created an adequate number of teams relative to the demand of sports fans and cities for franchises, (2) ensured all teams have the opportunity to earn sufficient revenues to remain competitive, and (3) minimized the utilization of subsidies for their operations.

The supply of teams

The ability of any community to support a team is a function of the size and wealth of its population. Preferences for different sports also are important. In 1995, the *New York Times* performed an analysis of the number of baseball teams that could be supported in the USA. This examination focused on four criteria enumerated for each metropolitan area: the number of men between the ages of 18 and 54, per capita incomes, population growth, and the potential for the sale of luxury suites (the number of firms and wealthy households in an area). The *Times* identified nine areas without MLB teams that could definitely support a team, five areas that could possibly support a team, and as many as five other areas with teams that could support at least one *additional* team. With 28 teams based in the USA, the analysis by the *New York Times* would suggest MLB should have at least 37 teams and possibly as many as 47 (Ahmed-Taylor, 1995) at the existing level of player salaries. Although the *New York Times* analysis was fairly simplistic, its basic conclusion is correct. There are many cities that do not have a team that are similar to the cities with MLB teams. Why shouldn't these cities be able to support a team?

The *New York Times* analysis is particularly interesting in light of the current financial difficulties confronting four or five baseball teams in North America and the suggestion made by the Commissioner of Major League Baseball (who is chosen by the owners) to simply eliminate some of these teams. The owners of the teams that would be disbanded would have their franchises purchased by the league and then the players would become **free agents**, able to sign with any of the other clubs. The teams currently in financial difficulty are the Florida Marlins, the Minnesota Twins, the Montreal Expos, the Oakland As and the Tampa Bay Devil Rays. As these teams currently receive a share of the revenues generated by the other teams, many have speculated that the other owners would be better off if they simply gave the owners of unsuccessful teams $250 million to permit their clubs to be disbanded. This figure would be a less than the present value of the revenues a team receives from the league. The other owners would benefit in that there would be fewer teams to receive a share of future revenues. Lost in this dialogue is a consideration of the inept management decisions of some of the teams' owners that led to declining levels of support from fans. An early owner of the Florida Marlins traded the best players to other teams to reduce his costs and maximize short-run profits. This action completely alienated fans, and it took years to undo this damage. After winning the World Series in 2003, the Marlins new owner issued a demand for a subsidized stadium which was subsequently met by the city and county. Nevertheless, the response from the league is not a commitment to maintain competitive and well-managed teams but to threaten communities and fans with the loss of a team because they have not performed to the standards demanded by a cartel.

If one focused only on the increased population of the USA there would also appear to be too few teams. There are nine metropolitan areas with populations larger than the smallest area with a MLB baseball team. If one focused on the number of large corporations in an area as a measure of the financial viability of a region to support a franchise, additional teams should exist in the Northern Virginia and Austin/San Antonio areas, Portland, and in the San Bernardino area. The current US population and the distribution of large businesses are sufficiently robust to support 33 or 34 major league baseball teams. In the NFL, Buffalo is the smallest market with an NFL team, but 13 other metropolitan areas with larger populations are without teams.[1] As many as 42 NFL teams could be supported if population and local wealth were the factors determining supply and demand; however, at the current time the NFL has 32 teams. Other analyses have identified several markets without NBA or NHL teams that could support either a major league hockey or basketball team (King, 2000). Using wealth and the size of the population in a region as critical variables indicates that too few teams exist with regard to demand. In a free market setting it is reasonable to expect that there would be more teams. The sports cartels have restricted the supply of teams.

The competitiveness of teams

The distribution of revenue is critical to the integrity of athletic competition in a league. If teams have very different levels of income, then high-income teams will have a greater potential to attract and retain the best players. If this occurs, a group of teams can dominate a league and effectively eliminate competition (Hughes, 2000). The degree of competitive balance in a league cannot be used to assess whether the league attends to fan interests or just the profits of the owners because both purposes are served by a high degree of balance. Maximizing league-wide profits would serve the interests of owners because the league-wide revenue gains from more competitive balance could be used to compensate the big city team owners for the lost local revenues when their teams lose the dominance.

As described in Table 7.1, team payrolls in MLB varied from a high of more than $92 million to a low of approximately $15 million in 1999. For the 2003 season the New York Yankees had a payroll in excess of $170 million, despite a new tax on spending imposed by the owners, while more than half of the teams in MLB spent less than half as much money on their players. Disparities of this nature destroy the competitiveness of the sport and this led Sandy Alderman, a member of the staff of the Commissioner of MLB, to conclude that 'small market teams are no longer in the business of competitive baseball – they're in the business of entertainment – because their knowledgeable fans know that these teams can't compete' (Costas, 2000, pp. 58–9).

In MLB lower payroll teams have won the World Series in recent years, but their payrolls immediately increased and the 2002 Angels could not repeat their success as they failed to reach the playoffs in 2003. The Angels' payroll increased by more than $20 million from 2002 to 2003. To keep the 2003 Merlins together their owner may need to spend in excess of $25 million. As a result he demanded a new stadium after winning the World Series and within three weeks of winning the championship local governments agreed to provide more than $150 million in subsidies for a new park. Of the final four teams that played for league pennants in 1998, only the San Diego Padres had a payroll below $60 million, while the league average was $41.1 million. In 1999, the Braves, Mets, Yankees and Red Sox were MLB's final four, and no team had a payroll below $71.5 million, while the league-wide average team salary was $48.6 million. In 2000 the Mets, St. Louis, Seattle and the Yankees comprised the four final teams and just one paid all of their players less than $89 million. The two final teams in the World Series had player payrolls in excess of $90 million. In 2002 two smaller market teams had successful seasons, but in the end a larger market team, the Anaheim Angels, defeated another large market team, the San Francisco Giants, for the World Series championship.

In the NBA since 1980, only five teams from market areas with fewer than 3 million people have made the NBA finals. The Portland Trail Blazers have appeared twice in the NBA finals (in a market area of 2.6 million people), while the Orlando Magic (2.7 million residents in their market area) and the Utah Jazz (in a regional market of 2.2 million people) have each made one unsuccessful appearance in the finals. In 1999 the San Antonio Spurs, playing in a market area of less than 2 million (3.2 million if the Austin area is added), won the NBA title and this team played for the championship again in 2003. However, the team threatened to leave the area after its first championship if a new subsidized arena was not built. Voters approved the subsidy even though the team's current home, the Alamo Dome, is but 7 years old. In contrast, between 1980 and 2003, the Los Angeles Lakers have been in the NBA finals eleven times, the Boston Celtics and Chicago Bulls five times, the Houston Rockets four times, and the Detroit Pistons, New York Knicks and Philadelphia 76ers three times each, and the New Jersey Nets twice. None of these markets has fewer than 4.6 million residents.

The NFL, with the most robust revenue-sharing program of the four North American leagues, does produce more champions from smaller markets. Since 1997, the NFL's champion has come from Denver, Green Bay, St. Louis, Baltimore and Tampa Bay. None of these markets has more than 3.2 million residents; the Baltimore/Washington, DC market does have more residents, but two teams share it. However, prior to the victories by the Packers, Broncos, Rams and Buccaneers, the last time a team from a region with fewer than 3 million residents won the Super Bowl was 1980 (Pittsburgh Steelers). In addition, after the Packers and Broncos won their titles, both teams needed to raise additional revenue, and the Tampa Bay team also plays in a new facility that substantially enhanced the revenues available to the owner. The Packers sold additional stock that has no real market value, and the Broncos renewed their demands for a publicly subsidized stadium. Under a threat that the Broncos would move if a new stadium were not built, voters agreed in November 1998 to subsidize a new facility for the team. In early 2000 the Packers also sought a public subsidy to remodel their aging stadium. The Wisconsin state legislature approved enabling legislation and by the end of the year the local residents of the NFL's smallest market voted to use tax money to ensure that the team would remain competitive. The Rams, who relocated to St. Louis from the Los Angeles/Orange County region, play their home games in a publicly subsidized stadium and receive one of the largest annual subsidies of any NFL team. As a result, even with extensive revenue-sharing, NFL teams in small markets seem to be able to compete for championships only if the local community provides a substantial subsidy.

While Scully and others have shown that there is a statistical association between revenues and winning, recent cases underscore this association. For more than two decades, the Cleveland Indians languished at the bottom of the American League. The team's revenues have increased dramatically since heavily subsidized Jacobs Field opened. In 1990, the team earned $34.8 million; in 1997, the team's earnings had increased to $134.2 million for a real increase of 214 per cent. In the same period, the team's payroll increased from $19.1 million to $66.9 million for a real increase of 250 per cent. In 1990, player salaries accounted for 44.3 per cent of total revenues; this figure increased to 49.3 per cent in 1997.

The team's increased expenditures for players and revenues have matched their increased winning percentages. From 1993 to 1994, the Indians increased player salaries by 30 per cent and the team had a successful season in 1994 for the first time in more than a decade. Since increasing salaries, the team has never had a losing season. In 1995 and 1997 the team won the American League pennant and in 1998 lost the American League pennant in the final round of the playoffs. Increased revenues and expenditures for players have changed Cleveland from a two-decade loser to an annual competitor for the American League pennant.

The importance of revenues for a winning team does not imply that managerial talent does not matter. Some teams in large markets have consistently done poorly and have also failed to win division titles and championships, despite a willingness to spend dollars to attract the best playing talent. The Yankees had several poor seasons in the 1980s and early 1990s, as have the Mets, the Chicago White Sox, the Dallas Cowboys and the Los Angeles Lakers. Philadelphia's sports teams each enjoy the ability to market their sports in a very large region but until recently they have frequently failed to provide local sports fans with winning franchises. Despite these important examples of the role of management, in recent years, when managerial issues have been addressed, the teams that consistently win have been those with access to either the largest markets, revenue sources that are not shared with other teams, or heavily subsidized facilities.

Implications of the North American framework for managing sports

Despite an economy described as market driven, professional team sports in North America are controlled by four cartels. The justification for this seeming contradiction has been the peculiar nature of sports as a business. Each team's financial success is dependent on the existence of other teams to attract fans to competitive games. In this regard, then, it would seem each team would want to be sure that other teams could win so that more fans would be attracted to games. Yet, as noted, team revenues and the ability of a team to pay players (increase its own revenues) is tied to winning more games. Hence there is an inherent conflict in the profit positions of teams and leagues. The leagues exist to ensure that competitive games attract fans, but individual team owners want to maximize their individual returns. How well have leagues resolved this conflict?

If success is measured by the wealth attracted to the games through attendance and media contracts, the leagues have been quite successful. Player salaries, once unfairly depressed by owners, have now soared. At the same time, franchises continue to escalate in value, generating substantial returns on every owner's investment. These two stakeholders then have clearly benefited from the cartel structure of sports. Other constituencies may not have fared as well.

For example, by manipulating the supply of teams, the four major leagues have been able to coerce lavish subsidies from communities that want teams. Essentially, teams have been able to extort public subsidies by threatening to move to a more pliable community if their requests are not met. Since 1985, more than $7 billion in public debt has been negotiated to build new facilities for teams (Noll and Zimbalist, 1997). Total state and local debt for sports facilities is now in excess of $15 billion (Cagan and deMause, 1998; Zimmerman, 1998). The money to support this public investment is produced by the levy of special sales or excise taxes, or the deflection of property, income and sales taxes from state and local governments to repay the bonds used to pay for the facilities used by teams. Thus, these taxes represent one of the costs of the cartel system to North American taxpayers and sports fans. The other costs involve the absence of teams in communities that yearn for one and the higher price of tickets to games caused by the artificial scarcity of the number of teams.

Fans are also being shortchanged in that the very essence of competition is being undermined. Despite paying increasing ticket prices, the competitiveness of some of the leagues is being undermined by a failure to share revenues. In baseball, where the highest-revenue teams consistently dominate play, ticket prices since 1991 have increased by 92.9 per cent, while the consumer price index has risen by just 25.9 per cent. 'The NFL's average ticket price has risen 81.0 percent' while the NBA's ticket prices have increased by 81.3 per cent (CNN Sports Illustrated (CNNSI.Com), 2000). Larger market teams have dominated winning, and those smaller market teams that have won championships all demand large subsidies from local communities to augment their revenues. If these communities fail to offer the demanded subsidy then teams leave for other areas. The NHL's roots are to be found in Canada, but recently teams in smaller Canadian cities have moved to the greener pastures of North America just as smaller American cities have lost their teams to larger areas.

The cartel is clearly not protecting the interests of the fans who are paying more for less competitive teams. Those communities that ultimately pay subsidies simply raise the cost of sports across cities as the teams play one city off against another. Some community residents may well see this as an appropriate investment. However, the actions by the cartels raises the costs of sport and some leagues are failing to ensure an environment in which teams from smaller markets can field competitive teams. As a result taxpayers and fans are spending more money to support a system that fails to produce competitive games.

Some have argued that if the current patterns continue and fans are truly dissatisfied with the structure of the sport they will eventually decide not to attend games. The ensuing economic losses will then force the owners to address each sport's problems. While there is certainly a degree of validity to this position, equally valid would be the position that if cartels, sanctioned by the government, are failing to address the needs of stakeholders, then reforms should be implemented that return market competition to the industry. Further, if the cartels are failing to meet the needs of fans, expecting this same group to make a sufficient response may be unrealistic. Sports are an important part of every society and if the structures fail to meet the needs of fans, such structures needed to be changed so that fans can articulate their demands through an unfettered marketplace. How could this be achieved?

The simplest and most direct action would be to eliminate all protections from the full application of existing antitrust laws to the four major leagues. A second response would be to create competing leagues; this is not a difficult option to implement. As each of the four existing leagues in North America was the product of mergers, the existing unions could be broken into their component parts. The two leagues (e.g., the American and National in MLB) could still schedule a championship between the best teams in each league, but with two competing leagues, attractive markets without teams would have a greater opportunity to secure a franchise as each league would fear the other would enter and secure income from a potentially profitable market. The existence of competing leagues would mean more teams in more markets.

The largest markets (New York and Los Angeles) could also become areas where existing leagues would want to place another team to preclude the existence of a second team from the other league. Currently, each of the four cartels has a very powerful incentive to keep at least one viable market without a team. The availability of a potentially profitable market for a team creates pressure on other cities to meet their team's demands. If those demands are not met the team could always move to the city without a team. But if there were two or more independent leagues in each of the four professional sports, each would want to capture the profits possible in a market without a team before another league did.

Creating competitive leagues and using market forces to establish the number of teams that should exist is but one response that could be made to end the cartel control of professional team sports. Another could involve a more proactive role for government. For example, currently only the leagues can award franchises giving the owners control over the supply of teams. This responsibility could be extended to include local governments in the process of establishing new teams. How could such a system work? It could be modeled on the system used by the NFL to place expansion franchises in such cities as Cleveland and Houston.

To establish a new Cleveland Browns' football team (to replace the one that had moved to Baltimore), the NFL held an **auction**. After bids were submitted, an ownership group acceptable to the NFL was granted a new franchise. The city agreed to build a new stadium, and the NFL helped the new owners finance their share or contribution to the facility's capital costs. The NFL gave the new franchise the first draft pick in 1999 and gave the new owners an equal share of all pooled revenues. The winning bid was $535 million and the revenues were then divided among the existing owners.

This system could be easily adapted to fit any sport and permit a larger role for local governments in the creation of franchises. Any city that wished to be home to a new team in a league could apply for a franchise and the league would then be required hold an auction to find a suitable owner. The bids received would reflect the present value of access to the league's pool of shared revenues and local profit potential. If the existing owners shared the franchise fee, as they did in the NFL's expansion into Cleveland, then no existing team owner would suffer a loss in the value of its franchise. With more franchises, there are more jobs and more teams to bid for players, so they too gain. The precise effect on players is complicated. Clearly, the number of players would expand; whether the salaries of star players would rise depends on how the expansion affects the marginal revenue product of the star players. More teams in every sport might dilute the revenue impact of a star player in one sport. For example, if a city went from having two to four major league teams, the revenue generated by a star on one team could easily be reduced. To protect the interests of existing owners, a minimum bid level equal to the median value of league franchises could be established. A minimum bid level would also ensure that markets too small to produce an adequate return would not attract investors.

Would such a system mean there would be hundreds of teams in each of the sports? The experience of numerous American cities with gaming enterprises illustrates that a bidding procedure is quite efficient. The first cities that award franchises for casinos are generally successful. But when too many franchises are awarded, the market shares required for each to be profitable are constrained and franchise auctions fail to attract bidders (Felsenstein, Klacik and Littlepage, 1999). In this regard, some cities may want teams, but when an auction is held it is possible that no acceptable bids will be received. If the public sector could require that an auction be held to determine if there are acceptable investors, areas could acquire the teams they want. In addition, larger metropolitan areas might be able to get an additional team if investors had interests in taking that risk.

These are just two public policies that can be considered to change the cartel structure of sports in North America. Existing laws and the cartel structure of the four major sports leagues have created excessive costs for taxpayers and fans (Wunderli, 1995). A return to a framework with competitive leagues would reduce the need to subsidize teams. Requiring the leagues to hold auctions for expansion teams would also eliminate the subsidy wars between cities. Allowing the current system to continue, however, will simply mean that the subsidies will continue.

Leagues and the management model in the UK

Sports leagues developed along a very different model in the UK, although recent trends suggest a format is emerging that is more similar to the one existing in the USA. Player mobility, the desire to place the most competitive teams on the pitch, and to maximize both team revenues and championships is driving the UK towards a new management model.

The establishment of leagues and the creation of professional teams (denoted by the paying of players) had a slightly different history in the UK as compared to developments in the USA. Modern football began in English schools much like American football in the USA. Between the 1820s and 1860s several dozen grammar schools (high schools in US terms) added teams and, as in the USA, rules and procedures varied among the schools. As a result, interschool games were difficult to stage as teams played different games and a unified league was impossible with so many different formats in existence. All of this changed in 1863 when several English clubs and schools met in London to codify the game's rules and the dimensions of the pitch. While negotiations would take 10 years, eventually the format of the game that is known today evolved and a Football Association was created. Scotland followed with the creation of an independent association in 1873 and the Welsh Football Association was formed three years later. In 1880 the Irish Football Association was created and the stage was set for the creation of an international football association. The first international board was appointed in 1882 and this led to the formation of FIFA in 1904, which today is the governing body for football across the world. Eight different individuals have served as president of FIFA since its founding with three of the eight presidents coming from England.

By the 1960s the English Football Association (FA) governed 92 clubs in four divisions. Despite its size, Szymanski and Kuypers (1999, p. 12) still described football leagues as 'classic, even textbook examples of business cartels'. However, this cartel and the cooperation by its members that made it successful did not endure. In 1992, several of the larger members of the FA realized they could make more money if they were part of a separate league. Led by the country's most successful clubs, 20 teams left the first division of the Football League and formed a new division, the English Premiership. Premiership teams retain 100 per cent of their ticket revenues in contrast to the partial sharing of gate receipts that had earlier existed. One factor driving the move to a new league was to raise revenue to attract and retain the best players. It was argued that without better pay the best players would eventually migrate to other countries.

There is one other significant element that defines football in Europe and places it in sharp contrast to the management models in North America: promotion and relegation. Each year the most unsuccessful team at any level faces relegation to a lower division. Hence, year-end games between teams that are at the bottom of the standings that would be largely meaningless in North America take on special interest in England and throughout Europe as all teams must strive to finish above the last one or two positions in their league's table. If they do finish at the bottom they are relegated to the next lower division and the best teams in the lower division are elevated. This process has permitted 'Wimbledon, a strong amateur club in the late 1950s and 1960s, to achieve promotion to the most senior league in the country' (Day, 2000, p. 72).

Financing problems, however, are not unknown to teams in the UK. Just as some baseball and basketball teams have struggled in North America, some soccer teams have over stretched their budgets. Fans had to establish a special fund to support AFC Bournemouth during the 1996/97 season. Similar funds have not been established in the USA. The subsidies for US teams usually go to profitable teams that are threatening to go to areas to where they can make even greater profits. It has been argued these forms of support (trust funds or tax subsidies) are simply market mechanisms reflecting the interests of local consumers in sports (Rosentraub and Swindell, 2002). Those communities that raise taxes or establish special funds are simply placing some of their disposable income into accounts for sports to ensure a team's existence in their area.

Football in the UK has recently endured two substantial calls for reform and one sharp decline in overall attendance. The calls for reform involved the increasing levels of hooliganism that led to deaths and injuries among supporters and the short-term banning of English clubs from matches in Europe. A 1983 report indicated that declining attendance at matches was a direct result of people's fears of the unruly behavior that had become a staple at FA matches. Regardless of the reason, attendance at football matches declined until a resurgence of fan interest and confidence began in the 1990s.

The second controversy that also contributed to a decline in attendance involved a fire in the terraces at a Bradford City match: 55 people died when the wooden facility caught fire. This tragedy promoted a call for the building of modern facilities that would be fireproof. Wherever new facilities were not built substantial renovations were undertaken. Szymanski and Kuypers (1999) reported that Premiership clubs spent no less than £12 million each to ensure that there would be no repeat of the Bradford City fire. The betting pools established in the 1920s which are still around today contributed more than £100 million to improve facilities. These improvements were designed to both reduce hooliganism as well as make the facilities safer for fans. Attendance first grew in the lower divisions but by the 1990s attendance was up across the nation (Szymanski and Kuypers, 1999).

Revenue-sharing, leagues and competitive balance

The most significant issue that now confronts all leagues in North America and the UK is competitive balance. The issue is relatively direct and emanates from a simple economic proposition. Unfortunately its resolution is quite complex and unclear. With all of the attention now directed at revenue-sharing and sustaining teams it might also be surprising to learn that the debate has endured for more than 100 years. When the English Football League was in its infancy, in 1888, William McGregor proposed that gate income be equally shared (Szymanski and Kuypers, 1999). In North America sharing gate revenues was part of the structure of MLB to ensure that teams could survive even if their biggest source of income was games played with the teams from the largest market areas. In Japan, the issue of competitive balance in its baseball league has also arisen and some have considered changing rules in an effort to promote more competition (La Croix and Kawaura, 1999).

In terms of the commitment to implement plans and programs to maintain competitive balance, at least in terms of soccer in England, Szymanski and Kuypers (1999, p. 250) concluded: 'Traditionally the football authorities have shown little interest in maintaining a competitive balance and have done little to promote it actively. Competitive balance was always used as argument to maintain the maximum wage and **retain-and-transfer system**.' In North America this retain and transfer system was known as the **reserve clause**. That element of the relationship between teams and players ended first in North America and then more recently in England and Europe.

If the value from sports is the entertainment and unpredictable nature of outcomes, then it would follow that the most value would be generated by games between equally matched teams. The longer the fans are held in suspense, the higher the excitement value. As a result, the notion of competitive balance dominates the discussion of leagues and their roles on both sides of the Atlantic. Part of the debate is over how to measure competitive balance. Finding the best ways to promote competitive balance presupposes a definition that all or a majority of interests can accept. At this point it is unclear that there is any resolution of this debate.

For example, is competitive balance the probability of winning a game or is it an opportunity to win a championship? The former is usually referred to as event or game uncertainly. The winning of a championship is seasonal uncertainty. El-Hodiri and Quirk (1971, p. 1, 303) have summarized the basic economic axiom with regard to event or game uncertainty by noting: 'as the probability of either team winning approaches one, gate receipts fall substantially, consequently, every team has an economic motive for not becoming too superior in playing talent compared to other teams in the league'. Virtually all leagues have debated the two primary tactics to ensure some level of competitive balance: (1) talent sharing; and (2) revenue-sharing. Talent-sharing plans have ranged from limiting the mobility of players to systems that bind players to teams to drafts for new players that are inversely tied to a team's performance. Teams that lose more games draft new talent before more successful teams. Across the past few decades the ability of any team in Europe or North America to retain a player has been sharply curtailed as courts have recognized the need for labor markets to be free so as not to restrain the ability of players to receive their market value. Each North American league does share talent in the sense that new players enter the league and are drafted by teams.

Research that has been done on the issue of competitive balance has illustrated what one might surmise. For example, as discussed earlier, in North America, larger market teams have dominated in baseball and basketball. Smaller market teams have had success in the National Football League, but this league shares the largest proportion of its wealth (Atkinson, Stanley and Tschirhart, 1988; Mason, 1997). Consequently the case for extended revenue-sharing seems to have been bolstered. Reviews of outcomes in the Premiership seem to also suggest that more revenue-sharing is needed as the championship has been rotated among a handful of the teams from the largest cities. Some commentators have noted that the Premiership is really three leagues. There is a group of four or five teams with the revenues required to acquire and retain the players needed to compete for the championship. There is also a middling group which competes but which cannot win the championship. These clubs have the ability to beat one of the more competitive teams but are unable to beat those teams on a regular basis. There is also a bottom group of clubs that competes among itself to avoid relegation. The dominance by four or five teams has caused some to fear that the four or five major or dominant teams will some day decide to join a European 'Super League'.

It would seem that, in principle, the value of revenue-sharing and these concepts is relatively crystal clear. There is, however, a severe 'fly in the ointment'. Dominance by a few teams with regard to championships has not diminished attendance or the measure of the quality that fans seek or enjoy from their interest in sports. Indeed, total league revenues are at record levels and many teams are enjoying substantial profits. This is sustained by the inability to statistically demonstrate that more revenue-sharing and competitive balance leads to more fan interest (as measured by attendance). League profits would be maximized if teams won close to 50 per cent of their games and cities were all of the same size. Since size varies, more wins by teams in larger areas could maximize league revenues. However, individual team revenues are also driven by wins so there is a conflict between the interests of an individual team owner and league revenues. Similar pressures are leading to the creation of European League for soccer teams as the owners of some franchises could maximize their position by leaving the Premiership. However, such an outcome would weaken the English Football Association while increasing the profits of an individual team owner.

As far as predicting market attendance is concerned, proxies for competitive balance have included the logarithms of the absolute difference in league positions prior to a match (Hart, Hutton and Sharot, 1975) and the absolute value of the difference in league positions prior to a match (Siegfried and Hinshaw, 1979). The major flaw in these examples is that they fail to compensate for the effects of home advantage or the possibility that recent performance differs from performance over the whole season. An alternative approach is to use fixed match betting odds prior to a match (Peel and Thomas, 1988). This implies that the betting market is an efficient and unbiased estimator of the match performance. As the authors themselves note in a later 1996 paper, because of the change of sign according to whether the away team is higher or lower in the league table, this estimate is more likely to capture the probability of success at home than uncertainty of outcome. These measures also fail to pick up whether a particular match is meaningful in the context of the overall championship outcome.

That brings us on to the second measure of uncertainty of outcome, namely seasonal uncertainty. One form of this occurs when individuals value the identity of the eventual winner of the championship being unknown for as long as possible, as implied in a close championship race. Another form occurs when fans value their own team remaining in the championship race. Ways of measuring this include average number of teams in contention (Demmert, 1973), the number of games required to win the league championship (Jennett, 1984). In practice it is rather difficult to find an adequate proxy to capture the proportion of meaningful games over the season.

Another measure of uncertainty of outcome is the absence of long-run domination by one or a few clubs, in the sense that the same or a few clubs win the league championship over a number of seasons. Thus in Scotland both Rangers and Celtic have won the Scottish league championship in soccer nine seasons in succession. This is not only likely to reduce the interest of fans from other clubs who lose hope that their own club will ever win anything, but ultimately may reduce interest in the successful clubs, as winning loses its novelty. In the latter respect qualification for play offs or international club competition may serve to maintain interest. Relatively few studies incorporate such a measure but Borland (1987), for example, uses a variable involving the number of different teams appearing in the finals over the previous three seasons in relation to the number of places available to measure long run domination in Australian Rules Football. No studies have attempted to incorporate all three measures in regressions attempting to explain variations in attendance or to examine the possibility that they may interact with one another.

Gratton (2000) recently provided a detailed review of the relationships between competitive balance and finances of professional teams. Commenting on the work completed by one of the authors of this book, he included the following observation on the state of the research: 'it is unfortunate that not only has empirical testing of the key relationship between demand and uncertainty been limited, but also that the discussion of this central concept has been unmethodical, if not confused' (Cairns, Jennett and Sloane, 1986, as quoted in Gratton, 2000, p. 12).

Given that spectators like uncertainty of outcome, but would prefer it if their own team won, we can portray the relationship between a representative individual supporter's preference map and the uncertainty of outcome constraints as shown in Figure 7.1. The proportion or probability of wins, p, is on the x-axis. The variance or uncertainty of outcomes, $p(1-p)$, is on the vertical axis. The theory of the distribution of a binary random variable with constant probability of success establishes a fixed relationship between the probability of winning p and $p(1-p)$ given by the inverted U shape labeled *cc*. We assume also a conventionally shaped indifference map with I_1, I_2 and I_3 representing higher and higher levels of utility. Then it can be seen that maximum uncertainty of outcome, where $p = 0.5$, is not the level of uncertainty that maximizes fans' utility. This occurs at p^* where the consumer is prepared to trade off some uncertainty of outcome in order to see the team win more often, and is more likely to win the league championship. If there is a monotonic relationship between consumer utility and attendance, then p^* is the level of

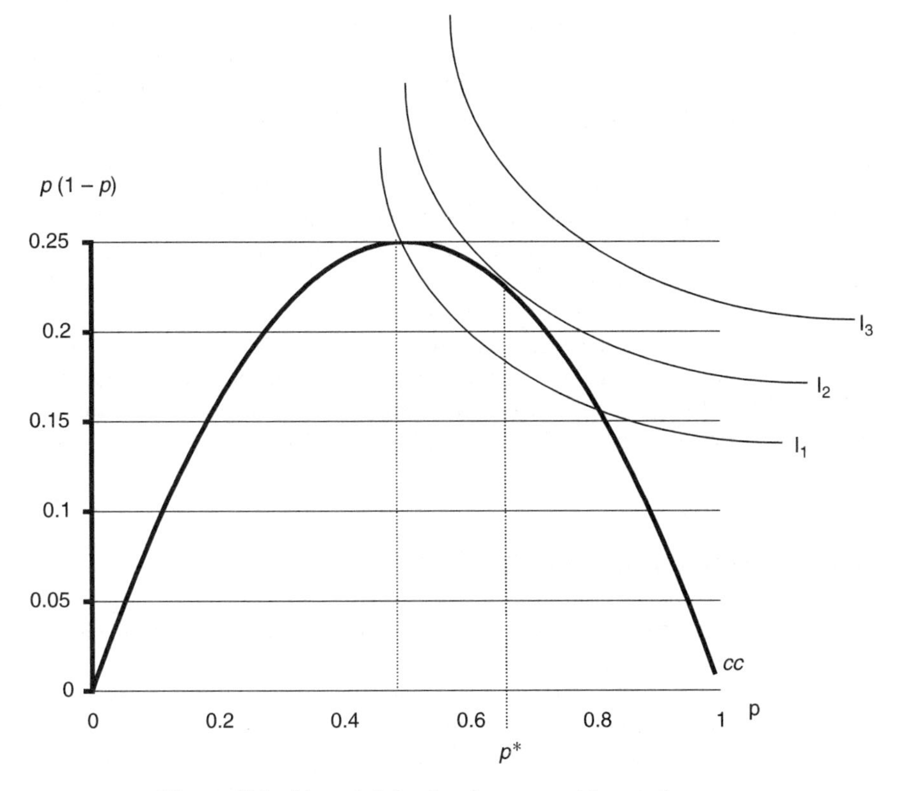

Figure 7.1 Uncertainty of outcome and fan preferences

winning that will maximize attendance. The graph describes a single team, as it is not possible for all franchises to win 62.5 per cent of their games.

The real issue may well be the inherent conflict between owners' self-interest and a league's self-interest. Individual owners maximize their position with the highest possible attendance, and that generally occurs when their team wins. Thus owners will do all that they can to maximize their position and that involves winning as often as possible. Winning has been shown to be associated with player expenditures, and player expenditures are associated with gross revenues. If winning produces the highest levels of gross revenues, an individual owner is not as interested in uncertainty of outcome as is a league. The league may well be focused on gross revenues, but here too there are examples of dominance by teams and rising revenue levels (the Premiership). Major League Baseball's championship has also been dominated by a handful of teams across the past several years, and attendance and gross earnings have also been at very high levels.

There can be no doubt that for supporters of several teams in the Premiership, MLB, the NBA, and the NHL that each season begins with merely a dream of a championship. However, how fundamental is winning a championship to total fan interest and support for a sport? At this time the answer is muddled. It may well be that through television fans can regularly enjoy the games of the best team, and hence they are fans of their local teams and sufficiently interested in the outcomes of games involving the most dominant teams.

The hypothesis that dominant teams do not endanger league revenues can be argued in the following fashion. In MLB, for example, fans across the USA root for the Yankees or root for any team playing against the Yankees. In this manner a fan may well root first for their local team and then, when the play offs begin, root for or against the Yankees. Similarly, in the Premiership, fans may enjoy rooting for their local mid-range team or their club that is fighting to avoid relegation. Then, when the championships begin, the fan may turn their loyalty to the team at the top of the table or the European teams playing this team. Empirical support for this argument, however, is lacking.

Summary and conclusions

Leagues began in an effort to codify rules and satisfy the essential precondition of changing sports from a game to an entertainment industry. This precondition is that for sports to generate entertainment benefits for which people are willing to pay for the privilege of enjoying games, teams of relatively similar skill are needed to stage 'competitive games'. Competition means that all or most teams can contend for individual victories in games and for league championships. To maintain levels of uncertainty and incentives to compete until a season ends, several teams joined together into leagues with the team having the most wins designated as champion. With some levels of uncertainty maintained across several months leagues have been able to attract and maintain substantial fan interest. In many nations, the value of teams in well managed leagues have risen to values that would have seemed to be nothing more than idle dreams when the sports organizations were initially founded. There are now several franchises or clubs in the UK and the USA worth in excess of $500 million. Values of that nature, sustained across several years, would suggest that the leagues have been immensely successful as economic entities for owners and players alike. Indeed the rising salaries paid to players in North America and the UK clearly suggests that they too have shared in the value created. While in times past a case could have been made that the players were largely underpaid relative to the wealth they have created, today it is probably fair to surmise that players and owners are roughly dividing in half the value earned from the staging of games.

While there is little debate in regard to the need for leagues, it is also clear that these organizations have secured immense power, especially in North America, and this power has been used to increase the subsidies and price of sports. Market forces do not drive the supply and location of teams. While team owners want to locate in the most profitable markets (and these tend to be the ones with the most residents), where smaller communities have desired teams and provided large subsidies, teams have moved from larger to smaller areas. Some of the most valued franchises in the National Football League are located in smaller regions because the governments in these areas have provided substantial locational incentives in the form of subsidies to support the cost and operation of a stadium.

England is now confronting its first exposure to the pressures that have long been a constant in North America. Wimbledon has moved to Milton Keynes, the first move of a soccer club in more than 100 years. It is likely that the English Football Association will be confronted with more and more issues which contrast league interests with those of individual club owners. The creation of the English Premiership was a clear indication that the most successful teams want a league and association that permits them far more control over profits and revenues.

The operation of leagues also highlights an inherent conflict in the different self-interests at work. At one level there is an interest among owners to ensure the existence of competitive teams so that entertainment value is maximized for fans. When entertainment values are maximized, it is argued, leagues and sports will be quite successful and profitable. The problem with this observation is that winning percentages are also associated with profitability for an individual owner and hence a league of owners seeks to ensure that all games are competitive so that teams then win about half of the games. An individual owner, however, seeks to win as many games as possible to maximize the revenues earned by an individual. Herein lies the conflict. If Manchester United or the New York Yankees shared more of their revenues with weaker clubs, those clubs would probably improve and offer more competitive matches and games to both the Yankees and Manchester United. However, if both the Yankees and Manchester United continue to dominate their respective leagues, profit for their owners will be maximized. In addition, there is no empirical evidence to suggest that leagues are far worse off when one or two teams dominate. In other words, it is not clear whether the fact that the Yankees have won four of the last six championships in baseball reduced attendance levels or gross revenues from what they would have been had different teams won the championship. Similarly, Manchester United's perpetual domination of the Premiership, and the likelihood that some of the clubs in this league will never challenge for a trophy, has not reduced the popularity of the league or football in general. We simply do not know what attendance levels or profits would have been had there been more teams competing for and winning championships.

This conflict of self-interest values or orientations has led to the relatively chronic competitive imbalance in professional sports. The teams able to secure larger levels of revenue as a result of market size, marketing acumen, public subsidies and long-term management success dominate most leagues. In some leagues teams from smaller market areas (if they have not received a large subsidy) have not won a championship in at least a decade, and in the Premiership there are a group of clubs that compete only to avoid relegation. These clubs have no realistic chance of winning a cup, and the same can be said for numerous teams in MLB. The National Basketball League has implemented a salary cap to help improve competitiveness, but to date no smaller market team has competed for a championship unless the public sector provided that team with a large subsidy. For example, the Indiana Pacers are in one of the NBA's smallest markets and the team's competitiveness across several seasons was a direct result of a $109 million public sector investment in a new arena for the team and owners willing to accept losses in exchange for a competitive team (Gruen and Lane, 2001; Rosentraub, 2000).

Yet, despite these issues and challenges, professional teams sports are now more popular in England, Canada and the USA than at any time in their histories. Prices have risen, but attendance, for the most part, has also increased in many markets. Leagues with the most dominant teams are still able to command handsome contracts from media outlets, indicating again that there is unmet demand for the games and matches even though the identity of the teams that will compete for championships is well known long before the first kick-off or pitch.

Note

1. The Green Bay Packers serve the Milwaukee region, giving the team a larger primary market area than the one available to the Buffalo Bills.

Exercises

1. Leagues are necessary for the delivery of competitive matches but, once established, would operate to maximize the profits of owners. What should a national government do to ensure that the interests of all stakeholders are protected without jeopardizing the competitive environment established by leagues?
2. The interests of leagues are served when all games are competitive, but the interests of individual owners may lie in winning as many games as possible. In addition, all teams in a league may also benefit from having one franchise that wins a majority of its games so that there is a strong incentive to attend games to see the favored team lose to a weaker franchise. Under what circumstances would a revenue-sharing program that divided all resources generate the most income for a league?
3. Under what circumstances would limited revenue-sharing, which also allows teams to spend more money than others for players, generate more income for a league?
4. The conflict between individual owners maximizing their profits and the league-wide profit maximization could be solved by eliminating the individual owners and having the league own all of the teams. What are the advantages and disadvantages of a single business entity owing the league? How do

these advantages and disadvantages differ between existing leagues with separate team ownership and newly formed leagues?

5. In each of the situations below in which tickets are being sold for a public performance, decide if there is conjoint production and explain why.
   (a) An independent orchestra and an independent choral society produce a concert.
   (b) A promoter creates a track and field event by offering appearance money and prize money to individual athletes.
   (c) The Harlem Globetrotters and the Washington Generals play a basketball game.
   (d) Textile companies in Georgia and South Carolina sponsor employee baseball teams. These teams compete in a league.
6. What considerations on the part of the owners favor having a league with more teams, and what factors limit the number of teams?
7. Pick a sport and look up the percentage of wins by the home team over the most recent season. Use Figure 7.1 to explain why this ratio is above 0.5. Is the home field advantage inherent in the nature of the sport or a result of decisions on rules made by the league?
8. Quoting this chapter,

   > The smallest city with a team in 1922, Cincinnati, had a population of 402,000. By 1960 the population of the USA had increased to 179.3 million, and Kansas City (with a population of 475,539) was the smallest with a major league team. In 1960 there were 11 cities with populations larger than Kansas City's that did not have a team.

   The comparison of city populations and the presence or absence of a baseball team in the above quotation is over roughly a 45-year period. Many economic factors changed over that period. For example, in 1922 the spectators would have walked or taken street cars to see the game and there was no broadcast revenue. List whatever economic changes you think are relevant and decide whether the minimum population that could support a baseball team increased or decreased over that period.
9. Why do fans in the UK donate money to a football club that is in financial trouble (e.g., AFC Bournemouth during the 1996/7 season) while US fans do not?
10. How can competitive balance be defined? What results have been found for the effect of competitive balance on team revenues for each of these measures?

8 Sports and economic development

Chapter goals

Many community leaders believe that sports events such as the Olympics, the World Cup tournament, or a season of games played by a home team generate substantial economic development. Sometimes the benefits are thought to extend to a region and sometimes to a smaller area such as a downtown (town centre). Community leaders often claim that sports activities can turn around run-down areas as well as transform a city's image. These claims have a common sense appeal given the spending that takes place when millions of fans attend matches. As a result, numerous cities and countries have used taxes to build facilities for teams or to attract events such as the Olympics and the World Cup.

This chapter examines the economic impact and **economic development** that sports teams and events bring to a region or a city, and the value of changing a city's image. Two basic questions are addressed: first, 'What are the benefits that are possible by using tax dollars to attract and retain teams and events?'; and second, 'Have communities realized these benefits?' If economic returns are received, or if a new city image is created, then the use of tax revenues for sports policies may be appropriate. If these benefits do not materialize, then the main effect of using public funds for sports is higher salaries for athletes and higher profits for team owners and event organizers.

Introduction

Many people believe sporting events and local professional teams generate substantial levels of economic development while enhancing the image of a city. The idea that sporting events promote development is rooted in the intuitive view that the spending by the hundreds of thousands or even millions of people who attend games must generate substantial economic benefits. The view that teams generate intangible and image benefits is rooted in another view of sports. Athletic competitions are an integral component in the life of every society. As a result, those communities that host teams or events are inevitably described as 'major league' or 'big time'. Communities without teams want this prestige and there is evidence that residents of a city may well place so much value on teams that their pride in living in the city is greater than it would have been without sports (Swindell and Rosentraub, 1998).

The combined expectations of economic development and enhanced prestige has encouraged community leaders from Western Europe and North America to include sports in strategies to revitalize stagnating economies and tarnished civic images. However, if sports cannot (1) improve an economy, (2) enhance a community's image, or (3) increase civic pride, the tax money supporting sports teams would not only be poorly invested, it would transfer money to wealthy team owners and players through the provision of government subsidies.

At first glance it would certainly appear that a team, a new stadium, or a national or international sporting event would have a major positive effect on an economy. The most popular baseball teams in North American (such as the New York Yankees and St. Louis Cardinals) attract more than 3 million fans to their games. Teams in the National Football League generally play in stadiums where all seats are sold, meaning that teams such as the Buffalo Bills, New York Giants, New York Jets and St. Louis Rams play before more than half a million fans each season. Real Madrid, FC Barcelona, Bayern Munich and Manchester United play in stadiums with more than 50,000 seats, so they too attract almost a million fans each season. Basketball and ice hockey teams in North America play in arenas that generally have fewer than 20,000 seats, but some teams (such as the Indiana Pacers, the Los Angeles Lakers, Detroit Red Wings and New York Rangers) have attracted more than 700,000 people to a season's games.

All of these fans spend a great deal of money before, during, and after games and events that generates **economic activity**. Does economic activity translate into economic development? Can teams and events change a city's image? What impact does a new image for a city have on business expansion and relocation? Since so many cities consider sports a critical component of their economic development programs, we now turn to these questions to understand what sport can and cannot do for an economy.

Defining terms: talking a common language when discussing the economic gains from sport

The key to understanding what sport can and cannot do for an economy lies in a clear set of definitions for the terms that are frequently used to discuss the contributions of sports and teams to an economy. All too often assessments of the value of teams and sport are confused by the use of terms as synonyms that have quite different meanings. If a team or an event's organizers are asking for a substantial investment from the public sector to build a stadium, the justification for the investment of tax money should involve a substantial economic benefit. The incentive to claim some economic benefit has led to a confusing use of technical terms which over-states the economic benefit of the spending that does take place at sporting events.

The numbers frequently reported do not measure economic development or the **welfare** gains for an economy. The total spending that takes place at a sports facility and by team, which is the *economic impact*, is quite different from *economic development* or welfare gains. In addition, some consultants utilize implausible assumptions with regard to the application of multipliers and this too leads to an over-estimation of the economic development. Local area multipliers will be discussed below. Many of the invariably favorable assessments of sport and regional economies focus on the economic impact and not the changes in either welfare levels or even the distribution of wealth. It is here where a major misunderstanding occurs; many people assume that economic activity means enhanced welfare levels for a community (see Box 8.1).

Box 8.1 Economic impact of a Major League Club in Houston

How widespread is the focus on economic impact instead of total welfare and economic development? Here is an example that can help you be sure that you do not fall victim to an over-estimation of the economic value of a sports team. This is representative of the work by consultants that over-estimates the value of teams to local economies. Other examples of this sort of error are cited by Siegfried and Zimbalist (2000).

In the early 1990s, the Houston Oilers of the NFL wanted a new stadium. The NFL shares more revenue than any of the four major North American sports leagues. Each league member receives an equal share of approximately four-fifths of the total revenues earned by all teams (Sheehan, 1996). However, each team retains the profits earned from the sale of luxury seating, advertising, naming rights and food and beverages. As a result, teams with the newest facilities are the most profitable as the newer designs contain more eating establishments, luxury suites and club seats, retail facilities, and space for advertisements. At the time of the study the Houston Oilers were playing in a 30 year-old facility that had been North America's first domed stadium for baseball and football. Dual use facilities frequently have poorer sight lines and put fans further from the field than single use facilities designed for a specific sport. In addition, Houston's Astrodome was economically obsolete as it lacked many of the revenue-generating attributes of newer facilities. The team wanted the public sector to pay more than 50 per cent of the cost of constructing a new stadium; hence a study was needed to reassure the public of the value of the team and the return that would be received for the public's investment of tax dollars in the facility.

There were two messages that the team wanted to convey. *First*, the team's owners wanted to make it clear that the team produced substantial economic benefits for Houston. *Second*, the team wanted to be sure that people understood that these benefits would be lost to the community and not replaced by other recreational or entertainment options if the team moved to another city. For additional incredibility, the internationally recognized accounting firm of Coopers & Lybrand was awarded the contract for the study.

Coopers & Lybrand reported that the team and its new facility would generate between $352 million and $406 million in economic impact for Houston each year. In presenting their findings Coopers & Lybrand opened the section of their report on the stadium's economic impact by

cont. overleaf

Box 8.1 continued

noting 'Throughout the country, increased emphasis has been placed on economic development by the public sector, particularly within downtown areas' (1994, p. 59). The balance of the report focused on the economic impact of the team and the facility and the authors were careful not to discuss any welfare or distributional issues. Indeed, even a careful reader of this report could be left with the impression that economic impact produced welfare gains for the community and all its residents. The report completely ignored substitution effects.

Economic activity

The broadest measure, economic activity, takes place whenever there is a transaction that leads to or involves a payment for services provided or goods produced. For example, when a community raises taxes to pay for the building of a bridge, economic activity takes place as the taxes collected are used to pay for the bridge. However, if the bridge were not built, taxpayers would have spent the funds on other goods and services, generating an offsetting level of economic activity. Consequently, the community is only better off if the new structure generates an increase in the welfare levels through (1) lower transportation costs or (2) attracting new businesses. The building of the bridge, by itself, generates economic activity, but no increase in welfare or change in economic value for a community. Without the construction of the bridge those paying the taxes for the bridge would most likely have spent the money paid in taxes to build the bridge or on other forms of consumption. Imagine a bridge being built where there is no road and thus no savings in transportation costs and no attraction to new businesses. This useless bridge would generate a measurable economic activity for its construction but no economic benefit to the community. It is difficult for people to realize that in the absence of one form of consumption – spending money on a sports facility – fans would simply spend their money on other things. Even if some of the money were saved, the corresponding investments would also generate incomes for other workers and hence new consumption.

Economic development or total welfare

The value that communities actually seek when they make an investment in a sports facility – real growth in their local economies – can only measured by determining the increment in total welfare due to real economic development. Intertwined in the concept of economic development is another term – growth

– but that is not the same as development. Economic growth does not necessarily mean that an individual or an economy is better off; what is actually desired is the real economic development that occurs only when there is a positive change in total welfare (Becker and Becker, 1996). The Beckers' concept provides a guideline of what is the real benefit from an investment. That concept focuses on increasing real wages and the number of hours people work. An example may help to illustrate the concept.

Suppose a new stadium is built in Manchester or Baltimore and workers are hired for a restaurant inside or adjacent to the facility. If a restaurant employs part-time staff who have other full-time jobs, then their extra income from the additional hours of work represents an exchange of leisure time for income. The loss of leisure time represents a cost; the income received represents a gain. It can be assumed that the workers are better off since they have made the decision to work extra hours and reduce their leisure time. However, as made clear by the concept of total welfare, the gain is not equal to the additional income earned from the extra hours worked, but the income earned less the value of the lost leisure time. The economic development or gain generated by the sports facility in terms of these workers is not their total earnings, but their earnings minus the value of their leisure time. If their total income is calculated as comprising economic development, the value of the team and sports facility for a regional economy is over-estimated. The total income earned is a measure of the economic impact of the facility, but the contribution to the increment in total welfare for the community is the income earned less the cost of the leisure time that was forfeited to earn the income.

A new business locating to an area provides another example. If a new business enters an area and productivity increases such that wage levels rise while profits either remain constant or also increase, total welfare increases. When economic activity generates higher salaries for the same number of hours worked, and profits do not decrease, the increase in income is equal to the increment in total welfare and is a real gain in economic development. If a business moves to an area and increases wage levels but the increased labor costs lead to lower profits, then there is no change in total welfare levels (the salary gains are offset by lower profits) and hence there is no real economic development. There are winners (workers) and losers (owners), but there is no change in the total welfare level of the community (Felsenstein and Persky, 1999; Fleischer and Felsenstein, 2000).

An evaluation of welfare gains also requires attention to *distributional* issues. John Blair (1995: 14–15) warns 'that income alone is an incomplete indicator of how well residents of a region are doing. Equity is another indicator of [welfare or] economic development.' He also expands welfare issues to include 'improvements in the quality of life such as better transportation systems, education, and cultural facilities are also indicators of economic development.' Seers (1969), an early proponent of this line of reasoning, argued economic development takes place only when unemployment and inequality are reduced. Others have also noted the evaluation of the value of any commitment of tax dollars to assist businesses should include an assessment of the resulting distribution of wealth between capital, all income groups, and different levels or types of workers (Goodwin, Duncan and Halford, 1993; Sassen, 1994). Consequently, reports that fail to focus on welfare gains and the distribution of these increments are not really studies of economic development. Blair succinctly defines economic development as welfare increases for residents coupled with a progressive distribution of benefits (1995). That definition may well be the best to be used in assessing the outcomes from the use of public resources for the support of professional sports. A consideration of the redistribution of economic activity could mean that if wages increase and profits decline there is a real increment in welfare as lower income individuals receive a benefit generating a progressive redistribution of the total economic welfare available in a community.

Separating substitution effects from new revenue

The last set of definitional issues are substitution effects and the export function of sports.

Substitution effects

Money spent at a sporting event is not necessarily new spending for a region. If most or all of the fans attending a game or event are from the local area, then most of their spending will simply be a transfer from other forms of recreation. In the absence of a professional sports team people do spend money on other forms of entertainment. If the money spent by Detroit's fans at a hockey game had been spent at a pub, theater, or restaurant in the city had the game not been played, then most of the money spent at the game is nothing more than a substitution of spending on hockey for other forms of recreation consumption. Under this scenario *no* economic development takes place. The portion of spending at a sporting event that would have taken place at any other recreational venue within a city or region had the team not existed is identified as the *substitution effect.*

Export functions

Sports produce economic development or increments in welfare in two ways. The example of a hockey game in Detroit can be used to illustrate development as contrasted to substitution effects. There are some residents of Detroit who would travel to other cities for matches if Detroit did not have a team. These individuals are not content to watch games on the television; they want to be at a live match. The spending by those 'real fans' that live in Detroit but who would have gone to another city for a game if Detroit did not have a local team is economic development. That spending is economic development as it would have been lost to the regional economy had a team not existed. If the presence of a team discourages people from spending their recreation dollars in another city, then some economic development does take place. In this example sport performs an **export function** through the deflection of spending into an economy and away from another regional economy through the provision of desired recreational activities.

Continuing with our example of hockey in Detroit, if the games in Detroit attract fans from surrounding cities, then sport again has an export function as people from other economies bring their money to the region. Manchester United may be a good example of this, as are the New York Yankees, as both teams have fans that live outside the local economy and come to their respective cities to see matches and games. International and national championships are other examples where sport has an export function through the attraction of recreational dollars from other economies. When people make a special or additional trip to Athens to see the Olympics, there is a clear export function that generates economic development.

Moving economic activity to achieve policy goals

While the movement of economic activity from within a region does not generate economic development, we cannot dismiss the mere movement of activity as being valueless. Many cities have tried to move recreation activities from their suburbs to downtown areas. While this generates no regional economic development, helping a declining area can still achieve important public policy objectives. If a blighted downtown embarrasses residents the relocation would have some value in spite of there being no increase in economic development for the region as a whole.

The multiplier game

Consultants hired by cities or teams to analyze the economic benefits of either a new stadium or of attracting or retaining a team usually multiply the initial extra spending by a factor in the range of 2 to 5. The rationale for the muliplier is that some of the new spending will be spent again locally and generate yet more economic benefits. As an example of the multiplier concept, consider the investment in an airfield on a Caribbean island intended to woo tourists to the island. The tourists pay for meals and hotel rooms and buy locally made souvenirs. Suppose 90 per cent of the money spent by tourists stays on the island and the rest goes on imported goods such Scotch whisky which the tourists also consume. Suppose, further, that 90 per cent of any new spending in the island is for local goods and services. No one on the island saves any money. If the new airport generated \$1 million of new tourist spending a year there would be a second round of local spending of \$900,000. That second round would generate a third round of local spending of 90 per cent of 900,000, or \$810,000. Eventually the total additional local spending would be \$10 million. In this example the multiplier is ten. In general the multiplier is one divided by the proportion not spent locally, $1/0.1 = 10$.

For the value of the multiplier to be accurate the following two assumptions must hold. First, the initial new spending must really be new spending rather than money that would have been spent locally on something else. This assumption is plausible in the island tourist example. Second, the proportion spent locally has to stay the same in every round. This assumption is a little shakier on the island. If goods and services on the island start to get more expensive because there is limited land, the islanders would start to import more of their food or take vacations on cheaper islands. In the context of sport the first assumption is suspect. Most professional sports events just draw local spectators. Because the sports events just substitute for other local recreation there is hardly any net new spending that would be subject to a multiplier effect. The assumption of the same percentage being spent locally in successive rounds is also unwarranted. The professional athletes, who have itinerant careers, live outside the local area and take their spending elsewhere. Their short and uncertain careers make them save most of their earnings. The owners often live outside the political jurisdiction supporting the stadium construction or the team. They are even wealthier than the athletes and save a high fraction of their income.

The Bureau of Economic Analysis (BEA) tries to estimate what is spent locally based on the source of the new income. The BEA looks at firm revenues on tax forms and creating input–output tables showing the between-industry flows of spending. For example, if there was additional spending by tourists on hotels in an area the BEA could estimate how much of that spending flowed into local bakeries, local laundries, etc. The basic assumption behind input–output tables is that spending patterns do not change. Adding spending will not raise wage rates and encourage some firms to leave the local area. Being richer will not cause anyone to spend more outside the area. New businesses will not raise land prices. There are no congestion costs to the new businesses.

The BEA is the main source of the multipliers used in the consultant reports. Their multipliers are sensitive to the size of the region being considered. The smaller the region, the more spending leaks out in any round. It is interesting that the BEA Handbook (1997) on how to use its RIMSII model illustrates the use of its multipliers with a new sports stadium in Kansas City that cost \$111.5 million to construct. The BEA estimated that the construction of the stadium would generate a regional impact of \$286.8 million. The BEA makes no deduction for lost local spending due to the taxes needed to finance the stadium. It treats the \$115 million as if it came from the sky. Thus, the term *impact* does not mean economic development. The value of the BEA's multiplier in their example is 2.57 (286.8 divided by 111.5). This multiplier value is for an entire region. The smallest area for which the BEA estimates multipliers is a county. The county values would necessarily be lower than the multipliers for a region. In turn, the multiplier for a city would be much smaller than for a county because more of the initial spending would leak away into the area surrounding the city than the area surrounding a county or a region. What makes the typically reported multipliers by private consultants so dubious is that the political jurisdiction that usually supports the team's operation or the stadium's construction is a city. The economic benefits that should be calculated are the benefits that apply to the community footing the bill.

The nature of multipliers highlights what sorts of sporting events have the greatest economic development effects. Events that draw very rich people from outside the region are ideal. Events that last many days also help. The NCAA Final Four, the Olympics, the World Cup and a Formula one race all fit this description of an ideal event because they draw free spenders from outside the area for a long stay. An NBA, NFL, MBL or NHL game does not. US professional league sports are almost entirely home-crowd affairs. In the UK there is always an away supporters' section in the stands but the distances between the cities tend to be less so that the away supporters do not always have to stay overnight to attend a match.

Sports and economic development: regions and cities

We now turn to the issue of what teams, facilities and sports mean to regions, cities and downtown areas. The intangible and image benefits of teams and sports will round out the discussion.

The issue of the economic value of sport to a region's economy has been studied with increasing frequency because of the increased spending by communities or sports facilities. After more than three decades of research on this topic there is virtually unanimous agreement among economists that there is no relationship between economic development and sports (Baade, 1996; Baim, 1994; Hudson, 1999; Noll and Zimbalist, 1997; Quirk and Fort, 1992; Rosentraub, 1999a; Siegfried and Zimbalist, 2000). Yet, if one looks at the aggregate size of different industries in any regional economy, this conclusion is hardly surprising.

Sport in a regional economy

The most valuable sports teams – such as Manchester United, Arsenal (a London-based team), the Washington Redskins and the New York Yankees – each earn sufficient revenues to have a market value in excess of $500 million.

Manchester United is currently regarded as the team with the most substantial revenues and market value, having surpassed the New York Yankees in 1999. Arsenal is estimated to have a value of $800 million, just $10 million less than Manchester United (Stuart, 2000). In 2000, the Washington Redskins surpassed the New York Yankees as the most valuable team in North America. *Forbes* magazine estimated that the Washington Redskins had a market value of $741 million in 2000. Below these four giants are teams such as the Dallas Cowboys, FC Barcelona, the Atlanta Braves, New York Mets, AC Milan, the Miami Dolphins, the Tampa Bay Buccaneers and the New York Knicks. These teams have revenues in excess of $100 million. Most teams in the National Football League have gross revenues at or above $100 million. Most basketball and hockey teams earn less than $100 million, and just a handful of baseball teams earn more than $100 million each year (Gruen *et al.*, 2000).

Businesses with gross revenues of approximately $100 million are certainly valuable. However, as a percentage of a region's economy, teams or businesses of this magnitude are really quite small. For example, colleges and universities receive far less attention and are rarely considered engines of a region's economy, yet the budgets of most universities are far larger than those of any sports team. One of the authors of this book is a member of the faculty at Indiana University-Purdue University Indianapolis (IUPUI). IUPUI has an enrollment of more than 27,000 students and, including its health center, has an annual budget in excess of $1 billion. While far more people have heard of the New York Yankees or Manchester United, IUPUI has a budget that is at least five times larger than the world's most successful sports teams.

Comparing sports teams with universities provides one benchmark for describing the size of teams as economic entities. On a national scale in the USA in 1995, fewer than 1 in 2,000 *private* sector jobs in cities over 300,000 were associated with professional sports teams (see Table 8.1). There are a substantial number of jobs in the nonprofit and public sectors. If these jobs are included in the measure of total jobs in an economy, employment opportunities related to sport, as a percentage of total employment, would be far less than the 0.07 per cent reported in Table 8.1.

The sports jobs identified in Table 8.1 did produce an annual payroll of $4.9 billion, but total private sector income in 1995 in all counties with more than 300,000 residents exceeded $1.79 trillion dollars. This means that professional sports accounted for slightly more than 0.25 per cent of the private sector payrolls in the USA in 1995 (see Table 8.1). The number of jobs and total payroll in the numerous sectors of the economy including services, manufacturing, finance, insurance, and real estate dwarfed the sports sector (Rosentraub, 1997b).

The importance of sport as an employment sector is no different in England or Scotland. Data from the 1998 Annual Employment Survey found 0.9 per cent of all jobs in England in the sports services sector. In Scotland, 1.2 per cent of all employees were classified as employed in the sports sector. These

Table 8.1 Private sector employment and payroll levels in all US counties with 300,000 or more residents, 1995

Standard Industrial Code Classification	*Employment as a percentage of total*	*Payroll as a percentage of total*
Eating and drinking places	6.67	2.20
Hotels and other lodging places	1.49	0.82
Amusement and recreation services	1.28	0.75
Professional sports	0.07	0.27
Remaining retail trade	12.79	8.06
Remaining services	34.14	32.56
Manufacturing	15.52	20.25
Wholesale trade	7.46	9.58
Transportation	6.43	7.81
Finance, insurance and real estate	8.30	11.48
Agriculture	0.58	0.40
Mining	0.34	0.52
Construction	4.82	5.23
Unclassified	0.10	0.07
Total for all counties	61,104,320	$1,790,160,862,000

Source: US Bureau of the Census, *County Business Patterns, 1996.*

proportions, considerably larger than those in the USA, could be the result of definitional differences between the three nations; yet, even if there is a broader inclusion of business in the sports business in England and Scotland, athletics accounts for approximately 1 per cent of the jobs in a country. By comparison, in Scotland 2.0 per cent of all jobs were associated with hotels and in England 1.1 per cent of all jobs were in hotels.

Not only are sports a small proportion of a national economy, but sports and teams also represent a small portion of the economy of communities that attempt to capitalize on sports or entertainment as a majority component of their identities. Arlington, Texas, with approximately 300,000 residents, is located between the cities of Dallas and Fort Worth, and south of the Dallas/ Fort Worth International Airport. Since the early 1979s, the city has tried to develop its identity through sports and recreation services. In 1973, the city's leadership was able to attract the Washington Senators, which then became the Texas Rangers. The Rangers played in Arlington Stadium, a former minor league stadium that was substantially improved in 1977 and then razed in 1994 as the city and team built 'The Ballpark in Arlington'. Arlington is also home to the Six Flags over Texas amusement park (the largest theme park in the Southwestern United States), and to the Wet'n'Wild water amusement park.

In 1992, the private sector payroll for the city of Arlington was estimated to be $1.9 billion. More than one-quarter of this income, 26.0 per cent, originated in businesses classified as services. The second largest industry group was manufacturing, accounting for 19.3 per cent of Arlington's private sector payroll. Retail trade was Arlington's third largest private sector industry, accounting for 12.8 per cent of all estimated payroll dollars in the city. The combined payrolls (citywide) for *all* sports-related businesses, amusement parks, recreation (theaters, etc.), hotels and restaurants amounted to 11.4 per cent of the private sector payroll. This made the *citywide* entertainment grouping the fourth largest industry in the city. Wholesale trade was almost as large as entertainment, accounting for 10.9 per cent of all private payroll dollars (see Table 8.2).

Arlington, located between the two larger markets of Dallas and Fort Worth, tried to use its location to become the regional recreation and tourism center. Despite this very favorable location and a clear public policy orientation to focus on sports and tourism, these data indicate that sports and entertainment are very small components of even small- and medium-sized cities (similar to Arlington) that seek to serve an entire metropolitan region.

Can sport improve the overall performance of an economy? In other words, do teams attract business because of the impact of sport on the quality of life or the image of a successful city created by a sports team? Across the last few years there have been several studies of the effect of teams and the presence of facilities on regional economic conditions. For example, in 1996 Baade looked at per capita income and the number of teams and new sports facilities in a region. Baade found that in only one city, Indianapolis, was the presence of teams associated with income growth. For all other cities and for the sample as a whole the presence of a team or new facilities was statistically insignificant. Baade and Sanderson (1997) then looked at employment in specific sectors of the economy and their relationship to the presence of teams and new facilities. In only five instances was the presence of teams and new facilities related to employment levels in the recreation and entertainment sectors. Hudson (1999) substantially expanded on this work with a model that had employment levels as the dependent variable and market size, labor costs, education levels, energy prices, and tax levels as independent variables. This general model was then refined and the number of professional sports teams was introduced along with education levels of the population, growth in tax

Table 8.2 Industry size as measured by private sector payrolls, Arlington, Texas, 1992 (total estimated private sector payroll, $1,885,222,215)

Industry grouping	*Estimated percentage of private sector payroll dollars*
Services	26.0
Manufacturing	19.3
Retail trade	12.8
Citywide entertainment[a]	11.4
Wholesale trade	10.9
Other (Combined)	7.6
Finance, Insurance and Real Estate	6.0
Transportation	6.0

[a] Includes all restaurant, recreation, and hotel spending throughout the city of Arlington.

Source: US Department of Commerce, *County Business Patterns*, 1992.

rates, and growth of the average wage and salary per employee. He concluded, 'in the US, the number of sports teams in a city has no statistical relationship to changes in employment' (Hudson, 1999, p. 407). Indeed, the correlation was statistically insignificant and negative. There is no evidence to indicate that the presence of a team in this sample of 17 cities was associated with job growth. Siegfried and Zimbalist (2000) argue that teams create as few as 30 full-time year-round jobs.

An export-based sports policy and economic change

The work performed by Baade (1996) and others has generally used the presence of a team or facility as an explanatory variable. With teams essentially adding to a community's range of recreation opportunities, there may be little reason to believe that the addition of one more recreational opportunity would change a region's economy. In the absence of the team residents would simply spend their money on other forms of recreation. Consequently much, but not all, of the spending that takes place at a sporting event would take place in a region's economy if the game were not played. One should not expect to find much economic development from one team or sports facility. What if a city adopted a comprehensive sports strategy? Under those circumstances, what are the overall benefits of a sports strategy for economic development? The idea here is that sports might work to foster economic developments of the city if the city had a coordinated program as they reached some critical mass.

The best answer to this question comes from studying the sports and downtown development program implemented by Indianapolis. Indianapolis, part of the rustbelt in the Midwest, was mired in the recession of the 1970s. Like most other cities in the region, Indianapolis was losing population to the suburbs. Downtown Indianapolis was deteriorating and replete with abandoned buildings and crime. The downtown was deserted by the end of the business day. In an effort to stem the loss of residents and coordinate redevelopment plans the Indianapolis city boundary expanded to the limits of the surrounding county. However, this reorganization of the public sector did not stop the flow of people and businesses to suburban areas. Between 1970 and 1980 the consolidated city of Indianapolis lost residents while the metropolitan area enjoyed a 17.6 per cent growth rate. By 1980, the consolidated city accounted for just 53.7 per cent of the region's population, far less than the 66 per cent that lived within the city after World War II. To reinvigorate the economy of Indianapolis and enhance its attractiveness, a new set of policies and programs were required.

Indianapolis launched a downtown redevelopment program anchored in a sports strategy that focused on national and international amateur sporting events and professional sports teams. An organization was created to produce a new image for the city and to encourage businesses to locate in the downtown area. An economic development corporation was created to assist companies considering a move to Indianapolis or to help local corporations that might want to expand their operations. Another group was created to market the city as a venue for sports events and as the headquarters location for amateur sports organizations.

Indianapolis's sports strategy differed from programs implemented elsewhere in that it focused on more than just the attraction or retention of a single team. As already noted, individual teams (such as the Indiana Pacers which decided to stay in the city or the Indianapolis Colts which moved to the city) create little economic development. However, the amateur sports strategy involved the attraction of national and international events with the potential to bring residents of other cities to Indianapolis for recreational consumption. These events included the Pan American Games, the World Gymnastics Championships, and several of the NCAA championships. It was also hoped that this sports strategy would become a magnet drawing other businesses to the revived downtown. This sports and downtown development strategy has been sustained for more than 20 years by three different city administrations.

From 1974 to 2000 more than $4 billion was spent on new construction projects as a result of the sports strategy (see Table 8.3). Eliminated from this tabulation were projects that would have taken place even if no specific strategy existed. More than one-fifth of these expenditures, or $998.6 million, was specifically related to the 'experience economy' of sports and entertainment facilities. Residential construction, a direct result of the renewed excitement from a vibrant downtown, accounted for another $88.9 million in new construction through 2000. This construction is particularly important as the downtown area had been abandoned as a site for residential development before the sports strategy was implemented. The projects identified in Table 8.3 do not include all the development that took place in the downtown area. Some developments (the city's monuments, a large park area, the state's refurbishing of the Capital building, new fire stations, etc.) probably would have taken place even if a sports strategy had not been implemented.

Before reviewing the impacts of Indianapolis's strategy on the region and its economy, several important elements should be underscored. *First*, there was the building of new facilities. In 1974 the Market Square Arena opened as the home for the Indiana Pacers, bringing the team downtown from its mid-city location. Earlier, the state and city had agreed to build a convention center. A modest facility was planned in 1966 and initiated after the private sector committed $2 million for the project. The balance of the center's costs was financed with a hotel room tax and with bonds guaranteed by the state. In latter years the Hoosier Dome would be added to the convention center, substantially increasing exhibition space and providing an anchor for the conventions. Not every project identified or included in Table 8.3 is sports-related. Indeed, if that were the case then the program would not have

Table 8.3 Projects and sources of funds for downtown development in Indianapolis (in $0,000,000)

Projects	*Year*	*Source of Funds*					*Total*
		Federal	*State*	*City*	*Private*	*Philanthropic*	
Sports Related							
Market Square Arena	1974	0.0	0.0	16.0	0.0	0.0	16.0
Sports Center	1979	0.0	0.0	4.0	1.5	1.5	7.0
IU Track and Field Stadium	1982	0.0	1.9	0.0	0.0	4.0	5.9
IU Natatorium	1982	1.5	7.0	0.0	0.0	13.0	21.5
Velodrome	1982	0.5	0.0	1.1	0.0	1.1	2.7
Hoosier/RCA Dome	1984	0.0	0.0	48.0	0.0	30.0	78.0
Nat'l Institute of Sports	1988	0.0	3.0	3.0	0.0	3.0	9.0
Conseco Fieldhouse	1999	0.0	38.0	71.0	69.0	0.0	178.0
Victory Field	1997	0.0	5.0	9.0	9.0	0.0	23.0
RCA Dome Improvements	1999	0.0	0.0	20.0	0.0	0.0	20.0
NCAA Headquarters	1999	0.0	5.0	0.0	0.0	70.0	75.0
Pan American Plaza	1987	0.0	0.0	5.7	25.0	4.5	35.2
subtotal		*2.0*	*59.9*	*177.8*	*104.5*	*127.1*	*471.3*
Culture/Entertainment							
Children's Museum	1976	0.0	0.0	0.0	0.0	25.0	25.0
Indiana Theater	1980	1.5	0.0	0.0	4.5	0.0	6.0
Zoo	1988	0.0	0.0	0.0	0.0	37.5	37.5
Zoo Additions	1999	0.0	0.0	0.0	0.0	6.6	6.6
Aquarium	1999	0.0	0.0	0.0	0.0	60.0	60.0
Eiteljorg Museum	1989	0.0	0.0	0.0	0.0	60.0	60.0
Eiteljorg Museum Expansion	2000	0.0	0.0	0.0	0.0	15.0	15.0
Indiana State Museum	2000	0.0	1.0	0.0	0.0	104.0	105.0
Walker Building	1985	2.0	0.0	0.0	0.0	1.4	3.4
Union Station	86–00	0.0	0.0	0.0	0.0	8.8	8.8
subtotal		*3.5*	*1.0*	*0.0*	*4.5*	*318.3*	*327.3*
Hotels/Commercial Buildings							
Hyatt Hotel/Bank	1977	0.0	0.0	0.0	55.0	0.0	55.0
2 W. Washington Offices	1982	1.2	0.0	0.0	11.8	0.0	13.0
1 N. Capitol Offices	1982	3.2	0.0	0.0	10.4	0.0	13.6
Embassy Suite Hotel	1985	6.5	0.0	0.0	25.0	0.0	31.5
Westin Hotel	1989	0.5	0.0	0.0	65.0	0.0	65.5
Farm Bureau Insurance Co.	1992	0.0	0.0	0.0	0.0	36.0	36.0
USA Funds, Incorporated	1996	0.0	0.0	0.0	16.6	0.0	16.6
Adam's Mark Hotel	2000	0.0	0.0	0.0	50.0	0.0	50.0
Marriott Hotel	2000	0.0	0.0	0.0	90.0	0.0	90.0
Anthem Corporation	2000	0.0	0.0	0.0	33.6	0.0	33.6
Heliport	1985	2.5	0.1	0.6	2.4	0.0	5.6
Lilly Corporate Expansion	92–00	0.0	0.0	0.0	893.5	0.0	893.5
subtotal		*13.9*	*0.1*	*0.6*	*1,253.3*	*36.0*	*1,303.9*
Retail Complexes							
Lockerbie Market	1986	1.8	0.0	0.0	14.0	0.0	15.8
Union Station	1986	16.3	0.0	1.0	36.0	0.0	53.3
City Market	1986	0.0	0.0	0.0	0.0	4.7	4.7
Circle Centre Mall[a]	1995	0.0	0.0	290.0	0.0	10.0	300.0
subtotal		*18.1*	*0.0*	*291.0*	*50.0*	*14.7*	*373.8*

Table 8.3 continued

Projects	*Year*	*Source of Funds*					*Total*
		Federal	*State*	*City*	*Private*	*Philanthropic*	
Convention Center							
Expansion	1999	0.0	0.0	0.0	45.0	0.0	45.0
Residential Projects							
Lower Canal Apartments	1985	7.9	0.0	10.3	0.0	2.0	20.2
Lockfield Apartments	1987	0.0	0.0	0.6	24.6[a]	0.0	25.2
Canal Overlook Apartments	1988	0.0	0.0	0.0	11.0	0.0	11.0
Canal Apartments	1999	0.0	0.0	0.0	10.0	0.0	10.0
Lombardi Row	1999	0.0	0.0	0.0	1.4	0.0	1.4
Meridian Row	1999	0.0	0.0	0.0	6.8	0.0	6.8
Ryland Homes	1999	0.0	0.0	0.0	9.1	0.0	9.1
Watermark Homes	1999	0.0	0.0	0.0	5.2	0.0	5.2
subtotal		*7.9*	*0*	*10.9*	*68.1*	*2.0*	*88.9*
State of Indiana Projects							
Capitol Tunnel	1982	1.4	0.0	0.0	0.0	0.0	1.4
Indiana University	75–00	0.0	357.0	0.0	0.0	0.0	357.0
State Office Center	1992	0.0	264.0	0.0	0.0	0.0	264.0
Subtotal		*1.4*	*621.0*	*0.0*	*0.0*	*0.0*	*622.4*
Other Projects	74–98	*0.0*	*0.0*	*0.0*	*1,066.9*	*0.0*	*1,066.9*
Property Tax Abatements	74–99	*0.0*	*0.0*	*98.0*	*0.0*	*0.0*	*98.0*
TOTAL		46.8	682	578.3	2,592.3	498.1	4,397.5
%		1.1	15.5	13.2	58.9	11.3	100

[a] This is the present value of the city's investment. The city is also responsible for a $33 million loan from the State of Indiana due in 2000. The data identifies the annual costs for the bonds negotiated for the city's investment. *Source*: Rosentraub (1999a).

achieved its objective of attracting and stimulating economic development. A review of the development projects between 1974 and 2000 indicates that slightly more than one-quarter of the buildings (measured in construction dollar terms), 26.0 per cent, or $1.2 billion, was specifically related to making downtown Indianapolis the recreation and entertainment center for the region. An early measure of the successful impact of the programs can be seen in the continuing increases in hotel rooms. In 1974, downtown Indianapolis was not a destination for tourists. By 1996 there were 3,557 rooms in downtown Indianapolis; in 2001 there were 5,225 hotel rooms in the downtown area.

Second, the data in Table 8.3 also underscore the extent to which Indianapolis's sports and downtown redevelopment program involved both governmental and nongovernmental funds. Squires (1989), among others, has identified a number of cities where the public sector's commitment of funds has created extraordinary subsidies for private sector ventures. To be sure, Indianapolis did provide subsidies for a number of projects (including the new home for the Indiana Pacers). However, the city of Indianapolis's expenditures accounted for just 13.2 per cent of the $4.4 billion expended to rebuild the downtown area. More than half of the funds, 58.9 per cent, came from the private sector and, when combined with the investments from the philanthropic sector, 70 per cent of the cost of the downtown redevelopment program came from private sources. Indianapolis was able to leverage more than $7.58 for every $1 its taxpayers committed. While it still remains to be seen if the burden of the investment was equitably shared or if the city received the returns it wanted, relative to the leveraging of funds, Indianapolis accomplished something that would be the envy of most cities in the USA. The city was able to rebuild its downtown area with the extensive support of the private and nonprofit sectors and the State of Indiana through its investments in the IUPUI campus and a new government center.

Third, all the development noted in Table 8.3 (with the exception of the Children's Museum) took place within two miles of the center of downtown Indianapolis. In this sense Indianapolis also concentrated its redevelopment efforts in a very narrow area and thus its tourism or sports policy established a set of resources or venues that can be easily accessed by pedestrians. The proximity of the venues also meant that tourists and area residents mingle when enjoying the activities hosted at the sites and in visiting the retail operations.

Fourth, there can be little doubt that the focus on sport, tourism and the hospitality industry led to a rebuilding of downtown Indianapolis and the investment of a substantial amount of private money in commercial and residential facilities. The $1.3 billion investment in new commercial buildings and hotels also slowed a trend toward development in the suburban sections of the region that would not have taken place without the concentrated focus on downtown and the sports strategy.

Evaluating the success of a city's sports strategy: moving economic activity or enhancing total welfare?

It is already evident what worked: downtown Indianapolis was rebuilt and a considerable amount of money from the private and nonprofit sector was used to accomplish this goal. Downtown Indianapolis is a far more inviting and pleasant place to be than it was 25 years ago. Did this movement of economic activity into downtown Indianapolis produce a change in total welfare?

For example, officials had hoped that the sports strategy would attract firms to Indianapolis leading to higher salary levels. The cities with which Indianapolis competes for business expansion in the Midwest, as identified by economic development and municipal leaders, are Columbus (Ohio), Minneapolis, St. Paul, St. Louis, Dayton, Cincinnati, Louisville, Milwaukee and Fort Wayne (Indiana). During the sports strategy period, Indianapolis had the third highest growth rate among these communities and the number of jobs in Indianapolis increased by 32.9 per cent, exceeded only by growth in Columbus and Minneapolis. However, in 1977, 10.1 per cent of all of the jobs in these ten communities were located in Indianapolis; in 1989, this share had increased by just 0.2 per cent, suggesting that sports strategy did not substantially shift the location of jobs among the 10 regions.

There is also little evidence that the jobs attracted to Indianapolis were high-paying positions. In 1977, for the ten counties studied, Indianapolis had the second highest average income. In 1989, Indianapolis's rank had declined to fifth among the 10 communities. At the regional level, the Indianapolis area fared somewhat better: ranked second in 1977, the Indianapolis region was fourth in 1989 with the seventh largest percentage increase. However, regardless of whether one looks at the county or region, the sports strategy did not bring higher-wage jobs to Indianapolis. By 1996, wage levels had improved but the Indianapolis region was still ranked third relative to the wealth of households among the competitor cities, clearly indicating that the sports strategy did not engender any changes in total welfare levels which surpassed those that took place in other Midwestern cities that did not focus on sports.

The concentration of sports facilities and a level of economic activity in downtown Indianapolis did not reverse the long-standing trend towards suburbanization in the region. In 1985, 18 per cent of the region's jobs were located in downtown Indianapolis; in 1995, the number of jobs in downtown Indianapolis accounted for 14.8 per cent of the region's opportunities. From 1985 to 1995 there was actually an increase of 3,239 jobs in the downtown area; the region, however, enjoyed more robust growth accounting for the reduction in the centrality of the core area (Rosentraub, 1999). In summary, then, Indianapolis was able to utilize a sports strategy to rebuild its downtown area, but in terms of changes in total welfare there was no evidence that the emphasis on sports had the hoped-for impact. The importance of this example is that Indianapolis represents the most extensive and sustained effort by any city to use sports as an engine for economic development. The cities with no professional teams did at least as well in job growth and per capita income growth. They also had revitalized downtowns, part of a national trend in the USA.

Sport and the choice of different locations for business

The statistical studies of the effect of sports on total welfare levels are also sustained by the observations of experts who provide services designed to find the best locations for businesses. PHH Fantus (now part of another business management and consulting company) helps corporate clients to find new locations for their business activities. Robert Ady, President of PHH Fantus Consulting, summarized the importance of the sports for business location when speaking to a group of Kansas City's community leaders at Arrowhead Stadium in 1993:

> In fact, the single most important location criterion today is grouped under operating conditions. No, I must tell you now that it is not the presence of a professional sports team it is in fact the availability of a qualified workforce. In today's competitive and ever-changing environment, companies are locating where they feel assured of securing such a workforce. Not only the availability of managerial talent but, more importantly, the availability of skilled and technical talent. Other typical operating condition criteria might include: proximity to an international airport, tranquil labor–management relations, sophisticated telecommunications availability, and dual-feed utility systems.

Ady also noted that sporting events are a great opportunity to bring prospective companies to a city and to highlight things the city has accomplished with the private sector. Since bringing a prospect to town is essential to any relocation process, sport can be a tool when making the deal, but corporate locations are dictated by economic factors that enhance profits.

Business location decisions seem to involve a two-stage process. At the first level or tier firms seek to maximize their profits or market shares. As a result, businesses select locations where their costs for producing a good or service, transportation, energy, taxes and labor are minimized. (The quality and level of public services also enters the decision process at this stage since taxes are payments for the quality of services received from the government.) Often, several areas have essentially identical profit potential (Bartik, 1991). The second tier, then, involves the choice of the specific location from this group of cities and may also involve an assessment of the quality of life. Sports teams contribute to the quality of life but so do the arts, museums, universities, libraries, public schools, public safety, parks and civic pride. In this regard, sport, through its contribution to the quality of life, can assist in establishing an area's value for businesses and their employees. This intangible benefit will be addressed in a later section.

Sport and downtown development: experience elsewhere

While teams and sports strategies seem to have little impact at the regional level, what can a team or sports do for a downtown area? Austrian and Rosentraub (1997) examined job creation in downtown Cleveland immediately after the opening of Jacobs Field (home to the Cleveland Indians) and Gund Arena (home to the Cleveland Cavaliers). Between 1992 and 1995 there was a 2.7 per cent increase in the number of downtown jobs, but growth elsewhere in the county and region was more robust at 4.1 per cent and 6 per cent respectively. However, by 1996, more than $700 million had been invested by the private sector in other downtown projects. Nevertheless, with the public sector's investment in both sports facilities exceeding $289 million, the cost per job created, at least up to 1995, was $231,000. If the number of jobs increased since 1995, the cost per job would still be in excess of $115,000 and, as Felsenstein and Persky (1999) have noted, it is not appropriate to count all of these jobs as a net gain as many people may have found other or similar positions in unsubsidized areas of the city or county.

These per-job costs from other economic development efforts are sometimes far less. For example, Tennessee's attempts to attract a Nissan plant in 1984 cost $11,000 per job, and South Carolina paid $68,000 per job for a BMW plant. However, Alabama provided almost $200,000 per job for a Mercedes-Benz plant (Eisinger, 1995). Goss and Phillips (1997) looked at economic development spending between 1986 and 1994 by state economic development agencies and found that the cost per job ranged from $64 to $8,698. Spending by cities for individual projects would inflate these numbers, but these data do provide some insight into the high expense associated with sports investments for job creation.

Phoenix is another city that sought to revitalize its downtown area. While a center of the fast-growth Sunbelt of the United States, the fate of Phoenix in its region and its downtown area closely mirrored the experiences of Indianapolis and Cleveland. As detailed in Table 8.4, Phoenix's share of Maricopa County's population has been steadily declining since 1960. In 1960, more than two-thirds of the county's population lived in Phoenix, but by 1998 slightly more than two-fifths of the county's population was concentrated in the city of Phoenix. Phoenix, despite its location in the booming Sunbelt, shares a common fate with rustbelt Indianapolis. Phoenix is now challenged to preserve its role in the economy of the region.

Phoenix followed a route similar to the one taken by Indianapolis to rebuild its downtown area. During the 1990s, almost $1.5 billion in new development was concentrated in downtown Phoenix (see Table 8.5). While the public sector provided almost 30 percent of these funds, private investors committed $1.3 billion to the projects that rebuilt downtown Phoenix. As a result, Phoenix was also able to leverage a substantial level of private sector support. Was the Sunbelt city of Phoenix any more successful than Indianapolis in terms of using sports for economic development?

Table 8.4 Population concentrations in Maricopa County, 1960–98

Year	*Population counts*		*Phoenix's population as a percentage of Maricopa County*
	Maricopa County	*Phoenix*	
1960	663,510	439,170	66.2
1970	967,522	581,562	60.1
1980	1,509,052	789,704	52.3
1990	2,122,101	991,711	46.7
1998	2,784,075	1,198,064	43.0

Source: Rosentraub (2000b).

Table 8.5 Projects and sources of funds for downtown development in Phoenix (in $0,000,000)

Projects	*Year*	*Source of funds*			*Total*
		State	*City*	*Private*	
First Interstate Bank Renovation	1993			40	40
Bank of America Renovation	1994			9	9
Phoenix Museum of History	1995		9.5		9.5
Downtown Streetscape	1995		8.8		8.8
AT&T and US West	1996			15	15
Phoenix Civic Plaza	1996		31		31
Phoenix Newspapers	1996			35	35
Abbey House Housing Project	1996			8.8	8.8
Orpheum Theatre	1997				14
Arizona Science Center	1997	48			48
Metropolitan Apartments	1997			10	10
New Phoenix Transportation Center	1997		7.5		7.5
411 N. Central Building	1997			8	8
AMC 24 Screen Theatre	1998			10	10
Ball One Ballpark	1998		238	113	351
Alice Cooper'stown Restaurant	1998			2.7	2.7
Holiday Inn Express Hotel & Suites	1998			8	8
Valley Youth Theatre	1998	7			7
Embassy Suites	1999			52	52
Civic Plaza Parking	2001		43		43
Roosevelt Square Housing	1999			75	75
Park at Arizona Center Housing	1999			25	25
Collier Center	2000			400	400
Marriott at Collier Center	2001			113	113
Phelps Dodge Center	2001			78	78
Total		55	337.8	1016.5	1409.3
Percentage		3.9	24.0	72.1	100.0

Phoenix's downtown area, like Indianapolis's core area, is now a destination for recreation and tourism. In addition, a number of businesses have moved to or expanded their offices in downtown Phoenix. Downtown Phoenix has indeed shed its image as a core area largely abandoned after the workday. However, this change in the image of downtown Phoenix has not produced the level of economic development or change that had been anticipated. If downtown Phoenix had become the engine or center of recreation and entertainment for the region, one would expect to find both a growing level of tax revenues and an increasing proportion of these taxes concentrated in the downtown area. Table 8.6 illustrates that there has indeed been a very large increase in the scale of business in the downtown area as reflected in the increasing levels of taxes collected from establishments in that area. Total tax collections from hotels and restaurants in downtown Phoenix increased from $1.7 million in 1991 to $3.3 million in 1998. However, when these increases are compared with the changes in business activity throughout Phoenix, it becomes clear that the sports strategy permitted the downtown area to retain its share of activity, but there was no change in development patterns.

Table 8.6 Sales tax revenues generated in downtown Phoenix by business type

Year	*Restaurants, bars*	*Hotels, motels*	*Retail*	*Total*
Rate	*1.3%*	*4.3%*	*1.3%*	
1991	$577,833	$808,698	$270,111	$1,656,642
1992	602,270	721,553	279,251	1,603,074
1993	695,613	785,293	344,150	1,825,056
1994	789,601	1,008,919	339,257	2,137,777
1995	806,963	1,105,665	309,789	2,222,417
1996	914,549	1,389,192	291,879	2,595,620
1997	930,476	1,411,185	291,527	2,633,188
1998	1,357,665	1,493,189	487,773	3,338,627

Source: City of Phoenix, Finance Department, Tax Division.

Table 8.7 Citywide sales tax receipts and the proportion from downtown Phoenix

Citywide sales taxes receipts by activity and year (in millions of dollars)	*1991*	*1992*	*1993*	*1994*	*1995*	*1996*	*1997*	*1998*
Restaurants, bars	12.0	12.7	13.3	15.5	16.8	18.2	19.4	21.0
Hotels and motels	10.0	10.3	11.3	13.3	14.8	16.9	18.4	19.2
Retail	72.2	73.5	77.3	92.7	100.4	108.1	113.5	122.2
Total	94.2	96.5	101.9	121.6	132.0	143.2	151.3	162.5
Sales taxes collected downtown as a percentage of the taxes collected throughout Phoenix								
Restaurants, bars of All eating Places	4.8	4.8	5.2	5.1	4.8	5.0	4.8	6.5
Hotels, motels of All Hotels	8.1	7.0	7.0	7.6	7.5	8.2	7.7	7.8
Retail of All Retail	0.4	0.4	0.4	0.4	0.3	0.3	0.3	0.4
Total of All Sales Taxes Collected*	1.8	1.7	1.8	1.8	1.7	1.8	1.7	2.1

* The Total refers to the city's sales tax downtown tax as a percentage of the total Sales tax.
Source: City of Phoenix, Finance Department, Tax Division.

In 1991, 1.8 per cent of all of the sales taxes collected from hotels and restaurants in the City of Phoenix came from outlets in the downtown area. In 1998, after the opening of the Bank One Ballpark and the completion of several other projects, the downtown area was generating only 2.1 per cent of the city's sales tax dollars (see Table 8.7). There was a slight increase in business activity in the downtown area as a result of the sports and entertainment policies, but most of the consumption that takes place at restaurants and hotels in Phoenix takes place outside the downtown area.

Teams, sport and total welfare: conclusions

Measured by the number of jobs or the total welfare of communities, sports teams have no ability to promote economic development. However, sports facilities – when coupled with other forms of recreation – have been able to relocate economic activity and to raise the visibility of downtown areas. At the regional level, all the available evidence suggests sports teams and the facilities they utilize have no positive effects on total welfare. The best estimates are that public investment in sport has a negative economic consequence. Indianapolis's sport strategy had a significant export component, but even with a rebuilding of the downtown area there were no real gains in total welfare levels. Indianapolis did not perform better than its counterpart cities.

In terms of the vitality of downtown areas, if vitality is measured by number of people coming to an area, the presence of teams and sporting events clearly rearranges recreation patterns within a metropolitan area. In Cleveland, for example, the two new sports facilities attract in excess of 5 million people to an area that a scant decade ago was largely avoided. Baltimore and Indianapolis are two other cities that can point to the new centrality of their downtown areas with regard to the consumption of recreation in their regions. However, none of the cities with specific downtown policies for development and sports can illustrate that the new destinations for recreation have altered the pattern of business and residential location. While there are indeed more businesses and residences in these downtown areas, the general trend in these areas is towards increased development in suburban areas (Rosentraub, 1997b). It could be argued that the extensive public sector investments at least helped downtown areas capture some of a region's development. Yet, given what the public sector has invested in professional sports facilities, this modest gain was secured as a result of a very large expenditure. Residents of each region will have to decide if the benefits received were worth the costs.

The intangible benefits

Assessments of development and the benefits from teams and sports cannot be limited to changes in a region's economic landscape or the vitality of the downtown area. Civic pride and image are important factors for a city's overall development. Sport, as an important part of the quality of life, can and does have an effect on civic pride and, given the media's interest in sports, the image of a community. Can this impact and value be measured and incorporated into an assessment of the economic benefits of teams?

In 1996, respondents from 1,500 randomly selected households in the Indianapolis region were asked a series of questions designed to measure the intangible benefits of the Indiana Pacers, the Indianapolis Colts, the Indianapolis 500, local museums, and other civic assets in the Indianapolis community. There is little reason to believe that results in other communities would be substantially different. Five different indicators of civic pride were used to assess the value of teams and other cultural assets. Respondents were asked the importance of assets in 'making you feel proud' to be a resident of the Indianapolis region. Responses were coded from a high of 5 for an asset that

Table 8.8 Measures of civic pride and identity

Asset or event	*Civic pride*	*National reputation*	*Others mentioned (%)*	*Visitors see (%)*	*Loss hurts reputation (%)*
Auto racing	3.94	4.49	31.7	14.5	85.1
Black Expo	3.17	3.55	0.8	2.1	36.8
Colts (NFL)	4.07	4.33	10.5	4.3	74.9
Ice (IHL)	3.22	–	0.2	0.4	–
Indians (AAA)	3.65	–	0.5	1.1	–
Museums	4.27	4.29	2.3	6.6	68.3
Music	4.02	4.03	0.4	3.2	59.4
Other Sports	3.98	4.17	1.1	2.4	59.5
Pacers (NBA)	4.26	4.47	15.5	5.0	81.1
Shopping	4.00	3.87	1.5	3.5	58.8

Source: Swindell and Rosentraub (1998).

was described as 'very important' to a 1 if a respondent believed the regional asset was 'very unimportant'. The results are shown in Table 8.8.

Sports teams clearly are critical in establishing the sense of pride respondents have in their communities. Although museums generated the most pride, professional sports teams ranked second and third. Indeed, the Pacers virtually tied with the museums as a source of pride for community residents. Respondents also were asked to describe the importance of these assets and events in defining Indianapolis's national reputation using the scale from the civic pride question. There are interesting differences in terms of how respondents view the role of these amenities in determining reputation. For instance, auto racing (the Indianapolis 500) is ranked highest in determining reputation although it ranks only seventh in terms of generating civic pride. This is the result of different dimensions of pride and identity. The greater importance of an amenity in the everyday life of individuals and families can account for a higher ranking on a question focusing on the pride associated with living in an area.

Respondents were also asked, 'When you tell people who do not live in the Indianapolis region that you live here, what organization or event do you hear them mention when you say Indianapolis?' Each respondent could list up to four events or organizations. The results presented in Table 8.8 show the percentage of all responses and the pattern is almost identical to the national reputation question. Auto racing, the Pacers, the Colts, and museums, in that order, were the most frequently noted assets. This may indicate that respondents' ideas of what determines a city's national identity is reflected or mirrored by those outside the area.

Similarly, all respondents were asked what activities, events, or amenities in Indianapolis brought friends and family members to the region. Thus, respondents were not asked where they took visitors, but what amenities, if any, brought their out-of-town family and friends to Indianapolis. Again, the pattern is generally consistent with the previous indicators. Most often, visitors requested to visit the Indianapolis 500 racetrack; however, the Pacers and Colts fall to third and fourth places behind museums with regard to out-of-town visitors. The final indicator we used to measure civic pride and identity asked respondents to report whether or not the loss of a given asset or event would hurt the reputation of the community. The percent of respondents reporting that a loss would hurt the community is reported in the final column of Table 8.8. Yet again, auto racing, professional sports, and museums ranked highest.

The results from Table 8.8 add support to the argument that residents enjoy substantial social spillover benefits related to the presence of the Pacers and the Colts. However, just as important as the individual scores for understanding the feelings of pride generated by cultural and other amenities are the values placed on each asset by different groups of respondents. In other words, who enjoys the benefits the most, or is enjoyment evenly distributed across the population? The data indicate that there are very distinct patterns in the pride respondents derive from different assets.

The most consistent set of differences was related to attendance or 'direct consumption' of an asset. This issue is particularly important when considering civic pride since sports proponents have argued that people receive a sense of pride or enjoyment from teams even if they do not attend games or events. For example, respondents who lived in households where at least one member had attended a Pacers game within the last 12 months gave the team a rating of 4.65 in terms of its importance in making them feel proud to be a resident of the area. If no one in the household had been to a game, the team's rating declined to 4.01 (see Table 8.9). Similarly, if someone in the household had been to a Colts game, the importance of the team rose from an average of 4.07 to 4.54. In households where people did not attend a game, the importance of the team to a person's pride in living in Indianapolis declined to 3.86. The relationship between frequent contact with an asset and a respondent's sense of its importance is probably best underscored by the different ratings accorded auto racing. If people had attended the Brickyard 400 or the Indianapolis 500 the importance of auto racing in establishing their pride as a resident increased from a rating of 3.94 to 4.40.

Table 8.9 The importance of different assets in establishing pride in living in Indianapolis by attendance

Asset or event	*Mean score**	*Attended*	*Did not attend*	*t-test*[a]
Museums	4.27	4.42	3.97	7.3
Indiana Pacers	4.26	4.65	4.01	12.3
Indianapolis Colts	4.07	4.54	3.86	12.6
Music	4.02	4.30	3.71	10.2
Auto racing	3.94	4.40	3.62	12.4
Indianapolis Indians	3.65	4.19	3.46	12.3
Indianapolis Ice	3.22	3.95	3.08	11.3

*Responses coded, 5 = very important, 4 = important, 3 = unsure, 2 = unimportant and 1 = very unimportant.
[a] All statistical tests exhibit significance ($p < 0.0001$).
Source: Swindell and Rosentraub (1998).

Table 8.10 Correlations of civic pride with attendance levels

Asset or event	*Number of times attended*[a]
Museums	0.19
Indiana Pacers	0.18
Indianapolis Colts	0.22
Music	0.20
Auto racing	0.11
Indianapolis Indians	0.17
Indianapolis Ice	0.19

[a] Statistically significant at the 0.001 level. *Source*: Swindell and Rosentraub (1998).

The overall pattern of more favorable impressions if the respondent or a household member had attended an event is consistent across each of the assets (for which specific attendance questions were asked). The differences are statistically significant. If respondents or members of their households visited the asset or attended a game (event), that asset was far more important to a respondent's pride in living in Indianapolis than if they or another household member had not attended an event (game) or visited the asset (see Table 8.9).

For several of the regional assets, there also is a linear effect from repeated attendance. As the directions of the correlations in Table 8.10 show, the more events attended, the higher the rating. In addition, the magnitude of the correlations indicates that attendance is an important element in determining pride. Overall, the regional assets were a greater source of pride for those who lived in households where individuals had attended events or games, and those who attended more events (games, concerts) had more feelings of pride from the presence of the asset. In other words, nonusers of different elements of the region's quality of life do not feel as positive or receive as much benefit from the existence of the asset as do direct users. Thus, these correlations suggest financing mechanisms should place more of the burden of paying for the asset on those who attend. With regard to professional sports, for instance, it is justifiable to make users pay at the door and treat these assets in large part as toll goods. Perhaps not all the costs should be assessed at the door, however, since nonusers still clearly receive some social spillover benefits from the teams' presence. Therefore, the question turns into one of identifying the best mechanism to support the public's investment to secure the social spillover benefits for nonusers.

Sport and development: what is possible?

Sports, teams and facilities clearly enhance the quality of life in a region. In addition, placing facilities in declining areas can shift patterns of recreation in the sense that people will come to an area that was avoided. The impact of sports and teams on the quality of life should not be minimized. Having a team does help to establish an area's identity, and the available evidence clearly suggests it means a great deal in terms of establishing or maintaining people's pride in their community. It is also clear that there is a concentration of these benefits among those who attend games or sporting events. While it is true that there is a general benefit enjoyed by all, those who attend sporting events have a greater emotional attachment to their teams.

These important benefits, however, do not conflict with the general conclusion that sports, teams and facilities have had no observable effects on total welfare levels. Downtown Cleveland, Phoenix and Indianapolis are indeed livelier places today then they were years ago, but there is no increment in welfare that can be attributed to the presence of sports facilities and team.

Exercises

1. Suppose a club attracts a free agent star by agreeing to pay a salary that exceeds all other offers made. Describe and analyze the circumstances under which a region's total welfare will increase as a result of the presence of a star player. Also illustrate how the addition of a star player who earns a hefty salary could lead to a decrease in welfare for a region.
2. A city is debating whether or not to build a new facility to retain a team or to secure a franchise. Develop the business plan that will be used to provide the city's leadership and voters with the information required to make an informed decision. (Do not perform the research needed; instead, develop the plan and illustrate the methods you would follow which identifies (a) the needed information for the business plans and (b) the procedures you would follow to collect the needed information.)
3. The gross revenues earned by the New York Yankees are approximately $250 million. The team pays its players approximately $175 million and an additional $15 million is spent on expenses for travel and management. Develop a research design that would let you answer a question about the welfare or economic development generated by the New York Yankees for (a) New York City and (b) for the borough in which Yankee Stadium is located (Bronx County).
4. In each case decide whether there is economic development or just economic activity and explain your reasoning.
   (a) Dick and Jane are married. Dick does the yard work. Jane does the cleaning. They get a divorce. Dick pays Jane to do his cleaning. Jane pays Dick to do her yard.
   (b) A city raises taxes and uses the revenue to hire residents who are homeless and unemployed. The new city workers pick up litter.
   (c) A city raises taxes and uses the revenue to lure an airline to locate an aircraft maintenance facility at the local airport. The tax money is used for

construction, infrastructure, and loan to the airline at below market rates. The maintenance facility hires 1,000 highly-paid airline mechanics.

(d) The NFL decides to hold the Super Bowl in a city. All the hotels in the city require a minimum one-week stay to book a room (this is real example) and double their room rates. Every hotel is booked and paid for but most rooms are empty except for the weekend of the game.

5. In each of the examples decide whether there has been a substitution of one type of local spending for another, whether there has been an export effect, and whether there has been a redistribution of income toward greater equality. Explain your reasoning.

   (a) A city raises taxes to build a new stadium in a blighted area. The new stadium attracts a major league team. The blighted area is revitalized but total employment in the city is constant.
   (b) A major league team moves to an city and it pays for the construction of a new stadium. (This is not a recent example.)
   (c) Vancouver, British Columbia (in Canada), loses the NBA Grizzlies to Memphis, Tennessee. Vancouver did not use tax money to construct an arena. Memphis did use tax money. Consider the situations of both Vancouver and Memphis.
   (d) A casino run by an Indian tribe opens in a city. The patrons are mostly low-income residents of the city. No tax dollars were used to subsidize the casino.

6. The proponents of a tax-supported new arena for an NBA team that already resides in a city claim that the spending inside the stadium will be $100 million per year. They use a multiplier of 2 and further claim that local spending will increase by $200 million if the city is able to retain the team by building the new arena. Critique these claims.
7. Economists have done a miserable job convincing people that subsidizing professional sports teams is a waste of public funds. It is not for lack of trying. For example, John Siegfried, an economist at Vanderbilt, organized a campaign to oppose using public funds to attract an NFL team to Nashville. His campaign failed. Why have economists done so poorly?
8. Suppose the same public money could be spent on a stadium to attract an NFL team or new dormitories and classrooms at a local university. The expansion of the university would either attract students from outside the city or keep city residents from attending universities in other locations. What are the plusses and minuses of the two alternatives?

9 Financing the facilities used by professional sports teams

Chapter goals

Each team's facility is a 'stage' on which its home matches are presented. If owned by the team, the stadium or arena is its largest physical capital asset. That ownership, or else a contract for the use of a publicly-owned stadium, allows the team to sell tickets, broadcast rights and Internet rights. Teams have an obvious economic interest in convincing the public authorities to pay for the stadium. To justify the public subsidy teams claim that the benefits generated by their presence extend beyond the fans that watch or listen to a game. Many economists claim that the benefits produced by teams are almost entirely private in nature and limited to the team's fans. The chapter explores these claims and develops a framework to determine the optimal portion of public sector support for a sports facility. Next, the chapter considers the benefits and costs of different financial instruments and strategies to pay for any public subsidy of stadiums and arenas. The model of optimal cost-sharing between the public and private sectors and least cost payment mechanism are then compared with recent contracts for building new facilities.

Introduction

Across North America and Europe there has been a boom in stadium and arena construction. In the USA many facilities have been built to ensure that a team stays in a city. Some communities have constructed a facility in the hope that a team would relocate from another city. Stadiums for major league teams with retractable domes, especially if built in areas prone to earthquakes or flooding, have cost as much as $500 million. The more typical price for a state-of-the-art facility for baseball or football without a retractable dome is approximately $375 million (2003 dollars). While the most expensive arena for a basketball or hockey team has cost in excess of $300 million, those facilities typically cost approximately $200 million. The cost of any street or road improvements and cost of parking facilities is generally not included in these estimates.

In addition to a dome, costs depend on the level of amenities included (suites, club seats), the cost of land, environmental remediation, and costs related to specific location (e.g., protection against earthquake or flooding damage) and other environmental factors. For a given sport the cost of most facilities falls within a narrow band because all of the new ones tend to have the same revenue-producing amenities. It does not make economic sense to build a new facility without including club seats, luxury suites and ample concession areas. The most important issue in stadium financing is, 'What is the appropriate portion of the cost of a sports facility that should be supported by the public sector?' Team owners would want the public sector to be responsible for all the costs for both constructing and maintaining a facility so that their incomes are maximized.

The most common justification for a stadium subsidy is that the team would otherwise leave the city. A second justification is that the subsidy will cause the owner of the team to hire better players and coaches and thus improve its performance. If a better team was the city's goal it would be much more efficient to simply pay the team a performance bonus. The impact of any stadium subsidy on team performance is complex. There is a well-established 'new stadium' effect, which at any given win percentage raises attendance in the first few years. Fans simply want to see the new facility. If the marginal revenues from wins, defined as the extra ticket revenue per additional victory, falls as some of the fans attend primarily to see the stadium, the owner has an incentive to field a weaker team. However, the novelty of the new stadium wears off fairly quickly. The long-term impact of the public subsidy on the win percentage then depends on how the public subsidy changed the design of the stadium. If the subsidy was used to create more club seats, more suites and more elaborate concession areas, the owner has an incentive to field a better team because the pay off for greater attendance is higher in a high-amenity stadium. A public subsidy that was used to build a larger stadium could also give the owner an incentive to improve the team. This result depends on the marginal revenue function. If profits were maximized at the capacity of what would have been built without a public subsidy, the owner may set prices at a level that leaves part of the new stadium empty (except perhaps for the most compelling opponents) and has no incentive to change team performance.

As was discussed in Chapter 2, some owners in some years do not follow **profit maximization**. In these instances putting more money in an owner's pocket will cause them to spend more on the team provided there are no 'hard' caps limiting spending on players' salaries. If a hard cap exists, then the public subsidy simply increases the owner's profits. Even in the absence of spending caps, reliance on the owner's pleasure from winning as a means of improving the team's performance through a public subsidy is problematic. Owners change. Most of the individual owners are old men and there is no guarantee that their heirs would share their motivations. Even if they are around for a while they can become bored with their team and devote themselves to some new toy.

Many economists consider a stadium as nothing more than a capital requirement for a private business that should be privately financed. Part of the team's revenue from all sources would support building maintenance and go toward retiring any construction bonds. Alternatively, the stadium could be financed by the team's cash reserves, although this is an unusual method. Either way, under private financing the team would pick the level of amenities and the size and design of the stadium. These choices would affect its marginal-revenue-of-wins function. The levels of yearly expenditures on maintenance and bond retirement are fixed costs that do not affect any decisions about ticket prices or team performance, unless the owner is a win maximizer.

In rare instances the polar positions of 100 per cent public subsidy or 100 per cent private financing are in fact what occurs. For example, all units of government in the St. Louis and Baltimore regions were convinced of the benefit of having an NFL team. Given the NFL's control over the supply of teams, it was decided to offer a state-of-the-art facility free to any team that would relocate. St. Louis was successful in convincing the Rams to move from Anaheim, California, and Baltimore was able to lure the Browns from Cleveland. At the other end of the spectrum, the value of the Washington, DC, market for a football team convinced the owner of the Washington Redskins to pay the full cost of a new facility. After voters rejected a planned investment in a new facility for the San Francisco Giants the team decided to pay all the costs of building a state-of-the-art facility with the public sector's investment being limited to the infrastructure needed to provide access to the site. The New England Patriots of the NFL tried twice to get referendums for a stadium subsidy (a ballot among all citizens who are registered to vote) passed. After the second referendum failed the team rejected an offer from Hartford, Connecticut, for a stadium subsidy and built its own new stadium in Foxboro, Massachusetts. The key to the team's decision was that the Boston area was more populous and much wealthier than Hartford.

Most new stadiums in the USA involve some public subsidy beyond infrastructure, such as sewers and access roads. This chapter establishes a framework for stadium financing that is tied to the public and private benefits produced by teams. Previous chapters have summarized the range of private and public benefits. However, before developing a framework it is helpful to review these benefits.

The private and public goods aspects of sports facilities

At first glance a professional sport's team stadium is a purely private good:

> Although someone watching a game in a stadium does not take away from someone else's enjoyment of the game (joint consumption), it is possible to package the good, attach a price to this benefit which becomes a consumption charge (ticket price) and exclude those unwilling to pay it.. Even those fans who watch games on television (or listen on the radio) are charged for this privilege through the commercials that are part of most broadcasts or the fees they pay for cable or satellite transmission services. Rather than being a public good, sports are similar to a toll good that can be produced in a private market. (Swindell and Rosentraub, 1998, p. 13)

However, important external benefits exist for individuals who do not attend games or watch broadcasts. These include the enjoyment that comes from talking and reading about teams and the celebrations that accompany championships. Danielson (1997) emphasized the image benefits that teams generate for regions: 'Art museums, symphony orchestras, theaters, and zoos are all marks of major cities, as are libraries and universities, leading law firms and banks, and great commercial and industrial corporations, but big city teams are seen by many as more easily and widely recognized symbols of a place's importance' (Danielson, 1997, p. 102). The benefits generated by a team's performance and presence have also been noted by Kearns and Philo (1993) and Shropshire (1995), who have documented the importance of teams and facilities for establishing a region's identity. Michener (1976) and Wilson (1994) placed the societal value of sports in a cross-cultural perspective based on the long-standing interest of societies in sports. Even the most casual observer notices the benefits generated when a team is successful in terms of the conversations and celebrations by individuals who do not attend games.

If there is an external benefit from the transactions that make the private goods aspect of sports possible, then it can be argued that an efficient solution (one that ensures an adequate level of sports in a society) would involve a public subsidy. Swindell and Rosentraub (1998) demonstrated the existence of these spillover benefits through a random survey of households in the Indianapolis region, although they noted that those households that valued these benefits most were those in which a member had attended a game. Hamilton and Kahn succinctly stated this case in their analysis of the subsidy provided for the building of Oriole Park at Camden Yards (1997, p. 274): 'the state and its subdivisions lose approximately $9 million a year on [Oriole Park at] Camden Yards. This is approximately $12 per Baltimore household per year; the public subsidy to the stadium is justified only if the public consumption benefits of the Orioles are at least this large.' Apropos of the civic pride and the excitement generated by a team's presence, Jacobs Field and Gund Arena in Cleveland, built in 1994, have attracted more than four million people to a part of the downtown area avoided for years. As a result:

> Downtown Cleveland is a far more lively place today than it was five years ago. There is a contagious vitality and excitement that should not be discounted or ignored.. Will this new recreational nexus create a great many jobs? No. Will the sports facilities encourage a substantial or significant change in development patterns? No. Is downtown Cleveland a more exciting place? Is there a greater sense of excitement and civic pride? Are people who long ago gave up on downtown returning for recreation? The answer to each of these questions is yes.. Are these benefits or returns worth the hundreds of millions of dollars spent by taxpayers to subsidize sports?.. the investment in sports amounts to less than $10 per person per year.. Did Cleveland and Cuyahoga County get good or adequate value for their investment? In a city with a full set of urban challenges, is the new image created by these public investments worth the commitments if there is no direct economic impact?...Those are questions only the residents of Cleveland and Cuyahoga County should answer. (Rosentraub, 1996, p. 26–7)

An expenditure of $12 per household per year, as in the case of Baltimore, might be justified by the external benefits produced by team. The key questions then in each instance when a sports facility is to be built are: (1) what is the complete range of external benefits; (2) what is the value of these benefits to the affected taxpayers; (3) is the proposed expenditure by the public more or less than the identified value; and (4) what are the equity implications of the external benefits and the proposed financing scheme? We add that last point to the analysis as the spillover benefits may be worth different amounts to different groups. Ticket prices may simply lock out low-income households from attending games and hence they will have less interest in talking or reading about the team, or watching broadcasts or celebrating championships. Swindell and Rosentraub (1998) found that those households that did not attend games reported fewer spillover or public consumption benefits. A broad-based tax such as sales or income taxes would reach lower-income residents even if the main recipients of the external benefits of the team's presence are upper-income individuals.

A point made in earlier chapters needs to be reiterated. Teams do not exist in a free market. In North America the supply and location of teams is not determined by market demand but by cartels that maximize their profits. Teams are kept artificially scarce so that local governments will subsidize stadium construction. Estimates of the external benefits of a team are raised because of this artificial scarcity that forces cities to subsidize teams to either locate or remain in their areas (Rosentraub, 2001). In Europe the movement of teams from one city to another is almost unknown. The move of the Wimbledon soccer team from London to Milton Keynes is one of few European examples of a US-style move. Yet, increasingly, in a search for identity and the establishment of international reputations, cities are engaged in the building of sports facilities for the establishment of an image (Shoval, 2002).

Analyzing the external benefits of a professional sports team to aid in the development of a plan for financing a sports facility is a substantial task. Considerable work has been done in developing methodologies for measuring public consumption benefits. Some of this work has been focused on measuring the public consumption benefits from professional sports (Irani, 1997; Swindell and Rosentraub, 1998). Other policy analysts studying environmental protection have also identified several ways to enumerate the intangible benefits through a process known as contingent valuation (Lindsey, Paterson and Luger, 1995).

Contingent valuation is a survey technique to estimate nonuse values by asking respondents how much they are willing to pay or to accept for a change in the good in a hypothetical market framework. The first identified description of contingent valuation was in 1944 in an article by S.V. Ciriacy-Wantrup about measuring the benefits of preventing soil erosion. Its first use was apparently by Robert Davis in his PhD dissertation in 1963 in order to measure the value of a recreation area to hunters and wilderness advocates. Since then, many studies have been conducted on a wide range of commodities, including environmental amenities, natural resources and public provision of health care (such as ambulances). Three significant studies are summarized here to illustrate several of the possible categories of nonuse values: altering visibility at the Grand Canyon; the *Exxon Valdez* oil spill; and changing the operating system at Glen Canyon Dam (Breedlove, 1999).

> The contingent valuation method is referred to as a 'stated preference' method, because it asks people to directly state their values, rather than inferring values from actual choices, as the 'revealed preference' methods do. The fact that contingent valuation is based on what people say they would do, as opposed to what people are observed to do, is the source of its greatest strengths and its greatest weaknesses. (Ecosystem Valuation Website, 2002)

Contingent valuation as a method to assess intangible benefits has limitations, but it identifies a way for a government to estimate the value of the intangible benefits to taxpayers and residents and thus provides a framework for assessing whether or not there is a sufficient level of benefits to warrant the use of public funds. As has already been noted, facilities and teams do not generate sufficient levels of economic benefits for a region to warrant the use of public funds. Teams and facilities can and do move **economic activity** and sometimes the transfer of this activity from suburban to inner-city areas is worthy of the public's support. But if additional support is required to sustain the level of investment that some franchises demand or seek, then that benefit must be found in the intangibles such as nonattendees talking about the team. If the intangible benefits are viewed as too small there is no other economic justification that can be used to sustain the use of public funds in the building or maintenance of a sports facility.

Contingent valuation involves the use of surveys of a random sample of citizens. The process has been refined sufficiently that the results can be relied upon to understand the value placed on some change by the general public. The results from the surveys could guide a financing plan or program for any city contemplating a facility. Two examples are, Groothuis, Van Houtven and Whitehead (1998) and Johnson, Groothuis and Whitehead (2001). The key finding in the 2001 paper is that the external benefits of an NHL team are unlikely to be high enough to justify a tax-supported arena even in a city as large as New York. Johnson and Whitehead (2000) also find not enough external benefits to justify taxing the public for a minor league baseball team. Thus, the published Contingent Valuation Method (CVM) studies on subsidizing stadiums conclude that the external benefits do not justify the public subsidy.

During the most recent expansion of the NFL, there were clear indications that the league preferred to place a team in the large Los Angeles market. Los Angeles had two teams, but both had moved to smaller cities offering higher subsidies. The other city competing for the expansion franchise was Houston. Houston had also lost an NFL team to a smaller city that was offering higher subsidies. Public officials in Los Angeles would not match Houston's offer. The NFL eventually awarded the franchise to Houston. The action by the mayor and other elected officials in Los Angeles was based on an assessment of the value of the intangible benefits of the team. Numerous surveys had been performed and the leadership understood what the city's taxpayers would accept and what they would not. On the other hand, Houston's leadership and voters enthusiastically supported (and voted for) the taxes needed to sustain the offer put forward by the franchise owner. The eventual franchise owner agreed to pay $700 million for the right to own the team. However, to do this he required a firm commitment from the public sector to pay a substantial part of the cost of a new stadium while permitting the team to retain most of the revenues generated from the amenities built into the new stadium. The actions of community leaders, elected officials and voters in both cities clearly demonstrated the different assessments of the contingent value of the franchise and facility. The responsibility for assessing the intangible value lies with the public sector's leadership.

The building boom in sports facilities: why, and how large?

The most frequently asked question when a new facility is proposed is, 'What is wrong with the existing stadium (or arena)?' This is a very appropriate question as in some instances the facilities to be replaced are less than 20 years old. In Miami the NBA Heat wanted a new facility within a decade, and the Hornets of the NBA moved to New Orleans when the Charlotte region refused to replace an arena built less than 15 years earlier specifically for the team. Many facilities become economically obsolete in relatively short periods of time. This obsolescence, however, is not too different from what occurs in many other businesses. Stadiums and arenas are the physical capital of sports teams. Just as any business must update its plant and machinery to ensure that it is efficient and profitable, sports teams have to ensure that their facility meets the changing demands of sports fans. In the past fans were indeed content to have a stadium or arena merely provide a seat or area for standing from which a match or game could be seen. But just as terraces with standing areas gave way to stadiums with seats, fans today are willing to spend far more money at an arena or stadium for more luxurious seating areas and other amenities.

In business terms, sports have undergone what is known as a 'Disneyfication phase'. What is meant by this term is drawn from comments alleged to have been made by Walt Disney when he viewed all the development of hotels, restaurants and other theme parks surrounding Disneyland in Anaheim in California. He declared that if he ever built another theme or amusement park it would be a Disney World sufficiently large to capture all of the facilities in which tourists spend money (hotels, restaurants, golf courses, and other parks for additional days of entertainment). Building multiple theme parks and including other tourist amenities such as golf courses, hotels, restaurants and convention centers in the midst of this Disney World accomplish this. The success of this business model can be seen from a casual inspection of the outcomes in Orlando, Florida (Fogelsong, 2001).

Team owners, while slow to accept and implement this concept, have now realized that they can capture a substantial portion of the total spending by fans by including luxury seating, suites for entertaining business clients, numerous restaurants, and large and diversified retail outlets within the stadium. Owners now seek to capture as much of the recreational spending associated with attending a game as possible. One irony of this trend is that in some cities the restaurants that are losing customers to the arena are being asked to charge a special sales tax to support their 'competition'. For an example, see the letter in Box 9.1.

Box 9.1 Downtown eateries lose on game days

September 24, 2002, letter to the *Indianapolis Star*

In discussing the possibility of a new home for the Colts or a direct subsidy for the team, many have been making the assumption that a new arena would mean a huge windfall for Downtown restaurants. A decision to give millions of dollars of public money to the team should be based on facts, and suggesting that a new dome or payments to the team can be subsidized from some financial benefit they bring to our industry is pure fiction. If the team is a benefit to the entire population, then the voters should pay the taxes directly and our customers should not be targeted.

Former Mayor Stephen Goldsmith first promoted this myth over many local restaurateurs' objections as justification for building Conseco Fieldhouse, when one of the prime motivators for any new sports facility is to enhance food and beverage sales for the facility itself by increasing sales opportunities. Those include wide hallways, broader menu options and various other amenities. Net per-person sales from event customers have substantially increased in the new fieldhouse and the market share has decreased for neighboring restaurants.

That was also a primary reason for 7 p.m. start times; people do not have time to eat outside as they must first find a place to park and claim seats. They most often eat inside the facility because of timing issues.

A recent survey of Downtown restaurant association members shows the majority experience a net decrease on fieldhouse event nights and a whopping 80 percent experience a chilling effect on even non-event nights as suburbanites fear that an event might be going on Downtown and parking prices will be absurdly high. This same phenomenon exists at the RCA Dome now.

Few of Sunday's football crowds eat Downtown before a noon game and most go directly home afterward. There are some Downtown restaurants that don't even bother opening on football Sundays.

A new football arena will exert every effort to take what little outside food and beverage sales exist and transfer that income to the team. There is little, if any, significant net contribution to the annual sales for the majority of Downtown restaurants from football, even though our customers are

cont. overleaf

Box 9.1 Continued

taxed 1 percent of our sales to pay for these facilities every day of the year, whether they use them or not.

The primary effect on the local economy from football is that parking companies reap a huge windfall when they inflate their rates by 1,000 percent or more during events. They again are the primary outside beneficiaries, certainly not restaurants.

If a better Downtown is the focus, then that money is better spent on many substantive real improvements, rather than paying for the bragging rights that we have an NFL team. I would be remiss in not pointing out that the restaurant industry fills 300 percent more downtown seats annually than the Colts, Pacers and Indians combined. And we do that every night of the year without being subsidized by public money and not just on a handful of Sunday afternoons and a few select evenings.

(The writer, Ted Bulthaup, owns Hollywood Bar & Filmworks in Indianapolis.)

With so many owners maximizing their income through a Disney-fication of the sporting experience, any team without these income possibilities is at a competitive disadvantage. Even with gate and broadcast revenue-sharing they cannot field a competitive or championship team. Fans for the most part also embrace these new facilities. This embrace is hardly surprising as the fans, as much as they might grouse about ticket prices, are usually not the ones paying for the facility. Attendees are a small fraction of the overall population.

The building frenzy in North America began with the opening of Oriole Park at Camden Yards in 1992. The city of Baltimore, seeking another jewel for a downtown revitalization program emphasizing tourism and entertainment, built the first of a wave of 'retro' parks. These facilities were designed to attract fans with an architecture that evoked memories of facilities that existed in the 1940s and 1950s. These stadiums reversed a trend in the 1960s and 1970s of building dual-use stadiums for baseball and football. The dual-use stadiums worked poorly in both sports. Building two single-use facilities that are specifically designed for particular sports can be more efficient than building one dual-use facility. Fans have been willing to pay the higher ticket prices and fees for services (luxury seating, food and souvenirs) at new facilities with excellent views of the action. Of course, when the stadium is built at the public's expense the owner of the professional team would prefer a single-use facility that yields more revenue for his or her team.

Baltimore had a typical dual-use facility for its football Colts and baseball Orioles franchises. When the city refused to build a football-only facility, the Colts moved to Indianapolis. In Indianapolis the Colts were able to use a domed facility designed for a football team. Within 20 years of their arrival in

Indianapolis the team was threatening to leave the city and break its stadium rental lease. They asked for a new stadium with more seats and more club seats and suites. Indiana does not have a referendum process so the issue will be settled in negotiations between the team and the mayor. The real 'referendum' on this issue will occur when the mayor seeks re-election. If the mayor gives the Colts a new stadium he will be criticized for raising taxes to subsidize wealthy owners, players and fans. If he refuses to give them a new stadium he will be the mayor who lost the Colts.

When the Colts moved away from Baltimore that city did not want to risk losing its other major league team, baseball's Orioles. Consequently, the city of Baltimore responded to the demands made by the Orioles, and built what became the new definition of a state-of-the-art baseball facility. What made Oriole Park at Camden Yards state-of-the-art? As was stated above, its design evoked memories of older baseball facilities. Second, the new facility was designed with a large number of amenities designed to increase the team's revenues. The facility has 144 luxury suites that rent for $75,000 to $175,00 per season. Three additional suites are available for rent on a per game basis. The facility also has 3,736 club seats where fans are offered services such as cocktails and a separate lounge area. Club seats cost $35 per game plus an annual fee of $500. The stadium also included extensive food and beverage outlets as well as large retail spaces for the sale of souvenirs. In response to the improved facility and the team's competitive play, attendance at Oriole games increased by more than 1 million, and in 1997 the team attracted a record 3.7 million paying fans to games.

The construction boom that began in Baltimore has continued unabated ever since. New facilities were built for the New England Patriots, the Philadelphia Eagles, the Philadelphia Phillies, the Pittsburgh Pirates, the Pittsburgh Steelers, the Cleveland Indians, the Cleveland Browns, the Cincinnati Bengals, the Cincinnati Reds, the Atlanta Braves, the Houston Astros, the San Francisco Giants, the San Diego Padres, the Seattle Mariners, the Seattle Seahawks, the Chicago White Sox and the Chicago Bears. There was also a wave of new arenas for basketball and hockey teams. These new facilities mimicked the new stadiums and included luxury seating, new and expanded restaurant facilities and retail outlets. Virtually every team in the NHL and NBA was playing in a new facility by the beginning of the 2003 season. European and South American cities were also the sites for several new sports facilities that sought to offer some of the revenue advantages so common in North American facilities.

Factors influencing financing plans for sports facilities

The first and most critical element in the financing of a sports facility has already been discussed: the estimation of the private and public benefits produced by a team's presence. To the extent that the benefits produced are private, then those consumers enjoying the private benefits should pay for the cost of a facility through fees added to ticket prices or the consumption of food, beverages and souvenirs associated with a visit to the facility or a team's existence. As noted, the public benefits include the intangible value of having a team as perceived by residents of a community. However, there are other public benefits that also need to be considered. For example, if a team's presence redistributes economic activity from a suburban location to a downtown area, and this enhances a particular city's revenue flow through the collection of local taxes or the attraction to the area of some other businesses, then an important public policy goal, balancing growth, may be achieved. That benefit is worth some level of public investment.

The recognition that positive externalities or public consumption benefits are produced by teams does not lead to the immediate conclusion that broad-based taxing instruments or other forms of public support should be used to pay for sports facilities. As important as the presence of public consumption benefits from sports is the distribution of these **externalities**. Communities must be careful to assess who enjoys the public consumption benefits from sports. If these benefits are unevenly distributed and concentrated only among the fans who attend games or higher-income individuals, then the use of broad-based taxes to support a sports facility is inappropriate. For example, if fans attending games also report the highest levels of enjoyment of public consumption benefits, then increasing ticket prices or user fees would be the appropriate way to finance the facility required to ensure the presence of the benefits. Similarly, if higher-income households report enjoying more of a team's externalities, then a taxing or finance instrument that assesses the costs of financing a facility against these households is warranted.

Regardless of the distributional issues, however, what contingent valuation studies disclose is that public sector subsidies toward a sports facility in order to generate external benefits should be much less than the full cost of the stadium. The appropriate amount to be supported by public investment depends on two factors: the public benefits and the distribution of public benefits. These factors will vary across communities leading to different decisions. For example, Los Angeles has enough sources of entertainment that the absence of an NFL team caused little concern. No one claimed that Los Angeles would lose it status as an important city if it went without an NFL team. Also, the political mechanism for setting the level of stadium subsidy, such as referendums, varies by jurisdiction.

The financing tools available to the public sector to subsidize a stadium include broad-based or general taxes, specific consumption taxes, user fees, tax increments, sports taxes, tourist taxes, and lottery or gaming revenues. The selection of the instrument used to finance the bonds should reflect the assessment of the distribution of public and private benefits. Some taxing instruments are more politically acceptable than others. The amount of new public debt used to finance a stadium is a separate issue from the choice of the best revenue source used to meet the annual bond payments.

General or broad-based taxes

There are two basic sets of commitments that the public sector can make to retire bonds. The revenue from a specific tax can be dedicated to the bond payments, or the public sector can add the annual payments required to retire a bond to all other obligations it has to fund. When a government pledges its full faith and credit to repay a bond, it is encumbering its general revenues and therefore using broad-based taxes, or taxes paid by all or most residents of the area. Communities that place a high value on public consumption benefits from sports, and those that mistakenly believe sports teams promote **economic development**, have used general taxing powers and taxes that apply to purchases or property to finance their share of a facility's cost. For example, voters in Arlington, Texas, approved an increase to their local sales tax to finance their share of the costs for the Ballpark in Arlington (see Chapter 8). All residents paid this sales tax. Arlington is a regional center for retail stores and as a result many nonresidents also paid the sales taxes required to finance the public sector's share of the sports facility. It might appear that the outsiders paying the increased sales tax are picking up some of the cost of building the stadium. However, the sales tax levied on revenues generated by outsiders could have been used to reduce property taxes within Arlington. If the property taxes the Arlington residents are paying for their police, fire and schools exceed the revenue generated by the portion of the 1 per cent sales tax paid by outsiders, the citizens of Arlington have the option of reducing their property or other taxes instead of building the stadium.

More generally, any tax that appears to be paid by outsiders, such as a hotel tax or a car rental tax, does not shift the cost of the stadium to outsiders. Stadium proponents often argue that taxes on outsiders shift the cost of the stadium away from local citizens. This is a fallacy. Local taxes also have incentive effects. A higher sales tax in Arlington will push some sales that otherwise would have occurred in Arlington to other cities. It is usually not worth driving to another city to save 1 per cent, but on big-ticket items such as a car, the 1 per cent could cause an Arlington buyer to make a purchase outside the city. Conversely, shoppers in other nearby cities are more likely to buy locally if they can avoid Arlington's sales tax. The implicit assumption behind the argument that taxes on outsiders shift the burden of stadium financing dollar-for-dollar in terms of the revenue the outsider tax generates is that the **elasticity of demand** for the good being taxed is zero. Under this assumption, no one chooses to rent a hotel room in another location in response to the hotel tax. Similarly, no one chooses to rent a car in another location and no one chooses to make retail purchases in another location in response to the tax. Again, this argument is fallacious.

Specific consumption taxes

It has become increasingly common to find governments pledging revenues from specific acts of consumption to pay for sports facilities. For example, several communities have used 'sin taxes', or extra taxes paid for the consumption of alcohol and tobacco products. Other communities have used parking taxes and taxes on consumption of food and beverages in restaurants. There have also been taxes placed on stays in hotels and on car rentals, but these are considered taxes on tourists. Taxes that are seen as 'voluntary' or paid by nonresidents have enjoyed more political support as many citizens do not consider taxes of that nature as a general burden. This political support is based on a poor understanding of economics.

User fees

The imposition of user fees refers to payments made by fans or spectators for the construction or maintenance of a facility. In Philadelphia, Pittsburgh and Indianapolis, entertainment taxes are collected on the sale of every ticket to events held in the facilities used by professional teams. These funds are then used to support the public sector share of the facility's cost. Another form of a user charge is an extra fee for parking in areas adjacent to a facility. Any fees assessed for advertising within a facility or for consumption of food and beverages inside a facility (extra sales tax) would also be classified as a user fee as the fans attending games or events pay these charges. From the point of view of the team owner, user fees are a disaster. They simply limit the revenue the team could otherwise generate. Consider the example of a fee on tickets. In Figure 9.1 the demand for tickets before a ticket tax is levied is labeled *D*1. The demand after a $10 per ticket tax is levied is labeled *D*2. The vertical distance between the two demand curves is $10 because the fans care only about the total ticket price, not how the ticket revenue is divided between the team and the city. As in Chapter 3, the diagram assumes zero marginal cost. Compared to not having the ticket tax the team gives up $10 of revenue on every ticket it had previously. This is shown as the cross-hatched area between the two demand curves.

If a new stadium were fully financed by ticket taxes, from the team's perspective this would be the same as the team paying for the stadium itself. The only difference is that if the team leaves the city it would still owe the bond-holders, if the stadium were team-financed, but if the city issued the bonds, the team could leave the city and the citizens would be stuck with the bond payments on the empty stadium. Cities try to tie teams to long term leases precisely to avoid being stuck with the bond payments for an empty stadium. Sometimes the language of the lease turns out to be less binding a tie than the city expected.

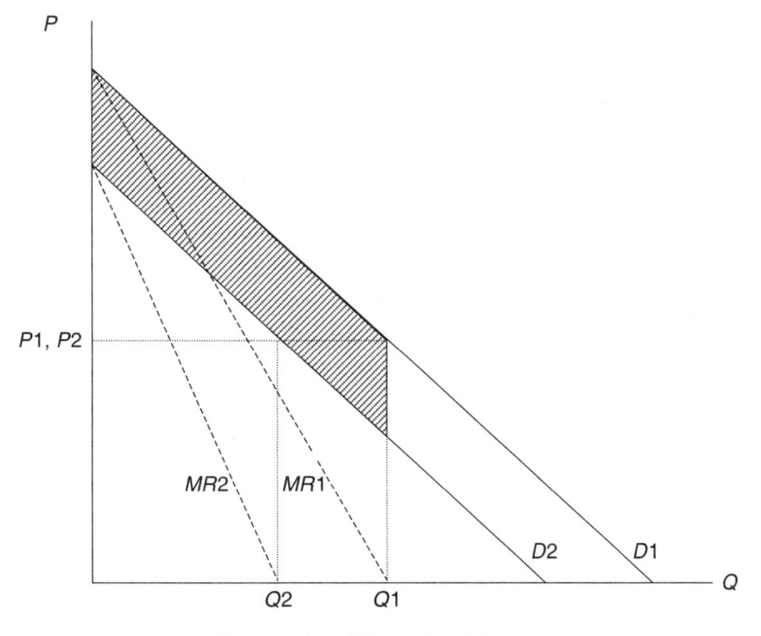

Figure 9.1 Effect of a ticket tax

Tax increments

Some communities have established base levels of taxation and then pledged the increments or extra tax dollars generated by a facility's presence. These plans are similar to tax increment-financing programs used for development in numerous states and countries. A base level of taxes, primarily income and sales taxes, is specified based on what would be generated if a team were not playing in the facility. The taxes collected above this base are considered the increment and then used to repay the loan. The real issue in the use of tax increment financing for a facility is the extent to which the taxes are actually an increment. For example, if in the absence of a team people still spent the same money for recreation but in other parts of a community, then there is no real increment.

Sports taxes

Sports taxes are those paid by the athletes. In states that assess income taxes, if there were no team in the area, then visiting as well as home athletes would not pay income taxes. As a result, several communities pledge these revenues as they are considered a pure increment due to the sport. Again, this logic may be flawed if fans' spending is offset by less consumption of other forms of entertainment. The lower level of consumption of other forms of entertainment would lead to lower wages and thus lower taxes collected at the other sites of recreation and entertainment. One example is Indianapolis, which has created a sports district tax by combining the income tax paid by athletes and those who work at the facilities with all the sales taxes paid in the region. This plan has a degree of political attractiveness as those who do not want to pay for the facility can simply consume services in other parts of the community and thus never pay the tax. However, to the extent that the consumption activities in the zone where the sports tax is collected is a substitution effect for activities that would have taken place elsewhere (and would have been taxed), this form of a tax increment charge can represent a net loss to overall tax collection levels. If that does occur then the sports tax becomes a broad-based income or sales tax.

Tourist and gaming taxes

Numerous communities use taxes on visitors to the area (hotel usage, short term car rental) to pay for sports facilities. These are politically attractive as surveys indicate that residents prefer assessments that do not appear to be paid by residents (Swindell and Rosentraub, 1998). Some communities and nations have used the revenues from lotteries to pay for sports facilities. This is a form of revenue generation used in many European countries and is frequently seen as some sort of a 'sin tax'. Increasingly, communities in North America have become attracted to this concept. There is less political opposition to sin taxes as compared to increases in income or sales taxes. Again, the lottery revenue could have be used to reduce other local taxes. As attractive as it might appear, the cost of the stadium is not paid by the sinners.

Outside North America it is also common to find clubs using revenues earned from betting on sporting events to finance facilities. In the UK, for example, leagues receive a fee for the publishing of lists or schedules of matches that are used in the nation's legalized gaming industry. That income helps to support the building of facilities and other aspects of a club's operations. Other nations operate lotteries or betting pools and the revenue from these operations helps to pay for the building of facilities and team operations.

Theory into practice: public sector financing of sports facilities

Often the concepts of contingent evaluation or matching tax sources with the individuals receiving the benefits are not used. The pressures on elected leaders to avoid the politically embarrassing event of a team leaving creates an environment in which teams control the negotiating process. Many public leaders find themselves in a situation in which competing cities are offering their team a bigger subsidy. It has been observed that hosting a sport team is much like the **winner's curse** in game theory (Swindell and Rosentraub, 2002). The city that bids the most for the team is the one with the most optimistic assessment of the team's benefits. Among a large set of bidders the most optimistic one usually over-estimates the value of the object. Cities can avoid the winner's curse if they understand both the value of their market to the team and the value of the team to their city. In that sense, then, the management tools discussed here are designed to ensure that an elected official knows what the team is worth to the community and then executes a financing plan which reflects that value. In a very direct political sense, if the team demands more than the community is willing to pay an elected official can carefully and skillfully explain the value placed on the team and the offer made to retain the team.

In terms of understanding the economic and political importance of the management tools discussed here it is useful to look at specific examples. First, the largest and wealthiest cities have a decided advantage in their negotiations and the ensuing deals; but this is not a constant as political forces sometimes emerge that lead officials to minimize the value of their markets. For example, the two largest markets for sports in the USA are the New York and Los Angeles metropolitan regions. A new arena was recently built in the City of Los Angeles for the Lakers and Kings. (Los Angeles is home to two NBA teams.) While the City of Los Angeles did pay for a small part of the facility, the public sector also receives a revenue stream from the facility that not only returns sufficient funds to offset this investment, but the City of Los Angeles has been able to earn a profit on its investment. There are enough event nights such as rock concerts for the arena to have been profitable as a private investment. This contrasts sharply with the public investment required in Indianapolis to ensure that the Pacers would remain in the community. To build the new Conseco Fieldhouse in downtown Indianapolis the public sector had to spend more than $100 million. Los Angeles was able to build its arena on far more favorable terms as its market size offers profit potential that is not available in smaller markets.

In a similar vein, the New York Yankees have long wanted the City of New York to provide a substantial subsidy for the building of a new facility. While the City has made investments to improve the existing stadium (built in the 1920s), it has successfully resisted the demand for more incentives because of the value of the New York market to the Yankees and the financial appeal of the current historic stadium to fans. As noted, a far smaller market, Baltimore, had to provide a substantial subsidy to ensure that its baseball team would not leave and then provide a second, larger subsidy to attract a football team.

The size and wealth of a market contributes to the ability of a community to resist paying a large subsidy, but politics can often intervene and remove any benefits from market size. For example, in Philadelphia, North America's fifth largest market for professional sports, a new arena was built for the Philadelphia 76ers and Philadelphia Flyers with a very modest investment from the public sector. In Philadelphia the community also receives a revenue flow from the arena that supports its investment so that no tax dollars or subsidies are necessary. When the city then turned its attention to building new stadiums for their baseball and football teams, despite a subsidy from the State of Pennsylvania for both facilities, the city's new mayor and council supported the provision of an additional $200 million in subsidies for the two facilities. These payments are unwarranted given the size and wealth of the Philadelphia market.

In general, if a league holds absolute control over the supply of franchises, one can expect that there will be constant pressure on cities to provide subsidies. In addition, team owners make large contributions to the campaigns of numerous elected officials. Donations have an impact on the support for subsidies by elected officials. Campaign support is especially important in the absence of data regarding the value of the team to the region.

The type of facility planned also has an impact on the financing plans. With arenas able to host numerous nonsports events, the owners of basketball and hockey teams can frequently enjoy revenue streams that are not available to owners of football and baseball teams. Fear of damage to the playing surfaces in ballparks and stadiums and scheduling problems limits the revenues that can be produced from nonsports events. Thus, with these additional profits for the owners of basketball and hockey teams, the public sector's share of the construction costs has generally been smaller (see Table 9.1).

The Boston Celtics/Boston Bruins paid for the new arena they use, as did the Washington Wizards/Washington Capitals, and the Toronto Raptors. In the case of Washington, DC, the value of that market assumed a large role in the team's owner deciding that a privately financed facility would be quite profitable. In Toronto, provincial laws prohibit public support for the facilities used by professional sports teams. The fact that an entrepreneur might still build a new arena in spite of this law underscores the profitability of larger markets for arenas that can be used for events every day of the week.

Baseball facilities, especially those built in smaller markets, have involved substantial public sector investments. In recent years voters in San Francisco were the only ones to resist demands for a subsidized stadium and to have had a team assume responsibility for building a new stadium. In 16 out of 17 other instances the public sector provided most of the support to build or remodel a baseball stadium. New York City has still not made any final decisions regarding new facilities for the Yankees and Mets. The public sector paid 100 per cent of the cost of remodeling the home of the Chicago White Sox. The situation involving the Atlanta Braves is unique. Atlanta hosted the Olympic Games in 1996 and built a new facility for the opening and closing ceremonies and the track and field competitions. The facility's cost was supported from revenue earned by hosting the Olympic games. The City of Atlanta then charged the Braves $50 million to remodel the Olympic Stadium for baseball. As the public sector did not pay for the Olympic Stadium, in a sense Atlanta's public sector did not make a significant contribution to the building of the facility

Table 9.1 Construction costs and the public sector share

Team	*Type of facility*[a]	*Opening year*	*Cost of construction*		
			Total	*% Public*	*% Private*
Major League Baseball					
Anaheim Angels	1	1998	100	30	70
Arizona Diamondbacks	1	1998	355	71	29
Atlanta Braves[b]	1	1997	235	100	0
Baltimore Orioles	1	1992	235	96	4
Chicago White Sox	1	1991	150	100	0
Cincinnati Reds	1	2003	361	83	17
Cleveland Indians	1	1994	173	88	12
Colorado Rockies	1	1995	215	75	25
Detroit Tigers	1	2000	395	63	37
Houston Astros	1	2000	266	68	32
Milwaukee Brewers	1	2001	322	66	34
Philadelphia Phillies	1	2003	346	50	50
Pittsburgh Pirates	1	2001	233	71	29
San Diego Padres	1	2001	411	57	43
San Francisco Giants	1	2000	306	5	95
Seattle Mariners	1	1999	517	72	28
Texas Rangers	1	1994	191	80	20
Toronto Blue Jays	1	1989	388	63	37
National Basketball Association					
Atlanta Hawks	4	1999	214	91	9
Boston Celtics	4	1995	160	0	100
Chicago Bulls	4	1994	150	7	93
Cleveland Cavaliers	2	1994	152	48	52
Dallas Mavericks	4	2001	325	38	62
Denver Nuggets	2	1999	165	3	97
Houston Rockets	2	2003	175	100	0
Indiana Pacers	2	1999	175	41	59
Los Angeles Clippers	4	1999	375	10	90
Los Angeles Lakers	4	1999	375	10	90
Miami Heat	2	1999	241	59	41
Philadelphia 76ers	4	1996	206	11	89
Phoenix Suns	2	1992	90	39	61
Portland Trail Blazers	2	1995	262	13	87
San Antonio Spurs	2	1993	186	100	0
Seattle SuperSonics	2	ren. 1995	110	100	0
Toronto Raptors	4	1999	180	0	100
Washington Wizards	4	1997	260	0	100
National Football League					
Atlanta Falcons	3	1992	214	100	0
Baltimore Ravens	3	1998	229	87	13
Buffalo Bills	3	ren. 1999	63	100	0
Carolina Panthers	3	1996	248	0	100
Cincinnati Bengals	3	2000	458	95	5
Cleveland Browns	3	1999	306	70	30
Denver Broncos	3	2001	364	73	27
Detroit Lions	3	2002	225	36	64
Green Bay Packers	3	ren. 2003	295	58	42
Houston Texans	3	2002	402	71	29
Jacksonville Jaguars	3	ren. 1995	135	90	10

Table 9.1 continued

Team	Type of facility[a]	Opening year	Cost of construction		
			Total	% Public	% Private
Miami Dolphins	3	1987	115	10	90
New England Patriots	3	2002	350	0	100
Philadelphia Eagles	3	2003	395	21	79
Pittsburgh Steelers	3	2001	244	69	31
Seattle Seahawks	3	2002	430	77	23
St. Louis Rams	3	1995	300	100	0
Tampa Bay Buccaneers	3	1998	190	100	0
Tennessee Titans	3	1999	292	100	0
Washington Redskins	3	1997	251	28	72
National Hockey League					
Atlanta Thrashers	4	1999	214	81	19
Boston Bruins	4	1995	160	0	100
Carolina Hurricanes	2	1999	160	87	13
Chicago Blackhawks	4	1994	150	7	93
Colorado Avalanche	4	1999	165	3	97
Columbus Blue Jackets	2	2000	150	0	100
Dallas Stars	4	2001	300	42	38
Florida Panthers	2	1998	212	87	13
Los Angeles Kings	4	1999	375	10	90
Minnesota Wild	2	2000	130	100	0
Montreal Canadiens	2	1996	156	0	100
Nashville Predators	2	1997	144	100	0
Ottawa Senators	2	1996	136	21	79
Philadephia Flyers	4	1996	206	11	89
Phoenix Coyotes	2	2001	180	0	100
Washington Capitals	4	1997	260	23	77

[a] 1 = ballpark; 2 = arena; 3 = stadium; 4 = shared arena; ren = renovated
[b] The Atlanta Braves facility was built for the 1996 Olympic Games. The Braves paid $50 million to covert it into a baseball stadium.

for the team. In contrast, the public sector played a major role in other facilities: at least 75 per cent of the construction costs of five other ballparks were funded by the public sector, while nine additional teams play in facilities where the public sector paid between 50 and 74 per cent of the construction costs. While it is possible for baseball stadiums to host other events, teams are quite reluctant to risk damaging the playing surface. As a result, teams are frequently the only source of revenue for a baseball facility.

Football stadiums are also frequently paid for by the public sector. As noted, the Washington Redskins built their new home just north of the District of Columbia. The owner of the Carolina Panthers also assumed responsibility for the costs of their new home while the public sector paid for the land and the necessary infrastructure. In contrast, in five other locations the facilities used by football teams were paid for by the public sector. Nine other football teams play in facilities where the public sector contributed funds to pay for more than half of the cost of construction. The New England Patriots are also paying virtually all of the costs for their new home with the public sector providing funds for the essential infrastructure. The lucrative nature of the Boston/Providence market supported this deal even after the owner sought permission from the NFL to accept a far better proposal from the State of Connecticut and the City of Hartford. The NFL and its television partners did not want the Patriots to abandon the lucrative Boston market and refused to permit the move. The NFL could have permitted the team to move and then placed a new or expansion franchise in the Boston region, but the market for this team was seen as too close to the market area of a Hartford team to support the notion of an expansion.

Financing tools used by the public sector

In most cases where the public sector funded some or most of the construction costs of sports facilities, bonds are issued by the public sector to repay their investment. The real issue for students of public finance, then, is the taxing instrument used to repay the obligations. In some instances revenues from more than one source are used. This section describes who issued the bonds and how bonds were repaid by using examples from the building of ballparks.

In several of the most recent construction projects, the public sector was involved through all three levels of government: city, county and state. These include the Milwaukee Brewers, Philadelphia Phillies, the Pittsburgh Pirates and the new ballpark proposed for the St. Louis Cardinals. In each of these instances, the public sector is paying for more than 50 per cent of the cost of the new facility. For example, in building Miller Park for the Milwaukee Brewers the infrastructure costs ($72 million) were shared by the city, county and state. In addition, Wisconsin issued $160 million in tax-exempt bonds that are paid through a five-county, 0.1 cent sales tax increase. In the case of the Phillies, in November 2000, the Mayor's Office in Philadelphia announced an agreement with both the MLB and the NFL to build two new stadiums at a cost of $1 billion. Under the agreement, the city will issue $304 million in bonds to finance its share; the money will be paid back by new tax revenue created by the stadiums and the new 2 per cent tax on car rental. The State of Pennsylvania will grant $170 million and the teams will provide $482 million.

It is also important to note that for some ballparks built in the 1990s, nonprofit organizations created by the public sector were established to deal with the financing, construction and maintenance of the facilities. For example, in Cleveland, the Gateway Economic Development Corporation was created to build a city sports complex, including a ballpark for the Cleveland Indians and an arena for the Cleveland Cavaliers. The nonprofit organization issued bonds to fund construction and owns the facilities. Another example is the Denver Metropolitan Major League Baseball Stadium District, which owns the Colorado Rockies facility, Coors Field. Covering the six counties surrounding Denver, the district was created by the Colorado legislature; it issued bonds and levied a 0.1 per cent sales tax in the six-county area to fund the ballpark.

Table 9.2 Financing tools used by the public sector to build baseball facilities

	Hotel/ motel taxes	*Sales tax*	*Car rental tax*	*City reserve funds/ general revenues*	*Sales tax on restaurants and bars*	*External facility advertising*	*Facility-generated revenues*	*Sports lottery tickets*	*Sin tax on alcohol and cigarettes*
Major League Baseball									
Anaheim Angels	*			*		*			
Arizona Diamondbacks		*					*		
Atlanta Braves									
Baltimore Orioles								*	
Chicago White Sox	*								
Cincinnati Reds		*							
Cleveland Indians									*
Colorado Rockies		*							
Detroit Tigers	*		*						
Houston Astros	*		*						
Milwaukee Brewers		*							
Philadelphia Phillies			*				*		
Pittsburgh Pirates	*	*							
San Diego Padres	*								
San Francisco Giants									
Seattle Mariners		*	*		*			*	
Texas Rangers		*							
Toronto Blue Jays									

Table 9.2 illustrates the different taxes utilized to repay bonds. The tax instruments most commonly used involve sales (all consumption), hotel and motel use, and car rental use. The public sector used at least one of these taxes to pay back debt for construction of new facilities for 13 of the 18 teams. Both hotel/motel and car rental taxes are used to pay back debt for the facilities of the Detroit Tigers and the Houston Astros. To pay for Comerica Park in Detroit, revenues from casinos operated by Native Americans (a gaming tax) were also utilized. Sales taxes, usually at the county level, are being used to pay for the facilities of seven teams, but in the case of the Ballpark in Arlington the sales tax is in one city. A 'sin tax' helped to pay for Jacobs Field.

Unique financing tools have also been used to supplement the tax revenues pledged to retire bonds. For example, fees from commemorative license plates are being used to build Safeco Field, the home of the Seattle Mariners. These contributions, as well as a 0.017 increment in the state sales tax and proceeds from the sale of sports lottery/gaming bets, are all part of the support provided by State of Washington. It should be noted that unique revenue sources are frequently viewed with caution by the bond market as reliable sources for repayment of obligations. As a result, a more traditional revenue source, such as a sales tax, has to be part of most bond packages. If a more traditional tax is not involved, interest rates will be higher and the market may well 'demand' bond insurance (in case of insufficient revenues to make payments) before the bonds are purchased. Another financial tool is a facility's admission tax or ticket surcharge. This is being used to pay for part of the cost of the facilities for the Seattle Mariners and the Texas Rangers, where a $1 surcharge was imposed to help pay for some of the cost of the Ballpark in Arlington.

Relationship between the share of public funding and selected economic variables

When communities analyze providing different levels of support for a sports facility, it is critical that the impact on the wealth of a team's owner is considered. In terms of establishing the appropriate share for both the public sector and the team, the issue of the possible increase in team owner's wealth may need careful consideration.

The examples presented here are all taken from Major League Baseball, although other sports were examined too. We have examined lagged as well as present and future relationships between the public sector's share of funding new construction and several economic variables relating to the teams and their markets.

Figure 9.2 describes the relationship between the public sector share and team values two years before completion of the new facility. In general, baseball teams with higher team values prior to building a facility received relatively less public support. In other words, teams with smaller values depend on a larger public share to build their ballparks. One team that highlights this relationship is the San Francisco Giants; the team had the third highest team value at $213 million, and the public sector contributed only 5 per cent of total costs. An exception to this negative relationship is the Baltimore

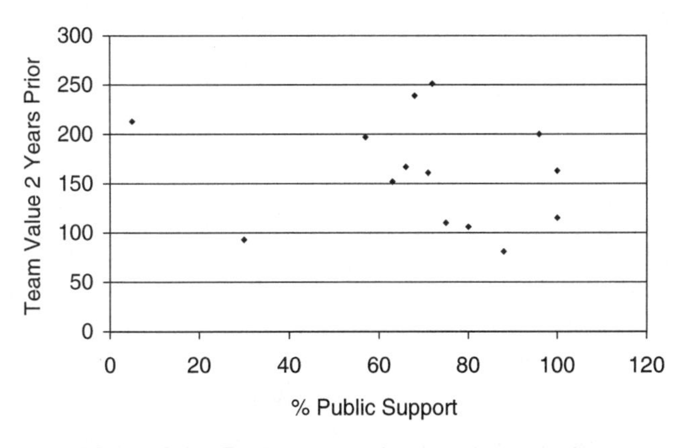

Figure 9.2 Public sector share and team value

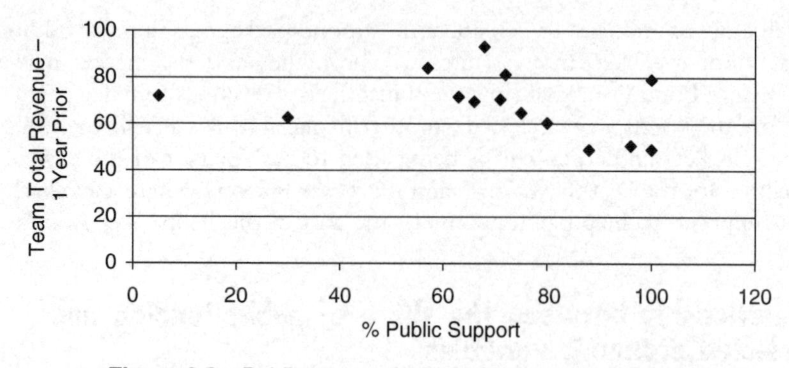

Figure 9.3 Public sector share and team total revenue

Orioles, where the public sector paid for 96 per cent of building Oriole Park at Camden Yards, although the team was valued at a high $200 million two years prior to opening of new facility.

Another interesting relationship is that between the share of the public sector and a team's total revenues one or two years prior to the opening of the new facility. Figure 9.3 shows this relationship for baseball teams. It illustrates that a negative relationship exists between the two variables. The lower the team revenues prior to the new construction, the higher the role the public sector played in financing the new facility. One exception (outlier) to be noted in the figure is the Atlanta Braves, where the team's revenue, $79.1 million, was relatively high, and the public sector paid all its facility cost. However, as noted, Turner Field was built for the 1996 Summer Olympics and was later converted for baseball by the Braves.

In theory, the market size in which a team plays has also an impact on the public sector role. We would expect that teams in the larger markets could pay a larger share of the cost, hence requiring a smaller share of the public sector. Several market size variables were tested, including the percentage of households with high incomes and the number of large firms. Figure 9.4 presents

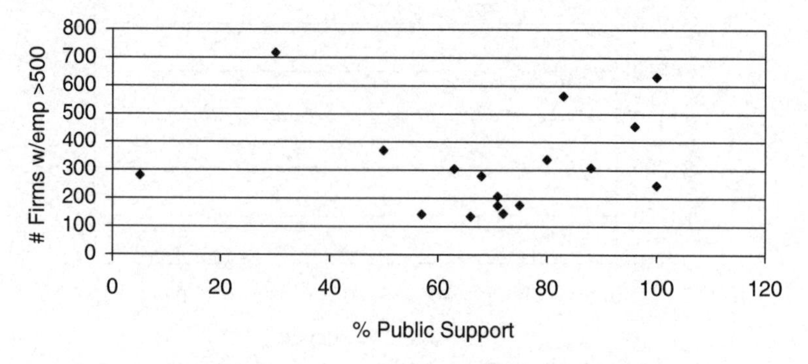

Figure 9.4 Public sector share and size of market

the relationship between the share of the public sector and number of large companies in the market.

The figure points to a negative relationship between the public sector share and the market size, although several exceptions suggest a less apparent relationship. The exceptions include the San Francisco Giants with a relative small market size and small public sector participation. At the other extreme are the Chicago White Sox and the Baltimore Orioles, all with large markets (458–632 companies with more than 500 employees) and a large public sector share (83–100 per cent) of financing for their ballparks. The White Sox, however, are not supported to the same extent as are the Cubs, and their owner threatened to move the team unless a large subsidy was provided.

Conclusions

The public sector's share of the costs for building and maintaining a professional sports facility should be proportionate to the share of benefits classified as positive externalities or public consumption benefits. The return to the team owners in terms of the franchise's increased value should also guide proposals for public/private partnerships, as should the ability of the facility to generate revenue from other entertainment activities.

To repay the bonds used by local governments to pay for a facility there is a pronounced tendency to use sales tax instruments. In some cities, taxes that do not affect local residents have been the favored choice (taxes on hotels, motels and car rentals), while in other areas increments to the general sales tax have been used. Taxes on the sale of alcohol and tobacco products have also been used in some areas to avoid increases in the general sales tax. Politically, gaming revenues are also seen as a desirable source of funding, but in some instances these resources have to be supplemented with other taxes to ensure the existence of a sufficient pool of revenue to repay the public's debt.

Exercises

1. A community is interested in estimating what its investment in a sports facility should be, and you are asked to determine the annual benefit of a team to the residents of a community. Discuss the process you would employ to measure the benefit and how you would translate in your findings in a recommended investment level. Using prevailing interests rates how much money could the community spend that would be justified based on the intangible benefits of a team?
2. Discuss the appropriate rationale for the use of the following financing tools to pay for a sports facility: (1) user fees, (2) a general sales tax, (3) a tax on

tourists, (4) a tax on the incomes earned by players, and (5) a tax on consumption that occurs in or near a sports facility.

3. What is the impact on team revenues from the utilization of each of these financial tools: (1) user fees, (2) a general sales tax, (3) a tax on tourists, (4) a tax on the incomes earned by players, and (5) a tax on consumption that occurs in or near a sports facility.
4. One argument for a public subsidy of a privately owned sports team is that there are intangible benefits to having the team, e.g. the team's success unifies members of the community and gives them pride and gives them something to talk about around the 'water cooler' in their offices. Since the private owners of teams cannot capture this external benefit through ticket prices or broadcast revenues the standard economic theory suggests the amount of the good will be lower than the optimal quantity. If athletic success is the underprovided good, does it make sense for cities to provide subsidies? If so, what form should these subsidies take?
5. What are the equity or redistribution implications of using a general sales tax to finance the construction of a stadium, i.e. who gains and who loses? How do these equity implications change if the tax used to support a stadium is levied on non-residents such as a car rental or hotel tax? How do the equity implications change if the stadium is supported by a ticket tax on events in the stadium?
6. Stadium deals offered to teams vary across cities. The best possible deal from the point of view of the team has the city pay all of the construction and infrastructure costs, and give the team all of the revenues generated by the stadium (concessions, naming rights, signage, parking, revenue from any non-sporting events at the stadium), give the team free police services for within-stadium security, and then charge the team nothing for rent. The worst possible deal from the point of view of the team is that the city pays the team nothing and provides no free services.

   Pick a recent stadium or arena deal and identify how the costs were split on the above items. What factors determined the actual split (e.g. market size, number of corporate headquarters, per capita income, number of other teams in the market)? Is the deal you analyzed atypically favorable to the team or the city?
7. The demand for tickets over a season, holding the quality of the team constant, is $P = 200 - 0.001Q$. The marginal cost of an additional ticket is zero. The fixed costs for the team are \$50 million. Use a diagram to show the effects of a \$5 per ticket tax on the optimal number of tickets. What are the team's profits after the ticket tax is imposed?
8. States that charge an income tax treat visiting athletes salaries as subject to their income tax. If an NBA player is on the roster over the regular 82-game season and he plays one game in a city, 1/82 of his salary is taxed by that city. Just two states that have major league teams have no an income tax, Texas and Tennessee. What are the consequences of this disparity?

10 Nonteam sports and incentives

Chapter goals

There are important differences between team sports and nonteam sports. In team sports the team owner assembles a team of players with complementary skills by offering long-term contracts. Also, a league promotes league-wide **profit maximization**. In individual sports the promoter of an individual event needs to attract individual athletes through prize and/or appearance money. Competition may involve seeding to improve the likelihood of the best players remaining in the competition. The prize money may be spread widely to ensure that a good field is attracted or the promoter may use appearance money to ensure the presence of star players. In product markets for individual sports, such as golf, some interesting economic questions are why membership fees predominate over per-use fees and what determines the structure of **auction** sales of race horses.

In labor markets tournament theory has been applied to explain the distribution of prize money in both US and European professional golf, while in other sports (such as boxing, athletics and motor racing) **principal-agent theory** has been applied to explain the structure of rewards in these sports. Although team sports have received much more attention from economists, non-team sport is a rich field for the application of economic analysis.

Introduction

Most of the economic analysis of sports has focused on team sports because of the requirement for competitive balance, which gives rise to a series of interesting issues such as the invariance principle, **cartel** behavior and the divergence between club and league objectives. In contrast, nonteam sports such as track-and-field events, boxing, golf, horse-racing and tennis have had much less attention. In individual sports competitive balance is important: fans still want to see close matches. However, if one individual dominates the sport one cannot reallocate players, as is possible in team sports, to make contests more even; one simply hopes that a new challenger will emerge. In some cases handicapping systems might help, as in horse-racing where previous winners have to carry heavier weights, or as in amateur golf where less successful players are allowed more shots compared to those who play off scratch. (For an example of handicapping as proposed in Formula One motor racing, see Box 10.1.)

There have been different views as to what are the crucial differences between team and non-team sports. Thus, Szymanski (2001) suggests for some team sports, such as baseball and cricket, the outcome of a match does not depend on teamwork. In these examples the individual marginal productivities are largely independent. In other team sports complementary players create a sum that is greater than the parts. One question in sports in which different

Box 10.1 Sporting dominance in Formula One racing

On October 7, 2002 the London *Times* reported that the dominance of Ferrari, and its leading driver, the German Michael Schumacher, in particular, had forced Formula One's ruling body, led by Bernie Ecclestone, and the president of the Federation, Max Mosley, to seek ways of redressing the imbalance between Ferrari and the also-rans in the World Championship. Schumacher had won 19 out of 33 grand prix over the previous two seasons, a victory rate of one out of every 1.7 races. He was also successful in the following event in Japan establishing a record of 11 victories in a season and finished on the podium (for those in the first three positions) in every race in 2002, including five seconds and one third place.

A consequence of this dominance was a decline in television audiences worldwide. ITV lost five million viewers for the grand prix competitions and, together with the sponsors, demanded to know what action was to be taken to arrest the decline.

Ecclestone's response was to suggest some form of handicapping. For example, adding a kilogram of weight to a car once a driver had passed a set number of points in the season would impose a penalty of around 0.3 seconds per lap, which is enough to make a difference. Technicians have become more significant than drivers as the eleven competing teams have spent increasing sums on research and development, but not all have the same financial resources.

Therefore, a second proposal is to impose a series of cost-cutting measures to reduce costs by up to £300 million per year, with proposed restrictions including less testing time and using one engine for half a season, rather than using three in one race weekend, or requiring that the aerodynamic shape of each car remains the same until mid-season. Ferrari's annual budget exceeds £250 million compared to just £30 million for the smallest team, Minardi. Some of these proposals were eventually implemented.

players have complementary skills is why groups of players with complementary skills do not offer their services jointly to particular clubs? With a group contract for a set of players, individuals in the group would bear some risk that other group members would be injured or free-riding on the group's performance. Instead the team assembles a roster of players with complementary skills and each player is an agent of the team. According to Szymanski the central distinction between team and non-team sports is the unit of competition. In the team case the player is an agent of the team, viewed from a principal-agent framework, while in individual sports the player is more like a contractor hired for one job. The relationship between a tournament organizer and the players is relatively straightforward and short term, whereas in team sports a long-run relationship between player and team is of special significance.

Forms of competition

In nonteam sports one may choose between two main forms of competition: match play or play against the entire field of competitors. In golf, competitions may take either form. In match play players tend to be seeded, as in the major tennis tournaments, which shields star players against early elimination. Scully (1995) suggests this distinction is important. When competing against the whole field of competitors (as in championship golf), the individual's performance variability will determine the variability of an individual's finish in the field (being higher than expected when performance is above average and lower than expected when the individual has a bad day). This is because the distribution of performance across the entire field of competitors will be relatively constant. The chance of a particular player winning the tournament is a different question from the variability of their finish position across tournaments. The chance of winning depends on that player's average performance and their luck in the particular tournament versus the average ability and luck of whichever individual has the best score across the remainder of the field. Although the distribution of performance for the entire field can be considered constant, the performance of the best player among all of the players entered is very much a matter of individual luck. In contrast, in seeded play the variance in finish around a star player's recent average performance is less than in against-the-field play because the star might perform relatively poorly early in the tournament, but still be capable of defeating players with low seeds. There is empirical support for this claim. Leband (1990) finds that the probability of a top ranked player finishing in first place is roughly four times higher in tennis, where seeding is the norm, compared with golf, where competition against the field is the norm. As a result the inequality in income among players is greater in tennis than in golf. A further implication is that if uncertainty of outcome is important to spectators then unseeded play should, other things being equal, attract more spectators than seeded play. If knowing that the star players will be around for the latter matches is important to the advance ticket buyers, seeding will draw more spectators for the entire tournament. There do not appear to have been any attempts to test these propositions.

In order to be attractive to spectators a tournament must have a good field of competitors in terms of the quality of the stars and the depth of the talent going down the ranking. Advertisements for tennis tournaments tend to highlight the names of the stars that have committed to play. The problem for the promoter is that if most of the tournament's award money is given out as appearance money the players have much less incentive to try to win. In 2002 a high-ranked tennis player was accused of not trying to win a match and the promoter refused to pay the appearance money (see, Federer's Dubai Delight, http://news.bbc.co.uk/sport2/hi/tennis/2813357.stm). Appearance money is common at second tier tennis tournaments. The top events do not have to worry about schedule conflicts and the prize money they offer is high enough to draw the stars. Appearance money is also important in golf. It can be higher than the first place prize. For example, Tiger Woods received $2 million for his appearance at the Deutsche Bank Open in Hamburg in 2002 but just $410,000 for winning the tournament. (http://www.msnbc.com/news/755468.asp?cp1=1). The problem of performance incentives when the appearance money exceeds the prize money applies to golf as well. Some top golfers are notorious for banking the money and 'tanking' the rounds. Empirical work on the impact of appearance versus prize money on performance is difficult because the amount of the appearance money is often secret. There was considerable controversy when a woman tennis player revealed that appearance money on the woman's tour was tied to appearance (i.e., which women looked better) rather than to tennis performance (http://slate.msn.com/id/114267/).

The promoter has to decide on: (1) the total amount to spend on players either as appearance money or as prizes; (2) how much to offer as appearance money and to which players; and (3) the gradient in prize money from first to second to third, and so on down to the last place to be given a prize. The appearance money for a star has to generate enough extra ticket revenue to cover the cost. An added complexity is that the drawing powers of the stars are not independent. Two players who have an intense rivalry will draw better than two equally good players who do not. Another complexity is that concentrating the prize money at the top may improve performance and provide closer contests. However, the prize distribution must be sufficiently flat to ensure that the marginal candidate for winning the lowest prize is induced to enter the competition. A winner-take-all competition would draw too few competitors. In sports such as track-and-field (athletics in the UK), golf and tennis the opportunity costs of entry are relatively low. A contestant may have to forgo alternative earnings opportunities and incur travel and accommodation costs. In other sports, however, opportunity costs may be relatively high. Scully cites the case of automobile racing, where it cost almost $10 million in the 1980s to run 'Indy' cars over the seventeen-race CART season. On average it cost about $3 million to run cars over the 24-race NASCAR circuit. For this reason sports promoters must offer greater prizes at the lower end of the field at the expense of prizes for the top finishers if they are to attract an adequate field. Relative to golf and tennis we expect to find a flatter distribution of winnings in automobile racing.

One difference between nonteam and team sports is that in the latter case every player will receive a basic salary, whereas in the former the least successful may earn very little if they consistently fail to finish in a prize position. Appearance money for nonstar players may be insufficient to live on. The concentration of prize and appearance money at the top in individual sports such as boxing or golf allows the stars in individual sports generally to earn more than the stars in team sports. Michael Schumacher, Tiger Woods,

Mike Tyson, Pete Sampras and other stars in these individual sports are certainly among the highest earners in sport. This is not universally the case, however, as (according to the *Forbes* 1997 list of the highest-paid sportsmen) the top earner was a basketball player, Michael Jordan.

Product markets in nonteam sports

Membership fees

The general principles of product market pricing outlined in Chapter 3 apply equally to nonteam sports. However, there are a number of additional factors to consider. Sports clubs, such as golf clubs or leisure centers, have to consider the impact of taking in additional numbers on the utility derived by existing members through congestion costs. This takes us into the area of **theory of clubs**. Buchanan (1965) argued that club members, or rather the committee representing their interests, could determine the optimal size of club by equating the marginal reduction in per capita total costs due to the additional members contributing to the fixed costs of the club (marginal benefits) with the negative effect that these new members have on existing members' levels of congestion (marginal costs).

Most golf clubs charge membership fees on an annual basis, but this does not vary according to the number of rounds played. Green fees are limited to nonmembers who wish to play on the course. It has been argued (Mulligan, 2001) that membership fees are inefficient when usage level is a choice variable for members. Per-use fees would have the advantage of helping to reduce congestion. In the absence of per-use fees members will determine the number of rounds of golf they play by equating the marginal benefit of the last round played with its marginal cost, which may be zero when membership fees are a sunk cost. With per-use fees the value of the marginal utility of the last round played would be equated to the price (cost) of a round of golf. With membership fees only the number of rounds played by each member will exceed the socially optimal amount.

Why, then, do we observe the prevalence of membership-fee-only golf clubs? Two potential explanations have been offered, the first relating to monopoly power and second relating to the presence of transaction costs in monitoring use. In the case of the latter Mulligan doubts whether these are likely to be large. Monitoring use is easy where members have to sign in or see the professional before playing. In a members-only club preventing individuals playing without paying should be relatively straightforward. The monopoly power argument has been put forward by Scotchmer (1985). Let us assume that clubs attempt to maximize their profits and consumers attempt to maximize their utility and that both membership fees and per-use charges apply. Then the utility function for each of N consumers is given by:

$$U(m, x, c) = m + h(x) - f(c)$$

$U =$ utility

where

$m -$ a round of golf

$c =$ total number of golf rounds played on the course (i.e., the level of congestion)

h and f are functions

$x =$ number of rounds per member

Scotchmer also assumes that there are a fixed number of homogeneous clubs, S, such that each club has N/s members, with N representing the total population of golfers. In equilibrium a profit-maximizing club will charge a per-use fee which equals marginal cost and fix a lump-sum membership fee which captures as much as possible of the **consumer surplus**. Scotchmer suggests the lump-sum fee directly measures the club's market power as in a competitive market this would fall to zero.

However, in practise, argues Mulligan, the evidence is at variance with this theory of profit-maximizing pricing. In the USA there are 400 ski resorts and 16,000 golf courses, so that the latter sport should be more competitive; yet per-use fees are more common in ski resorts than membership fees are in golf. According to Mulligan the explanation for this state of affairs lies in the positive **externalities** resulting from limits on the number of golfers through membership fees. This means that one can vet players to ensure that those who have the appropriate code of conduct are allowed to become members, raise the probability of playing on a particular day and give better protection to the course. Golf clubs also serve nonsport functions. The high membership fees serve to keep out the riff-raff and convey prestige. The clubs are also a means of conducting business and catering for social functions, so that membership fees should not be analyzed on purely sporting criteria. Similar issues apply to clubs of the nonsporting variety.

The price of race-horses

Another kind of pricing issue relates to the prices paid for thoroughbred race horses. This has been analyzed by Gamrat and Sauer (2000) in the USA where the principal market for racing talent centers around the yearling auctions, which take place prior to proof of actual ability, so that price is entirely governed by pedigree. This market structure is explained as a means of minimizing **transaction costs**, since acquiring information after performance had been revealed would be costly given that **adverse selection** means that horses available for sale would have a greater probability of physical ailments. This is one of the many applications of Akerlof's theory of the market for lemons.

Data for the period from 1980 to 1993 show that average prize money over a horse's racing career was lower than the price paid for yearlings in each year, not taking into account the costs of maintenance and training or the residual value of the horse after racing. For brood-mares, taking into account these costs and the average prize money, the cumulative rates of return were minus 28.5 per cent for the 1982 auction sales and minus 77.8 per cent for the 1989 auction sales. This negative average rate of return is inconsistent with profit-maximizing behavior and suggests that owners derive utility simply from owning race horses. The evidence is also inconsistent with championship models of sports ownership as the better female race-horses (as measured by their price) yield a higher return to their owners, whereas we would expect their prices to rise to eliminate the higher return, given that the auction market is competitive. An alternative explanation is that horse owners are notorious gamblers: that is, they are risk-seeking. They are willing to take a gamble on owning a horse with a negative expected value for the chance of a big pay off.

Labor markets in non-team sports

Tournament theory and golf

Most sports display elements of the **rank order tournament model** developed by Lazear and Rosen (1981). In this model individual performance is treated as a serially repeated and rewarded event. Among individuals competing in professional sports the distribution of earnings will be determined by the distribution of rewards or prizes for performance, the distribution of talent and work effort (which may be proxied by the number of competitions entered). Given a prize differential for winning each player can be assumed to choose this effort level in order to maximize his expected utility. Thus we can write for performance in a given tournament:

$$Q_{ij} = U_{ij}[(w_{1j} - w_{2j}), A_{io}, A_{ic}] + \delta_j + \varepsilon_{ij}$$

where

Q_{ij} represents individual i's score in the jth tournament
U_{ij} is the utility obtained by player i in tournament j as a function of the prize differential
$w_1 - w_2$ is the prize differential for coming in first instead of second
A_{io} is the player's own ability
A_{ic} represents other competitors' ability
δ_j represents tournament-specific factors, and
ε_{ij} is a random error term

In general expected earnings will be positively related to the difference in talent among competitors and the inequality in relative rewards for finishing in different positions in the rank order. Higher levels of player's i's ability, A_{io}, will improve player i's score. Higher levels of the opponent's ability, A_{ic}, will also improve player i's score because it induces greater effort. Porter and Scully (1996) reason that when there is sufficient randomness in match-to-match performance to permit upsets, the distribution of earnings will be more equal than the distribution of rewards across the order of finishers in tournaments. They provide two illustrations of greater randomness making the earnings distributions more equal. In professional tennis men generally play five sets and the women three. Their argument implies that the distribution of earnings in the men's circuit should be more unequal than that on the women's circuit. Second, in seeded match play, whether in tennis or golf, as we have seen above, where past performance is used to rank competitors there will be a less equal distribution in earnings than where the highest ranked players play the lowest ranked players in the earliest rounds of a tournament. This is because matching the best against the worst players has the effect of increasing the difference in talents and reducing the probability of an upset.

Some of these arguments about the distribution of earnings can be applied to the distribution of earnings across teams. In professional team sports it is common to share revenues between competing teams. The more equal the **gate-sharing** the less the inequality in income. There will be greater inequality in the size distribution of income among clubs in sports such as professional baseball and basketball (where the home team retains all the gate income) than in professional football and hockey where this is shared. Further, where the production performance of an individual is easier to separate from that of team colleagues we would expect greater inequality in earnings (e.g., in baseball relative to other North American team sports). Finally, since labor effort is more variable in individual sports than team sports, because players can vary the number and level of contests entered, in the former case one would predict the distribution of earnings will be wider in individual sports than in team sports. Using Lorenz dominance tests[1] for the entire distribution of earnings in the four major North American team sports, plus men's and women's golf and tennis, Porter and Scully are able to confirm a majority of these predictions.

Tournament theory has been tested in relation to golf in both the USA and Europe. One can view a two-person tournament as a situation in which one contestant competes against the rest of the field. Each individual's score can be assumed to depend on effort or concentration, luck and tournament-specific factors such as the weather. While one might argue that a professional player will always try his best to win, it is likely that fatigue will play a part. A typical golf tournament consists of four rounds of 18 holes each, with half the field cut at the end of the second round. Fatigue may well set in in the last two rounds and more concentration will be required as only the best players are left in contention. Across tournaments the structure of prize money by order of finish is virtually identical in both the USA and Europe, although the level of prize money varies across tournaments. A critical aspect is that the marginal returns from moving up the order of finish are much higher for players close to the leaders after three rounds than for players at the back of the field. As indicated in Figure 10.1, the marginal prize for finishing first rather than second is much greater than, say, finishing twenty-second rather than twenty-third.

Ehrenberg and Bognanno suggest that, given the structure of prizes and variations in the level of prizes across tournaments, there are two tests of the hypothesis that tournament-type prize structures have incentive effects. First, as the structure of prizes is constant across tournaments, the prize differential for winning depends only on the level of the total prize money as this determines the absolute difference in winnings between finishing first rather than second, and so on. Second, one can focus on the last round of a tournament and test whether a player's performance depends on the marginal return to effort. The latter, in turn will depend on the total prize money offered in the tournament, the player's position in the field at the end of the third round and how closely the leaders are bunched after that round. Given the nature of the reward system this is perhaps not a strong test of the model as the outcome may simply imply that higher first prizes increase effort. A stronger test would occur if golf tournaments varied in the share of prize money distributed among the field. Nevertheless it is one of the few direct tests of tournament theory in the literature.

Using data for the 1984 US PGA Tour, Ehrenberg and Bognanno (1990a) find that (as predicted) increasing total prize money leads to a lower stroke average. Increasing total prize money by $100,000 leads to each golfer taking 1.1. fewer strokes during a tournament. In the final round a player whose marginal return to effort was one standard deviation above the mean would take between 1 and 1.7 fewer strokes in this round of the

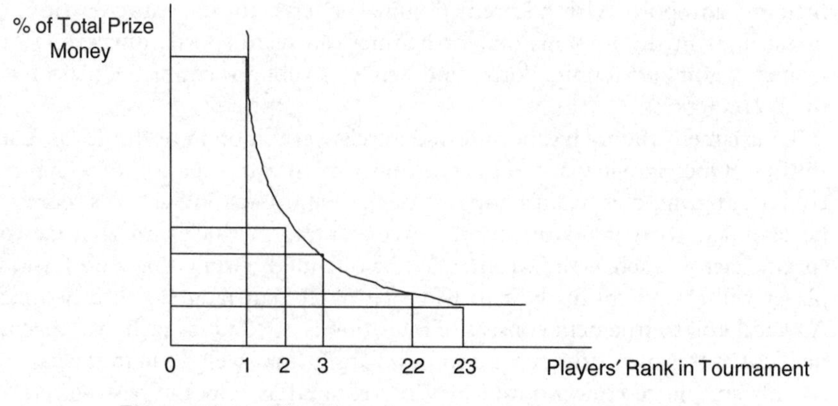

Figure 10.1 Allocation of prize money in the PGA tours

tournament. An identical study (Ehrenberg and Bognanno, 1990b) was carried out for the 1987 European Men's PGA tour and it was found that performances were even more sensitive to prize levels than in the US Tour. Increasing prize money by £60,000 would be associated with a reduction of 3 strokes per golfer over a tournament and the final round effect was between 1.9 and 3 strokes. However, some doubt has been cast on these results by Orzag (1994), who addressed the first only of the above hypotheses for the 1992 US PGA tour and was unable to replicate the findings. He attributes the difference to the impact of the weather variable in the Ehrenberg and Bognanno (1990a) study, which seems to be (unexpectedly) correlated with the total prize money in a tournament. Other possibilities are increased prize money and television exposure between 1984 and 1992, which may have increased stress and led to higher scores; or perhaps the effort/concentration assumption is incorrect in the first place.[2] Therefore, further tests need to be carried out on the application of tournament theory to golf. It is also interesting to speculate if widening the structure of rewards in some tournaments relative to others would have the predicted effect on performance.

Principal-agent theory in boxing and running

It is not only tournament theory that has relevance to incentives in sports labor markets. Another approach is *principal-agent theory* since it may not always be easy for club-owners or managers to detect shirking behavior on the part of players. The principal-agent theory supposes that the objective of the principal is to get the agent to act in his (the principal's) own best interests in a situation in which there is **information asymmetry** and a difference in objectives. Thus the owner or manager of a company wishes to obtain the highest degree of effort from an employee, but does not have full information on whether the worker is exerting maximum effort. The worker has an incentive to withhold information about what level of performance is possible, so that he can operate at a lower level of efficiency without retribution (**shirking behavior**). One example of this approach is provided by horse-racing (see Box 10.2).

Shirking behavior can only be overcome if appropriate incentives are provided, but this is not always the case. This is most clearly seen in boxing, where payment (or the boxer's 'purse') for a given fight is entirely guaranteed. This amounts to full insurance in any given fight against poor performance. According to economic theory this will give rise to a **moral hazard** problem because the agent (boxer) has no incentive to exert himself fully with regard to preparation for the contest. Tenario (2000), one of the few economists to analyze boxing, reports one prime example of such behavior:

> On October 25, 1990, James 'Buster' Douglas was scheduled to defend his heavyweight boxing title against Evander 'Real Deal' Holyfield. Douglas, who was

Box 10.2 Pay and performance in horse-racing

Horse-racing is a sport which is closely associated with the betting industry. This gives ample scope for moral hazard in relation to jockeys. The principal (the owner) cannot easily gauge the effort, quality and commitment of the agent (the jockey). A jockey could, for instance, claim that the going did not suit the horse or the distance. He might do this simply to cover for a poor performance or because he has accepted a side payment from a bookmaker, or to obtain better odds the next time the horse raced, though betting by jockeys is forbidden by the rules. The British horse-racing industry has developed an array of measures (monitoring) to combat the moral hazard problem. The regulating body, the Jockey Club, monitors performance and may fine jockeys for inappropriate behavior. More importantly perhaps, the official payment system for jockeys is a classic example of using contingent pay to deal with the moral hazard problem. Pay is directly related to prize money as well as a fixed-fee for each ride, the fractions of prize money and the riding fee being constant across jockeys. Thus a winning jockey receives some 7 per cent of the total prize for any race.

A study by Fernie and Metcalf (1999) has attempted to ascertain how far the payment system has been able to align the interests of principals and agents in the industry. They were able to compare the performance of an unbalanced panel of jockeys subject to the above payment scheme over the period 1988–1995 ($n = 413$), as well as a balanced panel of jockeys in the sample throughout the eight years ($n = 184$) with a sample of jockeys who received non-contingent retainers over the period 1983–1995 ($n = 37$).

When they regress current racing research performance, which is based on an exhaustive examination of each horse's performance when ridden by different jockeys throughout a season, and earnings they find that a jockey who performs 10 per cent better than another will receive £5,700 more in payment. There are, therefore, appropriate incentives. When they compare the performance of jockeys subject to noncontingent retainers for part of the period with their performance under the contingent pay system, they find that performance is unambiguously worse when retained than when not retained. They conclude: 'All in all our data strongly suggest that these large non-contingent retainer payments re-introduced moral hazard into a payment system which had previously proved to be very successful at overcoming such behavior.'

guaranteed more than $20 million for the match, showed up visibly out of shape and delivered a lack-luster performance, while being knocked out in three rounds. He did not fight again for six years. Many boxing fans felt ripped off by Douglas' performance. From the fans' perspective, the contract Douglas was given did not elicit appropriate work incentives.

Tenario analyses a large sample of boxing champions across the various weights from the start of the implementation of Queensberry rules under which the modern sport operated up to 1994. On average championship purses are larger for heavier weight classes and given that high wealth deters effort this leads to the prediction that lighter weight champions will exert more effort than heavier weight champions. It is observed that heavier weight champions wait longer before defending their title than their lighter brethren and also, in line with the theory, make fewer successful defenses per year. An alternative explanation is that heavier weight boxers cause each other more than proportionate damage compared to lighter weight boxers and thus require more time to recover.

Incentive effects may operate in two ways. First, they may induce higher quality performers to enter the competition and, second, they may induce greater effort from each entrant. Let us suppose we have three athletes, A_1, A_2 and A_3, of varying abilities with A_1 representing the highest and A_3 the lowest ability, and three athletics races offering varying prizes, D_1, D_2 and D_3, with D_1 representing the highest prize and D_3 the lowest. Further, we suppose willingness to enter a race is a function of the minimum expected prize. Then the supply curve will have two components: the response of athletes in deciding whether or not to compete and the response of entrants to higher prizes in terms of effort expended. This is illustrated in Figure 10.2. The runner with the highest opportunity cost, A_1, requires the highest entry prize level, D_1, to induce him to enter. It is assumed that (barring accidents) if he enters he is likely to win. He will not enter races with lower prizes and some other runner will then win.

Maloney and McCormick (2000) have attempted to test the effect of such incentives on athletes using a sample of over 1,400 individual runners in 115 open invitational road races in the Southeastern USA over the period 1987–91. It is assumed that average prizes, which varied between $10 and $8,000, capture the market response in terms of the quality of athletes

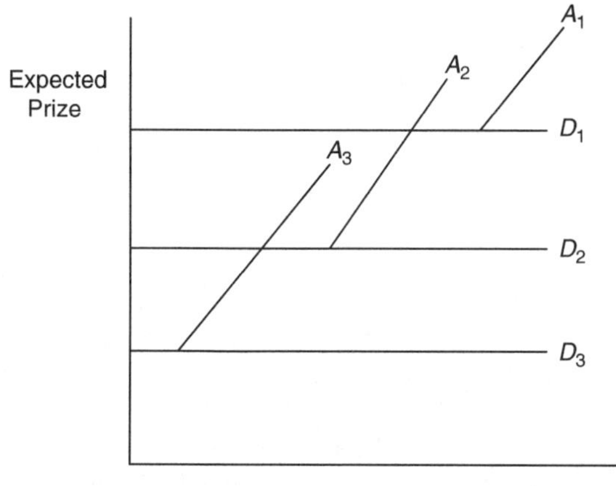

Figure 10.2 The response of runners with different abilities to differential prizes

entering each competition and that the prize spread captures the amount of effort expended. They find that if the average prize doubles, average finishing times fall by 2 per cent, which they attribute to the participation effect, while if the prize spread doubles average finishing times fall by 4 per cent, which they attribute to increased effort. Male athletes appear to respond more strongly to such incentives than female athletes. This greater prize–greater effort result has been confirmed by Lynch and Zax (2000). They used data provided by the USA Track and Field Running Information Center for road races in both the USA and abroad. Holding distances constant, the effects are substantial. A $100 increase in the prize spread decreases finishing times by 50 seconds (3 per cent of the average) in 8 kilometer races. However, when they control for runner ability using a fixed effects approach, the prize money variables tend to lose significance. This they attribute to the **sorting hypothesis**: better athletes are attracted to races offering better prizes.

Where costs of entering competitions are considerable other factors may impinge on the reward system. This is most clearly seen in relation to motor racing. In this case variations in driver ability are likely to be less important than in road racing, for example, because of the importance of contributions from other factors of production such as car capability and that of mechanics. In the USA professional stock car racing (NASCAR) has grown considerably in popularity both in terms of attendance and television ratings. Cars are required to meet shape requirements based on 18 different templates in an attempt to ensure that aerodynamically no one car has any advantage over another. The NASCAR season consists of 34 races. Drivers have to qualify for these through a series of time trials as the number of cars starting a race is limited to 43. Cash prizes are awarded to drivers in each race based on order of finish, but there are also season championship points and a pay-out from a season-end points distribution. Von Allmen (2001) points out that in many races some drivers may earn more than those finishing in front of them. This arises from the award of bonuses from sponsors which are based on factors such as leading in the most laps in a race, winning the first ('pole') starting position or moving up the most positions during a race. In addition there are two bonuses open only to a limited number of drivers. The Winston Cup leader bonus is awarded to the current points leader, provided he wins the race; and the Winston 'No Bull 5 Program', covers five major races over the season in which the top five finishers win a $1million bonus. Some drivers are paid fixed salaries and do not receive any share of race winnings, while others receive up to 50 per cent of winnings, with the remainder going to the team. These arrangements are not consistent with the tenets of tournament theory and seem to be inefficient given that the marginal cost of effort is increasing and the marginal return associated with a higher finish is rather low. Von Allmen suggests that tournament theory would not operate successfully in this sport for a number of reasons. First, the need for sponsorship income requires incentives for consistency above winning. Second, motor racing may be too dangerous for a winner-takes-all type of incentive system. Third, motor racing is very expensive with the marginal cost of reducing lap times being strongly upward sloping. This implies that nonlinear rewards may reduce competitive balance.

Conclusions

Nonteam sports cover a disparate array of activities and this can explain the rather different incentives that apply in each case. In sports such as motor racing or boxing the danger of serious injury or even death is ever present, so that one does not want to utilize incentives that may encourage participants to take excessive risks. Tournament theory has more relevance for sports such as golf and tennis. Nonteam sports also have to ensure that individual tournaments are sufficiently attractive to persuade star performers to participate. In team sports this aspect does not arise as individual players do not choose how many games they will take part in, though coaches may decide to rest particular players from time to time.

Notes

1. A Lorenz curve relates the cumulative proportion of earnings recipients ordered from the poorest to the richest to the cumulative proportion of total earnings received by the population. One curve dominates another if it at no point intersects the other. Scully (2002) shows that in PGA golf the frequency distribution of golfers scoring averages is normally distributed, while the prize structure is highly skewed with a Gini coefficient, measuring the area between the diagonal and the Lorenz curve, of 0.566. It follows that payment in this case is not based on the value of the marginal product.
2. He quotes Fred Couples as stating 'You try real hard and you can't make anything, and you don't try at all, and everything goes in the hole – go figure!' Many amateur golfers will concur.

Exercises

1. What are the distinguishing features of team sports and nonteam sports?
2. What determines the optimal size of a golf club in terms of the number of members?
3. What is the rank order tournament model? How might it affect athletic performance?
4. Why might it be more appropriate to seed particular players in particular tournaments rather than allow them to compete against the whole field?

5. In nonteam sports is it more important to offer incentives to participate or incentives to participate more keenly in the competition itself?
6. 'In sports where there is danger to life and limb incentives should be limited.' Discuss.
7. In team sports a player's *marginal revenue product* (MRP) depends on his or her athletic ability, which affects the team's win percentage which in turn affects the team's ticket revenue. How can the MRP of a player in an individual sport be determined? Does a player who collected no prize money in a year have a zero MRP?
8. Most individual sports sell tickets. In some individual sports, such as marathon races, the prize money and appearance money comes from corporate sponsors because it is impractical to sell tickets to an event held on a 26-mile road course. How does this different source of funds change the incentive structure?
9. Some individual sports events are sponsored by nonprofit organizations, such as the US Masters Golf Tournament in Augusta, Georgia. There is no question here of profit maximization versus utility maximization because the nonprofit organization is not allowed to retain any profits. However, utility maximization in this context does not mean maximizing wins because there is always one winner who is independent of the sponsoring organization. How does the non-profit structure change, if at all, the incentives of paying prize and appearance money?
10. The world's record holder for a footrace of a certain distance has a best time of 230 seconds. A race is held with the record holder and seven competitors. The competitors have identical and independent normal distributions of running times with an average of 240 seconds and a standard deviation of 5 seconds. If the record holder is able to match his best time, what is the probability that he will not come in first?

11 College sports in the USA and the role of the NCAA

Chapter goals

On any financial measure college sports programs in the USA dwarf college sports programs in all other countries combined. Even if the figures for the developmental professional sports programs in other countries for the 18–22-year-old age group were added to the non-US collegiate sports total, the USA figures would still dwarf those in other countries. In overall attendance and ticket revenues college sports in the USA is close to any of the four major US professional leagues. Because there is little media coverage of US college sports in other countries most people outside of the USA do not realize its scale. Conversely, most Americans have no idea that there is nothing like it any- where else.

Why is the USA so different? This chapter proposes two hypotheses: that the autonomy of local schools districts and colleges in the US facilitated the big-budget sports programs and the second is that youth sports programs are sensitive to *per capita* income. The second broad question this chapter discusses is what are the main objectives of the major governing body of the collegiate sports in the USA, the NCAA. That organization claims that its objectives are to promote fair competition, high academic standards for students and the ideals of amateurism. Economists generally describe it as a **cartel** whose main objective is to make money. Is it possible for both views to be accurate?

The next topic is one on which economists have split. Do colleges with big time sports programs make or lose money on their athletic programs? The accounting procedures for nonprofit enterprises in the US are sufficiently arbitrary that a school that was making a substantial profit on its sports program could organize its books so that they would be covered in red ink. We will try to figure out what is really happening. The last topic is competitive balance in collegiate sports. The main issue here is again the NCAA. Does it foster competitive balance or favor the entrenched high-profile programs?

Why are intercollegiate sports so big?

The scale of intercollegiate sports

How big is intercollegiate sport in the USA? In the 1998–9 academic year there were 360,000 athletes in the sports in which the NCAA recognizes and sponsors a championship (see http://www.ncaa.org/participation_rates/1998-99_m_partrates.pdf and http://www.ncaa.org/participation_rates/1998-99_w_partrates.pdf). Schools affiliated to a competing college sports sanctioning body, the National Association of Intercollegiate Athletics (NAIA), had approximately 50,000 athletes in 1998–9. The NAIA sanctions programs in about 350 small colleges. Between them the NCAA and the NAIA athletes represent 3 per cent of the undergraduate enrollment in the USA in baccalaureate degree-granting institutions. Of the 360,000 athletes in the NCAA 146,064 were in the Division I programs.

Two sports, men's basketball and football, are commonly termed the 'revenue sports'. Three hundred and eighteen schools have Division I programs in basketball and 236 schools have Division I programs in football. Division I football is further subdivided into a Division IA and IAA. There are 114 programs at the more competitive IA level. The two revenue sports usually generate more gate and broadcast revenue than the costs that universities assign to those sports. Note, however, that the 'assigned costs' may have little to do with the actual costs. A few other college sports at the Division I level, such as men's ice hockey and men's baseball, can often break even according to a university's accounting scheme. At each school the surpluses from the revenue sports are used to cover deficits in the nonrevenue sports, such as golf and water polo. A nonrevenue sport is any sport that consistently loses money. Again, to 'lose money' here means showing a deficit under a university's fairly arbitrary assignment of costs and revenues. The number of athletes in the two Division I revenue sports is 28,742. These net-revenue-generating athletes ostensibly 'pay the freight': that is, they carry most of the book costs of the other NCAA 331,000 athletes as well as the coaches, trainers and support staff for the nonrevenue sports.

Another way to quantify the size of intercollegiate sports is to look at the attendance figures. A comparison that might be striking for UK readers is that the attendance at college football games is greater than all the professional soccer attendance in England. In 1999, US college football attendance was 39.5 million (see http://www.ncaafootball.net/News+Release/Football/1998/01/14/). The teams with the highest average home game attendance figures, Tennessee and Michigan, had 106,500 people per game. Added across its four divisions (premier, first, second, and third), English professional soccer had almost the same attendance (38 million). The other revenue sport, men's basketball, had an attendance of 24 million in 1999 (see http://www.ncaa.org/stats/m_basketball/2000_basketball_attend.pdf).

Table 11.1 compares attendance for the two revenue sports at the top level of intercollegiate sports, Division I, to attendance in the top levels of the US professional sports, the four major leagues. The figures were all taken from public sources on the web.

An overall revenue comparison among the NCAA Division I revenue sports and the major league professional sports is more difficult than a comparison of attendance figures and ticket revenue. More than 95 per cent of Division IA programs require a 'donation' to the foundation supporting its athletics programs either as a condition for being allowed to buy a season ticket or (for the slightly less popular programs) a season ticket in a desirable location (Shulman and Bowen, 2001). The real ticket revenue for a college is the sum of the donation and the price of the season ticket.

There are many advantages to breaking a season ticket price into two parts, an explicit charge for the ticket and a 'donation'. First, since college sports teams are part of a not-for-profit educational institution, under the US tax code the donations are treated the same as donations to a charity: that is,

Table 11.1 1999 attendance and average ticket prices

Sport	*Total attendance*[a]	*Average ticket prices*[b]	*Total ticket revenue*[c]
MLB	45	14.91	671
NCAA Division I Football and Men's Basketball	59	12.83	757
NBA	20	48.37	967
NFL	16	45.63	730
NHL	16	45.70	731

[a] in millions.
[b] in dollars.
[c] in millions of dollars.

they are made with before-tax dollars. This tax deductibility makes potential ticket buyers, especially the ones facing the highest marginal tax rate, more willing to donate. Second, the donations help colleges price discriminate. They can set up levels of donations with fancy titles such as the 'Founders Circle' or the 'Varsity Club' with a ladder of privileges for the higher donation levels. The same sort of perks used by the professional teams, such as exclusive lounges, receptions with the coaches, and first call on an large number of post-season tickets, are offered as an inducement for higher levels of donations. Although this pricing scheme is technically not price discrimination, which requires selling exactly the same good at different prices, it has the same effect as price discrimination. The perks cost very little but they neatly separate those with the highest reservation prices from their money as well as physically separating them from the less well-heeled fans. Lastly, the foundations have much more latitude about how they can spend money and what records they have to make public than the regular athletics departments that run the programs. Public access laws in the US open the books of all publicly funded US colleges but their affiliated foundations are more or less free of any scrutiny.

In addition to participation and ticket revenues, a third way to measure how big intercollegiate sports are is with broadcast revenues. The NCAA controls the revenue from the end-of-season basketball tournament but broadcast revenues from football games are negotiated by individual schools or groups of schools organized into athletic conferences. The broadcasts rights to the Men's NCAA Basketball Tournament have increased dramatically. They were sold for $143 million per year from 1991 to 1998, $243 million per year for 1995 to 2002 (the years overlap because of a contract extension), and $546 million per year for 2003 to 2014. For comparison purposes, the worldwide broadcast rights for the 2002 and 2006 soccer World Cup tournaments, the sporting event with the largest viewing audience, sold for £1.1 billion (about $1.7 billion for both years or $825 million dollars per year). It appears that the US broadcast rights to just the annual NCAA basketball tournament are worth almost as much worldwide broadcast rights to the World Cup.

At this point it is clear that intercollegiate sports programs are 'big' in ticket revenue, participation and broadcast revenue. Why is the USA different?

The effects of local fiscal control and higher per capita incomes

Before discussing the differences between US colleges and those in other countries it is worth taking a step back and considering the differences between high schools in the USA and other nations. Educational spending in the USA is largely left to the decisions of local or State governments and nonprofit institutions. Varsity sports at the high school level in the USA had 6,657,257 participants in the 2000–1 academic year (see http://www.nfshsa.org/press/participation%20survey01.htm). This figure double-counts athletes who participate in more than one sport. The total number of high school students in the same year was 14.8 million. A rough guess (provided by an official at the National Federation of State High School Associations) is that 20 per cent of the participants are involved in more than one sport. Using that figure for double counting would put the fraction of high school students who participate in varsity sports at around one-third of all high school students. These high school athletes are the 'feed stock' for the intercollegiate athletics programs. In every other country local high school officials do not have the autonomy to build giant football stadiums and basketball arenas. National ministries of education determine local spending priorities. In contrast, in the USA there is tremendous autonomy in all aspects of education. They are just beginning to bring in national standards for the curriculum and these are voluntary. In other countries national education ministries would be appalled if tax dollars for education were diverted to sports programs for a tiny fraction of the students. They would be even more appalled at the common practice in the USA of hiring high school social studies teachers primarily, if not entirely, for their coaching ability. National ministries of education might care about the physical fitness of the general student body, an issue historically connected with the availability of young men healthy enough to serve in the armed forces. They might be interested in prestige garnered by a program of elite athletes (an example would be Communist East Germany's program for training Olympic athletes); but US high school programs are aimed at neither military preparedness nor Olympic glory. In the USA the physical fitness of nonathletes is a low priority. (See the President's Council on Physical Fitness website for a lament on the decline of required courses in physical education.) What the US high schools offer is the opportunity to participate in the training, camaraderie and competition of organized sports for any student with a modicum of athletic skill, or roughly the top one-third of the athletic talent distribution.

The USA's autonomy goes back to the States providing free public elementary education in the mid nineteenth century and free high school education in the early twentieth century. In turn the States let local communities set and raise their own taxes (usually property taxes) to finance the local schools. State-level interventions to equalize per pupil funding across local districts are also a recent phenomenon. Local autonomy is a necessary condition for the emphasis on varsity athletics in US high schools but not the full explanation. Clearly, the parents who are paying the local real estate taxes and who serve on local school boards have the autonomy to choose to offer varsity sports programs. Why do they do it? An answer is that when these programs were first set up, generally after World War I, the USA was much richer than every other country. US high schools could afford to cater to varied student interests from athletics to college preparation to industrial/ mechanical training. During the same interwar period high schools in Europe were charging tuition and limiting their curriculum to college preparation. Even when European high schools first gave tuition free, generally after the World War II, entrance was by examination and the curriculum remained college preparatory. The exams were set to let in the top 10 or 20 per cent of the academic ability distribution. The claim here is not that US parents are more interested in sports or that they are more interested in seeing their children compete in sports; it is that they could both better afford to pay for it and had the freedom to set up elaborate high school sports programs.

The autonomy of colleges in the USA is even greater than the autonomy of high schools. Other than some constraints tied to Federal funds, such as having to provide equal educational opportunities for women under **Title IX**, private colleges are completely autonomous. The public universities depend on State legislatures for basic funding and their boards often have members appointed by the State's Governor, so there is some public control. However, intercollegiate sports programs are not a burning issue at the State level. Governors like to be seen at the traditional big rivalry football games. When it is an intra-state rivalry they make an elaborate point of demonstrating their neutrality by walking across the field at half time so that they can sit with both sets of fans. That governors attend these games is scarcely an endorsement of college football because they are wont to show up at any event that draws 100,000 possible voters. Occasionally a college is embarrassed by a scandal such as its football players getting organized help from the athletics department to plagiarize term papers. The coach in the affected sport resigns and maybe the athletics director, but university presidents seem to be immune to any scandal in their athletics department.[1] The continuing immunity of public college presidents from any public ire over these scandals is a strong indicator that taxpayers and State legislatures do not think that the scandals are important. In academic terms the scandals call into question the integrity of college's teaching and grading. The graduation rates for minority basketball players in men's Division I programs also calls into question the academic integrity of the colleges that allow sham courses and retain athletes who are not progressing toward a degree. The combination of autonomy and public indifference lets colleges collectively run whatever athletics programs they want.

Is the NCAA a cartel?

What is a cartel?

A cartel is an agreement among independent firms not to compete in either the product or factor market. The most famous cartel is OPEC, the Organization of Petroleum-Exporting Countries. OPEC controls the price of crude oil by setting output quotas for its members. A factor market cartel would be an agreement by independent firms not to offer more than an agreed price for labor or a raw material. Cartels are illegal in the USA and in the EU. An example of a recent illegal product market cartel is the agreement between Hoffman-LaRoche and BASF (along with 11 other pharmaceutical companies) to raise the prices of vitamins. A recent factor market example is Sotheby's and Christie's price-fixing agreement reducing how much they would pay sellers of the lots offered for **auction** by raising their commission shares. These firms were fined when their schemes were discovered. OPEC is not subject to fines or criminal sanctions for price fixing because it is outside the jurisdiction of the USA and EU.

Does the NCAA qualify as a cartel?

Colleges in the USA are all not-for-profit firms. In one price-fixing scheme a college took the position that since the price fixing was intended to be for the **public good** and to further the college's educational mission, and because it was not a profit-making firm, it should be exempt from the US **antitrust** laws. The 'price fixing' was an agreement by Ivy League colleges and the Massachusetts Institute of Technology (MIT) not to compete in terms of the scholarships they offered to students. Every student accepted by more than one of these colleges got an identical scholarship offer because the admissions officers had previously met in private and agreed upon a common offer. When the conspiracy was discovered the Ivy League colleges agreed to stop. They knew they were in a weak legal position because they also colluded on faculty salaries and agreed not to hire away each other's star professors. MIT had only participated in the price fixing on scholarships (see *U.S.* v. *Brown University et al.*). All of the colleges except MIT settled out of court. MIT contested the charges, lost, had the case sent back on appeal and then settled. The courts did not accept MIT's defense. Price fixing was illegal per se.

The relevance of the MIT case to the intercollegiate sports is that colleges cannot claim that agreements not to compete in financial offers are legal because the colleges are not-for-profit firms.

The NCAA has lost several cases for price fixing. One involved trying to hold down the wages of assistant coaches. Both the trial and appellate courts ruled that the NCAA owed 1900 coaches back wages and treble damages totaling $67 million (see http://sports.findlaw.com/sports_law/makethecall/summer98/law/). The NCAA settled out of court for $54.5 million (see http://sportsillustrated.cnn.com/basketball/college/news/1999/03/09/ncaa_settlement/). The other big case that went against the NCAA was over its restrictions on how often a college could have its football games on television over a season. This is a product rather than factor market cartel. Restricting the number of games raised the prices that the television networks would pay for a game. Two colleges sued the NCAA and the restrictions were declared a violation of the antitrust laws. That is why individual schools and conferences now control the broadcasts of their football games. The NCAA controls the broadcast rights to the basketball tournament because it set up the tournament. This example was discussed in Chapter 6.

The most important way that the NCAA restricts factor market competition is its rules against paying athletes anything beyond tuition, room and board. Athletes who leave college early for professional sports are paid millions of dollars. The same athlete was getting the equivalent of $30,000 worth of tuition, room and board when he played for a college. Since the drawing power of top college teams is not very different from the drawing power of professional sports teams, the NCAA is clearly able to hold down the pay of these athletes (Brown, 1993). So far the courts have treated the restrictions on payments to athletes as part of the NCAA effort to set sporting rules (e.g., how many players can be on the field and how long teams can practise). Obviously, some entity has to set up the rules for the games. The restrictions on hours of practise are meant to benefit the athletes so that they have time to study. Under the hours restrictions, if an individual athlete wanted to spend more time training he or she could. The restriction just prevents a coach from requiring more hours. In contrast, the rules against paying athletes are not necessary to organize the games and are not in the interest of all athletes, and certainly are not in the interest of the star athletes. It seems likely that an athlete who sues the NCAA over its restrictions on payments will win in court. In the meantime the NCAA is considering payment schemes, such as small fixed stipends so that the athletes can have some pocket money, or allowing athletes to do commercials and save the money until they graduate. The NCAA recently allowed athletes to hold part time jobs during the academic year.

Holding down expenses by capping assistant coaches' salaries or restricting output by limiting the number of games on television is clearly cartel behavior. Some of the NCAA's other restrictions have more than one interpretation. Rules on the minimum number of sports and the minimum number of scholarships raise the costs of participating at a given level. These rules vary across NCAA divisions with the most competitive divisions, IA and IAA and IAAA, having the highest requirements. Fleisher, Goff and Tollison (1992) see these rules as cartel enforced entry barriers. Why else would the cartel impose these costs on its members when some schools would be content to just field men's football and basketball teams and the minimum number of women's teams to satisfy Department of Education's interpretation of Title IX? We will argue below that the sports programs, including the nonrevenue sports, draw more students and higher-quality students. An individual college might have a private interest in fielding 20 teams and offering grants-in-aid to 400 or even 500 athletes. That incentive depends on what student drawing power the college would have without its big time athletics program. Harvard and the Ivy League schools in general have enough drawing power that a big time sports program would be superfluous. While more is always better, there is little pay off to a college going from 10 applicants for every slot in its freshman class to 20 applicants for every slot, especially if the quality of the applicant pool is so high that every slot could be filled with high school valedictorians. The problem with colleges that have less drawing power is that they cannot field teams in nonrevenue sports unless they have opponents in those sports. The NCAA's minimum number of sports requirements takes care of that problem.

How can the 'entry barrier' versus the 'guaranteeing competitors' explanations of the NCAA's minimum number of sports teams requirements be distinguished? One possibility is to consider how effective as a barrier the requirements have been. Later in this chapter there is a table showing the recent flows into higher levels of sports program affiliation. This flow might better be described as a mad dash to Division I than a cartel determined to limit the spoils to its current members.

There is no doubt that the NCAA pursues cartel goals. After opposing Title IX and losing that battle, the NCAA simply smashed the rival Association of Intercollegiate Athletics for Women (AIAW) that had 800 member colleges. The NCAA instituted competing national championships in women's sports, offered free trips to its championship games, waived membership fees to any college that was already an NCAA member, and scheduled its championship at exactly the same time as the AIAW. Similarly, the NCAA went after the National Invitational Tournament (NIT) in men's basketball by expanding the NCAA Basketball Tournament field and forbidding participation by teams playing in the NIT tournament. In terms of attendance the NIT went from being the premier post-season basketball tournament to living off the leavings from the 64-team NCAA Championship field. In 2002, the NIT suffered the indignity of having a team left out of the NCAA tournament refuse its invitation. In 2001 the NIT sued the NCAA under the antitrust laws. The case is still pending. The attorney representing the NIT, Jeffrey Kessler, claimed: 'Now that the NCAA is in effect declaring war on the NIT and is going to drive it all out of existence, there's no longer any need to pull their punches.' (see http://www.sportslawnews.com/archive/Articles%202001/NITNCAAsuit.htm).

Yet another predatory action by the NCAA is to supplant its long time rival for organizing intercollegiate athletics among small colleges, the NAIA. The movement of colleges out of the NAIA into NCAA Division II and Division III (along with movements up the affiliation ladder among existing NCAA schools) has been so rapid that the NCAA declared a two-year moratorium on membership changes in 2001. It claimed that the number of new programs was overwhelming its staff. During the moratorium it tweaked its membership requirements, raising the minimum number of sports sponsored for a Division II program from eight to ten.

The NCAA requirements both hold down costs, primarily by limiting payments to star athletes, and force a series of cross-subsidies. Within each college the NCAA forces the revenue sports to subsidize the nonrevenue sports. Across its Divisions the high profile, high revenue Divisions subsidize the lower Divisions by paying for the post-season tournaments and insurance costs. Thus, the NCAA appears to be a mix of a traditional cartel while at the same time fostering some noncartel goals (e.g., more athletic competition in the lower Divisions and the name recognition and recruiting goals of its member colleges). As a complex organization representing schools with diverse interests, it should not be surprising that the NCAA's actions fit more than one description.

In the field of industrial organization there is a concept called the *capture hypothesis*. The idea is that an industry that is regulated by a government agency will try to control that agency by getting members of the industry appointed to the regulatory board. The NCAA can be viewed as a regulatory agency that tries to enforce standards such as the athletes being real students who attend classes and make progress toward graduation. The capture hypothesis can be applied to this description of the NCAA. The industry group that has supposedly captured the NCAA is the head coaches of the revenue sports, the athletic directors and the senior staff of the NCAA. In this description the NCAA operates so that any surplus revenues college sports programs generate are paid to these coaches, athletics directors and the staff.

This description should not be dismissed out-of-hand. The head of the NCAA is the highest paid administrator of any nonprofit organization in the USA. The NCAA staff of 330 is tiny compared to other nonprofit organizations such as the Red Cross and the US Postal Service. The NCAA also gave its senior staff large zero-interest loans. The salaries of coaches are complicated. In addition to their university pay they earn money by hosting television shows that review recent games and discuss the prospects for upcoming games, and by running summer camps (usually on campus facilities) for high school or middle school athletes, and from athletic apparel companies. These additional sources of income are largely outside the control of universities. Total earnings in excess of a million dollars a year are not uncommon. It is reasonable to assume that the coaches are concerned about the value of the total package of payments rather than the component parts. Further, the outside sources of income would vanish if the coach lost his or her university coaching position. A college that knew that its football or men's basketball coach could earn $500,000 in outside income presumably could hire a coach for a token $1 a year. The capture hypothesis ascribes the high university salaries, say another $500,000 a year, to the structure of the NCAA. The strictures on paying athletes and the limitations on recruiting expenses creates more of a surplus to pay these coaches, and the NCAA's payment system (which heavily rewards Bowl games and NCAA basketball appearances) raises the marginal revenue product of successful coaches. The athletic directors tend to be former coaches and their salaries are tied to overall level of coaches' salaries.

The problem with the capture hypothesis is that all the money going to the NCAA's senior staff and the highly successful coaches and to the athletic directors of the biggest programs, while in some eyes appearing to be overly generous or even obscene, is nevertheless a small share of the pot. With more than 1,000 member colleges no one college has much of an incentive to move to limit head coaches' salaries or senior NCAA staff salaries. Moreover, in trying to limit head coaches' salaries the NCAA would run foul of the antitrust laws. It seems more plausible to describe the NCAA as largely serving the interests of its members. There is so much money sloshing around that a little money slips through the cracks.

Do colleges make or lose money on their sports programs?

Framing the debate

James L. Shulman and William G. Bowen (2001) are the latest economists to conclude that almost all colleges lose money on sports programs. Because they have proprietary data no one else has gathered and because they consider every financial aspect of college athletics, their work merits careful discussion. Although Murray Sperber is not an economist, he is the most prominent writer on the impact of college sports programs on universities. In four books that assess different aspects of the college sports he has argued that almost all programs lose money. Some other economists on the 'lose money' side of the issue are Roger Noll (1999) and Andrew Zimbalist (1999). The 'make money' side includes Arthur Fleischer, Brian Goff and Robert Tollison (1992) and Melvin Boreland, Brian Goff and Robert Pulsinelli (1992). There is clearly controversy over what is essentially an accounting issue. To give the reader fair warning of where we are going, the authors of this textbook are also on the 'make money' side of the debate.

That making or losing money on sports is a matter of any concern begins with a premise about what colleges ought to be doing. Almost all colleges lose money by accepting students and teaching classes. Even the highest private school undergraduate tuition rates are not high enough to cover the costs of faculty, staff and facilities. The most expensive undergraduate majors in colleges include the physical sciences (which require laboratories) and health programs (such as nursing and physical therapy). A few colleges avoid all physical science and health majors. Instead they offer just the majors that can be taught cheaply (i.e., in large classes and with minimal equipment and books), such as business. Even these 'low rent' colleges cannot hold their costs of providing instruction below their tuition rates. The only way a college can make money from teaching is by avoiding the overhead costs of libraries, classrooms, tutors and most instructors (e.g., having all classes web-based). The fact that almost all universities routinely lose money on teaching elicits no discussion. Teaching is what these not-for-profit private enterprises or public bodies were set up to do.

The complaints about losing money on college sports begin with the premise that varsity sports are not a necessary part of the university's educational mission and may impede that mission. Supporters of the classical Greek view of education, specifically that it requires a physical as well as mental training, would be hard pressed to justify a varsity athletics program that trained the bodies of 3 per cent of the students while exempting the remainder. If the benefits often attributed to athletic training and team competition (e.g., that it promotes cooperation and sacrifice, life-long health, discipline, and resourcefulness) are true, why not require participation and training in team sports for all able-bodied students? No university administrator is advocating universal mandatory participation in team sports because the expense of student-body wide athletic teams would be astronomical. Thus, defenders of varsity programs either have to show that they at least cover their costs *or* that the subsidiary benefits (such as student and alumni identification with the school's teams and favorable publicity) more than justify any financial losses.

Since colleges are not-for-profit institutions in the USA it is important to understand their objectives before deciding whether college sports programs are a financial burden holding colleges back from achieving those objectives; otherwise it would make no more sense to criticize colleges for losing money on sports programs than for teaching classes. Colleges and universities (we use these terms interchangeably) can be modeled as maximizing the present value of future revenue streams. The revenue stream is made up of tuition, donations, research grants, royalties on patents, licensing the sale of the college's logo, ticket sales to athletic events and, for public universities, state government payments tied to either the number of students or the growth in student numbers, and State capital allocations. Most of these sources depend on the college's reputation, which is why all universities are in a prestige race. Every college would like to have a reputation for outstanding teaching and for path-breaking research. The more prestige a college has the better students it can draw, as measured by high school grades and Standard Assessment Test (SAT) scores, and the better faculty it can hire, as measured by research visibility and/or teaching ability. Better faculty will generate more grant income and keep raising the college's prestige profile. The better students graduate at a higher rate and go on to earn more money and donate more to the college. To a college a pool of wealthy alumni is a capital asset just as season ticket holders are to a professional franchise.

Depending on a college's position in the prestige pecking order, its varsity athletics program can attract better students to the campus or crowd out more academically-able students whose families are rich enough to pay the 'full freight' (the list price on tuition and room and board). The real cost of offering varsity athletes 'full ride' grants-in-aid (full tuition, books, and room and board) depends on how much the college charges for tuition and how much it has to discount that rate to get an additional student of a given quality to attend. Colleges do not talk about discounts on tuition – the preferred terms are 'financial aid' or 'scholarships' – but they are discounts nonetheless. If a college has excess capacity (empty dorm rooms and empty seats in classrooms) and no one is standing in line to take the slot occupied by a varsity athlete, then the cost of handing out the full-ride scholarship is much less than its list price. In this situation the real cost of the athletic scholarship or grant-in-aid is the marginal cost associated with serving that student. These marginal costs are the increased food purchases to cover what the additional student will eat if he or she is in a dormitory, plus any extra staff required for teaching and advising.

Shulman and Bowen concentrate on colleges near the top of prestige rankings. The list of Division IA universities for which they collected detailed data, along with their *US News and World Report* 2001 ranking, is Stanford (6), Duke (8), Northwestern (13), Rice (13), Notre Dame (19), Vanderbilt (22), Georgetown (23), Michigan (25) and North Carolina (25), Penn State (44), Tulane (45), and Miami of Ohio, which is out of the top 50. Recall that there are 114 Divison 1A football programs and 318 Division I basketball programs. Obviously, many programs do not even make the *US News and World Report* national rankings, the top division in the prestige race that has just 210 universities. Indeed, many of the universities with Division I sports programs are near the bottom of the *US News and World Report* regional rankings. Not surprisingly, given the schools they consider, Shulman and Bowen treated the athletic tuition grant-in-aids as costing universities the face value of their tuition charges. However, even some of the schools on their list toward the lower end in the rankings would have a difficult time replacing athletes with students whose families both could pay the full tuition and who had academic records near the average of their current students. If Shulman and Bowen had a list of more typical Division I schools (say, Boise State in Iowa which has a Division IA football program and is ranked in the third tier of the regional universities), their decision to ignore the true costs of providing grants-in-aid would have been blindingly conspicuous. A large public university with a low prestige ranking and excess capacity could have a marginal cost close to zero for adding a varsity athlete. The relevance of the university being public instead of private is that public universities have much lower tuition rates. Conversely, a highly ranked private university, such as Northwestern or Stanford which are on the Shulman and Bowen list, does give up a real $30,000 in revenue every time it hands out a grant-in-aid because it could easily let in an equally qualified (or perhaps a better qualified) applicant for the same slot.

A major difference between high-prestige versus low-prestige schools in the effects of giving full-ride scholarships to varsity athletes is the impact of the athletic program on applications. Low ranked schools are generally anxious to attract more applicants. A highly ranked school that gets five applications from candidates with similar qualifications for every opening does not mind getting even more applicants, but increasing its applicant pool it is not a major concern.

A varsity athletics program brings in more applicants simply because the athletes have usually have friends who want to attend the same college. Admissions directors are familiar with the estimates of how athletics programs draw applications from prospective athletes, their friends, students who want to attend college games, and even students who have no interest in athletics. These last are simply interested because the publicity from athletics programs make it more likely that students will have heard of the university and thus more likely to bother to open advertising mail from university. One 'window' into how admissions directors at modestly ranked universities view athletics programs is a new computer program that simulates managing a university's enrollment (see http://www.virtual-u.org/index.php). It is meant to guide the planning of actual admissions directors. Upgrading the athletics programs is one of the ways the simulation allows administrators to boost enrollments.

Athletic success and student quality

There are many anecdotes which support the hypothesis that athletic success attracts better students, but the statistical evidence is more problematic. A series of papers has been devoted to this issue. The anecdotal evidence usually takes the form of an institution that is not a perennial power in either football or basketball winning an unexpected conference title or going to a major Bowl game (e.g., Northwestern and the Rose Bowl) or the NCAA basketball championship (e.g., Villanova). The most famous example is Doug Flutie winning the Heisman Trophy at Boston College. The year after a 'big win' the admissions office announces how many more applications it received. Two implicit assumptions in this process are that these institutions have little excess capacity and that the additional applicants are of similar quality to the institution's usual applicant pool. The implication of these assumptions is that the admissions officers use the surge of applications to raise the SAT scores of the next freshman class.

The first empirical paper on that looked for a statistical relationship between athletic success and SAT scores (McCormick and Tinsley, 1987) set the pattern of focusing on major conference football programs and of measuring the quality of the freshman class by SAT scores. McCormick and Tinsley had a cross-sectional model and a change-in-change model. The cross-sectional model estimated the effect of the presence of a major sports program on SAT scores controlling for:

- tuition rates
- library volumes
- full professor salaries
- the age of the institution
- private versus public status
- student/faculty ratio
- total enrollment
- per capita endowment
- PhDs awarded per faculty member
- proportion of male undergraduates.

The presence of a major sports program was strongly associated with higher SAT scores. McCormick and Tinsley also regressed the change in SAT scores over three years on the changes in:

- student/faculty ratio
- in-state tuition
- out-of state tuition
- enrollment
- size of the library
- an indicator variable for private/private status
- fifteen-year trend variable for the change in win percentage in football.

They had observations on 44 schools. The estimated gains in SAT score were small. In the specification with the highest coefficient on the trend term, 302.37, and for the college with the highest value for the trend term, the University of Iowa at 0.05596, the estimated gain in SAT scores was 16.9 points. The coefficient was not estimated with much precision. The *t*-ratio was 1.55.

The next paper on this topic (Bremmer and Kesselring, 1993) also had a cross-sectional model and a change-in-change model. Bremmer and Kesselring added some other measures of having a major football program: the number of appearances in a major football Bowl game and the number of appearances in the NCAA basketball tournament over a ten-year period. In every specification including separate regressions for public and private universities none of the sports program variables were significant. The covariates were the changes in:

- library volumes
- faculty salaries

- student-to-faculty ratios
- enrollment
- endowment per student
- Statewide average SAT for public institutions
- acceptance percentage.

In their change-in-change model over a nine-year period none of the sports variables was significant at a 0.05 level. Bremmer and Kesselring raised the issue of whether an institution's acceptance rate, which is clearly a choice for the institution, should be treated as an exogenous determinant of its SAT score. They concluded that at least for the instruments they tried as determinants of the acceptance rate, the acceptance rate could be treated as an exogenous explanatory variable.

In the same year as the Bremmer and Kesselring paper, Tucker and Amato (1993) used another measure of athletic success, a variable based on end-of-season Associated Press (AP) top 20 rankings over a ten-year period for both football and basketball. In the cross-section regressions the AP-based variables were not significant but in the change-in-change regression the football AP variable was significant. Their covariates for the change-in-change model were the changes in:

- library volumes
- faculty salaries
- student-to-faculty ratios
- enrollment
- tuition.

Tucker and Amato followed McCormick and Tinsley and had an indicator variable for public versus private status.

Looking across the three papers with change-in-change models, McCormick and Tinsely used the trend over fifteen years in athletic success to predict a change in SAT scores over three years. The fifteen-year trend included the three years over which the changes were measured. Bremmer and Kesselring used the change from the first year to the ninth year in athletic success in athletic success to predict the change in SAT scores from the first to the ninth year. Tucker and Amato used the used the change from the first year to the tenth year athletic success in athletic success to predict the change in SAT scores from the first to the tenth year. None of these specifications aligns with the standard anecdotes. A model testing for responses in SAT to deviations from the institution's historic average athletic success in the year after the 'success' or 'failure' would be closer to the anecdotes.

The next paper on this topic is by Franklin G. Mixon (1995). It is the first to show a positive effect on SAT scores of basketball success. His cross-section model includes variables for

- enrollment
- entrance selectivity
- student/faculty ratio
- percentage of faculty holding PhDs
- indicator variable for private versus public
- indicator variable for historically black college
- basketball success as measured by the number of rounds in the NCAA Basketball Tournament over a fifteen-year period.

There is no football success variable. The paper does not have a difference-in-difference model. A cross-sectional framework cannot address the central question: if an institution invested in a more prominent football program by increasing its football budget and no other institution responded in kind, would it be able to raise its SAT scores? The reason that a cross-section regression cannot answer this question is that unobserved differences in an institution's 'drawing power' can cause the high SAT-to-football-success association to appear in a cross-section. For example, Stanford has a prominent athletics program and very high SAT scores but its drawing power may have little to do with its athletics program. Stanford could fill its entire freshman class with students who have scored 1,500 or more on the SAT. The university presumably has goals other than SAT maximization, such as racial or social diversity or the loyalty of the alumni. Similar arguments could be made for Michigan and UCLA on the public side. Quoting Leeds and von Allmen (2002, p. 378):

> Studies suggest, for example, that schools that belong to major athletic conferences attract freshmen with higher SAT scores, and that the more successful a school's football program is, the higher the scores rise. The reason for the higher SATs appears to be that success on the football field expands a school's applicant pool (at least for Division IA programs), allowing for a school to generate more revenue by admitting more students or to generate greater prestige by being more selective in its admissions process.
>
> The studies, however, rely on assumptions that may invalidate their conclusions. For example, when a study equates a big-time football program with one that belongs to a major athletic conference, it includes many of the nation's premier state universities. Finding that such programs attract more and better students may reflect the impact of the school's position in the state rather than the prominence of its football program.

These papers have not established a connection between athletic success and improvements in the student body. Also, the pattern over time of the relationship between SAT scores and athletic success is not clear. Is the response contemporaneous or lagged, and does it have 'staying power', (i.e., does the applicant pool shrink as soon as the team slips back)?

Predicting the level of a college's sports program

Intercollegiate sports programs are organized into tiers of affiliation. In descending order these are NCAA Divisions IA, IAA, IAAA, II, III and NAIA. Each tier has different requirements for the minimum number of sports teams and the number of athletes on grants-in-aid. The lowest NCAA tier, Division III, does not allow grants-in-aid. The NCAA IA programs have the large football stadiums and require the most grants-in-aid. The NCAA also requires schools to meet a number of qualifying criteria for IA status. Thus in football these include a requirement that a college has at least 30,000 permanent seats in its home stadium and an average attendance of at least 17,000 in any single year and an average of 20,000 over the previous four years. The NCAA IAA schools usually have football teams but at a much lower level. The NCAA IAAA programs are known as 'basketball schools'. The NCAA website, www.ncaa.org, lists the basic facts on different tiers. In 1999 for Division IA, IAA and IAAA the average operating budget for intercollegiate athletics is $6,425,827. For Division II schools with football programs the average budget is $1,950,00. For Division III schools the average budget is $663,000. The NAIA does not list the average operating budget on its website. A random sample of 30 NAIA schools from the US Department of Education website, http://ope.ed.gov/athletics/, yielded an average expenditure on athletics of $385,781. Most NCAA II schools have football, but at a modest level. The NAIA allows grants-in-aid but does not specify school minimums.

The costs of sports programs at a given school are primarily determined by the level of affiliation because of the NCAA requirements on the number of sports and the minimum number of scholarships. The travel expenses and the recruiting expenses are also tied to the level of affiliation. For example, Division III schools have minimal travel costs because that Division is set up around local or within-State rivalries. At the other end of the spectrum, the Division IA schools routinely recruit athletes internationally and schedule out-of-conference matches across the USA. While there are a few 'power house' programs such as the University of Michigan, which funds 700 athletes and competes for national championships nearly every year in nearly every sport, most schools have one or two sports with consistent winning records while the rest of their teams hover around 50 per cent wins. Since there is little promotional benefit and perhaps some loss to fielding a full complement of teams with consistent losing records, the choice of the level of affiliation constrains the schools to spend enough to have at least mediocre athletic success at that level.

Colleges have some discretion over their level of affiliation. Clearly, any of them could opt for no participation. The smallest and most resource-constrained colleges would find it impossible to meet the minimum stadium size, average attendance at home football games, and minimum number of grants-in-aid required of NCAA IA, but colleges as small as 2,807 undergraduates (Rice University) are in Division IA. Figure 11.1 shows box-and-whisker plots for the number of undergraduates for colleges in Divisions IA, IAA, IAAA, II, III, NAIA and no affiliation. The data are for 1999. The respective counts of the number of colleges in the seven categories are: 114, 122, 85, 293, 420, 254 and 170. These 1,458 colleges are the universe of accredited baccalaureate degree-granting colleges in the USA in 1999. The line inside each box represents the median undergraduate enrollment in that category. The boxes cover the central 50 per cent of each distribution. The circles and asterisks mark respectively outliers and extreme outliers. Even though there is a clear downward trend in the median enrollment going from IA to the 'no affiliation', category Figure 11.1 also shows that there is a wide overlap in enrollments across the categories.

If colleges are trying to maximize the present value of future revenues, they must adjust the level of their intercollegiate sports program according to whether they are gaining or losing money at a given level. Thus the level of affiliation should be precisely predicted by factors tied to costs and revenues. In a study by two of the authors of this book, variables with an obvious connection to costs and revenues were used to proxy costs and revenues to predict at a particular point in time the level of sports affiliation (Sandy and Sloane, 2003). These variables included undergraduate enrollment, tuition rates, room-and-board rates, dormitory capacity, etc. It also included variables measuring the college's prestige and selectivity such as the *US News & World Report* ranking, SAT scores and acceptance rates. A high-quality student body is effectively a capital asset to a college because these students are more likely to graduate, have higher lifetime earnings, and donate money to their alma mater. Holding tuition and room and board rates constant, colleges that could fill their current physical capacity with high-quality full-fee paying students give up much more money when they offer athletic grants-in-aid than colleges that draw low-quality students and have unused dorm space and classroom space. The colleges with empty dorm rooms and empty class seats may have a marginal cost for grants-in-aid close to zero. In the cross-section results there was a very close fit between cost/revenue proxies and the level of affiliation. Highly-selective/highly-ranked colleges had lower levels of sports programs. The combination of factors that are associated with a college being more likely to have a higher level sports program are being a very large, public, historically-black college offering remedial classes and having a high acceptance rate and a low SAT average.

The point-in-time results leave open the question of causation. A college with a high enrollment may be able to afford a big time sports program but the program itself may reduce enrollment. The point-in-time positive association may be due to unobserved characteristics that both raise enrollment and the level of the sports program. A way of getting around this problem is to look at response of enrollments to switches in the level of affiliation. If colleges maximize the present value of future revenue streams, switches to higher levels of affiliation for a given college must raise student numbers or student quality or both in order to justify their higher costs. The one clear result from the other

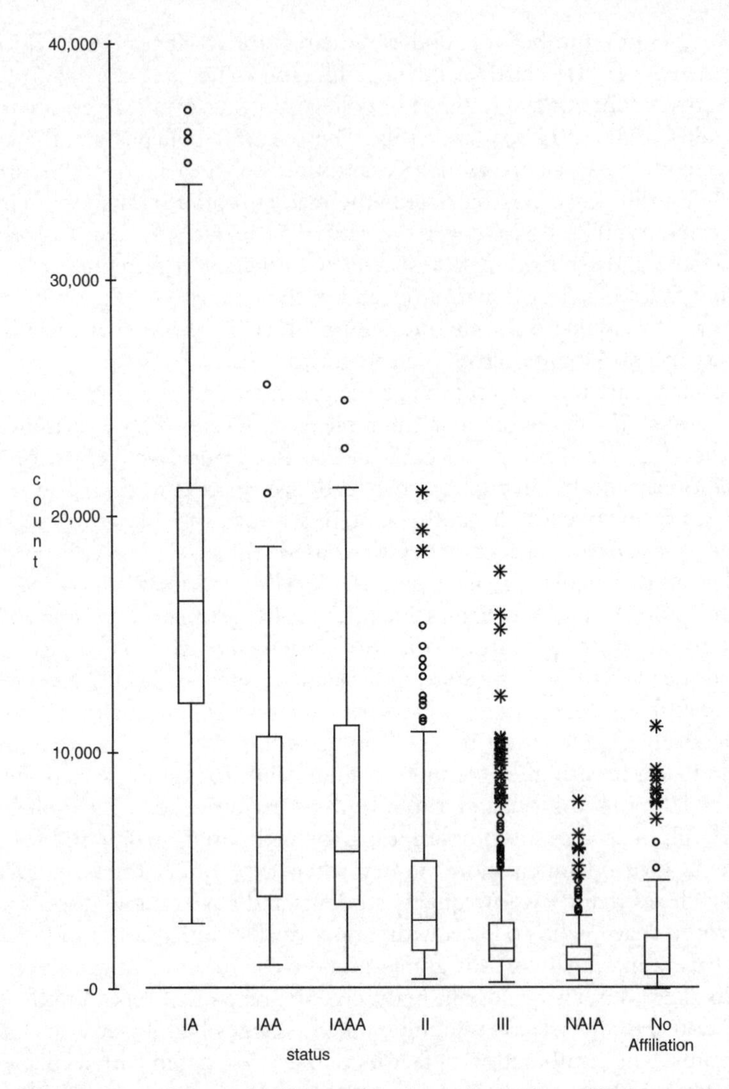

Figure 11.1 Box-and-whisker plot of enrollment by affiliation level

studies is that the gains in donations and ticket revenue are, on average, simply too small to cover the added costs. Some 124 colleges, or roughly 13 per cent of all colleges, changed the level of their sports affiliation between 1991 and 1999 (see Table 11.2). Of these 124, some 109 raised their level of affiliation. A statistical technique called fixed-effects panel estimates found substantial gains in student numbers and in student quality when a given institution raises the level of its sports affiliation, on the order of 2,000 additional students within five years of moving to Division IA. Colleges also raised their average SAT scores by moving up the sports affiliation ladder. The financial benefits from the gains in enrollment and student quality are far greater than the typical 'book'

Table 11.2 Counts of status changes

	1991–5	*1995–9*
Shifts Up		
NAIA to III	10	24
NAIA to II	19	16
NAIA to IAAA		2
III to II	2	2
II to IAAA	1	1
II to IAA	5	5
IAAA to IAA	14	3
IAA to IA	1	4
Total	52	57
Shifts Down		
IA to IAAA	1	
III to NAIA	2	
II to NAIA		6
II to III	2	2
IAA to IAAA		2
Total	5	10

losses (around $2 million dollars a year) that colleges assign to Division IA programs. With annual tuition at public universities costing around $4,000 a year the gain in tuition revenue would be around $8 million. Most public colleges gain additional State support by raising enrollments. The formulas vary widely but they more often reward gains in enrollment rather than pay a fixed amount per student. Clearly, the enrollment effect is a major part of the motivation for these programs (see Box 11.1)

Box 11.1 Sport provision and student recruitment

An example of the recruitment effect of intercollegiate athletics is the University of Mary Hardin-Baylor, which was a women's college until 1971. In 1997 it had 2,313 students, of which 70 per cent were women. Mary Hardin-Baylor wanted to attract more male students so it started a football team in 1998. It competes at the no-athletics-scholarships NCAA Division III level. The new team attracted 200 additional men who wanted to play football, enrolled in Mary Hardin-Baylor, and tried out for the team. The college started a junior varsity football squad to accommodate the overflow. (See Associated Press, 'Texas school to play first game', August 21, 1998 18:17 EDT.)

Other small colleges have one-third of the students participating in intercollegiate sports teams, such as the University of Indianapolis, a small private college of about 2,700 students, which is affiliated to NCAA Division II. The University of Indianapolis fields 19 teams, more than double the minimum of 8 teams currently required by the NCAA for a

cont. overleaf

Box 3.1 continued

Division II program. The enrollment aspects of the sports program are clear from the college's website, which includes the statement 'We offer more varsity sports than any other Division II school in the state of Indiana.' Indeed, the campus's 'extensive recreational complex for intercollegiate and intramural athletics' is highlighted in the short description of the college at under the link about UIndy (see http://www.uindy.edu/aboutuindy/).

The aggressive campaigns to promote small time athletics programs by colleges such as Mary Hardin-Baylor and the University of Indianapolis only make sense in the context of enrollment management.

The high responsiveness of student quality and numbers to increasing the level of sports affiliation raises some interesting questions. Why don't all colleges that can possibly beg or borrow the money start Division IA programs? One response is that they are doing that. It is difficult (if not impossible) to jump many steps on the sports affiliation ladder at the same time but the 109 net increases in affiliation level from 1991 to 1999 suggest that colleges are charging up the ladder at a rapid pace. The NCAA has placed new restrictions on entry to Division IA, such as increases in average attendance at football games, as a way of slowing down this flow. Another puzzle is why any college would lower its level of sports affiliation. This decision may be due to severe financial pressures forcing a college to cut anything that is expendable. The most interesting question is why is there such an apparently strong response to level of sports affiliation. There is a high income-elasticity to all leisure activities. A generation ago in the USA children would play pick-up games of baseball and basketball or football. Now most parents can afford uniforms for their five year olds along with trophies and victory banquets. The increased sensitivity of college students to the availability of intercollegiate sports as a participatory activity is just an extension of increased interest in sports. College age students would like to continue with the uniforms and camaraderie of youth sports.

Competitive balance in intercollegiate sports

The effects of the NCAA

The main way that the NCAA is thought to promote competitive balance is by limiting the number of athletic grants-in-aid in a sport. There is one empirical paper on this issue. Sutter and Winkler (2003) discuss the effects of the NCAA capping the number of scholarships in Division IA football at 95 in 1977 and then further reducing the limit to 85 in 1992. Division IA football is the highest revenue sport and the most expensive to operate. Their regression results yield mixed evidence on competitive balance effects of the caps. Within-year parity as measured by the standard deviation of the distribution of wins seems to have fallen compared to the pre-cap period (the years 1952 to 1976), while parity as measured by the Associated Press top 20 end-of-year standings has increased. They suggest two possible explanations. One is that the caps of respectively 95 to 85 grants-in-aid are too high to have any impact on competitive balance. Under that explanation the schools would not offer much more than 95 or 85 scholarships even if they were free to offer any number. Sutter and Winkler's second explanation is that while the caps do reduce the number of grants-in-aid which colleges would offer, the effect has been largely neutral across low and high profile Division IA football programs. They do not have the data to distinguish between these hypotheses.

Do these caps cut costs? Although being in Division IA helps attract more and better students, there appears to be little benefit to an individual IA college to increase the number of football grants-in-aid beyond the current cap of 85. Given the abysmal graduation rates of Division IA football players, once a reasonably competitive football program is in place it makes more financial sense in a college that has excess dorm and classroom capacity to use the grants-in-aid to attract athletes with better academic credentials.

Under the reasonable assumption that most athletes are interested in getting an education because the chances of a professional career are remote, the NCAA restrictions on payments to athletes help the colleges that have the highest tuition and room and board rates. Each college in Division I and II is limited to awards equal to the tuition, room and board. Presumably the higher tuition prices reflect some quality differences such as smaller classes, better labs, and more experienced or more famous professors. Ever since the NCAA clamped down on the athlete-only dorms with room service, the colleges that charged higher room and board rates have had an advantage in recruiting athletes. Again, this is under the assumption that the price differences reflected a difference in quality.

The NCAA also affects competitive balance through its rules on eligibility and its enforcement procedures. High academic standards would favor schools with the ability to draw athletes who are also good students. Imagine the effect of an NCAA rule that required football and basketball players to have SAT scores of at least 1,200 and to graduate within four years in an Arts and Science major. Harvard would be resurrected as a national football power. The actual rules recently in place are much more modest, such as a SAT score of 700 under Proposition 48. That score is so modest that it simply avoids scandals such as star basketball players admitting that they cannot read. Currently, the NCAA is considering a proposal to shift the enforcement from student quality standards such as SAT scores or the number of high school college preparatory classes the athlete passed to academic performance at the college level. Colleges that had low graduation rates would be penalized by reductions in the number of athletic scholarships they could offer or by being ineligible for post-season competition. Given the headaches the NCAA staff had in trying to evaluate the descriptions of thousands of high school courses to decide if they were indeed college-preparatory, the mechanics of either rewards or penalties based on percentages of athletes in a sport graduating is attractive. The problem will be policing sham degrees and hollow majors.

The NCAA has a tiny 'police force' to investigate infractions. Its main mechanism is to rely on competitors to 'rat' on each other. Coaches who lose a prize recruit to another school are often in a good position to know if there was an under-the-table payment. Fleisher, Goff and Tollison have argued that this enforcement mechanism holds down new schools while perpetuating the 'haves'. Any college that has a dramatic increase in the standing of its football or basketball program generates infraction complaints from its competitors and comes under intense scrutiny. They further argue that the traditional big athletic powers have captured the NCAA's enforcement committee. Identical infractions by a big power results in a 'slap on the wrist', while the punishment for a no-name program is draconian.

A third way that the NCAA affects competitive balance is its rules on transferring from one college to another. A student who transfers gives up one year of sports eligibility. Some of the transfers are unrelated to the quality of the school's athletic program: for example, the athlete is homesick, or loses his girlfriend, or hates his coach. Other transfers are due to a mismatch between the athlete's skill level and the program's level: an athlete who thought he would be a starter wants to leave after discovering that he is unlikely to even play. Conversely, an athlete who turns out to be a star in a low profile program might decide that he could increase his chances of a professional career by transferring to a higher profile program. The loss of one year's eligibility out of a possible four years greatly discourages transfers. Since young athletes tend to be optimistic about their potential one would expect to find more disappointed athletes sitting on the bench at high profile colleges than unexpected stars seeking to transfer out of low-profile programs. If this expectation is correct, the restrictions on transfers help the high-profile programs and hold down the low-profile programs that would love to recruit these transferees.

Other factors determining competitive balance

Conferences are groups of colleges that play amongst themselves for conference championships in a variety of sports. The conferences have a great deal of autonomy over **gate-sharing** and the sharing of television revenue or bowl revenue. Colleges hop from one conference to another as their circumstances change. The conference structure in the USA is a free-for-all scramble with some conferences having stable memberships for decades and others changing year-by-year. Conferences have a number of functions that reduce the costs of operating a sports program. Conferences guarantee a set of competitors, usually by setting up a series of home and away games against every conference member. Conferences facilitate the creation of traditional rivalries. Teams that drew poorly all season can sell out when their hated rival comes to campus. Conferences reduce risk by letting teams having a run of bad luck retain some conference revenue. Conferences also reduce travel costs because they are organized around nearby colleges. To entice a high profile program some conferences cut special deals such as allowing a particular college to retain more of its television revenue or appear on television more often or keep a larger fraction of its gate. Such arrangements would diminish competitive balance. It is difficult to assess the overall effect of conferences on competitive balance because often these arrangements are not public knowledge and they change frequently. Lastly, the conferences and the NCAA interact in complex ways, with conferences as well as individual colleges having voting rights in some contexts. Also, the NCAA gives automatic entry to its basketball tournament to every team that wins a conference championship. The 318 Division I basketball teams are organized into 30 conferences. The guarantee of at least one invitation to the NCAA tournament is an important incentive for to a college to belong to a conference.

Conclusions

Intercollegiate sports systems are several things at the same time. They are cartels holding down costs and restricting output. They are a means of managing enrollment affecting the ratio of male to female students, the number of students, and the quality of the students. They are a regulatory body that has at least partially been captured by the industry they regulate. It is also a tremendous eyesore for many colleges. Most Division I college presidents have made a Faustian bargain with their sports programs of the form 'give me visibility, enrollment gains, donations, and better students and I won't ask too many questions about why so few male basketball players graduate'. Some colleges have had no black basketball players graduate within four years of their matriculation in recent cohorts (Benson, 1999). This bargain with the devil seems largely unnecessary because the NCAA could enforce progress toward graduation.

Note

1. This claim illustrates the dangers of making generalizations. Since the sentence was first written the President of St. Bonaventure resigned in 2003 after it was discovered that he had intervened with his college's admissions office in favor of a basketball-playing 'junior college' transfer student whose sole academic qualification was a certificate in welding.

Exercises

1. Who would gain and who would lose if an athlete successfully sued the NCAA under the antitrust laws for its restrictions against paying athletes? How would professional sports be affected?
2. The diagram showing the percentage of wins in a two-team professional league could be applied to a two-team collegiate league. In the professional league the two teams hire enough talent to equate their marginal revenues from an additional win and league-wide total revenue is maximized. Does it make sense to apply this diagram to colleges?
3. College sports have followed professional sports in seeking money from commercial sponsors. College stadiums are named after companies that pay for the naming rights. Apparel companies pay to have their logo appear on the college athletes' uniforms, and signs for sponsors are appearing inside college arenas. Besides a gain in revenue, what are the consequences of this trend?
4. It is fairly common for the athletic department to spend every penny of the money earned on a post-season Bowl appearance. The athletics department pays for the travel and hotel and ticket expenses of an entourage of 50 administrators and spouses, a marching band of 250 students, and some lavish parties. It is also fairly common for faculty to complain about excessive spending by the athletics department. Other than for their immediate pleasure, why do athletics departments have an incentive to spend the bowl money as fast as it comes in?
5. One long-standing proposal to reform college athletics is to eliminate athletic scholarships. Under this proposal all scholarships would be based solely on financial need. The NCAA used to forbid athletic scholarships but it had a hard time enforcing that requirement. The financial aid forms, the Free Application For Federal Student Aid (FAFSA), now filed with the Federal government would make it easier to establish who qualifies for financial aid with a common formula. The colleges would save the money they now spend on grants-in-aid to athletes who have well-off parents. What would be the consequences of this reform?
6. The following quote is from Murray Sperber (2000, p. 227):

> Every year, the largest financial drain on NCAA members results from the association's requirement that the schools field a minimum number of teams to remain in good standing – for Division I, at least fourteen teams in seven sports. This is a compulsory stake in a very expensive poker game. The motive behind this rule is self-interest: NCAA executives, mainly former athletic directors and coaches, regard the NCAA as a trade association, in business to promote college sports; they are empire-builders, they want athletic programs to be as large as possible, and to employ as many athletic administrators and coaches as possible.

Even if the NCAA administrators had a free hand in setting up requirements that are, according to Sperber, against the interests of its member colleges, why would they impose costs on the colleges that would use up some of the possible surplus from intercollegiate athletics? What explanations other than empire building can account for the minimum number of sports requirements?

7. James Duderstadt (2000, p. 139) claims that most public Division IA colleges understate the true cost of their athletics grants-in-aid by using the in-State tuition rates that are one-third to one-quarter of the out-of-State rate of tuition. Does this claim make economic sense?
8. The following quote is from Andrew Zimbalist (1999, p. 171). After reviewing all sources of revenues and costs including donations to colleges that have successful sports teams, Zimbalist concluded:

> The only possible institutional justification, then, for supporting athletic success is that it might enable a university to expand the size of its student body. Of course, the positive correlation between athletic success and applications also means that poor athletic performance will lead to fewer applications. Thus, this is a risky strategy for a school to follow.

It seems reasonable to assume that new entrants into Division I will do miserably in terms of athletic success in football or basketball, at least for the first few years. Why? Even if the initial miserable performance is the case, does it make financial sense for a college to transfer to Division I?

9. The NCAA is considering a proposal for Division I that will permit an athlete to participate and be paid by a professional sports team and then enroll in a college and participate in varsity athletics in the same sport. The proposal will be put to a vote by the full NCAA Division I membership this Spring. Here is the rationale given by the NCAA's subcommittee on Agents and Amateurism of its Division I Academics/Eligibility/Compliance Cabinet.

> This proposal is part of a deregulation package of the amateurism legislation designed to enhance the welfare of precollege prospective student-athletes. Currently, any individual who signs a contract to participate in professional athletics no longer remains eligible for intercollegiate athletics competition *in the same sport.* Many prospects often have misguided aspirations to sign professional contracts to participate in elite level competition; however, the simple act of signing a contract does not, in and of itself, provide any competitive advantage. Thus, individuals prior to initial full-time college enrollment should not be denied the opportunity to participate in intercollegiate athletics simply by entering into a contractual arrangement to participate in professional athletics. It should be noted that the prohibition against the use of an agent would remain applicable and would continue to jeopardize the eligibility of any individual who agrees (orally or in writing) for such representation. (emphasis added)

(a) In what sense are 'aspirations to sign professional contracts to participate in elite level competition' misguided?
(b) What explanation other than 'enhancing the welfare' of high school graduates who sign with a professional team but don't make the roster could account for this proposal?
(c) Is the tolerance of contracts with professional sports teams along with an absolute bar to the use of an agent consistent with the NCAA stated rationale of enhancing the welfare of pre-college prospective student-athletes? Why is the NCAA dead set against athletes hiring agents?

10. How can the NCAA be both a cartel and serve the interests of its member colleges? What evidence is there that the NCAA is a cartel? How does it serve its member colleges?
11. Universities outside the USA have adopted many of the money raising strategies of US universities. Buildings are named after big donors, all of the alumni receive solicitation for gifts, high tuition rates are set for foreign students, and even higher tuition rates are set for popular programs such as an international finance MBA. The stark exception is US style college sports programs. What are the reasons for this exception?
12. The NCAA sells 10,000 tickets to the Final Four by lottery for $110 each. According to the *Indianapolis Star/News* these tickets can be resold for $1,200. The explanation that we used for below-market clearing ticket prices by professional sports teams, risk aversion by season ticket holders, does not apply to this situation as there are no season ticket holders. Why does the NCAA have below-market clearing ticket prices for the Final Four? (Some answers to avoid: the NCAA doesn't need the money, or they want to keep ticket prices low enough to be affordable for the average fan.)
13. Describe the evidence for the NCAA being a cartel.
14. Economists have a theory of least-cost criminal deterrence called the 'boil them in hot oil' theory. According to this theory the least costly enforcement mechanism combines small expenditures on catching criminals (few policemen) with huge penalties (boiling them in hot oil). Recently the NCAA put a university on probation that cost the university millions of dollars for giving a recruit a t-shirt. To what extent does the NCAA's enforcement mechanism fit and to what extent does it not fit the 'boil them in hot oil' theory.?
15. Northwestern University has a very high academic reputation yet the number of applicants to the school increased sharply after its football team won the Big Ten. Ohio State has a much more modest academic reputation but its applications hardly varied after it won the Big Ten. It seems paradoxical that students interested in a school with a high academic reputation would be so sensitive to football prowess. How would you explain this paradox?

Government and sports policy

Chapter goals

Governments intervene in the provision of a whole range of sporting activities stretching from grass-roots participation to international sporting events. This chapter attempts to explain why. In the case of participant sports it is believed that such activities are **merit goods** for which there are efficiency and equity considerations. Governments therefore attempt to prevent under-provision. In the case of international sporting success there is an element of **public goods** with a similar potential problem of under-provision. Governments, both local and national, provide subsidies in the form of aid for mounting bids or constructing stadiums in order to host international sporting events such as the Olympic Games and the World Cup. However, **cost-benefit analyses** of such events suggests that often the economic gains are much smaller than predicted.

A final reason for government involvement is the possibility that professional sports may infringe **antitrust** or competition laws, as many of their activities can be regarded as anticompetitive. In some cases governments have passed legislation to exempt certain sporting activities from such constraints.

Introduction

Why do governments intervene?

National governments are responsible for a diverse range of sports-related policies. Given that sports expenditure is only about 2 per cent of household spending in the European Union and just over 1 per cent of US gross national product, the extent of government policy is perhaps surprising. But about 125 million EU citizens and 87 million US citizens regularly participate in sporting activities. It should be noted that grass-roots participation policies and programs both in Europe and the USA are frequently under the jurisdiction of state and local governments.

Major realms of government sports initiatives include 'sport for all' policies aimed at grass-roots participation; elite sports programs aimed at securing long-term success in international competition; construction of major capital projects such as the development of sports centers at the local level or national stadia for housing prestige events; antidoping policies; antihooligan initiatives in relation to fan behavior, particularly in relation to international sporting events; the regulation of athletic labor markets and the sale of sporting goods and services; contributing to the bidding for, planning and implementation of international sporting events such as the Olympic Games or the World Cup; sport and education policies linked to young persons and perhaps linked to ideas about social inclusion; overseeing the functioning of specific bodies for sports administration such as national sports councils or Olympic Committees; sports broadcasting policy, notably the balance between subscription and free-to-air televised sport; acquiring and disbursing funding for sports programs including funds from national lotteries; the establishment of policies permitting local governments to pass taxes to finance sports facilities for professional sports teams (in most US states), and providing a framework for sports in the context of antitrust (competition) policy.

Why are there so many government interventions? Even in the USA Chalip, Johnson and Stachura (1996) note that, while the rhetoric of US policy is that sport should be independent of government, each branch of government is responsible for policies that have implications for both amateur and professional sports. It is important to distinguish between amateur/participatory sports and professional/spectator sports as the reasons for government involvement in each case are quite distinct. The basis of government policy towards participant sports is that such activity is a merit good, subject to two potential sources of market failure: efficiency and equity. Clearly, if sport generates external social benefits it is possible that private decisions may lead to a less than socially optimal output. In theory, governments can maximize social welfare by encouraging more consumption through subsidies or by directly providing such services at lower prices. The social benefits might include reduced public spending on health care and crime prevention. The historical reason for promoting participatory as opposed to spectator sports, going back to ancient Greece and Rome, was national defense. The military needed males who were physically fit. Although few countries still have a military draft, the issue of the fitness of the draft pool is not ancient history. In World War II many young men in the USA failed the physical for draftees because of childhood diseases associated with poor nutrition, such as rickets. They had grown up during the Great Depression. After the war Congress passed the Food Stamp program because a minimal nutrition standard would increase the pool of fit draftees.

Another example of a public good is international sporting success such as finishing first in the World Cup or gaining a large number of gold medals in the Olympic Games. Such success meets the strict definition of a public good because it is both **nonexcludable** and **nonrival**. The equity issue implies that resources should be targeted at young people from low income and socially deprived backgrounds, possibly in minority city areas on the grounds that their parents cannot afford to pay for equipment or training. Governments also support bids to host major sporting events such as the World Cup and the Olympic Games or provide funds for the refurbishment of existing stadia or the construction of new ones. The safety of spectators has been an important issue, particularly in the UK where there have been a number of fatalities in soccer games. Another issue that has increased in significance is the stance taken by competition authorities towards certain practices that may be regarded as anticompetitive, such as the collective selling of television rights for games.

Amateur sport

The distinction between amateur and professional sport has long been an issue of public policy concern. The development of professional sports has not been universally welcomed. Thus, Teddy Roosevelt in 1905 was reported as saying 'when money comes in at the gate, sport flies out of the window', (see http://www.baseball-almanac.com/prz_qtr.shtml). As we saw in the previous chapter the NCAA rules bar the payment of salaries to college athletes. The primary effect of not paying players is that payments will be transferred from players to coaches, administrators, or athletes in nonrevenue sports. In the Olympic Games, too, there was a requirement that players should not be paid. The ban on paying athletes served a class function. Only the rich could afford to train full time and become world-class athletes. During the 1960s and 1970s the Soviet Union and its satellite states had a vast training system. 'Amateur' athletes trained full time while holding down fictitious jobs. In response the International Olympic Committee (IOC) started to allow cash allowances to be paid to athletes. The rules against pay were first weakened in 1981 when the International Amateur Athletic Board agreed to allow athletes to benefit from advertisements providing the proceeds were disbursed by the national athletic bodies in the form of trust funds or social benefits. When IOC allowed professional athletes such as NBA players to compete in the Olympics the distinction between amateurs and professional was largely obliterated. A few minor sports such as archery still outlaw pay for athletes. In rugby, the question of whether players should be paid or not led to the formation of a competing professional rugby league and eventually the amateur Rugby Union itself became professional in 1995. The International Rugby Football Board declared that Rugby Union was an 'open game with no prohibition on remuneration for any persons involved in the sport, whether as players or officials'. This was a response to the fact that players were frequently paid 'boot money': that is, players were paid even though the rules forbade it. To compete at the highest levels in amateur sports requires a major input of time and effort, which might otherwise be invested in the athlete's career outside sports. Given the strong incentives by amateur athletes to seek support and the strong incentives of teams and sanctioning bodies to use under-the-table payments to attract the best athletes, the outcome is inevitable. A black market will exist for such services, policing costs will be high and the hypocrisy of the situation will lead to a loss of confidence among the public. The examples above were repeated in tennis, badminton and bowls where the distinction between amateur and professional players was also abolished. In US collegiate sports the widespread hypocrisy continues.

The merit good argument

Most amateurs engage in sports because they enjoy them. The issue for the government is whether private enjoyment results in enough sports activity or whether there are potential social benefits which are not internalized. Such benefits include improved health, crime reduction or other elements of public goods. In terms of health a number of studies have found that regular exercise can reduce the probability of heart disease, obesity and other ailments. Even if the main benefits are private, given the public benefits such as a reduction in public health care expenditures and a longer pay off to public investments in education, there would still be a case for subsidies of amateur sports facilities. If the benefits are entirely private then there is no case for direct government intervention. If there is under-utilization due to imperfect information, health promotion may be the relevant policy response. It has also been argued that the provision of sporting opportunities for young people can reduce the incidence of antisocial activities such as crime and vandalism. However, at least as far as the UK is concerned, Gratton and Taylor (2000) suggest that hard evidence is difficult to come by, and in particular the inference that prevention is less costly than curing crime needs to be demonstrated.

As noted earlier, if international sporting success raises morale and inspires young people to take an active part in sport such success would be a public good. However, a more compelling argument is that participation in sport may help to improve labor market outcomes, in which case it should be treated in the same way as other types of investment in human capital. A recent US study by Barron, Ewing and Waddell (2000) has shown, using the National Longitudinal Survey of Youth (NLSY), that men who participated in high school athletics were paid 31 per cent more at age 32 than those who had not done so. Other evidence from the NLSY of the high school class of 1972 pointed to a 12 per cent wage gain at age 31 for those who had participated in high school athletics. However, interpretation of these results is complicated by the fact that they could be explained by ability and/or a preference for leisure, in which case athletic participation could simply be a signal of individuals with higher ability or a higher work ethnic. Yet, when controlling for ability, Barron, Ewing and Waddell still found that there was a relationship between athletic participation and labor market outcomes, if somewhat reduced in size. Further, they found that athletic participation contributed to raising productivity over and above that of other extra-curricular activities. Other studies have found that male university athletes receive higher incomes after college than their nonsporting counterparts and that they are more likely to graduate than the latter. This is explained by Long and Caudill (1991) as a result of the fact that participation in sports can enhance discipline, self-confidence, motivation and other behavioral traits which encourage success. However, not all effects of participation in sport are desirable. In the UK it is estimated that over two million people are affected by some sort of sports injury every year and serious medical problems can arise due to inadequate preparation for activities such as marathons and weightlifting.

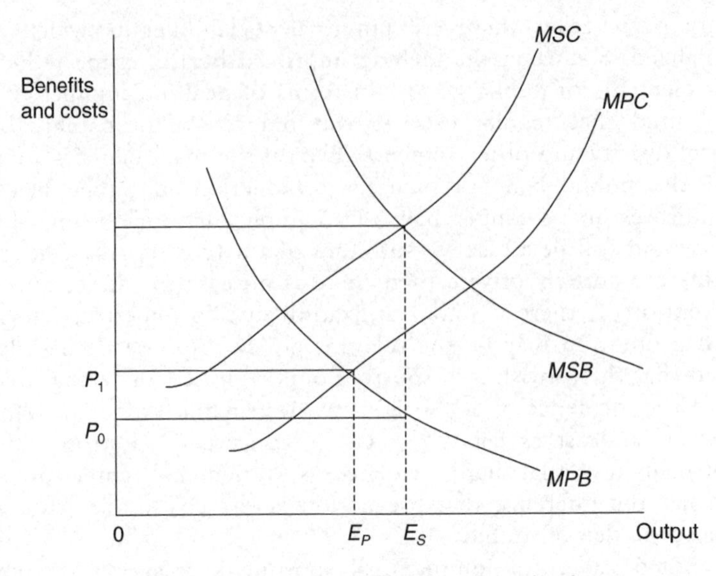

Figure 12.1 Costs and benefits of participation in sport

Given the latter we face the possibility that marginal social cost (*MSC*) could exceed marginal private costs (*MPC*) as in Figure 12.1, in which case under-provision would only occur if marginal social benefits (*MSB*) exceeded marginal private benefits (*MPB*), and this difference was greater than the difference between *MSC* and *MPC*. Given the positions of these schedules in Figure 12.1 the private equilibrium E_P lies to the left of the social equilibrium E_S, suggesting an under-provision of sports participation, but it is possible that E_S could lie to the left of E_P, in which case over-provision would occur. Even in the former case the costs of shifting participation from one equilibrium to the other need to be considered as well as the form that such intervention should take. One possibility is to introduce a subsidy equal to $P_1 - P_0$, which would encourage the consumer to consume at E_S rather than E_P.

The equity argument

Equity arguments have also been used to defend government intervention in the sporting market place. Thus, the UK Department for Culture, Media and Sport (2002) notes that the most disadvantaged groups are least likely to participate in sport and physical activity, with professional workers three times more likely to participate than manual workers, women being 19 per cent less likely to participate than men, and ethnic minority participation being 6 per cent lower overall than the national average.

However, there are a number of different equity strategies that governments might pursue. Le Grand (1982), for example, distinguished five such strategies:

- equality of expenditure, so that all consumers receive equal shares of public expenditure
- equality of final income, so that expenditure favours the poor to equalize (or reduce differences in) incomes
- equality of use, so that 'relevant' groups of individuals consume the same amount of the service after the payment of subsidies
- equality of cost, which requires that subsidies are allocated in such a way that consumers face the same cost (reflecting both time and money) as a result of the subsidies
- equality of outcome: that is, consumers end up with equal status as a result of the subsidies.

In practice, it appears that the concern of many governments has been to target resources at young people from low income, socially deprived backgrounds, often in inner-city areas. However, even when sports facilities are provided for free, nonprice barriers – such as lack of private transport – may limit participation. The evidence suggests that the main beneficiaries of such expenditures are not the most disadvantaged. One noticeable feature of sports and recreation consumption is the heterogeneity of tastes and any attempt to ensure equal shares for each activity appears somewhat misguided. Thus, sociologists suggest that working class culture (or tribalism) tends to lead to a preference for team sports such as football, cricket and baseball, while the middle or professional classes have a preference for nonteam sports such as golf and squash in line with the ethos of personal advancement. In economic terms, golf and squash require more money such as fees on public courses or for memberships. In contrast, it is possible to play soccer and baseball on bare fields with minimal equipment. The poor are also likely to choose nonteam sports where their opportunity cost is lower. Thus, concern for the poor should in general direct resources toward team sports. But what if the segments of the poor prefer boxing, where the risk of injury is high, or snooker and billiards or darts which in turn may increase consumption of alcohol? All of this points to the possibility of government failure in the sports market, either through the inefficient provision of services or through a failure to mirror accurately individual preferences. One means of avoiding this dilemma proposed in the UK is to use market-based strategies such as vouchers, which allow the individual to select the most appropriate form of expenditure in relation to their own demand function. A simpler mechanism is public provision. Cities build swimming pools, bicycle trails, ice skating rinks, indoor and outdoor basketball courts, jogging trails, etc., and adjust the mix of services over time as utilization varies. For example, Indianapolis has been building soccer fields as more Hispanics have moved into the city and more youths have taken up soccer.

Sporting infrastructure and international sporting events

The Olympic Games

Public sector support for major sporting events is a highly contentious issue but this has not prevented cities and countries bidding in large numbers for events such as the Olympic Games and the World Cup. Historically, hosting the Olympic Games served political and prestige purposes. For example, Germany used the 1936 Olympics to showcase the achievements of the Nazi Party. The Chinese government viewed the selection of Beijing as an affirmation of China's modernity and acceptance. The first Olympics to actually make money were the 1984 games in Los Angeles. The local organizing committee was so successful in lining up corporations to sponsor the games that it had an unexpected surplus of funds by the end of the games. Los Angeles became the model. Carefully managed events and lavishly sponsored events can be operated at a substantial gain. The Atlanta games fit this model. When losses occur, however, it often involves the national government. The investment in new facilities, some of which may be paid for by central government or the sports authorities themselves, represents a net addition to the local economy that will continue into the future. Often the investment is linked to urban regeneration, as was the case with the Commonwealth Games held in Manchester, England, in 2002.[1] Governments themselves may sponsor bids for such events and this may include assistance in the construction or refurbishment of national stadia, which are felt to be an essential part of a realistic bid. Thus in the UK there was government support for the reconstruction of two soccer stadiums, Wembley in England (see Box 12.1) and Hampden Park in Scotland, both of which proved to have political as well as economic problems. Economic theory casts doubt on the likelihood of a substantial windfall for the host city for such events. Cities competing with one another for such a privilege would theoretically bid until their expected return was zero and the monopoly organizer such as the IOC would appropriate any economic rents, either directly through accepting bribes or indirectly through mandating that the host assumes the full cost of putting on the event (Baade and Matheson, 2002). Yet, under the existing revenue-sharing agreement with the host country for media revenues, if those funds are judiciously used and the cost of facilities built roughly equals that revenue stream, losses can be and are avoided. Japan and Korea for nationalistic reasons ignored that management philosophy and were willing to expend extra dollars on grand stadia for image purposes. New York City's bid for the Olympics in 2012 could result in a profitable games given the number of facilities that exist in the region.

Box 12.1 The reconstruction of Wembley Stadium

Wembley Stadium in London was built in 1923 with a capacity of over 100,000 and traditionally housed home games of the English National Team, the FA Cup Final and the Rugby League Cup Final. In 1966 the Sports Council decided that the time was opportune to build a new national stadium for football, athletics and rugby league, given that the first National Lottery grants for capital projects were being distributed. After examining several sites Wembley was chosen, mainly because it was felt that its location would help in securing major international events such as the World Cup or the Olympic Games. Wembley Stadium was consequently purchased with £106 million of lottery money in 1999 (with an additional sum of £14 million for design costs) with the intention of knocking down the old stadium and building a completely new stadium at an estimated cost of £355 million. However, given the relative importance of football, a wholly-owned subsidiary of the Football Association, Wembley National Stadium Ltd (WNSL), was formed to manage the project. WNSL determined that the inclusion of an athletics track would detract from the stadium's atmosphere for football games by causing spectators to be further from the pitch, and the Secretary of State for Culture, Media and Sport agreed to support the construction of a separate athletics stadium at Picketts Lock, estimated to cost £60 million. WNSL agreed to give back £20 million to facilitate the construction of this stadium, though to date no progress has been made on this project.

Meanwhile the estimated costs of constructing the new Wembley Stadium escalated. In August 2001 the estimated cost had risen to just under £600 million and there were difficulties in persuading financial institutions to lend the required £400 million. Eventually, the demolition of the old stadium began in September 2002, but the estimated cost of the project had risen to £757 million, with a German bank, West LB, providing a £485 million loan. The 90,000 seat stadium was estimated to generate £229 million for the local area, but doubts remain whether the stadium will be able to cover its costs, as has proved to be the case with respect to the National Millennium Stadium in Cardiff, which hosts Welsh Rugby Union internationals, is the temporary home for the FA Cup Final, and was built for a much smaller sum. The costs of Wembley can be compared to the Euro 2004 capital costs. This soccer tournament will be held in Portugal and in preparation four existing stadiums were revamped and six new grounds constructed at a total cost of £299.7 million. In the 2002 World Cup, held jointly in Korea and Japan, the Koreans raised £1.03 billion and built 10 stadiums with an aggregate capacity of 500,000, and half of these were built within three years. Japan built 10 new stadiums for the World Cup at an estimated cost of almost £3 billion. These have multi-purpose facilities that can double up for track and field athletics, baseball and other

cont. overleaf

Box 12.1 continued

sporting events. It is clear that if an alternative site had been selected the cost of Wembley would have been much reduced. A House of Commons Select Committee was scathing of the roles of the government and Sport England, suggesting that the project had suffered from 'self-inflicted injuries, ambiguous government support and poor supervision by Sport England'. This is a clear example of government failure.

The World Cup

The World Cup is now the largest sporting and communications event in the world involving over 12,000 media personnel and attracting television audiences measured in the billions. This event is organized by FIFA, the world governing body, which has 204 national associations as members. The competition is generally held every four years and 17 competitions have so far been held in the 72 years of its existence, with seven countries having won the Jules Rimet trophy. In the 2002 World Cup, split between Japan and Korea at 20 venues, 32 qualifiers participated in 64 games over a four-week period, involving 736 players. Some 3,200,000 tickets were distributed. As in other mega sporting events it has been suggested that the economic benefits include the direct windfall from investment in stadiums and other facilities and substantial expenditure by visiting fans, teams, media and sponsors. Indirect benefits arise from improvements to the infrastructure, including transport networks, hotels, sport facilities and the development of leisure and other service sectors, such as tourism.

Income is obtained not just from ticket sales but also from the sale of broadcasting and sponsorship rights. The broadcasting rights for the 2002 competition were sold for £580 million and for the 2006 competition for £670 million. In addition the 15 top-tier sponsors paid FIFA a total of £375 million to have their products associated with the competition. All of this, however, does not tell us whether the total benefits outweigh the total costs of the competition.

Cost-benefit analysis

Preuss (2000) has attempted such an approach in his book, *The Economics of the Olympic Games*. The basis of the cost-benefit analysis is the **Pareto** or **Kaldor-Hicks criteria** regarding social **welfare**, recognizing that there are both negative and positive effects and winners and losers. Pareto defined an increase in total welfare as occurring under those conditions in which some people are better off as a consequence of the change, without at the same time anyone being worse off. Kaldor and Hicks argued, however, that if some individuals are made worse off, total welfare could still be increased by the change if those who gain from it can compensate the losers to their mutual satisfaction.

It is necessary to use **multiplier** analysis to determine the overall impact of the Games in relation to the host city. Several years prior to the Games the selected city will experience an increased demand after being awarded the Games. These game-related expenditures will last for several years after the games, mainly sustained by post-Olympic tourism. In estimating the full multiplier effects we must allow for outflows from the region (leakages), which will be determined by the resulting imports and taxes. Hence the multiplier is given by

$$dy = \frac{1}{1 - c(1 - t) + m} dA$$

where

dy = the change in income
dA = the change in autonomous expenditure
c = marginal propensity to consume
t = marginal tax rate
m = marginal propensity to import

Let us suppose that dA represents an expenditure of £1 billion, that $c = 0.9$, $t = 0.3$ and $m = 0.2$, then the expenditure increase of £1 billion will result in an increase in total income for the host city of £1.174 billion in income. However, we must also consider the possibility of crowding-out effects. If the host city finances the necessary investment itself (rather than incurring debt) the Games-related expenditure may substitute for other public projects. Even supposing there are positive effects for the host city in the form of improved infrastructure and increased income and employment, it is still possible that there is an opportunity cost in the form of alternative projects which might have led to a higher benefit for the city or lower costs for the same benefit. The same issue was raised in the discussion of the Bureau of Economic Analysis impact study of a new stadium in Kansas City in Chapter 8. Impact studies typically do not address the issue of alternative uses of public funds. The multiplier is also based on the assumption that the new spending does not change prices in the host city. However, Baade and Matheson (2002) attempted to estimate the effects of the Los Angeles and Atlanta games on employment growth by looking at deviations in this variable from long-run trends. The estimated coefficients for the Games did not emerge as statistically significant in either case. It should be noted, however, that while there was no economic gain for the region, neither city lost money since as an economic venture the revenues from the games supported the investments made. Hence, if people believed the intangible benefits were also valuable, these cities came out ahead.

In another study the same authors (Baade and Matheson, 2001) attempted to measure the impact of Baseball's All-Star game, an event which brings together the most talented and popular players in MLB. There are associated events including a baseball convention lasting five days that attracts large attendances. In order to encourage the construction of new stadiums by cities eager to host the All-Star game, MLB routinely estimates its economic impact. For Boston in 1999 this was estimated to be $62 million and for Milwaukee in 2002, $70 million. Using the same approach as in their Olympic Games study and a second model based on sales tax data, Baade and Matheson find no support for MLB's assertion of a positive impact on income and hence employment of hosting the All-Star game. Support for subsidizing such events must rest on the presence of nonobservable externalities. Another mega event that has been described as a 'mega bust' is the NFL's Super Bowl (Porter, 1999).

Antitrust and public policy

US antitrust policy

The treatment of professional team sports by competition policy is partly a function of their perceived structure. According to Neale (1964), professional sports leagues are natural monopolies and we may regard teams simply as individual plants in a common enterprise. In that case competition policy would focus on the league as a whole, while generally ignoring individual clubs. Other economists regard leagues as **cartels** that constrain the activities of individual teams through various rules. Rules that influence market structure and conduct, such as controls on league size, on the distribution of league franchises and various forms of labor market controls, are considered anticompetitive. Here the competition authorities would focus on the activities of the individual clubs as well as the league as a whole. A third possibility is to regard a sports league as a **joint venture** that produces sporting competition (Flynn and Gilbert, 2001). Then, from the point of view of competition policy, the central issue is whether the coordination of professional sports leagues harms competition, and if so, whether this effect is more than offset by the benefits consumers obtain from such coordination. For conventional antitrust analysis Flynn and Gilbert argue that the most important organizational feature of such leagues is whether teams are owned by separate economic entities or jointly owned by a single economic entity. Recent newly formed US leagues such as Major League Soccer and the Women's National Basketball Association have a structure in which the league, rather than its individual teams, owns all player contracts and negotiates player salaries collectively. Such arrangements may well lead to a more benign view of restrictive controls by antitrust regulators than would be the case under the first two alternatives.

Antitrust policy in the US is much longer established than competition policy in Europe and sport appears to be treated as a special case, whereas in Europe, though lip service is paid to the notion that sport is different, the European Union competition authorities appear in practise to have taken a much firmer line in relation to player contracts, the collective selling of broadcasting rights and other forms of restriction. In the USA the relatively lenient approach can be traced back to the 1922 Supreme Court case, *Federal Baseball* v. *National League*, already referred to in Chapters 4 and 7, which made a highly controversial judgment that baseball was exempt from the federal antitrust laws as it did not engage in interstate commerce. Thus, in the 1972 *Flood* v. *Kuhn* baseball case, the court refused to prohibit the **reserve clause** on the grounds that it was the responsibility of Congress to over-turn the antitrust exemption granted by the Supreme Court. While some important cases have gone against the owners in the other major team sports, including the finding that the reserve clause was unlawful, protection is offered under the National Labor Relations Act which shields collective bargaining agreements from antitrust legislation. Provisions such as the **player draft** and **salary caps** have similarly been protected. Also, as noted in Chapter 6, in 1961 Congress passed the Sports Broadcasting Act, which exempted collectively negotiated sponsored broadcasting agreements from antitrust coverage.

The one antitrust law in the US that went against the owners was the Curt Flood Act of 1998. Curt Flood unsuccessfully sued MLB over the reserve clause. The Act was named in his honor but he has no direct connection to the Act. MLB had such a public black eye after the last baseball strike that Congress decided to eliminate baseball's antitrust exemption as applied to labor matters. The only shield MLB now has against the antitrust laws related to hiring and wages is its collective bargaining agreement with the players' union. If the players were to vote to decertify their union two aspects of MLB's relations with players might be liable to a court challenge. These are the player draft and the luxury tax, which is based on team payrolls. The intent of the Curt Flood Act was to avoid another baseball strike. It was thought that MLB would have a difficult time functioning without a collective bargaining agreement. It is too early to tell what impact the Act will have (Edmonds, 1999).

European competition policy

In Europe domestic laws on competition policy, as in other areas, are subject to European control. The Competition Directorate (DG IV) of the European Commission has examined a range of sports issues in recent years. A landmark was the 1995 **Bosman case** (referred to in Chapter 4) before the European Court of Justice concerning the UEFA retain and transfer labor market rules, which were found to be incompatible with Article 34 of the Treaty of Rome, as the latter requires free mobility of labor. Subsequently, the European Commission decided that requiring a transfer fee for a player within, as opposed to the end of, a contract period represented a restriction on the free mobility of labor. A new system was agreed in March 2001 following negotiations between FIFA, UEFA and the EU. Players' contracts could range from 1 to 5 years with movement within the first three years of a contract, which occurred without the agreement of the parties, subject to civil remedies. Compensation fees for players aged 18–23 could be used to offset the costs of training and player development. In 2001 the Commission issued a statement objecting to the collective sale of broadcasting rights to UEFA's European Champions League Competition, though eventually this was agreed to subject to significant restrictions. In 1999 the UK Restrictive Practices Court upheld the right of the English Premier League to negotiate on behalf of all member clubs in a case involving BSkyB.[2]

However, the European Commission still has concerns about exclusivity over a long duration and for a wide range of rights. In December 2002, the Commission opened a formal investigation, suggesting that the Premier League was being anticompetitive by selling exclusive rights to a single domestic broadcaster (BSkyB) and by preventing its 20 member clubs from making their individual deals. The joint selling arrangements were held to be anticompetitive because they foreclose the market for other broadcasters to the detriment of the consumer. It seems clear, therefore, that European Union competition policy has been much harsher on the owners of professional sports teams than antitrust policy in North America. It seems unlikely, for instance, that approval would be given for the introduction of player drafts or salary caps. The latter have, in fact, already been introduced in Rugby Union, Rugby League and ice hockey, but these sports have much lower profiles than soccer, which is also seriously considering their introduction. If a player draft was instituted it would be likely to draw the attention of the Commission. It is also likely that nonteam sports will find it more difficult than team sports to justify restrictions on competitions (see, for example, the case of British horse-racing in Box 12.2).

Box 12.2 The British Horse-Racing Board and the Jockey Club

The Jockey Club (founded in 1752) was, until 1993, when it transferred certain functions to the British Horse-Racing Board (BHB) of which it is a constituent member, solely responsible for the governance and regulations of horse-racing in Great Britain. It also owns 13 of the 59 race-courses in Britain. Among the BHB's responsibilities is the control of the fixture list, including the power to fix the date at which all races may be held and to cancel or alter these at its own discretion. This practice was

Box 12.2 continued

investigated by the Office of Fair Trading (OFT) under the 1998 Competition Act, which prohibits anticompetitive agreements. In April 2003, the OFT issued a Rule 14 Notice setting out its preliminary view that certain orders and rules infringed the Act on the grounds that they

- limited the freedom of race-courses and the type of racing they staged
- fixed the amounts race-courses must offer owners to enter their horses in a race and
- monopolized the supply of race and runners data supplied to bookmakers by foreclosing competition from alternative suppliers.

The OFT recognised that noncommercial sporting rules such as the specification of the earliest age at which horses can run, how starting stalls should be operated, the use of whips by jockeys and tests for doping were legitimate rules for the two bodies to impose, and that the application of competition rules should take into account the distinctive characteristics of the sport. However, it believed the rules specified above had significant economic and commercial consequences and were not essential for achieving the objectives of the governing bodies. In effect they restricted the output of race-courses, restricted and distorted the balance between types of racing (e.g., national hunt and flat racing) and shared the market between race-courses by ensuring that race-courses located within 50 miles of another did not stage races of the same type at the same time.

There is a natural tendency for politicians to involve themselves in the activities of sporting organizations, as many of them are fans themselves. One particularly extreme example was the decision of the UK Minister of Sport in 1997 to set up a Football Task Force under the Chairmanship of David Mellor, a Conservative MP and supporter of Chelsea Football Club, to address public concerns about the organization of English football. Among the concerns to be addressed were the level of ticket prices, the increasing commercialization of the game, encouragement of greater supporter involvement in the running of clubs, and the reconciliation of the potential conflict between the legitimate needs of shareholders, players and supporters when clubs are floated on the Stock Exchange. This represents a remarkable and unprecedented degree of intervention in a private sector industry.

In reporting back to the government the Task Force recommended a Football Audit Commission to ensure greater accountability of clubs, a Financial Compliance Unit to introduce a 'fit and proper persons' requirement for anyone wishing to own a substantial number of shares in a football club, and a Code of Practice to set out minimum standards to be met by clubs in their treatment of spectators. Among very detailed recommendations on ticketing policies was the proposal that fans paying the highest prices should cross-subsidize those paying the lower prices (for whom prices should increase by no more than the rate of inflation), an extension of the use of low-priced tickets for children and the elderly, limits on the sale of season tickets, and an increase in the proportion of tickets issued to away fans (who should not be subject to price discrimination). An Independent Football Commission (IFC) was eventually set up under the Chairmanship of Professor Derek Fraser, the Vice-Chancellor of the University of Teeside, to review and report on the adoption by the FA, the FA Premiership and the Football League of best practices in commercial and financial matters within professional football, particularly with regard to customer service. The IFC has a particular interest in ticket prices, admission to matches, merchandise and supporter and other shareholder involvement.

Such intervention is unheard of in the USA. A contrasting example is the Commissioner's Blue Ribbon Panel on Baseball Economics (Levin *et al.*, 2000). Essentially, the panel was MLB's attempt to heal itself. The panel was appointed by the Commissioner of Major League Baseball to consider whether baseball's current economic system had created a problem of competitive imbalance in the game and to recommend solutions to the sport itself designed to address identified problems. The independent members included Senator George Mitchell, and Paul Volker, former Chairman of the Board of Governors of the Federal Reserve System, presumably to give substance to the belief that the public interest would be taken into account. In the event the panel found that large and growing revenue disparities existed, causing problems of severe competitive imbalance. The only problem with this conclusion is that it is contradicted by the evidence. Baseball in the 1990s was at least as competitively balanced as it had been in earlier decades using a variety of measures. Further, the limited revenue sharing and payroll tax that have been approved as part of the MLB's 1996 Collective Bargaining Agreement with the players' association had failed to produce the intended moderation in payroll disparities. This prompted a new luxury tax and revenue-sharing plan established in 2002. This new program has had little effect on the spending by one team, the New York Yankees. Its long-term effectiveness is, however, unknown. Finally, the panel found that in a majority of franchise markets the cost to clubs of trying to be competitive was causing an increase in ticket and concession prices, jeopardizing MLB's ability to be an affordable family sport.[3] In the view of the panel, proper competitive balance required that every well-run club should have a reasonable prospect of reaching the play-offs on a regular basis. As a consequence the panel recommended increased revenue-sharing (particularly local revenue), a competitive balance tax on club payrolls above a fixed threshold, central fund distributions, a competitive balance draft redistributing players from the eight clubs qualifying for the play offs to the weakest eight clubs, reforms in the rules for drafting for young players and franchise relocations. Most of these recommendations have not been acted upon.

Conclusions

Governments are actively involved in the production and regulation of sport. While some might be tempted to argue that sports are no different from any other recreational activity or form of recreation, the importance of sport to all societies has virtually guaranteed a prominent role for the public sector in sporting activities. In terms of sports as a recreation activity, local and regional governments are involved in the provision of park space and the organization of amateur leagues throughout North America. In Europe there are prominent roles for government in the formation of recreational policy and the building and maintenance of recreational land and facilities. All of this is justified in terms of the public benefits produced from sports that range from improved health to social benefits from learning teamwork.

Governments are also involved in professional sports through their role in ensuring a competitive environment and avoiding monopolistic control by groups of owners that seek to control a very profitable industry. Governments are also involved in the attracting of teams and sporting events as a result of the public benefits anticipated from the presence of a team or the hosting of a prestigious and popular sporting event. These hoped-for public benefits range from prestige and recognition of an area or city as 'big time', to the possibility of securing some form of economic advantage for an area as a result of a team's presence or the hosting of an event.

The pervasive role of government in sports makes the question of whether this involvement should exist largely academic. Governments are involved and will continue to play a strong role as a result of the importance of sport as a social institution and the publicly accepted view that sport is an important aspect of life with at least the potential for generating critical economic advantages. Local and regional governments should play a large role in the planning for and maintaining of space for recreational activities. This includes responsibility for parklands and the building of pitches or fields where activities can be held. These activities fall under government's responsibility for land use and zoning; representation of the balance between the use of land for economic development and preservation of open space continues to be an accepted role for the public sector, so that the public good aspects of recreational land can be balanced with the imperatives expressed by developers seeking to change land use to ensure expanded opportunities for profit and individual gain.

It is also important to note that governments can and do play a role in protecting the health of athletes. In the USA President Theodore Roosevelt threatened government intervention if colleges were unable to protect college football players from death and severe injuries. The NCAA grew from this challenge and while some of its activities have been questioned it is clear this organization outlawed dangerous tactics such as the flying wedge. The NCAA is not a quasi-governmental organization; it is entirely independent and self-governing. State Boxing Commissions are an example of government organizations that have made some effort to protect athletes and ensure that the injuries so rampant in the early part of the twentieth century are minimized.

Governments encounter a far more complicated environment when the desire of owners of professional sports franchises to secure monopoly control of markets and particular sports is encountered. Here governments have had less success in achieving goals related to the supply of teams and have actually helped individual leagues improve their control at the public's expense. Periodically there are calls for reform and one can and should anticipate that the issue of how governments can ensure more market-like solutions without jeopardizing the fiscal health of leagues will continue. There is also a need for international cooperation, especially with regard to the working arrangements involving the youngest athletes. As teams and leagues continue to seek the best players, some of the programs in South and Central America to attract and train young players would not be legal in the USA or in several European countries; yet teams and leagues operate in those environments as some governments are unable or unwilling to pass or enforce child protections laws that have become commonplace in more developed nations.

Government attitudes toward sport seem to vacillate between regarding them as no different from any other economic activity and regarding them as a special case, requiring various forms of intervention, though the reasons for such intervention vary between participant and spectator sports. As far as amateur sport is concerned almost all governments regard such activities as merit goods which justify subsidies. The Taliban government seems to have been an exception: it banned soccer outright. Little attempt has been made, however, to estimate the benefits of promoting participatory sports, compare them with costs and determine whether the distribution of resources between various activities is optimal. It is also doubtful whether targeting is sufficiently accurate to ensure that government efficiency objectives have been met.

Governments also seem to believe that there are considerable externalities to be derived from the hosting of major international sporting events and are often prepared to devote considerable resources to assist their own sports authorities in the bidding process.[4] Sometimes these beliefs lead them to provide resources for the construction of new or reconstruction of old national stadiums. In North America the equivalent is the subsidies offered to major league clubs by local governments to relocate.

An issue growing in importance is the appropriate stance to be taken by antitrust or competition policy-makers towards the activities of professional sports leagues, which are ostensibly designed to promote competitive balance. More particularly, should competition policy make special provision for such sports, which is more evidently the case in North America than in Europe? Current policy in Europe seems ill-defined and contradictory across countries. While there are some arguments in favor of special treatment for professional team sports given their distinctive nature, some degree of regulation might be regarded as an appropriate quid pro quo and a more equal sharing of income between large and small clubs may be one of them.

Notes

1. The Commonwealth Stadium was built in a run-down part of Manchester at a cost of £110 million. The National Lottery administered by Sport England contributed £77 million and the remainder was provided by the local council. After the event the stadium was extended and redesigned to be the new home for Manchester City football club, which would pay a rent based on a percentage of ticket sales. The stadium would also be made available for 100 days' community use per year. Other facilities cost £44 million and were similarly supported by lottery money. An independent report claimed that staging the games had helped Manchester secure more than £600 million of public and private investment and predicted that an additional 300,000 people would visit the city each year as a result, spending an additional £12 million. The Games would generate the equivalent of 6,100 full time jobs and nearly 30 million people worldwide would consider the city as a possible business and visitor destination because of its improved image. These sorts of figures are not atypical in investigations of the pay offs for such events, but are difficult to substantiate.
2. Similar challenges occurred in Germany (which was given an exemption from competition law by the German Government), Denmark, the Netherlands, Italy and Spain.
3. This, in fact, is a dubious proposition. See Chapter 3.
4. However, there are signs of some reassessment of this in the UK. In the Department for Culture, Media and Sport (2002) it is suggested that there should be a more cautious approach to the hosting of mega sporting events with a set process for government involvement, including a clear assessment of the benefits.

Exercises

1. Outline the arguments why governments should intervene in the market for sporting activity.
2. Is international sporting success a public good?
3. Should any distinction be made between amateur and professional sports men and women in terms of their ability to compete in competitions within their sport?
4. If amateur sports men or women attract large attendances to competitions in which they compete, what consequences are likely to follow if they are denied financial rewards for their participation?
5. Should involvement in sports or physical exercise be made compulsory in schools?

6. What externalities are likely to arise from participation in sports and physical activities?
7. Under which circumstances might it be appropriate for a government to support financially a bid by the sports organizations in a particular county to attract a mega sporting event?
8. Should sports be given special treatment with regard to the implementation of antitrust policy?
9. Should politicians intervene in the operation of sporting enterprises?
10. How have politicians intervened in the operation of sporting enterprises?
11. How do US and European antitrust policies differ? Which regime makes more sense?
12. There is a movement in the USA to provide education vouchers for children in primary and secondary schools that could be used to pay private school tuition. The advocates claim that the public schools in many US cities have utterly failed and that exposing them to private competition would force them to improve. Milton Friedman, the Nobel Laureate economist, is one of these advocates. He and his wife, Rose Friedman, have established the Milton and Rose Friedman Foundation to support the voucher movement. Paradoxically perhaps, given the social benefits claimed in this chapter, a political movement to provide publicly funded vouchers for private sports facilities to low-income children does not exist in the USA. Can you account for this difference?

Glossary of terms

Adverse selection: The problem that in certain markets the inability of one trader to assess the quality of the other makes it likely that poor quality traders will predominate (see lemons model below).

Antitrust: Governments have passed antitrust laws to prohibit corporations from engaging in activities that prevent entry into a market by a potential competitor or interfere with the operation of a free market.

Auctions: Sales in which the auctioneer elicits bids by starting at a low price and raising the price until only one bid remains (ascending price auction). Alternatives include sealed bid auctions where the amount rivals are prepared to bid is unknown to the other bidders.

Barnstorming: This refers to the practice where a team tours from city to city to play matches with loosely organized or irregular teams. In the late nineteenth and twentieth centuries these games were frequently played in rural areas in America and usually against a barn. Fans stood alongside the field and, since the barns were part of the field, the games came to be called 'barnstorming'.

Bilateral monopoly: A market in which a single seller (a monopoly) is confronted with a single buyer (monopsonist) leading to uncertainty in the determination of price and output.

Blackouts: The prevention of live television coverage of a game in the geographical area in which the game is being played.

Bosman ruling: A decision by the European Court of Justice in 1995 that the UEFA rules concerning the transfer of players were unlawful as they infringed the requirement for free mobility of labor under the Treaty of Rome. Further, restrictions on the number of foreign-born players were unlawful.

Broad exclusivity: An agreement with an exclusive purchaser of broadcasting rights that it will not show any other live broadcasts outside the agreement.

Capture hypothesis: Control of the regulatory agency that governs a industry by members of the industry.

Cartel: An association of producers designed to control prices by regulating output and restricting competition

Cartel bargaining: Bargaining by a representative of the league as a whole with television companies for broadcasting rights (sometimes referred to as collective selling).

Closely held shares: A situation in which a small number of people own enough shares to control a company.

Coase theorem: On the assumption of zero transactions costs and neutral wealth effects the allocation of resources is both efficient and invariant with respect to the initial assignment of ownership rights (see also invariance thesis).

Conjoint or joint production: Sport, unlike most other businesses, requires two or more producers to cooperate or ensure that the individual product of each firm exists. Matches require two teams (or athletes in nonteam sports), and without the participation of both firms and their agreement on rules the match cannot take place, eliminating the ability of either team to delivery a consumable product.

Consumer surplus: The difference between what consumers would be prepared to pay for a good or service and what they actually pay.

Contingent valuation method: A method by which consumers are asked to put a valuation on different policies which they might be faced with.

Contract compliance: The extent to which an organization has met the targets set by the Office of Civil Rights under affirmative action for representation of different groups in employment or activities.

Cost-benefit analysis: The appraisal of an investment project which includes all private and social costs and benefits accruing to the project.

Co-worker discrimination: The extent to which members of the majority group have an aversion to being employed with members of a minority group and are prepared to sacrifice income in order to exclude members of the minority group.

Cross-player complementarities: The extent to which the productivity of one player increases the productivity of another player.

Cross-price elasticity of demand: The proportionate change in the quantity demanded of one good divided by the proportionate change in the price of another good.

Customer discrimination: The extent to which members of a particular group have an aversion to being served by members of another group and are prepared to pay a higher price for a good or service to avoid such an outcome.

Customers: For sporting events these are ticket buyers plus buyers who pay to watch on pay-per-view television, plus those who 'pay' for regular television broadcasts by being part of the audience for commercials.

Derived demand: The fact that the demand for labor depends on the demand for the product which it helps to produce.

Demand: A function that relates the number of tickets sold to the price. More generally, a function that relates the quantity buyers will purchase of any good or service as a function of its price.

Economic activity: Economic activity is the value of any transaction such as the purchase of tickets for a sporting event or the consumption of food at a sporting event. Economic activity does not mean that new income for a community has been generated as a result of the transaction that has taken place.

Economic development: Economic development means there has been a positive increment in level of economic activity in an area that is not offset by a loss of some other form of economic activity in the same geographic area.

Effective price discrimination: Charging higher prices for variants of goods that have small or no increases in the cost of production.

Elasticity of demand. The percentage change in the quantity divided by the percentage change in the price.

Employer discrimination: The extent to which an employer has an aversion to members of a particular group and is prepared to sacrifice profit rather than employ members of that group.

Exploitation: The degree to which the wage for a unit of labour is less than its marginal revenue product as a function of the degree of inelasticity in the supply of labor.

Export function: As applied to sporting events, export function refers to the retention of fans' activities (as opposed to fans going to other areas for sports) or to the attraction of fans from other areas, thus producing economic development for a specific geographic area.

Externalities: The consequences for welfare of the inability of the market to capture fully all the costs and benefits to be derived from a particular activity.

Final offer arbitration: A situation in which the parties engaged in collective bargaining agree that in the event of a dispute a third party (the arbitrator) will determine the outcome on the basis of the final offer of the employer or the final demand of the trade union, as opposed to splitting the difference.

Free Agency: A North American term for players who have reached the end of their contract and have sufficient experience under the collective bargaining agreement to sell their services to the highest bidder without restriction.

Gate-sharing: The arrangements for dividing up the revenue obtained from spectators at a game between the home and away team and the rest of the league teams.

Growth maximization: The policy of allowing a company to grow as fast as possible given financial constraints.

Hiring discrimination: The tendency to prefer to hire members of one group rather than another, given the level of productivity.

Increasing the demand: Shifting the demand function to the right so that a greater quantity is demanded at any given price.

Information asymmetry: The extent to which one party possesses more information than another in negotiation.

Invariance thesis: The principle that the distribution of talent is unaffected by whether the market for players is free or restricted (see Coase theorem).

Irreversibility proposition: The idea that a player's talent may be team-specific so that he is worth more to his current club than to other clubs.

Joint venture: An arrangement by which two or more companies combine together in order to achieve some commercial objective.

Kaldor-Hicks criterion: This states that a project is desirable if it leads to a potential Pareto improvement: that is, the gainers could in principle fully compensate the losers and still have a net gain, even though in practise they do not pay any compensation.

Law of diminishing returns: The tendency for the marginal productivity of labor with capital fixed to decline as the quantity of labor increases.

Lemons model: The idea associated with George Akerlof that where sellers can judge the quality of a product but buyers cannot, all products will sell for the same price regardless of their quality. This will result in a lower price, so that sellers of high quality products will be less inclined to put them on the market (see adverse selection).

Lorenz curve: A graphical representation showing the degree of inequality of a frequency distribution in which the cumulative percentages of a population are plotted against the cumulative percentage of the variable under analysis.

Marginal revenue product: The increase in value of the total product associated with a one unit increase in a factor of production, with other factors of production fixed.

Market dominance: The extent to which one producer (team) wins more games within a season or over a number of seasons than the remaining teams in the leagues.

Merit good: A commodity whose consumption is regarded as socially desirable irrespective of consumer preference.

Mincer human capital model: An earnings equation in which earnings are measured in logarithmic form and the explanatory variables include years of education or qualifications plus experience and its square.

Monopoly model: A description of the prices charged and the quantity provided by a single sellar in a market for a good or service based on demand and the cost of production.

Monopsony: A market in which there is only one buyer of the good or service sold.

Moral hazard: The tendency of an agent to choose an option favorable to himself, but not in the interests of the principal. More generally, it is a perverse effect due to a payment mechanism. For example, someone renting a car that includes fully comprehensive insurance coverage has no incentive to worry about scratching the car.
Multiplier: The extent to which an increase in expenditure is believed to increase income.
Mutual interdependence: The extent to which the economic performance of a firm is influenced by the economic performance of other firms within its own sector.
Narrow exclusivity: An agreement to award exclusive rights to particular live matches to a single broadcaster.
Nash bargaining: A bargaining situation in which each party adopts its optimal strategy given the optimal strategy of the other party.
Nonexcludability: Once public goods are provided it is not possible to exclude anyone from using them, so that some individuals can free ride.
Nonrivalness: The consumption of a good by one person does not affect the ability of others to consume the same good.
No-shows: The non-appearance at a live game of fans who have already purchased a ticket to see the game.
Oaxaca decomposition: A method of estimating discrimination by decomposing earnings for two groups into differences resulting from varying endowments and differences resulting from varying coefficients. The unexplained residual is assumed to be the result of discrimination.
Opta index: The official performance statistics for English Premier League football providing detailed match statistics, quantifying every touch of the ball by each player during active play based on live and off-tape analysis of every match by a team of expert analysts.
Pareto criterion: A situation in which a change makes some people better off without at the same time making anyone worse off.
Pay-per-view: A situation in which the viewers pay a separate fee to see a live broadcast of a particular sporting event.
Perfect competition: A model in which there is free entry of new firms, common information on production technology and prices, and a homogeneous good. The model predicts that individual firms are price takers.
Perfect price discrimination: Charging each customer his or her *reservation price*.
Player draft: A system whereby teams bid for the services of the most promising new players in reverse order of their finish in the previous season's league competition.
Positional segregation: The tendency for different positions in a team to include members of particular ethnic groups disproportionately to their numbers in the population.
Price discrimination: Selling the same good or service at different prices according to how much a customer is willing to pay.
Principal agent-theory: The problem of a principal (e.g., the owner of a company) making sure that the agent (e.g., an employee) acts in the principal's interest when the agent has information that the principal does not possess and the objectives of the two parties are different.
Profits: Total revenue minus total cost.
Profit maximization: The assumption that the owner of firm's decisions are based on earning the highest possible long-term profits.
Public good: A good which yields nonrivalrous consumption and is nonexcludable in the sense that if one person consumes it one cannot exclude others from consuming it.
Rank order tournament model: A system under which prizes are fixed in advance and are independent of absolute performance, relative performance being the crucial determinant in determining incentives.
Relative wage demand curve: A demand curve representing the supply and demand for members of majority and minority groups in terms of their relative wage rates.

Reservation price: The most that a customer would pay for a good.
Reserve rule/clause: A league agreement in US major team sports that allowed team owners to continue to employ players under the previous contract if they informed a player of their intention to do so by a particular date.
Retain and transfer system: The European equivalent in soccer to the reserve clause.
Salary cap: A mechanism originating in the USA whereby a fixed percentage of allowable revenue, equally allocated across all teams, is permitted to be spent on the player wage bill.
Salary discrimination: The tendency to pay different levels of earnings for given productivity to players according to their membership of particular ethnic groups.
Sales revenue maximization: The assumption that the owner of a firm's decisions are based on the goal of sales revenue.
Say's Law: The idea, due to Jean Baptiste Say, that supply creates its own demand, because every provider of any new goods is seeking other goods in payment. In consequence that there can be no general over-supply of goods in the long run.
Shirking behavior: The tendency of workers to operate at a lower level of efficiency or effort than they have contracted to provide.
Sorting hypothesis: The notion that greater incentives will attract better competitors.
Stacking: The over-representation of members of certain ethnic groups in key positions on the field of play (see positional segregation).
Substitutes: Any two goods that as the price of one increases the quantity demanded of the other increases.
Stakeholders: Groups or individuals with interests in the existence of a good or service.
Taste for discrimination: An aversion to contact with members of a minority group by members of the majority group such that individuals are prepared to pay a price to avoid contact with minority members.
Team roster limits: A limit on the number of players a team is allowed to have under contract at any one time.
Theory of clubs: The determination of the optimal size of club in terms of membership on the basis of marginal costs and benefits.
Title IX: A law passed by the US Congress in 1972 which outlaws discrimination by sex in educational programs or in activities receiving federal financial support.
Toehold effect: The prediction under auction theory that when a bidder in an auction has an ownership stake in the asset being sold (or a toehold) that bidder is more likely to win the auction than other bidders who do not possess such a toehold.
Transaction costs: The costs involved in the exchange of goods and services.
Utility maximization: In sports the assumption that an owner is primarily motivated by the pleasure of having his or her team win and tries to hire enough talent to have a maximum number of wins or championships.
Vertical integration: The extent to which successive stages in the production process are controlled by a single enterprise.
Welfare: Welfare, as used in this chapter and the study of sports and economic development, refers to the wealth or economic state of individuals or a region considering the income earned and any forfeiture of leisure time.
Winner's curse: The tendency of a winning bid to be in excess of the real value of the asset sold in an auction.
Yankee paradox: The tendency for teams to fail to take into account the benefits from close competition giving rise to undue dominance. The term is used by Vrooman.

Bibliography

Adams, Henry (1982) *Mont-Saint-Michel and Chartres*, Columbia and Princeton, USA. University Presses of California.

Ahmed-Taylor, T. (1995) 'Who is Major Enough for the Major Leagues?', *New York Times*, April 2, p. E5.

Akerlof, G. (1970) 'The Market for Lemons: Quality Uncertainty and the Market Mechanism', *Quarterly Journal of Economics*, Vol. 84, pp. 488–500.

Alexander, D.L. (2001) 'Major League Baseball: Monopoly Pricing and Profit Maximising Behavior', *Journal of Sports Economics*, Vol. 2, No. 4 (November), pp. 356–68.

Alexander, D.L., Kern, W. and Neill, J. (2000) 'Valuing the Consumption Benefits from Professional Sports Franchises', *Journal of Urban Economics* (September), pp. 321–37.

Amato, L.H., Gandar, J.M. and Zuber, R.A. (2001) 'The Impact of Proposition 48 on the Relationship between Football Success and Football Player Graduation Rates', *Journal of Sports Economics*, Vol. 2, No. 2 (May), pp. 101–13.

Anderson, T. and La Croix, S.J. (1991) 'Consumer Racial Discrimination in Major League Baseball', *Economic Inquiry*, Vol. XXIX, No. 4 (October), pp. 665–77.

Andreff, W. and Staudohar, P.D. (2000) 'The Evolving European Model of Professional Sports Finance', *Journal of Sports Economics*, Vol. 1, No. 3 (August), pp. 257–76.

Arnold, A.J. and Beneviste, I. (1987) 'Wealth and Poverty in the English Football League', *Accounting and Business Research*, Vol. 17, pp. 195–203.

Atkinson, S., Stanley, L. and Tschirhart, J. (1988) 'Revenue Sharing as an Incentive in an Agency Problem: An Example from the National Football League', *Rand Journal of Economics*, Vol. 19, No. 1 (Spring), pp. 27–43.

Audas, R., Dobson, S. and Goddard, J. (1999) 'Organisational Performance and Managerial Turnover', *Managerial and Decision Economics*, Vol. 20, No. 6 (September), pp. 305–18.

Austrian, Z. and Rosentraub, M. (1997) 'Cleveland's Gateway to the Future', in R. Noll and A. Zimbalist (eds), *Cities, Sports, and Taxes*. Washington, DC: The Brookings Institution, pp. 355–84.

Baade, R.A. (1996) 'Professional Sports as a Catalyst for Metropolitan Economic Development', *Journal of Urban Affairs*, Vol. 18, No. 1, pp. 1–17.

Baade, R.A. and Matheson, V.A. (2001) 'Home Run or Wild Pitch? Assessing the Economic Impact of Major League Baseball's All-Star Game', *Journal of Sports Economics*, Vol. 2, No. 4 (November), pp. 307–27.

Baade, R.A. and Matheson, V.A. (2002) 'Bidding for the Olympics; Fools Gold?', in C.P. Barros, M. Ibrahimo and S. Szymanski (eds), *Transatlantic Sport; The Comparative Economics of North American and European Sports*. Cheltenham, UK, and Northampton, MA: Edward Elgar, pp. 127–51.

Baade, R. and Sanderson, A. (1997) 'The Employment Effects of Teams and Sports Facilities', in Noll and Zimbalist (1997), Sports, Jobs and Taxes: *the Economic Impact of Sports Teams and Stadiums*, pp. 92–188.

Baim, D. 1994. *The Sports Stadium as a Municipal Investment*. Westport, CT: Greenwood Press.

Baimbridge, M. (1997) 'Match Attendance at Euro 96: Was the Crowd Waving or Draining', *Applied Economics Letters*, Vol. 4, No. 9 (September), pp. 555–8.

Baimbridge, M. (1998) 'Outcome Uncertainty in Sporting Competitions: The Olympic Games 1896–1996', *Applied Economics Letters*, Vol. 5, No. 3 (March), pp. 161–4.

Baimbridge, M., Cameron, S. and Dawson, P. (1995) 'Satellite Broadcasting and Match Attendance: The Case of Rugby League', *Applied Economics Letters*, Vol. 2, pp. 343–6.

Baimbridge, M., Cameron, S. and Dawson P. (1996) 'Satellite Television and the Demand for Football: A Whole New Ball Game', *Scottish Journal of Political Economy*, Vol. 43, No. 3 (August), pp. 317–33.

Bairam, E.I. (1991) 'Functional Form and New Production Functions: Some Comments', *Applied Economics*, Vol. 23, pp. 1247–50.

Bairam, E.I. (1996) 'Production Functions and the Strategy Implications of Cricket in New Zealand', *Sporting Traditions: Journal of the Australian Society of Sports History*, Vol. 6, pp. 202–17.

Bairam, E.I. and Howells, J.M. (1991a) 'The Probability of Winning and Maximising Behaviour for One Day International Cricket', *University of Otago Economics Discussion Papers*, 01 (October), p. 21.

Bairam, E.I. and Howells, J.M. (1991b) 'The Probability of Winning and Maximising Behaviour in Cricket: The New Zealand Experience', *University of Otago Economics Discussion Papers*, 01 (October), p. 15.

Bairam, E.I., Howells, J.M. and Turner, G.M. (1990) 'Production Functions in Cricket: The Australian and New Zealand Experience', *Applied Economics*, Vol. 22, pp. 871–9.

Baler, M.R. (2002) 'Inter-League Play and Baseball Attendance', *Journal of Sports Economics*, Vol. 3, No. 4 (November), pp. 320–34.

Barron, J.M., Ewing, B.T. and Waddell, G.R. (2000) 'The Effect of High School Athletic Participation on Education and Labour Market Outcomes', *Review of Economics and Statistics*, Vol. 83, No. 3 (August), pp. 409–21.

Barros, C.P. (2001) 'Economic Return on Schooling for Soccer Players', *Journal of Sports Economics*, Vol. 2, No. 4 (November), pp. 356–68.

Barros, C.P., Ibrahimo, M., and Szymanski, S. (eds) (2002) *Transatlantic Sport: The Comparative Economics of North America and European Sports*. Cheltenham, UK, and Northampton, MA: Edward Elgar.

Bartik, T. 1991. *Who Benefits from State and Local Economic Development Policies?* Kalamazoo, Michigan: Upjohn Institute.

Battacharya, M. and Smyth, R. (2003) 'The Game is Not the Same: The Demand for Test Match Cricket in Australia', *Australian Economic Papers*, Vol. 42, No. 1 (March), pp. 77–90.

Baumol, W. (1959) *Business Behaviour, Value and Growth*. New York: Macmillan.

Becker, G. (1971) *The Economics of Discrimination* (2nd edn). Chicago, IL: Chicago University Press.

Becker, G. and Becker, G.N. (1996) *The Economics of Life*. New York: McGraw-Hill.

Bellemore, F.A. (2001) 'Racial and Ethnic Employment Discrimination: Promotion in Major League Baseball', *Journal of Sports Economics*, Vol. 2, No. 4 (November), pp. 356–68.

Bennett, R.W. and Fizel, J.L. (1995) 'Telecast Deregulation and Competitive Balance: Regarding NCAA Division I Football', *American Journal of Economics and Sociology*, Vol. 54, pp. 183–99.

Benson, Marty (1999) *1999 NCAA Division I Graduation Rates Report*. Indianapolis: NCAA.

Bergman, G., Brooks, R. and Davidson, S. (2000) 'The Sydney Olympic Games Announcement and Australian Stock Market Reaction', *Applied Economics Letters*, Vol. 17, No. 12 (December), pp. 781–4.

Bergmann, T.J. and Dworkin, J.B. (1978) 'Collective Bargaining vs. the Rozelle Rule: An Analysis of Labor–Management Relations in Professional Football', *Akron Business and Economic Review*, Vol. 9, No. 2, pp. 35–80.

Berri, D.J. (1999) 'Who is Most Valuable? Measuring the Player's Production of Wins in the National Basketball Association', *Managerial and Decision Economics*, Vol. 20, No. 8 (December), pp. 411–28.

Bien, D.D. (1975) 'An Analysis of the Skiing Industry', in S.P. Ladany (ed.), *Management Science Applications to Leisure-time Operation*. Amsterdam: North-Holland.

Bird, P.J.W.N. (1982) 'The Demand for League Football', *Applied Economics*, Vol. 14, No. 6, pp. 637–49.

Blass, A.A. (1992) 'Does the Baseball Labor Market Contradict the Human Capital Model of Investment?', *Review of Economics and Statistics*, Vol. LXXIV, No. 2 (May), pp. 260–8.

Blair, J. 1995. *Local Economic Development: Analysis and Practice*. Thousand Oaks, CA: Sage.

Blum, M.P. (1976) 'Valuing Intangibles: What are the Choices for Valuing Professional Sports Teams?', *Journal of Taxation*, Vol. 45 (November), pp. 286–8.

Bodvarsson, O.B. and Banavan, K. (1998) 'The Value of Arbitration Rights in Major League Baseball, Implications for Salaries and Discrimination', *Quarterly Journal of Business and Economics*, Vol. 37, pp. 65–80.

Bodvarsson, O.B. and Brastow, R.T. (1998) 'Do Employers Pay for Consistent Performance? Evidence from the NBA', *Economic Enquiry*, Vol. 36, pp. 145–60.

Bodvarsson, O.B. and Brastow, R.T. (1999) 'A Test of Employer Discrimination in the NBA', *Contemporary Economic Policy*, Vol. 17, No. 2 (April), pp. 243–55.

Bodvarsson, O.B. and Partridge, M.D. (2001) 'A Supply and Demand Model of Co-worker, Employer and Customer Discrimination', *Labor Economics*, Vol. 8, No. 3 (June), pp. 389–416.

Bodvarsson, O.B. and Pettman, S.P. (2000) 'Racial Wage Discrimination in Major League Baseball: Do Free Agency and League Size Matter?', *Applied Economics Letters*, Vol. 9, pp. 791–6.

Borland, J. (1987) 'The Demand for Australian Rules Football', *Economic Record*, (September), pp. 221–30

Borland, J. and Lye, J. (1992) 'Attendance at Australian Rules Football: A Panel Study', *Applied Economics*, Vol. 24, No. 9 (September), pp. 1053–8.

Borland, J. and Lye, J. (1996) 'Matching and Mobility in the Market for Australian Rules Football Coaches', *Industrial and Labor Relations Review*, Vol. 40, No. 1 (October), pp. 143–58.

Borland, Melvin V., Goff, Brian L. and Pulsinelli, Robert W. (1992) *College Athletics: Financial Burden or Boon?* Greenwich, JAI Press.

Bourgheas, S. and Downward, P. (2003) 'The Economics of Professional Sports Leagues: Some Insights on the Reform of Transfer Markets', *Journal of Sports Economics*, Vol. 4, No. 2 (May), pp. 87–107.

Boyd, D.W. and Boyd, L.A. (1995) 'Strategic Behaviour in Contests: Evidence from the 1992 Barcelona Olympic Games', *Applied Economics*, Vol. 27, No. 1 (November), pp. 1037–44.

Boyes, W.J. (ed.) (1994) 'The Economics of Sports Enterprises', Special Issue, *Managerial and Decision Economics*, Vol. 15, No. 5 (September–October), pp. 399–400.

Breedlove, Joseph (1999) *Assessing Nonmarket Values through Contingent Valuation.* Congressional Research Service, RL 30242, Library of Congress, Washington, DC.

Bremmer, Dale S. and Kesselring, Randall G. (1993) 'The Advertising Effect of University Athletic Success: A Reappraisal of the Evidence', *Quarterly Review of Economics and Finance*, Vol. 33, No. 4 (Winter), pp. 409–21.

Brooks, R.D., Faff, F.W. and Sokulsky, D. (2002) 'An Ordered Response Model of Test Cricket Performances', *Applied Economics*, Vol. 34, No. 18 (15 December), pp. 2353–65.

Brower, J. (1976) 'Professional Sports Team Ownership: Fun, Profit and Ideology of the Power Elite', *Journal of Sport and Social Issues*, Vol. 1, No. 1, pp. 16–51.

Brown, E., Spiro, R. and Keenan, D. (1991) 'Wage and Non-wage Discrimination in Professional Basketball: Do Fans Affect It?', *American Journal of Economics and Sociology*, Vol. 50, pp. 333–45.

Brown, K.H. and Abraham, F.J. (2002) 'Testing Market Efficiency in the Major League Baseball Over-Under Betting Market', *Journal of Sports Economics*, Vol. 3, No. 4 (November), pp. 311–19.

Brown, R.W. (1993) 'An Estimate of the Rent Generated by a Premium College Football Player', *Economic Inquiry*, Vol. XXX1, No. 4 (October), pp. 671–84.

Brown, R.W. (1994) 'Measuring Cartel Rents in the College Basketball Player Recruitment Market', *Applied Economics*, Vol. 26, No. 1 (January), pp. 27–35.

Brown, W.O. and Sauer, R.D. (1993) 'Does the Basketball Market Believe in the Hot Hand? A Comment', *American Economic Review*, Vol. 83, No. 5 (December), pp. 1377–86.

Bruggink, T. and Rose Jr, D. (1990) 'Financial Restraint in the Free Agent Labor Market for Major League Baseball: Players Look at Strike Three', *Southern Economic Journal*, Vol. 56, No. 4 (April), pp. 1029–43.

Buchanan J. (1965) 'An Economic Theory of Clubs', *Economica*, Vol. 32, No. 1, pp. 1–14.

Burdekin, R. and Idson, T. (1991) 'Customer Preferences and the Racial Structure of Professional Basketball Teams', *Applied Economics*, Vol. 23, pp. 179–86.

Burdekin, R.C.K. and Idson, T.L. (1995) 'Customer Preference, Attendance and Racial Structure in the Market for Baseball Memorabilia', *Journal of Business*, Vol. 68, pp. 215–30.

Burger, J.D. and Walters, S.J.K. (2003) 'Market Size, Pay and Performance: A General Model and Application to Major League Baseball', *Journal of Sports Economics*, Vol. 4, No. 2 (May), pp. 108–25.

Burkitt, B. and Cameron, S. (1992) 'Impact of League Restructuring on Team Sports Attendances: The Case of Rugby League', *Applied Economics*, Vol. 24, No. 2 (February), pp. 265–72.

Butler, M.R. (1995) 'Competitive Balance in Major League Baseball', *The American Economist*, Vol. XXXIV, No. 2 (Fall), pp. 46–52.

Butler, M.R. (2002) 'Inter-League Play and Baseball Attendance', *Journal of Sports Economics*, Vol. 3, No. 4 (November), pp. 320–34.

Cagan, J. and deMause, N. (1998) *Field of Schemes: How the Great Stadium Swindle turns Public Money into Private Profit*. Monroe, Maine: Common Courage Press.

Cain, M., Law, D. and Peel, D. (2000) 'The Favourite–Longshot Bias and Market Efficiency in U.K. Football Betting', *Scottish Journal of Political Economy*, Vol. 47, pp. 25–36.

Cairns, J.A. (1987) 'Evaluating Changes in League Structure: The Re-organisation of the Scottish Football League', *Applied Economics*, Vol. 19, pp. 259–75.

Cairns, J., Jennett, N. and Sloane, P.J. (1986) 'The Economics of Professional Team Sports: A Survey of Theory and Evidence', *Journal of Economic Studies*, Vol. 13, No. 1 (February), pp. 1–80.

Canes, M.E. (1974) 'The Social Benefits of Restrictions on Team Quality', in R.G. Noll (ed.), *Government and the Sports Business*. Washington, DC: Brookings Institution.

Carmichael, F., Forrest, D. and Simmons, R. (1999) 'The Labour Market in Association Football: Who Gets Transferred and For How Much?', *Bulletin of Economic Research*, Vol. 51, No. 2 (April), pp. 175–80.

Carmichael, F., Millington, J. and Simmons, R. (1999) 'Elasticity of Demand for Rugby League Attendance and the Impact of B Sky B', *Applied Economics Letters*, Vol. 6, No. 12 (December), pp. 797–800.

Carmichael, F. and Thomas, D. (1993) 'Bargaining in the Transfer Market: Theory and Evidence', *Applied Economics*, Vol. 25, pp. 1467–76.

Carmichael, F. and Thomas, D. (1995) 'Production and Efficiency in Team Sports: An Investigation of Rugby League Football', *Applied Economics*, Vol. 27, No. 9 (September), pp. 859–69.

Carmichael, F., Thomas, D. and Ward, R. (2000) 'Team Performance: The Case of English Premiership Football', *Managerial and Decision Economics*, Vol. 21, No. 1 (January–February), pp. 31–45.

Carmichael, F., Thomas, D. and Ward, R. (2001) 'Production and Efficiency in Association Football', *Journal of Sports Economics*, Vol. 2, No. 4 (November), pp. 369–78.

Cassing, J. and Douglas, R.W. (1980) 'Implications of the Auction Mechanism in Baseball's Free Agent Draft', *Southern Economic Journal*, Vol. 47, No. 1, pp. 190–212.

Cave, M. and Crandall, R.W. (2001) 'Sports Rights and the Broadcast Industry', *Economic Journal*, Vol. 111, No. 469 (February), pp. F4–F26.

Chalip, L., Johnson, A. and Stachura, L. (eds) (1996), *National Sports Policies: An International Handbook*. Westport, CT: Greenwood Press.

Chapman, K.S. and Southwick, L. Jr (1991) 'Testing the Matching Hypothesis: The Case of Major League Baseball', *American Economic Review*, Vol. 81, No. 5 (December), pp. 1352–60.

Chatterjee, S., Campbell, M.R. and Wiseman, F. (1994) 'Take That Jam! An Analysis of Winning Percentages for NBA Teams', *Managerial and Decision Economics*, Vol. 15, pp. 521–35.

Chelius, J.R. and Dworkin, J. (1980) 'An Economic Analysis of Final Offer Arbitration as a Conflict Resolution Device', *Journal of Conflict Resolution*, Vol. 24 (June), pp. 293–310.

Chiappori, P.A., Levitt, S. and Grosedose, T. (2002) 'Testing Mixed Strategy Equilibria when Players are Heterogeneous; The Case of Penalty Kicks in Soccer', *American Economic Review*, Vol. 92, No. 4 (September), pp. 1138–51.

Ciriacy-Wantrup, S.C. (1944) 'Taxation and the Conservation of Resources', *Quarterly Journal of Economics*, Vol. 58 (February).

Clement, R. and McCormick, R. (1989) 'Coaching Team Production', *Economic Inquiry*, Vol. 27, No. 2 (April), pp. 287–304.

Coates, D. and Humphreys, B.R. (2001) 'The Economic Consequences of Professional Sports Strikes and Lock-outs', *Southern Economic Journal*, Vol. 67, No. 3 (January), pp. 737–47.

Coates, D. and Humphreys, B.R. (2002) 'The Economic Impact of Post-season Play in Professional Sports', *Journal of Sports Economics*, Vol. 3, No. 3 (August), pp. 291–9.

Coleman, B.J., Jennings, K.M. and McLaughlin, F.S. (1993) 'Convergence or Divergence in Final Offer Arbitration in Professional Baseball', *Industrial Relations*, Vol. 32, No. 2 (Spring), pp. 238–47.

Conlin, M. (1999) 'Empirical Test of a Separating Equilibrium in National Football League Contract Negotiations', *Rand Journal of Economics*, Vol. 30, No. 2 (Summer), pp. 289–304.

Cooco, A. and Jones, J.C.H. (1997) 'One Going South: The Economics of Survival and Relocation of Small Market NHL Franchises in Canada', *Applied Economics*, Vol. 29, pp. 1,537–52.

Cooke, A. (1994) *The Economics of Leisure and Sport*. London: Routledge.

Coopers and Lybrand, LLP (1994) 'Market and Economic Impact Analysis Associated with the Proposed Multi-purpose Facility Presented to the Houston Oilers', Dallas, Texas, Coopers and Lybrand, Professional Sports Industry Services.

Costas, B. (2000) *Fair Ball: A Fan's Case for Baseball*, New York: Broadway Books.

Cottle, R.L. (1981) 'Economics of the Professional Golfers' Association Tour', *Social Science Quarterly*, Vol. 62, No. 4, pp. 721–34.

Cottle, R.L. and Lawson, R.S. (1981) 'Leisure as Work: A Case Study in Professional Sports', *Atlantic Economic Journal*, Vol. IX, No. 3, pp. 50–9.

Coughlin, C.C. and Erekson, O.H. (1984) 'An Examination of Contributions to Support Intercollegiate Athletics', *Southern Economic Journal*, Vol. 51, No. 1, pp. 180–95.

Cowie, C. and Williams, M. (1997) 'The Economics of Sports Rights', *Telecommunications Policy*, Vol. 21, pp. 619–34.

Craig, P.S. (1953) 'Monopsony in Manpower: Organised Baseball Meets the Anti-trust Laws', *Yale Law Journal*, Vol. 62, No. 4, pp. 576–639.

Curtis, J. and Loy, J.W. (1978) 'Positional Segregation in Professional Baseball: Replicating, Trend Data and Critical Observation', *International Review of Sport Sociology*, Vol. 13.

Cymrot, D.J. (1983) 'Migration Trends and Earnings of Free Agents in Major League Baseball 1976–1979', *Economic Inquiry*, Vol. XXI, No. 4, pp. 545–56.

Cymrot, D., Dunlevy, J. and Even, W. (2001) 'Who's on First? An Empirical Test of the Coase Theorem in Baseball', *Applied Economics*, Vol. 33, pp. 593–603.

Cyrenne, P. (2001) 'A Quality-of-Play Model of a Professional Sports League', *Economic Inquiry*, Vol. 39, pp. 444–52.

Dabscheck, B. (1975a) 'Sporting Equality: Labour Market versus Product Market Control', *Journal of Industrial Relations*, Vol. 17, No. 2, pp. 174–90.

Dabscheck, B. (1975b) 'The Wage Determination Process for Sportsmen', *Economic Record*, Vol. 51, No. 133, pp. 52–65.

Dabscheck, B. (1976a) 'Industrial Relations and Professional Team Sports in Australia', *Journal of Industrial Relations*, Vol. 18, No. 1, pp. 28–44.

Dabscheck, B. (1976b) 'Sporting Equality: A Reply', *Journal of Industrial Relations*, Vol. 18, No. 1, pp. 85–6.

Dabscheck, B. (1979) 'Player Associations and Professional Team Sports', *Labour and Society*, Vol. 4, No. 3, pp. 225–39.

Dabscheck, B. (1993) 'Rugby League and the Union Game', *Journal of Industrial Relations*, Vol. 35, No. 2 (June), pp. 242–73.

Dabscheck, B. (1996) 'Playing the Team Game: Unions in Australian Professional Team Sports', *Journal of Industrial Relations*, Vol. 38, No. 4 (December), pp. 600–28.

Daly, G. and Moore, W.J. (1981) 'Externalities, Property Rights and the Allocation of Resources in Major League Baseball', *Economic Inquiry*, Vol. XIX, No. 1, pp. 77–95.

Danielson, Michael N. (1997) *Home Team: Professional Sports and the American Metropolis*. Princeton, NJ: Princeton University Press.

Davenport, D.S. (1969) 'Collusive Competition in Major League Baseball: Its Theory and Institutional Development', *American Economist*, Vol. 13 (Fall), pp. 6–30.

Davies, B., Downward, P. and Jackson, I. (1995) 'The Demand for Rugby League, Evidence from Causality Tests', *Applied Economics*, Vol. 27, No. 10 (October), pp. 1003–7.

Davis, L.E. (1974) 'Self-regulation in Baseball, 1909–71', in R.G. Noll (ed.), *Government and the Sports Business*. Washington, DC: Brookings Institution, pp. 349–86.

Davis, L. and Quirk, J. (1975) 'Tax Writeoffs and the Value of Sports Teams', in S.P. Ladany (ed.), *Management Science Applications to Leisure-time Operations*. Amsterdam: North-Holland.

Davis, R. (1963) 'The Value of Outdoor Recreation: An Economic Study of the Maine Woods', PhD thesis, Harvard University, Cambridge, MA.

Dawson, P., Dobson, S. and Gerrard, B. (2000) 'Estimating Coaching Efficiency in Professional Team Sports: Evidence from English Association Football', *Scottish Journal of Political Economy*, Vol. 47, No. 4 (September), pp. 422–30.

Dawson, P., Dobson, S. and Gerrard, B. (2000) 'Stochastic Frontiers and the Temporal Structure of Managerial Efficiency in English Soccer', *Journal of Sports Economics*, Vol. 1, No. 4 (November), pp. 341–62.

Day P. (2000) 'The Administration of Football in the 21st Century', in Garland J., Malcolm D. and Rowe M. (eds), *The Future of Football; Challenges For the 21st Century*, London, Frank Cass, pp. 72–8.

Daymont, T.N. (1975) 'The Effects of Monopsonistic Procedures on Equality of Competition in Professional Sports Leagues', *International Review of Sport Sociology*, Vol. 10, No. 2, pp. 83–99.

Debrock, L.M. and Roth, A.E. (1981) 'Strike Two: Labor–Management Negotiations in Major League Baseball', *Bell Journal of Economics*, Vol. 12, No. 2, pp. 413–25.

DeGennaro, R.P. (2003) 'The Utility of Sport and the Returns to Ownership', *Journal of Sports Economics*, Vol. 4, No. 2 (May), pp. 145–53.

Dell'osso, F. and Szymanski, S. (1991) 'Who Are the Champions? (An Analysis of Football and Architecture)', *Business Strategy Review*, Vol. 2, No. 2 (Summer), pp. 113–30.

Demmert, H.G. (1973) *The Economics of Professional Team Sports.* Lexington, MA: Lexington Books, D.C. Heath.

Department for Culture, Media and Sport (2002) *Game Plan: A Strategy for Delivering Government's Sport and Physical Activity Objectives.* London: Department for Culture, Media and Sport Strategy Unit Report, December.

Depken, C.A. (1999) 'Free-Agency and the Competitiveness of Major League Baseball', *Review of Industrial Organisation*, Vol. 14, pp. 205–17.

Depken, C.A. (2000) 'Fan Loyalty and Stadium Funding in Professional Baseball', *Journal of Sports Economics*, Vol. 1, No. 2 (May), pp. 124–38.

Depken, C.A. (2001) 'Fan Loyalty in Professional Sports: An Extension to the NFL', *Journal of Sports Economics*, Vol. 2, No. 3 (August), pp. 275–88.

Depken, C.A. (2002) 'Free Agency and the Concentration of Player Talent in Major League Baseball', *Journal of Sports Economics*, Vol. 3, No. 4 (November), pp. 335–53.

Dietrich, M. (1999) 'The Political Economy of Sport: An Introduction', *New Political Economy*, Vol. 4, No. 2 (July), p. 267.

Dobson, S., Gerrard, B. and Howe, S. (2000) 'The Determinants of Transfer Fees in English Non-League Football', *Applied Economics*, Vol. 32, No. 9 (15 July), pp. 1,145–52.

Dobson, S.M. and Goddard, J.A. (1992) 'The Demand for Standing and Seated Viewing Accommodation in the English Football League', *Applied Economics*, Vol. 24, No. 10 (October), pp. 1,155–64.

Dobson, S.M. and Goddard, J.A. (1994) 'The Demand for Football in the Regions of England and Wales', *Regional Studies*, Vol. 30, No. 5 (April), pp. 443–54.

Dobson, S.M. and Goddard, J.A. (1995) 'The Demand for Professional League Football in England and Wales, 1923–1992', *Journal of the Royal Statistical Society*, Series D, Volume 44, pp. 259–77.

Dobson, S.M. and Goddard, J.A. (1998a) 'Performance, Revenue, and Cross-Subsidisation in the Football League, 1927–1994', *Economic History Review*, Vol. L1, No. 4 (November), pp. 763–85.

Dobson, S.M. and Goddard, J.A. (1998b) 'Performance and Revenue in Professional League Football: Evidence from Granger Causality Tests', *Applied Economics*, Vol. 30, No. 12 (December), pp. 1041–52.

Dobson, S.M. and Goddard, J.A. (2001) *The Economics of Football.* Cambridge, UK: Cambridge University Press.

Dobson, S., Goddard, J. and Ramlogan, C. (2001) 'Revenue Convergence in the English Soccer League', *Journal of Sports Economics*, Vol. 2, No. 3 (August), pp. 257–74.

Dobson, S., Goddard, J. and Wilson, J. (2001) 'League Structure and Match Attendances in English Rugby League', *International Review of Applied Economics*, Vol. 67, No. 3 (July), pp. 335–52.

Downward, P. and Dawson, A. (2000) *The Economics of Professional Team Sports.* London and New York: Routledge, p. 247.

Drever, P. and MacDonald, J. (1981) 'Attendances at South Australian Football Games', *International Review of Sports Sociology*, Vol. 16, No. 2, pp. 103–13.

Duderstadt, James (2000) *Intercollegiate Athletics and the American University.* Ann Arbor, MI: University of Michigan Press.

Dworkin, J.B. (1976) 'The Impact of Final Offer Arbitration on Bargaining: The Case of Major League Baseball', *IRRA 29th Annual Proceedings*.

Dworkin, J.B. *Owners Versus Players: Baseball and Collective Bargaining*. Auburn Books, Boston, Mass.: USA.

Dworkin, J. and Bergman, T. (1978) 'Collective Bargaining and the Player Reservation/Compensation System in Professional Sports', *Employee Relations Law Journal*, Vol. 4, pp. 241–56.

Eastman, B.D. (1981) 'The Labor Economics of the National Hockey League', *Atlantic Economic Journal*, Vol. IX, No. 1, pp. 100–1.

Eber, N. (2003) 'Sports Practice, Health and Macro-Economic Performance; An Endogenous Growth Model', *Journal of Sports Economics*, Vol. 4, No. 2 (May), pp. 126–44.

Eckard, E.W. (1998) 'The NCAA Cartel and Competitive Balance in College Football', *Review of Industrial Organisation*, Vol. 13, pp. 349–69.

Eckard, E.W. (2001a) 'Free Agency, Competitive Balance and Diminishing Returns to Pennant Contention', *Economic Inquiry*, Vol. 39, pp. 403–43

Eckard, E.W. (2001b) 'The Origin of the Reserve Clause: Owner Collusion Versus "Public Interest"', *Journal of Sports Economics*, Vol. 2, No. 2 (May), pp. 113–30.

Eckard, E.W. (2001c) 'Baseball's Blue Ribbon Economics Report: Solutions in Search of a Problem', *Journal of Sports Economics*, Vol. 2, No. 3 (August), pp. 213–27.

Ecosystem Valuation Website (2002) *Contingent Valuation Method*. http// www.cbl.cees.edu/-dkingweb/contingent_valuation.htm.

Edmund P. Edmonds (1999) 'The Curt Flood Act of 1998: A Hollow Gesture after All These Years?', *Marquette Sports Law Journal*, Vol. 9, pp. 315–46.

Ehrenberg, R.G. and Bognanno, M.L. (1990a) 'Do Tournaments Have Incentive Effects?', *Journal of Political Economy*, Vol. 98, No. 6 (December), pp. 1,307–24.

Ehrenberg, R.G. and Bognanno, M.L. (1990b) 'The Incentive Effects of Tournaments Revisited: Evidence from the European PGA Tour', *Industrial and Labor Relations Review*, Vol. 43, pp. 74–88.

Eisinger, P. 1995. 'State Economic Development in the 1990s: Politics and Policy Learning', *Economic Development Quarterly*, Vol. 9, No. 2, pp. 146–58.

El-Hodiri, M. and Quirk, J. (1971) 'An Economic Model of a Professional Sports League', *Journal of Political Economy*, Vol. 79, pp. 1,302–19.

El-Hodiri, M. and Quirk, J. (1975) 'Stadium Capacities and Attendance in Professional Sports', in S.P. Ladany (ed.), *Management Science Applications to Leisure-time Operation*. Amsterdam: North-Holland.

Ericson, T. (2000) 'The Bosman Case: The Effects of the Abolition of the Transfer Fee', *Journal of Sports Economics*, Vol. 1, No. 3 (August), pp. 203–18.

Esteller-Moré, A. and Eres-Garcia, M. (2002) 'A Note on Consistent Players' Valuation', *Journal of Sports Economics*, Vol. 3, No. 4 (November), pp. 354–60.

Faurot, D.J. (2001) 'Equilibrium Explanation of Bargaining and Arbitration in Major League Baseball', *Journal of Sports Economics*, Vol. 2, No. 1 (February), pp. 22–34.

Feess, E. and Muehlheusser, G. (2003) 'The Impact of Transfer Fees on Professional Sports: An Analysis of the New Transfer System for European Football', *Scandanavian Journal of Economics*, Vol. 105, No. 1, pp. 139–54.

Felsenstein D., Littlepage L., and Klacik, D. (1999) 'Casino Gambling as Local Growth Generation: Playing the Economic Development Game in Reverse', *Journal of Urban Affairs*, Vol. 21, No. 4, pp. 409–22.

Felsenstein, D. and Persky, J. (1999) 'When is a Cost Really a Benefit? Local Welfare Effects and Employment Creation in the Evaluation of Economic Development Programs', *Economic Development Quarterly*, Vol. 13, No. 1, pp. 46–54.

Fleischer, A. and Felsenstein, D. (2000) 'Support for Rural Tourism: Does it Make a Difference?', *Annals of Tourism Research*, Vol. 27, No. 4, pp. 1007–24.

Ferguson, D.G., Jones, J.C.H. and Stewart, K.G. (2000) 'Competition within a Cartel: League Conduct and Team Conduct in the Market for Baseball Player Services', *Review of Economics and Statistics*, Vol. 82, No. 3 (August), pp. 422–30.

Ferguson, D., Stewart, K., Jones, J.C.H. and Le Dressay, A. (1991) 'The Pricing of Sporting Events: Do Teams Maximise Profits?', *Journal of Industrial Economics*, Vol. XXXIX, No. 3 (March), pp. 297–310.

Fernie, S. and Metcalf, D. (1999) 'It's Not What You Pay It's the Way That You Pay It and That's What Gets Results: Jockeys' Pay and Performance', *Labour*, Vol. 13, No. 2 (June), pp. 385–412.

Ferrell, C. and Smith, A. Jr. (1999) 'A Sequential Game Model of Sports Championship Series: Theory and Estimation', *Review of Economics and Statistics*, pp. 704–14.

Financial Intelligence and Research (1982) *English League Football Clubs – Financial Status and Performance*. London: Financial Intelligence and Research.

Findlay, J., Holahan, W.L. and Oughton, C. (1999) 'Revenue Sharing from Broadcasting Football: The Need for League Balance', in S., Hamil, J. Michie and C. Oughton (ed.), *The Business of Football: A Game of Two Halves*. Edinburgh: Mainstream.

Findlay, D.W. and Reid, C.E. (2002) 'A Comparison of Two Voting Models to Forecast Election into the Baseball Hall of Fame', *Managerial and Decision Economics*, Vol. 23, No. 3 (April–May), pp. 99–114.

Fizel, J.L. and Bennett, R.W. (1989) 'The Impact of College Football Telecasts on College Football Attendance', *Social Science Quarterly*, Vol. 70, No. 4, pp. 980–8.

Fizel, J., Gustafson, E. and Hadley, J. (1996) *Baseball Economics: Current Research*. Westport, CT: Greenwood Press.

Fizel, John L. Gustafson, E. and Hadley, J. (eds) (1999) *Sports Economics: Current Research*. London: Praeger.

Fleischer, Arthur A. III, Goff, Brian L. and Tollison, Robert D. (1992) *The National Collegiate Athletic Association: A Study in Cartel Behavior*. Chicago, IL: University of Chicago Press.

Flynn, M. and Gilbert, R. (2001) 'An Analysis of Professional Sports Leagues as Joint Ventures', *Economic Journal*, Vol. 111, No. 469, pp. F27–F46.

Fogelsong, Richard E. (2001) *Married to the Mouse: Walt Disney World and Orlando*. New Haven, CT: Yale University Press.

Football Task Force (1999) *Football: Commercial Issues*, A submission to the Minister for Sport, 22 December.

Forrest, D. and Simmons, R. (2000) 'Forecasting Sport: The Behaviour and Performance of Football Tipsters', *International Journal of Forecasting*, Vol. 16, pp. 317–31.

Forrest, D. and Simmons, R. (2002) 'Outcome Uncertainty and Attendance Demand in Sport: The Case of English Soccer', *The Statistician*, No. 51, Part 2, pp. 229–41.

Forrest, D., Simmons, R. and Feehan, P. (2002) 'A Spatial Cross-Sectional Analysis of the Elasticity of Demand for Soccer', *Scottish Journal of Political Economy*, Vol. 49, No. 3 (August), pp. 336–55.

Fort, R. (2000) 'European and North American Sport Differences', *Scottish Journal of Political Economy*, Vol. 47, No. 4 (September), pp. 456–70.

Fort, R. (2003) *Sports Economics*. Englewood Cliffs, NJ: Prentice Hall.

Fort, R. and Gill, A. (2000) 'Race and Ethnicity Assessment in Baseball Card Markets', *Journal of Sports Economics*, Vol. 1, No. 1 (February), pp. 21–38.

Fort, R. and Maxcy, J. (2001) 'The Demise of African American Baseball Leagues: A Rival League Explanation', *Journal of Sports Economics*, Vol. 2, No. 1 (February), pp. 35–49.

Fort, R. and Quirk, J. (1992) *Pay Dirt: The Business of Professional Team Sports*. Princeton, NJ: Princeton University Press.

Fort, R. and Quirk, J. (1995) 'Cross-Subsidisation, Incentives and Outcomes in Professional Team Sports', *Journal of Economic Literature*, Vol. 33, No. 3 (September), pp. 1265–99.

Furst, T.R. (1971) 'Social Change and Commercialization of Professional Sport', *International Review of Sports Sociology*, Vol. 6, pp. 153–70.

Gabriel, P.E., Johnson, C. and Stanton, T.J. (1995) 'An Examination of Customer Racial Discrimination in the Market for Baseball Memorabilia', *Journal of Business*, Vol. 68, No. 2 (April), pp. 215–30.

Gabriel, P.E., Johnson, C.D. and Stanton, T.J. (1999) 'Customer Racial Discrimination for Football Memorabilia', *Applied Economics*, Vol. 31, No. 11 (November), pp. 1,331–6.

Gamrat, F.A. and Sauer, R.D. (2000) 'The Utility of Sport and Returns to Ownership: Evidence from the Thoroughbred Market', *Journal of Sports Economics*, Vol. 1, No. 3 (August), pp. 219–235.

Gandar, J.M., Zuber, R.A. and Dare W.H. (2000) 'The Search for Informed Traders in the Totals Betting Market for National Basketball Association Games', *Journal of Sports Economics*, Vol. 1, No. 2 (May), pp. 177–86.

Garcia, Jaume and Rodriguez, Placido (2002) 'The Determinants of Football Match Attendance Revisited: Empirical Evidence from the Spanish Football League', *Journal of Sports Economics*, Vol. 3, No. 1 (February), pp. 18–38.

Gartner, M. and Pommerehne, W.W. (1978) 'Der Fussballzuschauer – ein Homo Oeconomicus?' ('Do football fans behave like economic man?'), *Jahrbuch fur Sozial Wissenschaft*, Vol. 29, pp. 88–107.

Gaviria, A. (2000) 'Is Soccer Dying? A Time Series Approach', *Applied Economics Letters*, Vol. 7 (April), pp. 275–8.

Gerrard, B. (1999) 'Team Sports as a Free Market Commodity', *New Political Economy*, Vol. 4, No. 2 (July), pp. 273–8.

Gerrard, B. and Dobson, S. (2000) 'Testing for Monopoly Rents in the Market for Playing Talent: Evidence from English Professional Football', *Journal of Economic Studies*, Vol. 27, No. 3, pp. 142–64.

Gilroy, T.P. and Madden, P.J. (1977) 'Labor Relations in Professional Sports', *Labor Law Journal*, Vol. 27 (December), pp. 768–76.

Glenn, A., McGarrity, J.P. and Weller, J. (2001) 'Firm Specific Human Capital, Job Matching and Turnover: Evidence from Major League Baseball, 1900–1992', *Economic Inquiry*, Vol. 39, No. 1 (January), pp. 86–93.

Glick, J. (1983) 'Professional Sports Franchise Movements and the Sherman Act: When and Where Teams Should Be Able to Move', *Santa Clara Law Review*, Vol. 23 (Winter), pp. 55–94.

Goff, B.L., McCormick, R.E., and Tollison, R.D. (2002) 'Racial Integration as an Innovation: Empirical Evidence from Sports Leagues', *American Economic Review*, Vol. 92, No. 1 (March), pp. 16–26.

Goff, B.L., Shughart II, W.F. and Tollison, R.D. (1997) 'Batter Up! Moral Hazard and the Effects of the Designated Hitter Rule on Hit Batsmen', *Economic Inquiry*, Vol. XXV, No. 3 (July), pp. 555–61.

Goff, B.L. and Tollison, R.D. (eds) (1990) *Sportometrics*, College Station, Texas: A & M University Press.

Golec, J. and Tamarkin, M. (1991) 'The Degree of Inefficiency in the Football Betting Market', *Journal of Financial Economics*, Vol. 30, pp. 311–23.

Goodwin, M., Duncan, S. and Halford, S. (1993) 'Regulation Theory, the Local State, and the Transition of Urban Politics', *Environment and Planning D*, Vol. 11, No. 1, pp. 67–88.

Goos, E.P. and Phillips, J.M. (1997) 'Effect of State Economic Development Agency Spending on State Income and Employment Growth', *Economic Development Quarterly*, Vol. 11, No. 1, pp. 88–96.

Gramlich, E.M. (1994) 'A Natural Experiment in Styles of Capitalism: Professional Sports', *The Quarterly Review of Economics and Finance*, Vol. 34, No. 2 (Summer), pp. 121–30.

Gramm, C.L. and Schnell, J.F. (1994) 'Difficult Choices: Crossing the Picket Line During the 1987 National Football League Strike', *Journal of Labor Economics*, Vol. 12, No. 1 (January), pp. 41–73.

Gratton, C. (1980) 'Public Subsidies to Sport and Recreation', *National Westminster Quarterly Review*, May, pp. 46–57.

Gratton, C. (2000) 'The Peculiar Economics of English Professional Football', in J. Garland and D. Malcolm (eds), *The Future of Football: Challenges for the 21st Century*. London: Frank Cass.

Gratton, C. and Lisewski, B. (1981) 'The Economics of Sport in Britain: A Case of Market Failure?', *British Review of Economic Issues*, Vol. 3, No. 8, pp. 63–75.

Gratton, C. and Taylor, P. (1991) *Government and the Economics of Sport*. Harlow, UK: Longman.

Gratton, C. and Taylor, P. (2000) *The Economics of Sport and Recreation*. London and New York: Spon Press.

Grauer, M.C. (1983) 'Recognition of the National Football League as a Single Entity Under Section 1 of the Sherman Act: Implications of the Consumer Welfare Model', *Michigan Law Review*, Vol. 82, No. 1, pp. 27–35.

Greenstein, T.N. and Marcum, J.P. (1981) 'Factors Affecting Attendance of Major League Baseball: I, Team Performance', *Review of Sport and Leisure*, Vol. 6, No. 2, pp. 21–34.

Gregory, P. (1956) *The Baseball Player: An Economic Study*. Washington, DC: Public Affairs Press.

Grier, K. and Tollison, R. (1994) 'The Rookie Draft and Competitive Balance: The Case of Professional Football', *Journal of Economic Behaviour and Organisation*, Vol. 25, pp. 293–8.

Grimes, A. (1991) 'A New Production Function Bowled by a Googly: Reply', *Applied Economics*, Vol. 23, pp. 1245–6.

Groothuis, P.A., Van Huitven, G. and Whitehead, J.C. (1998) 'Using Contingent Valuation to Measure the Compensation Required to Gain Community Acceptance of a LULU: The Case of a Hazardous Waste Disposal Facility', *Public Finance Review*, No. 26, pp. 231–49.

Gross, E. (1979) 'Sports Leagues: A Model for a Theory of Organizational Stratification', *International Review of Sports Sociology*, Vol. 14, No. 2, pp. 103–12.

Gruen, D.T., Phillips, J.S., Friedman, A. and Lane, M.P. (2000) *Inside the Ownership of Professional Sports Teams.* Chicago IL: Team Marketing Report.

Gustafson, E. and Hadley, L. (1995) 'Arbitration and Salary Gaps in Major League Baseball', *Quarterly Journal of Business and Economics*, Vol. 34, No. 3 (Summer).

Guis, M. and Johnson, D. (2000) 'Race and Compensation in Professional Football', *Applied Economics Letters*, Vol. 7, (February), pp. 73–75.

Gwartney, J. and Haworth, C. (1974) 'Employer Costs and Discrimination: The Case of Baseball', *Journal of Political Economy*, Vol. 82, No. 4 (July–August), pp. 873–81.

Hadley, L., Poitras, M., Ruggiero, J. and Knowles, S. (2000) 'Performance Evaluation of National Football League Teams', *Managerial and Decision Economics*, Vol. 21, No. 2 (March), pp. 63–70.

Hall, C.D. (1990) 'Market Enforced Information Asymmetry: A Study of Claiming Races', *Economic Inquiry*, Vol. 24, No. 2 (April), pp. 271–91.

Hall, R.I. and Menzies, W.B. (1983) 'A Corporate System Model of a Sports Club', *Management Science*, Vol. 29, No. 1, pp. 52–64.

Hall, S., Szymanski, S. and Zimbalist, A. (2002) 'Testing Causality between Team Performance and Payroll: The Cases of Major League Baseball and English Soccer', *Journal of Sports Economics*, Vol. 3, No. 2 (May), pp. 149–68.

Hamil, S., Michie, J. and Oughton, C. (eds) (1999) *The Business of Football: A Game of Two Halves.* Edinburgh: Mainstream.

Hamilton, B.H. (1997) 'Racial Discrimination and Professional Basketball Salaries in the 1990s', *Applied Economics*, Vol. 29, No. 3 (March), pp. 287–96.

Hamilton, Bruce W. and Kahn, Peter (1997) 'Baltimore's Camden Yards Ballparks', in Roger Noll and Andrew Zimbalist (eds), *Cities, Sports, and Taxes.* Washington, DC: Brookings Institution, pp. 245–82.

Hanssen, A. (1998) 'The Cost of Discrimination: A Study of Major League Baseball', *Southern Economic Journal*, Vol. 64, No. 3, pp. 603–27.

Hanssen, F.A. and Anderson, T. (1999) 'Has Discrimination Lessened Over Time? A Test Using Baseball's All Star Vote', *Economic Inquiry*, Vol. 37, No. 2 (April), pp. 326–52.

Happel, Stephen K. and Jennings, Maniane (1995) 'The Folly of Anti-Scalping Laws', *The Cato Journal*, Vol. 15, No. 1 (Spring/Summer), pp. 65–80.

Happel, Stephen K. and Jennings, Maniane (2002), 'Creating a Futures Market for Major Event Tickets: Problems and Prospects', *The Cato Journal*, Vol. 21, No. 3 (Winter), pp. 443–61.

Hausman, J.A. and Leonard, G.K. (1997) 'Superstars in the National Basketball Association: Economic Value and Policy', *Journal of Labor Economics*, Vol. 15, No. 4 (October), pp. 586–624.

Hart, R.A., Hutton, J. and Sharot, T. (1975) 'A Statistical Analysis of Association Football Attendance', *Journal of the Royal Statistical Society*, Series C (Applied Statistics), Vol. 24, No. 1, pp. 17–27.

(1967) 'The Superbowl and the Sherman Act: Professional Team Sports and the Antitrust Laws', *Harvard Law Review*, Vol. 81, pp. 418–34.
Heilmann, R.L. and Wendling, W.R. (1976) 'A Note on Optimum Pricing Strategies for Sports Events', in R.E. Machol *et al.* (eds), *Management Science in Sports*. Amsterdam: North-Holland.
Henderson, P.A. and Bruggink, T.H. (1985) 'Will Running Baseball as a Business Ruin the Game?', *Challenge*, March–April, pp. 53–7.
Higgins, R., Shughart, W. and Tollison, R. (1985) 'Free Entry and Efficient Rent Seeking', *Public Choice*, Vol. 46, pp. 247–58.
Hill, J.R. (1985) 'The Threat of Free Agency and Exploitation in Professional Baseball: 1976–1979', *Quarterly Review of Economics and Business*, Vol. 25 (Winter), pp. 68–82.
Hill, J.R. and Groothuis, P.A. (2001) 'The New NBA Collective Bargaining Agrement, the Median Voter Model, and a Robin Hood Rent Redistribution', *Journal of Sports Economics*, Vol. 2, No. 2 (May), pp. 131–44.
Hill, J.R., Madura, H. and Zuber, R.A. (1982) 'The Short-run Demand for Major League Baseball', *Atlantic Economic Journal*, Vol. 10, No. 2, pp. 31–5.
Hill, J.R. and Spellman, W. (1983) 'Professional Baseball: The Reserve Clause and Salary Structure', *Industrial Relations*, Vol. 22, No. 1, pp. 1–19.
Hill, J.R. and Spellman, W. (1984) 'Pay Discrimination in Baseball: Data from the Seventies', *Industrial Relations*, Vol. 23, No. 1, pp. 103–12.
Hochberg, P. and Horowitz, I. (1973) 'Broadcasting and CATV: The Beauty and the Bane of Major College Football', *Law and Contemporary Problems*, Vol. 38 (Winter-Spring), pp. 112–28.
Hoehn, T. and Szymanski, S. (1999) 'The Americanisation of European Football', *Economic Policy*, Vol. 28 (April), pp. 207–40.
Hoffman, Saul D. (1986) *Labor Market Economics*. Englewood Cliffs, NJ: Prentice Hall.
Hofler, R.A. and Payne, J.E. (1996) 'How Close to the Offensive Potential Do National Football Teams Play?', *Applied Economics Letters*, Vol. 3, pp. 743–7.
Hofler, R.A. and Payne, J.E. (1997) 'Measuring Efficiency in the National Basketball Association', *Economics Letters*, Vol. 55, No. 2, pp. 293–9.
Holohan, W.H. (1978) 'The Long-run Effects of Abolishing the Baseball Players' Reserve System', *Journal of Legal Studies*, Vol. 7, No. 1, pp. 129–37.
Horowitz, I. (1974) 'Sports Broadcasting, in R.G. Noll (ed.), *Government and the Sports Business*. Washington, DC: Brookings Institution.
Horowitz, I. (1978a) 'Market Entrenchment and the Sports Broadcasting Act', *American Behavioural Scientist*, Vol. 21, No. 3, pp. 415–30.
Horowitz, I. (1978b) 'The Implications of Home Box Office for Sports Broadcasts', *Antitrust Bulletin*, Vol. XXIII, No. 4, pp. 743–68.
Horowitz, I. (1997a) 'Pythagoras's Petulant Persecutors', *Managerial and Decision Economics*, Vol. 18, No. 4 (June), pp. 343–4.
Horowitz I. (1997b) 'The Increasing Competitive Balance in Major League Baseball', *Review of Industrial Organisation*, Vol. 12, pp. 373–87.
Horowitz, I. (2000) 'The Impact of Competition on Performance Disparities in Organizational Systems: Baseball as a Case Study', *Journal of Sports Economics*, Vol. 1, No. 2 (May), pp. 151–76.
Horowitz, I. and Zappe, C. (1998) 'Thanks for the Memories: Baseball Veteran's End of Career Salaries', *Managerial and Decision Economics*, Vol. 19, No. 6 (September), pp. 377–82.

Houston, R.G. Jr and Wilson, D.P. (2002) 'Income, Leisure and Proficiency; An Economic Study of Football Performance', *Applied Economic Letters*, Vol. 9, No. 14, (November 1), pp. 939–44.

Hudson, I. (1999) 'Bright Lights, Big City: Do Professional Sports Increase Employment', *Journal of Urban Affairs*, Vol. 21, No. 4, pp. 397–407.

Hughes, R. (2000) 'Manchester Displays its Wealth of Talent', *International Herald Tribune*, March 17, p. 22.

Humphreys, B.R. (2000) 'Equal Pay on the Hardwood: The Earnings Gap between Male and Female NCAA Division I Basketball Coaches', *Journal of Sports Economics*, Vol. 1, No. 3 (August), pp. 299–307.

Humphreys, B.R. (2002) 'Alternative Measures of Competitive Balance', *Journal of Sports Economics*, Vol. 3, No. 2, (May), pp. 133–48.

Hunt, J.W. and Lewis, K.A. (1976) 'Dominance, Recontracting and the Reserve Clause: Major League Baseball', *American Economic Review*, Vol. 66, No. 5, pp. 936–43.

Hylan, T.R., Lage, M.J. and Treglia, M. (1996) 'The Coase Theorem, Free Agency and Major League Baseball: A Panel Study of Pitcher Mobility from 1961–1992', *Southern Economic Journal*, Vol. 62, No. 4 (April), pp. 1,029–42.

Hylan, T.R., Lage, M.J. and Treglia, M. (1997) 'Institutional Change and the Invariance of Behaviour in Major League Baseball', *Applied Economics Letters*, Vol. 4 (May), pp. 311–14.

Hynds, M. and Smith, I. (1994) 'The Demand for Test Match Cricket', *Applied Economics Letters*, Vol. 1, No. 7 (July), pp. 103–6.

Idson, T.L. and Kahane, L.H. (2000) 'Team Effects on Compensation: An Application to Salary Determination in the National Hockey League', *Economic Inquiry*, Vol. 38, No. 2 (April), pp. 345–57.

Irani, D. (1997) 'Public Subsidies to Stadiums: Do the Costs Outweigh the Benefits?', *Public Finance Review*, Vol. 25, No. 2, pp. 238–53.

Jacobs, M.S. and Winter, R.K. Jr (1971) 'Antitrust Principles and Collective Bargaining by Athletes: Of Superstars or Peonage', *Yale Law Journal*, Vol. 81, pp. 1–29.

Janssens, P. and Késenne, S. (1987) 'Belgian Soccer Attendances', *Tidschift voor Economie en Management*, Vol. 32, pp. 305–15.

Jeanrenaud, C. and Késenne, S. (eds) (1999) *Competition Policy in Professional Sports: Europe after the Bosman Case*. Antwerp: Standard Editions.

Jennett, N. (1982) 'The Economics of Sport in Britain: A Comment', *British Review of Economic Issues*, Vol. 4.

Jennett, N. (1984) 'Attendances, Uncertainty of Outcome and Policy in the Scottish Football League', *Scottish Journal of Political Economy*, Vol. 31, No. 2, pp. 176–98.

Jennett, N. and Sloane, P.J. (1985) 'The Future of League Football: A Critique of the Report of the Chester Committee of Inquiry', *Leisure Studies*, Vol. 4, No. 1, pp. 39–56.

Johnson, A.T. (1983) 'Municipal Administration and the Sports Franchise Relocation Issue', *Public Administration Review*, No. 6.

Johnson, B.K., Groothuis, P.A. and Whitehead, J.C. (2001) 'The Value of Public Goods Generated by a Major League Sports Team: The CVM Approach', *Journal of Sports Economics*, Vol. 2, No. 1 (February), pp. 6–21.

Johnson, B.K., and Whitehead, J.C. (2000) 'The Value of Public Goods from Sports Stadiums: the CVM Approach', *Contemporary Economic Policy*, Vol. 18, No. 1, pp. 48–58.

Johnson, N.R. and Marple, D.P. (1973) 'Racial Discrimination in Professional Basketball: An Empirical Test', *Sociological Focus*, Vol. 6, No. 4, pp. 6–18.

Jones, J.C.H. (1969) 'The Economics of the National Hockey League', *Canadian Journal of Economics*, Vol. 2, No. 1, pp. 1–20.

Jones, J.C.H. (1984) 'Winners, Losers and Losers: Demand and Survival in the National Hockey League', *Atlantic Economic Journal*, Vol. XII, No. 3, pp. 54–63.

Jones, J.C.H. and Davies, D.H. (1978) 'Not even Semi-tough: Professional Sports and Canadian Antitrust', *Antitrust Bulletin*, Vol. XXIII, No. 4, pp. 713–42.

Jones, J.C.H. and Ferguson, D.G. (1988) 'Location and Survival in the National Hockey League', *Journal of Industrial Economics*, Vol. XXXVI, No. 4, pp. 443–57.

Jones, J.C.H., Ferguson, D.G. and Stewart, K.G. (1993) 'Economics of Violence in the National Hockey League', *American Journal of Economics and Sociology*, Vol. 52, No. 1 (January), pp 63–78.

Jones, J.C.H., Nadeau, S. and Walsh, W.D. (1999) 'Ethnicity, Productivity and Salary: Player Compensation and Discrimination in the National Hockey League', *Applied Economics*, Vol. 31 (May), pp. 593–608.

Jones, J.C.H., Schofield, J.A. and Giles, D.E.A. (2000) 'Our Fans in the North: The Demand for British Rugby League', *Applied Economics*, Vol. 32, No. 14 (November), pp. 1879–90.

Jones, J.C.H. and Walsh, W.D. (1988) 'Salary Determination in the National Hockey League: The Effects of Skills, Franchise Characteristics and Discrimination', *Industrial and Labor Relations Review*, Vol. 41, pp. 295–310.

Jozsa, F.P. Jr and Guthrie, John J. Jr. (1999) *Relocating Teams and Expanding Leagues in Professional Sports: How the Major Leagues Respond to Market Conditions.* London: Quorum Books.

Kagan, P. (1998) *Kagan's Media Sports Business Data Book.* Carmel, CA: Kagan.

Kahane, L.H. (2001) 'Team and Player Effects in NHL Player Salaries; A Hierarchical Linear Model Approach', *Applied Economics Letters*, Vol. 8, No. 9 (September), pp. 629–32.

Kahane, L. and Shmanske, S. (1997) 'Team Roster Turnover and Attendance in Major League Baseball', *Applied Economics*, Vol. 29, No. 4 (April), pp. 425–32.

Kahn, L.M. (1991) 'Discrimination in Professional Sports: A Survey of the Literature', *Industrial and Labor Relations Review*, Vol. 44, No. 3 (April), pp. 395–418.

Kahn, L.M. (1992) 'The Effects of Race on Professional Football Players' Compensation', *Industrial and Labor Relations Review*, Vol. 45, No. 2 (January), pp. 295–310.

Kahn, L.M. (1993a) 'Free Agency, Long Term Contracts and Compensation in Major League Baseball: Estimates for Panel Data', *Review of Economics and Statistics*, Vol. LXXV, No. 1 (February), pp. 531–44.

Kahn, L.M. (1993b) 'Managerial Quality, Team Success and Individual Player Performance in Major League Baseball', *Industrial and Labor Relations Review*, Vol. 46, No. 3 (April), pp. 531–47.

Kahn, L.M. (2000) 'The Sports Business as a Labor Market Laboratory', *Journal of Economic Perspectives*, Vol. 14, No. 3 (Summer), pp. 75–94.

Kahn, L.M. and Sherer, P.D. (1988) 'Racial Differences in Professional Basketball Players' Compensation', *Journal of Labor Economics*, Vol. 6, pp. 40–61.

Kanazana, M.T and Funk, J.P. (2001) 'Racial Discrimination in Professional Basketball; Evidence from the Nielsen Ratings', *Economic Inquiry*, Vol. 39, No. 4 (October), pp. 559–608.

Kearns, G. and Philo, C. (eds) (1993) *Selling Places: The City as Cultural Capital, Past and Present.* New York: Pergamon Press.

Kennedy, S. and Rosentraub, M.S. (2000) 'Public Private Partnerships, Professional Sports Teams, and the Protection of the Public's Interests', *American Review of Public Administration*, Vol. 30, No. 4, pp. 436–59.

Késenne, S. (1994) 'Win Maximisation and the Distribution of Playing Talent in Professional Team Sports', *University Faculty of St Ignatius, Antwerp, Studiecentrum voor Economisch en Sociaal Onderzoek*, 01–09: 94, p. 22.

Késenne, S. (1995) 'League Management in Professional Team Sports with Win Maximising Clubs', *European Journal for Sports Management*, Vol. 2, pp. 14–22.

Késenne, S. (1999) 'Player Market Legislation and Competitive Balance in a Win Maximising Scenario', in Jeanrenaud and Késenne (1999), pp. 117–32.

Késenne, S. (2000a) 'Revenue Sharing and Competitive Balance in Professional Team Sports', *Journal of Sports Economics*, Vol. 1, No. 1 (February), pp. 56–65.

Késenne, S. (2000b) 'The Impact of Salary Caps in Professional Team Sports', *Scottish Journal of Political Economy*, Vol. 47, No. 4 (September), pp. 431–55.

King, B. (2000) 'Sun Sets on Expansion Era', *Street and Smith's Sports Business Journal*, Vol. 1 (February 28–March 5), pp. 56–9.

Knowles, G., Sherony, K. and Haupert, M. (1992) 'The Demand for Major League Baseball: A Test of the Uncertainty of Outcome Hypothesis', *American Economist*, Vol. 36, pp. 72–80.

Koch, J.V. (1971) 'The Economics of "Big Time" Intercollegiate Athletics', *Social Science Quarterly*, Vol. 52 (September), pp. 248–60.

Koch, J.V. (1973) 'A Troubled Cartel: The NCAA', *Law and Contemporary Problems*, Vol. 38 (Winter–Spring) pp. 135–50.

Koch, J.V. (1983) 'Intercollegiate Athletics: An Economic Explanation', *Social Science Quarterly*, Vol. 64, No. 2, pp. 360–74.

Koch, J.V. and Leonard, W.M. (1978) 'The NCAA: A Socioeconomic Analysis of the Development of the College Sports Cartel from Social Movement to Formal Organisation', *American Journal of Economics and Sociology*, Vol. 37, No. 3, pp. 225–39.

Koning, R.H. (2000) 'Balance in Competition in Dutch Soccer', *The Statistician*, Vol. 49, pp. 419–31.

Koning, R.H. (2003) 'An Economic Evaluation of the Effect of Firing a Coach on Team Performance', *Applied Economics*, Vol. 35, No. 5 (20 March), pp. 555–64.

Kotlyarenko, D. and Ehrenberg, R.G. (2000) 'Ivy League Economic Performance: Do Brains Win?', *Journal of Sports Economics*, Vol. 1, No. 2 (May), pp. 139–50.

Kowaleski, S. and Leeds, M.A. (1994) 'The Impact of the Salary Cap and Free Agency on the Structure and Distribution of Salaries in the NFL', in J. Fizel, E. Gustafson and L. Hadley (eds), *Sports Economics: Current Research.* Westport, CT: Praeger, pp. 213–28.

Krasnow, E. and Levy, H. (1963) 'Unionisation and Professional Sports', *Georgetown Law Review*, Vol. 53, pp. 762–4.

Krautmann, A.C. (1999) 'What's Wrong with Scully's Estimates of a Player's Marginal Revenue Product', *Economic Inquiry*, Vol. 37, No. 2 (April), pp. 369–81.

Krautmann, A.C., Gustafson, E. and Hadley, L. (2003) 'A Note on the Structural Stability of Salary Equations: Major League Baseball Pitchers', *Journal of Sports Economics*, Vol. 4, No. 1 (February), pp. 56–63.

Krautmann, A. and Oppenheimer, M. (1994) 'Free Agency and the Allocation of Labor in Major League Baseball', *Managerial and Decision Economics*, Vol. 15, No. 2 (September/October), pp. 459–69.

Krautmann, A.C. (1990) 'Shrinking or Stochastic Productivity in Major League Baseball?', *Southern Economic Journal*, Vol. 56, pp. 961–8.

Krohn, G.A. (1983) 'Measuring the Experience-Productivity Relationship: The Case of Major League Baseball', *Journal of Business and Economic Statistics*, Vol. 1, No. 4, pp. 273–9.

Kuypers, T. (1995) 'The Beautiful Game? An Economic Study of Why People Watch English Football', *University College, London, Department of Economics Discussion Paper*, December, p. 38.

Kuypers, T. (2000) 'Information and Efficiency: An Empirical Study of a Fixed Odds Betting Market', *Applied Economics*, Vol. 32 (15 September), pp. 1353–63.

La Croix, S.J. and Kawaura, A. (1999) 'Rule Changes and Competitive Balance in Japanese Professional Baseball', *Economic Inquiry*, Vol. 37, No. 2 (April), pp. 353–68.

Lavoie, M. (2000) 'The Location of Pay Discrimination in the National Hockey League', *Journal of Sport Economics*, Vol. 1, No. 4 (November), pp. 401–11.

Lavoie, M. and Grenier, G. (1992) 'Discrimination and Salary Determination in the National Hockey League, 1977 and 1989 compared', in G.W. Scully (ed.), *Advances in the Economics of Sport*, Vol. 1. Greenwich, CT: JAI Press, pp. 151–75.

Lavoie, M., Grenier, G. and Coulombe, S. (1992) 'Performance Differentials in the National Hockey League: Discrimination Versus Style of Play Theories', *Canadian Public Policy*, Vol. XVIII, No. 4 (December), pp. 461–9.

Lavoie, M. and Leonard W.M. (1992) 'The Search of an Alternative Explanation of Stacking in Baseball: The Uncertainty Hypothesis', *University of Ottawa, Department of Economics Research Paper*, August, p. 20.

Lazaroff, D.E. (1984) 'The Antitrust Implications of Franchise Relocation Restrictions in Professional Sports', *Fordham Law Review*, Vol. 53, No. 2, pp. 157–220.

Lazear, E. (2000) 'The Power of Incentives', *American Economic Review*, Vol. 90, No. 2 (May), pp. 410–14.

Lazear, E.P. and Rosen, S. (1981) 'Rank Order Tournaments as Optimal Labor Contracts', *Journal of Political Economy*, Vol. 89, pp. 841–64.

Lazear, E. and Rosen, S. (1995) 'Rank-Order Tournaments as Optimum Labor Contracts', in O.C. Ashenfelter and K.F. Hallock (eds), *Labor Economics. Vol. 2. Employment, Wages and Education.* Aldershot: Edward Elgar, pp. 422–45.

Le Grand, J. (1982) *The Strategy of Equality; Redistribution and the Social Services.* London: George Allen & Unwin.

Leband, D.N. (1990) 'How the Structure of Competition Influences Performance in Professional Sports: The Case of Tennis and Golf', in B. Goff and R. Tollison (eds), *Sportometrics*, College Station, Texas: A & M University Press.

Leeds, M. and Kowalewski, S. (2001) 'Winner Take All in the NFL: The Effect of the Salary Cap and Free Agency on the Compensation of Skill Position Players', *Journal of Sports Economics*, Vol. 2, No. 3 (August), pp. 213–27.

Leeds, M. and Von Allmen, P. (2002) *The Economics of Sports.* Boston: Addison-Wesley.

Lehn, K. (1982) 'Property Rights, Risk Sharing and Player Disability in Major League Baseball', *Journal of Law and Economics*, Vol. XXV, No. 2, pp. 343–66.

Lehn, K. (1984) 'Information Asymmetries in Baseball's Free Agent Market', *Economic Inquiry*, Vol. 12, No. 1 pp. 37–44.

Leifer, E. (1996) *Making the Majors: The Transformation of Team Sports in America.* Cambridge, MA: Harvard University Press.

Leonard, J. and Prinzinger, J. (1983) 'A Theoretical Exposition of Monopsonistic Exploitation in NCAA Sports', *Atlantic Economic Journal*, Vol. 11, No. 4, p. 80.

Levin, R.C., Mitchell, G.J., Volcker, P.A. and Will, G.F. (2000) *The Report of the Independent Members of the Commissioner's Blue Ribbon Panel on Baseball Economics.* MLB.

Levine, D.I. (1991) 'Cohesiveness, Productivity and Wage Dispersion', *Journal of Economic Behaviour and Organisations*, Vol. 15, pp. 237–54.

Lindsey, G., Paterson, R. and Luger, M. (1995) 'Using Contingent Valuation Surveys in Environmental Planning', *Journal of the American Planning Association*, Vol. 61, No. 2, pp. 252–62.

Long, J. and Caudill, S. (1991) 'The Impact of Participation in Inter-Collegiate Athletics on Income and Graduation', *Review of Economics and Statistics*, Vol. 73, No. 1, pp. 525–31.

Longley, N. (2000) 'The Under-representation of French Canadians on English Canadians NHL Teams: Evidence from 1943 to 1998', *Journal of Sports Economics*, Vol. 1, No. 3 (August), pp. 236–56.

Loy, J.W. and Kenyon, G.S. (eds) (1969) *Sport, Culture and Society.* New York: Macmillan, 1969.

Loy, J.W. and McElvogue, J.F. (1970) 'Racial Segregation in American Sport', *International Review of Sports Sociology*, Vol. 5, pp. 5–24.

Lucifora, C. and Simmons, R. (2003) 'Superstar Effects in Sport: Evidence from Italian Soccer', *Journal of Sports Economics*, Vol. 4, No. 1 (February), pp. 35–55.

Lynch, J.G. and Zax, J.S. (2000) 'The Rewards to Running: Prize Structure and Performance in Professional Road Racing', *Journal of Sports Economics*, Vol. 1, No. 4 (November), pp. 323–40.

MacMillan, J. (1997) 'Rugby Meets Economics', *New Zealand Economics Papers*, Vol. 3, No. 1, pp. 93–114.

Madura, J. (1980) 'Discrimination in Major League Baseball', *Atlantic Economic Journal*, Vol. VIII, No. 2, pp. 70–1.

Madura, J. (1981a) 'A Note on Risk Averse Baseball Contracts', *Atlantic Economic Journal*, Vol. 9, No. 2.

Madura, J. (1981b) 'Collective Bargaining Modifications in the Professional Basketball Industry', *Atlantic Economic Journal*, Vol. IX, No. 3, p. 117.

Madura, J. (1982) 'The Theory of the Firm and Labour Portfolio Choice in Professional Team Sports', *Business Economics*, Vol. 17, No. 4, pp. 11–18.

Malenfant, C. (1982) 'The Economics of Sport in France', *International Social Science Journal*, Vol. 34, No. 2, pp. 233–46.

Maloney, M.T. and McCormick, R.E. (2000) 'The Response of Workers to Wages in Tournaments: Evidence from Foot Races', *Journal of Sports Economics*, Vol. 1, No. 2 (May), pp. 99–123.

Marburger, D.R. (1994) 'Bargaining Power and the Structure of Salaries in Major League Baseball', *Managerial and Decision Economics*, Vol. 15, pp. 433–41.

Marburger, D.R. (1997a) 'Gate Revenue Sharing and Luxury Taxes in Professional Sports', *Contemporary Economic Policy*, Vol. XV (April), pp. 114–23.

Marburger, D.R. (1997b) 'Optimal Ticket Pricing for Performance Goods', *Managerial and Decision Economics*, Vol. 18, No. 5 (August), pp. 375–82.

Marburger, D.R. (2002) 'Property Rights and Unilateral Player Transfers in a Multi-conference Sports League', *Journal of Sports Economics*, Vol. 3, No. 2 (May), pp. 122–32.

Marburger, D.R. (2003) 'Does the Assignment of Property Rights Encourage or Discourage Shirking? Evidence from Major League Baseball', *Journal of Sports Economics*, Vol. 4, No. 1 (February), pp. 19–34.

Mariti, P. and Smiley, R.H. (1983) 'Co-operative Agreements and the Organisation of Industry', *Journal of Industrial Economics*, Vol. 31, No. 4 (June), pp. 437–52.

Markham, J.W. and Teplitz, P.V. (1981) *Baseball Economics and Public Policy*. Lexington, MA: Lexington Books, DC Heath.

Markmann, J.M. (1976) 'A Note on Discrimination by Race in Professional Basketball', *American Economist*, Vol. 20, No. 1, pp. 65–7.

Marris, R. (1964) *The Economic Theory of 'Managerial' Capitalism*. London: Macmillan.

Mason, C.S. (1975) 'Racial Discrimination in Professional Basketball – A Comment', *American Economist*, Vol. 19, No. 2, p. 81.

Mason, C.S. (1997) 'Revenue Sharing and Agency Problems In Professional Team Sport: The Case of the National Football League', *Journal of Sport Management*, Vol. 11, pp. 203–22.

Mason, T. (1980) *Association Football and English Society 1863–1915*. Brighton, UK: The Harvester Press.

Maxcy, J.G., Fort, R.D. and Krautmann, A.C. (2002) 'The Effectiveness of Incentive Mechanisms in Major League Baseball', *Journal of Sports Economics*, Vol. 3, No. 3 (August), pp. 246–55.

McBride, D.K., Worcester, L.L. and Tennyson, S.L. (1999) 'Women's Athletics and the Elimination of Men's Sports Programmes: A Re-evaluation', *The Cato Journal*, Vol. 19, No. 2 (Fall), pp. 323–44.

McCormick, Robert E. and Tinsley, Maurice (1987) 'Athletics versus Academics? Evidence from SAT Scores', *Journal of Political Economy*, Vol. 95, No. 5, pp. 1103–16.

McCormick, R.E. and Tollison, R.R. (1984) 'Crime on Court', *Journal of Political Economy*, Vol. 92, No. 2, pp. 223–35.

McDonald, D. and Reynolds, M. (1994) 'Are Baseball Players Paid their Marginal Products?', *Managerial and Decision Economics*, Vol. 15, No. 2 (September/October), pp. 443–57.

McGarrity, J., Palmer, H.D. and Poitras, M. (1999) 'Consumer Racial Discrimination: A Re-assessment of the Market for Baseball Cards', *Journal of Labor Research*, Vol. XX, No. 2 (Spring), pp. 247–58.

McLean, R.C. and Veall, M.R. (1992) 'Performance and Salary Differentials in the National Hockey League', *Canadian Public Policy*, Vol. XVIII, No. 4 (December), pp. 470–75.

Medoff, M.H. (1975a) 'Racial Discrimination in Professional Baseball', *Atlantic Economic Journal*, Vol. 3 (April), pp. 37–44.

Medoff, M.H. (1975b) 'A Reappraisal of Racial Discrimination against Blacks in Professional Baseball', *The Review of Black Political Economy*, Vol. 5 (Spring), pp. 259–68.

Medoff, M.H. (1976a) 'On Monopsonistic Exploitation in Professional Basketball', *Quarterly Review of Economics and Business*, Vol. 16, No. 2, pp. 113–21.

Medoff, M.H. (1976b) 'Racial Segregation in Baseball: The Economic Hypothesis vs. the Sociological Hypothesis', *Journal of Black Studies*, Vol. 6, No. 4, pp. 393–400.

Medoff, M.H. (1977) 'Positional Segregation and Professional Basketball', *International Review of Sports Sociology*, Vol. 12, No. 1, pp. 49–56.

Meyer, B.S. (1975) 'Racial Discrimination in Professional Basketball – A Comment', *American Economist*, Vol. 19, No. 2, pp. 79–80.

Meyer, B.S. (1982) 'Racial Discrimination in Professional Basketball: Hopefully a Final Comment', *American Economist*, Vol. 26, No. 1, pp. 67–8.

Michener, James A. (1976) *Sports in America*. New York: Random House.

Miller P.A. (2000a) 'A Theoretical and Empirical Comparison of Free Agency and Arbitration Eligible Salaries Negotiated in Major League Baseball', *Southern Economic Journal*, Vol. 67, No. 1, pp. 87–104.

Miller, P.A. (2000b) 'An Analysis of Final Offers Chosen in Baseball's Arbitration System: The Effect of Pre-Arbitration Negotiations on the Choice of Final Offers', *Journal of Sports Economics*, Vol. 1, No. 1 (February), pp. 39–55.

Mixon, Franklin G. (1995) 'Athletics versus Academics? Rejoining the Evidence from SAT Scores', *Education Economics*, Vol. 3, No. 3 (December), pp. 277–84.

Mogull, R.C. (1973) 'Football Salaries and Race: Some Empirical Evidence', *Industrial Relations*, Vol. 12, No. 1, pp. 109–12.

Mogull, R.C. (1974) 'Racial Discrimination in Professional Basketball', *American Economist*, Vol. 18, No. 1, pp. 11–15.

Mogull, R.C. (1975) 'Salary Discrimination in Major League Baseball', *The Review of Black Political Economy*, Vol. 5 (Spring), pp. 269–79.

Mogull, R.C. (1977) 'A Note on Racial Discrimination in Professional Basketball: A Re-evaluation of the Evidence', *American Economist*, Vol. 21, No. 2, pp. 71–5.

Mogull, R.C. (1979) 'Discrimination in Basketball Revisited', *Atlantic Economic Journal*, Vol. 7 (July), pp. 66–74.

Mogull, R.C. (1981) 'Salary Discrimination in Professional Sports', *Atlantic Economic Journal*, Vol. IX, No. 3, pp. 106–11.

Monopolies and Mergers Commission (1999) *British Sky Broadcasting Group plc and Manchester United PLC: A Report on the Proposed Merger*, Cmnd 4305. London: HMSO.

Morris, J.P. (1973) 'In the Wake of the Flood', *Law and Contemporary Problems*, Vol. 38 (Winter–Spring), pp. 85–98.

Morrow, S.H. (1992) 'Putting People on the Balance Sheet: Human Resource Accounting Applied to Professional Football Clubs', *Royal Bank of Scotland Review*, No. 174 (June), pp. 10–19.

Morrow, S.H. (1999) *The New Business of Football: Accountability and Finance in Football*. London: Macmillan.

Muldovanu B and Sela, A. (2001) 'The Optional Allocation of Prizes in Contests', *American Economic Review*, Vol. 91, No. 3 (June), pp. 542–58.

Mulligan J.G. (2001) 'The Pricing of a Round of Golf: The Inefficiency of Membership Fees Revisited', *Journal of Sports Economics*, Vol. 2, No. 4 (November), pp. 328–40.

Mullin, C.J. and Dunn, Lucia F. (2002) 'Using Baseball Card Prices to Measure Star Quality and Monopsony', *Economic Inquiry*, Vol. 40, No. 41 (October), pp. 620–32.

Murray Sperber (2000) *Beer and Circuses: How Big-time College Sports is Crippling Undergraduate Education*. New York: Henry Holt.

Nalbautian, H.R and Schotter, A. (1995) 'Matching and Efficiency in the Baseball Free Agent System: An Experimental Examination', *Journal of Labor Economics*, Vol. 13, No. 1 (January), pp. 1–31.

Nardinelli, C. and Simon, C. (1990) 'Customer Racial Discrimination in the Market for Memorabilia: The Case of Baseball', *Quarterly Journal of Economics*, Vol. 105, pp. 575–96.

Neale, W.C. (1964) 'The Peculiar Economics of Professional Sports', *Quarterly Journal of Economics*, Vol. 78, No. 1, pp. 1–14.
Newson, G. (1984) 'Three Points for a Win: Has it Made any Difference?', *The Mathematical Gazette*, Vol. 68, No. 444, pp. 87–91.
NFLPA (1993) http://www.nflpa.org/Media/main.asp?subPage=CBA+Complete
Nixon, H.L. (1974) 'The Commercial and Organizational Development of Modern Sport', *International Review of Sports Sociology*, Vol. 9, No. 2, pp. 107–37.
Noll, R.G. (ed.) (1974a) *Government and the Sports Business.* Washington, DC: Brookings Institution.
Noll, R.G. (1974b) 'The US Team Sports Industry: An Introduction', in Noll (1974a).
Noll, R.G. (1974c) 'Attendance, Prices and Profits in Professional Sports', in Noll (1974a).
Noll, R.G. (1974d) 'Attendance and Price Setting', in Noll (1974a).
Noll, R.G. (1982) 'Major League Sports', in W. Adams, (ed.), *The Structure of American Industry* (6th edn). London: Macmillan.
Noll, Roger (1999) 'The Business of College Sports and the High Cost of Winning', *Miliken Institute Review* (third quarter), pp. 24–37.
Noll, R.G. (2002) 'The Economics of Promotion and Relegation in Sports Leagues, The Case of English Football', *Journal of Sports Economics*, Vol. 3, No. 2 (May), pp. 169–203
Noll, R.G. and Zimbalist, A. (eds) (1997) *Sports, Jobs and Taxes: The Economic Impact of Sports Teams and Stadiums.* Washington, DC: Brookings Institution.
Oettinger, G.S. (1999) 'An Empirical Analysis of the Daily Labor Supply of Stadium Vendors', *Journal of Political Economy*, Vol. 107, No. 2 (April), pp. 360–92.
Oettinger, G.S. (2001) 'Do Piece Rates Influence Effort Choices? Evidence from Stadium Vendors', *Economics Letters*, Vol. 73, No. 1 (October), pp. 117–23.
Ohkusa, Y. (1999) 'Additional Evidence for the Career Concern Hypothesis with Uncertainty of the Retirement Period – The Case of Professional Baseball Players in Japan', *Applied Economics*, Vol. 31, No. 11 (November), pp. 1481–8.
Ohkusa, Y. (2001) 'An Empirical Examination of the Quit Behavior of the Professional Baseball Players in Japan', *Journal of Sports Economics*, Vol. 2, No. 1 (February), pp. 80–8.
Okner, B.A. (1974) 'Subsidies of Stadiums and Arenas', in Noll (1974a).
Olson, L.A. and Schwab, A. (2000) 'The Performance Effects of Human Resource Practices: The Case of Inter-Club Networks in Professional Baseball, 1919–1940', *Industrial Relations*, Vol. 39, No. 4 (October), pp. 553–77.
Oorlog, D.R. (1995) 'Marginal Revenue and Labour Strife in Major League Baseball', *Journal of Labour Research*, Vol. XVI.
O'Roark, J.B. (2001) 'Capital Structure and Team Performance in Professional Baseball', *Journal of Sports Economics*, Vol. 2, No. 2 (May), pp. 168–80.
Orzag, J.M. (1994) 'A New Look at Incentive Effects and Golf Tournaments', *Economics Letters*, Vol. 46, No. 1, pp. 77–88.
Osbourne, E. (2001) 'Efficient Markets? Don't Bet on It', *Journal of Sports Economics*, Vol. 2, No. 1 (February), pp. 50–61.
Pacey, P.L. (1985) 'The Courts and College Football: New Playing Rules off the Field?', *American Journal of Economics and Sociology*, Vol. 44, No. 2, pp. 145–54.
Palacios-Huerta, I. (2003) 'Professionals Play Minimax', *Review of Economic Studies*, Vol. 70, pp. 395–415.
Pascal, A.H. (ed.) (1972a) *Racial Discrimination in Economic Life.* Lexington, MA: DC Heath.

Pascal, A.H. and Rapping, L.A. (1972b) 'The Economics of Racial Discrimination', in A.H. Pascal, (1972a).

Paul, R.J. and Weinbach, A.P. (2002) 'Market Effriciency and a Profitable Betting Rate: Evidence from Totals in Professional Football', *Journal of Sports Economics*, Vol. 3, No. 3 (August), pp. 256–83.

Peel, D.A. and Thomas, D.A. (1988) 'Outcome Uncertainty and the Demand for Football: An Analysis of Match Attendance in the English Football League', *Scottish Journal of Political Economy*, Vol. 35, pp. 242–9.

Peel, D.A. and Thomas, D.A. (1992) 'The Demand for Football: Some Evidence on Outcome Uncertainty', *Empirical Economics*, Vol. 17, No. 2, pp. 323–31.

Peel, D.A. and Thomas, D.A. (1996) 'Attendance Demand: An Investigation of Repeat Fixtures', *Applied Economics Letters*, Vol. 3 (June), pp. 391–4.

Peel, D.A and Thomas D.A. (1997) 'Handicaps, Outcome Uncertainity and Attendance Demand', *Applied Economics Letters*, Vol. 4, pp. 567–70.

Phillips, J.S. and Much, P.J. (2000) 'Sports Teams and the Stock Market', in Gruen *et al.* (2000), pp. 18–25.

Porter, Phillip (1999) 'Mega-Sports Events as Muncipal Investments: A Critique of Impact Analysis', in John Fizel, Elizabeth Gustafson and Laurence Hadley (eds), *Sports Economics: Current Research.* Westport, CT: Praeger.

Porter, P.K. and Scully, G.W. (1982) 'Measuring Managerial Efficiency: The Case of Baseball', *Southern Economic Journal*, Vol. 48, No. 3, pp. 642–50.

Porter, P.K. and Scully, G.W. (1996) 'The Distribution of Earnings and the Rules of the Game', *Southern Economic Journal*, Vol. 63, No. 1 (July), pp. 149–62.

Preston, I. and Szymanski, S. (2000) 'Racial Discrimination in English Football', *Scottish Journal of Political Economy*, Vol. 47, No. 4 (September), pp. 342–63.

Preuss, H. (2000) *Economics of the Olympic Games.* Sydney: Walla Walla Press.

Price, B. and Rao, A.G. (1976) 'Alternative Rules for Drafting in Professional Sports', in R.E. Machol, S.P. Ladany, and D.G. Morrison (eds), *Management Science in Sports.* Amsterdam: North-Holland.

Prisinzano, R. (2000) 'Investigating the Market Hypothesis: The Case of Major League Baseball', *Journal of Sports Economics*, Vol. 1, No. 3 (August), pp. 277–98.

Putnam, D.T. (1999) *Controversies of the Sports World.* Westport, CT: Greenwood Press.

Putsis Jr, W.P. and Sen, S.K. (2000) 'Should NFL Blackouts be Banned?', *Applied Economics*, Vol. 32, pp. 1495–509.

Quirk, J. (1973) 'An Economic Analysis of Team Movements in Professional Sports', *Law and Contemporary Problems*, Vol. 38 (Winter–Spring), pp. 42–66.

Quirk, J. and El Hodiri, M. (1974) 'The Economic Theory of a Professional League', in Noll (1974a).

Quirk, J. and Fort, R.D. (1992) *Pay Dirt, The Business of Professional Team Sports.* Princeton, NJ: Princeton University Press.

Quirk, J. and Fort, R.D. (1999) *Hardball: The Abuse of Power in Pro-Team Sports.* Princeton, NJ: Princeton University Press.

Raimondo, H.J. (1983) 'Free Agents Impact on the Labor Market for Basketball Players', *Journal of Labour Research*, Vol. 4, No. 2, pp. 183–93.

Reilly, B. and Watt, R. (1995) 'English League Transfer Prices: Is There a Racial Dimension?', *Applied Economics Letters*, Vol. 2, No. 7 (July), pp. 220–2.

Reisner, C.L. (1978) 'Tackling Intercollegiate Athletics: An Antitrust Analysis', *Yale Law Journal*, Vol. 88, pp. 655–79.

Restrictive Practices Court (1999) *Judgment of the Court on the Agreement Relating to the Supply of Services Facilitating the Broadcasting on Television of Premier League Football Matches and the Supply of Services Consisting in the Broadcasting on Television of Such Matches*, July. London, HMSO.

Richards, D.G. and Guell, R.C. (1998) 'Baseball Success and Structure of Salaries', *Applied Economics Letters*, Vol. 5, No. 5 (May), pp. 291–6.

Richmond, B.M. (1975) 'Sportsgarden: A Simulation Approach for Planning a Multi-activity Recreational Facility', in S.P. Ladany (ed.), *Management Science Applications to Leisure-Time Operations*. Amsterdam: North-Holland.

Rishe P.J. (2001) 'Differing Rates of Return to Performance: A Comparison of the PGA and Senior Golf Tours', *Journal of Sports Economics*, Vol. 2, No. 3 (August), pp. 285–96.

Rivett, P. (1975) 'The Structure of League Football', *Operational Research Quarterly*, Vol. 26, No. 4, pp. 801–12.

Rockwood, C.E. and Asher, E. (1976) 'Racial Discrimination in Professional Basketball Revisited', *American Economist*, Vol. 20, No. 1, pp. 59–64.

Rosen, S. (1981) 'The Economics of Superstars', *American Economic Review*, Vol. 71 (December), pp. 845–98.

Rosen, S. (1986) 'Prizes and Incentives in Elimination Tournaments', *American Economic Review*, Vol. 76, No. 4 (September), pp. 701–15.

Rosen, S. and Sanderson, A. (2001) 'Labour Markets in Professional Sports', *Economic Journal*, Vol. III, No. 469, pp. F47–F68.

Rosentraub, Mark S. (1996) 'Does the Emperor have new Clothes?', *Journal of Urban Affairs*, Vol. 18, No. 1, pp. 23–31.

Rosentraub, M.S. (1997a) *Major League Losers: The Real Costs of Sports and Who's Paying for it*. New York: Basic Books.

Rosentraub, M.S. (1997b) 'Stadiums and Urban Space', in R. Noll and A. Zimbalist. (eds), *Cities, Sports, and Taxes*. Washington, DC: The Brookings Institution, pp. 178–207.

Rosentraub, M.S. (1999a) 'Are Public Policies Needed to Level the Playing Field between Cities and Teams?', *Journal of Urban Affairs*, Vol. 21, No. 4, pp. 377–95.

Rosentraub, M.S. (1999b) *Major League Losers: The Real Cost of Sports and Who's Paying for It*, (2nd edn). New York: Basic Books.

Rosentraub, M.S. (2000a) 'City–County Consolidation and the Rebuilding of Image: The Fiscal Lessons from Indianapolis's Unigov Program', *State and Local Government Review*, Vol. 32, No. 3, pp. 180–91.

Rosentraub, M.S. (2000b) 'Sports Facilities, Redevelopment and the Centrality of Downtown Areas: Observations and Lessons from Experiences in a Rustbelt and Sunbelt City', *Marquette Sports Law Journal*, Vol. 10, No. 2, pp. 219–35.

Rosentraub, Mark S. (2001) *Major League Losers: The Real Cost of Sports and Who's Paying for it* (rev. edn). New York: Basic Books.

Rosentraub, Mark S. (2003) 'Private Control of a Civic Asset: The Winners and Losers from North America's Experience with Four Cartels for Professional Team Sports', in T. Slack (ed.), *The Commercialisation of Sport*. London: Frank Cass.

Rosentraub, M.S. and Nunn, S.R. (1978) 'Suburban City Investment in Professional Sports', *American Behavioral Scientist*, Vol. 21, No. 3, pp. 393–414.

Rosentraub, M.S. and Swindell, D. (2002) 'Negotiating Games: Cities, Sports and the Winner's Curse', *Journal of Sport Management*, Vol. 16, No. 1 (January), pp. 18–35.

Ross, G.N. (1975) 'The Determination of Bonuses in Professional Sports', *American Economist*, Vol. 19, No. 2, pp. 43–6.

Ross, S. and Lucke, R. (1997) 'Why Highly Paid Athletes Deserve More Anti-trust Protection than Unionised Factory Workers', *Antitrust Bulletin*, Vol. 42, No. 3, pp. 641–79.

Rottenberg, S. (1956) 'The Baseball Player's Labor Market', *Journal of Political Economy*, Vol. 64, No. 3, pp. 242–58.

Rottenberg, S. (2000) 'Resource Allocation and Income Distribution in Professional Team Sports', *Journal of Sports Economics*, Vol. 1, No. 1 (February), pp. 11–20.

Ruddock, L. (1979) 'The Market for Professional Footballers: An Economic Analysis', *Economics*, Vol. 15, No. 3, pp. 70–2.

Ruggerio, J., Hadley, L. and Knowles, S. (1997) 'A Note on the Pythagorean Theorem of Baseball Production', *Managerial and Decision Economics*, Vol. 18, No. 4 (June), pp. 335–42.

Sack, A.L. and Staurowsky, E.J. (1998) *College Athletes for Hire: The Education and Legacy of the NCAA's and Amateur Myth.* Westport, CT: Praeger.

Sahota, G. and Sahota, C. (1984) 'A Theory of Human Investment in Physical Skills and its Application to Achievement in Tennis', *Southern Economic Journal*, Vol. 51, pp. 642–64.

Sanderson, A. (2002) 'The Many Dimensions of Competitive Balance', *Journal of Sports Economics*, Vol. 3, No. 2 (May), pp. 204–28.

Sanderson, A. and Siegfried, J.J. (1997) 'The Implications of Athletic Freedom to Contract: Lessons from North America', *Economic Affairs*, Vol. 17, No. 3 (September), pp. 7–12.

Sandy, Robert and Sloane, Peter (2003) 'Why Do US Colleges Have Sports Programs? Intercollegiate Sports as Enrollment Management', in John Fizel and Rodney Fort (eds), *Economics of Collegiate Sports.* Westport, CT: Greenwood Press.

Sassen, S. (1994) *Cities in a World Economy*, Thousand Oaks, CA: Pine Forge Press.

Schaffer, W.A. and Davidson, L.S. (1975) 'The Economic Impact of Professional Football on Atlanta', in S.P. Ladany (ed.), *Management Science Applications to Leisure-Time Operations.* Amsterdam: North-Holland.

Schmidt, M.B. and Berri, D.J. (2001) 'Competitive Balance and Attendance: The Case of Major League Baseball', *Journal of Sports Economics*, Vol. 2, No. 2 (May), pp. 145–67.

Schmidt, M.B. and Berri, D.J. (2002) 'The Impact of the 1981 and 1994–1995 Strikes on Major League Baseball Attendance; A Time Series Analysis', *Applied Economics*, Vol. 34, pp. 471–8.

Schofield, J.A. (1982) 'The Development of First-class Cricket in England: An Economic Analysis', *Journal of Industrial Economics*, Vol. XXX, No. 4, pp. 337–60.

Schofield, J.A. (1983a) 'The Demand for Cricket: The Case of John Player League', *Applied Economics*, Vol. 15, No. 3, pp. 283–96.

Schofield, J.A. (1983b) 'Performance and Attendance at Professional Team Sports', *Journal of Sport Behaviour*, Vol. 6, No. 4, pp. 196–206.

Schulman J.L. and Bowen, W.G. (2001) *The Game of Life; College Sports and Educational Values.* Princeton, NJ, and Oxford, UK: Princeton University Press.

Schwartz, B. and Barsky, S.F. (1977) 'Home Advantage', *Social Forces*, Vol. 55, No. 3, pp. 641–61.

Scoggins, J.R. (1993) 'Shirking or Stochastic Productivity in Major League Baseball: A Comment, and Reply by A.C. Krautman', *Southern Economic Journal*, Vol. 60, No. 1 (July), pp. 239–43.

Scotchmer, S. (1985) 'Two Tier Pricing of Shared Facilities in a Free Entry Equilibrium', *Rand Journal of Economics*, Vol. 16, No. 4, pp. 456–72.

Scott, F.A. Jr, Long, J.E. and Somppi, K. (1983) 'Free Agents, Owner Incentives and the NFL Players Association', *Journal of Labor Research*, Vol. 4, No. 3, pp. 257–64.

Scoville, J.G. (1974) 'Labor Relations in Sports', in Noll (1974a).

Scoville, J.G. (1976) 'Wage Determination and the Development of Collective Bargaining in Baseball', in *Proceedings of the 29th Annual Meeting of the Industrial Relations Association*, pp. 317–23.

Scully, G.W. (1973) 'Economic Discrimination in Professional Sports', *Law and Contemporary Problems*, Vol. 38 (Winter-Spring), pp. 67–84.

Scully, G.W. (1974a) 'Pay and Performance in Major League Baseball', *American Economic Review*, Vol. 64, No. 6, pp. 915–30.

Scully, G.W. (1974b) 'Discrimination: The Case of Baseball', in Noll (1974a).

Scully, G.W. (1978) 'Binding Salary Arbitration in Major League Baseball', *American Behavioral Scientist*, Vol. 21, No. 3, pp. 431–50.

Scully, G.W. (1989) *The Business of Major League Baseball.* Chicago, IL: University of Chicago Press.

Scully, G.W. (ed.) (1993/5) *Advances in the Economics of Sport*, Westport, CT: JAI Press; Vol. I, 1993; Vol. II, 1995.

Scully, G.W. (1994) 'Managerial Efficiency and Survivability in Professional Team Sports', *Managerial and Decision Economics*, Vol. 15, pp. 403–11.

Scully, G.W. (1995) *The Market Structure of Sports*, Chicago, IL: University of Chicago Press.

Scully, G.W. (2002) 'The Distribution of Performance and Earnings in a Prize Economy', *Journal of Sports Economics*, Vol. 3, No. 3 (August), pp. 235–45.

Seers, D. (1969). 'The Meaning of Development', *International Development Review*, Vol. 11, pp. 2–6.

Seitz, P. (1976) 'Are Professional Team Sports Sports or Business? Or How Much Would You Pay for Catfish Hunter?', *IRRA 29th Annual Proceedings.*

Sheehan, R. (1996) *Keeping Score: The Economics of Big Time Sports.* South Bend, Indiana: Diamond Communications.

Shmanske, S. (1992) 'Human Capital Formation in Professional Sports: Evidence from the PGA Tour', *Atlantic Economic Journal*, Vol. 20, No. 3 (September), pp. 66–80.

Shmanske, S. (2000) 'Gender, Skill and Earnings in Professional Golf', *Journal of Sports Economics*, Vol. 1, No. 4 (November), pp. 385–400.

Shoval, N. (2002) 'A New Phase in the Competition for Olympic Gold: The London and New York Bids for the 2002 Games', *Journal of Urban Affairs*, Vol. 24, No. 5, pp. 583–600.

Shropshire, Kenneth L. (1995) *The Sports Franchise Game: Cities in Pursuit of Sports Franchises Events, Stadiums, and Arenas.* Philadelphia, PA: The University of Pennsylvania Press.

Shulman, James L. and Bowen, William G. (2001) *The Game of Life: College Sports and Educational Values.* Princeton, NJ: Princeton University Press.

Siegfried, J.T. and Eisenberg, J.D. (1980) 'The Demand for Minor League Baseball', *Atlantic Economic Journal*, Vol. VIII, No. 2, pp. 59–69.

Siegfried, J.T. and Hinshaw, C.E. (1979) 'The Effects of Lifting TV Blackouts on Professional Football No-shows', *Journal of Economics and Business*, Vol. 32, No. 1, pp. 1–13.

Siegfried, J.J. and Peterson, T. (2000) 'Who is Sitting in the Stands? The Income Levels of Sports Fans', in W. Kern (ed.), *The Economics of Sports: Winners and Losers.* Kalamazoo: Upjohn Institute.

Siegfried, J. and Zimbalist, A. (2000) 'The Economics of Sports Facilities and their Communities', *Journal of Economic Perspectives*, Vol. 14, No. 3 (Summer), pp. 95–114.

Siegfried, J. and Zimbalist, A. (2002) 'A Note on Local Economic Impact of Sports Expenditures', *Journal of Sports Economics*, Vol. 3, No. 4 (November), pp. 361–6.

Sigelman, L. and Brookheimer, S. (1983) 'Monetary Contributions to Big-time College Athletic Progress', *Social Science Quarterly*, Vol. 64, No. 2, pp. 347–59.

Simmons, R. (1996) 'The Demand for English League Football: A Club Level Analysis', *Applied Economics*, Vol. 28, No. 2, pp. 139–55.

Singell, L.D. Jr (1991) 'Baseball-specific Human Capital: Why Good But Not Great Players Are More Likely to Coach in the Major Leagues', *Southern Economic Journal*, Vol. 58, No. 1 (July) pp. 77–86.

Singell, L.D. Jr (1993) 'Managers, Specific Human Capital and Firm Productivity in Major League Baseball', *Atlantic Economic Journal*, Vol. 21, No. 3 (September) pp. 47–59.

Sloane, A.A. (1977) 'Collective Bargaining in Major League Baseball: A New Ball Game and its Genesis', *Labor Law Journal*, Vol. 28, pp. 200–10.

Sloane, P.J. (1969) 'The Labour Market in Professional Football', *British Journal of Industrial Relations*, Vol. 7, No. 2, pp. 181–99.

Sloane, P.J. (1971) 'The Economics of Professional Football: The Football Club as a Utility Maximiser', *Scottish Journal of Political Economy*, Vol. 18, No. 2 (June), pp. 121–46.

Sloane, P.J. (1976a) 'Sporting Equality: Labour Market versus Product Market Control – A Comment', *Journal of Industrial Relations*, Vol. 18, No. 1, pp. 79–84.

Sloane, P.J. (1976b) 'Restriction of Competition in Professional Team Sports', *Bulletin of Economic Research*, Vol. 28, No. 1, pp. 3–22.

Sloane, P.J. (1980) *Sport in the Market?*, Hobart Paper No. 85. London: Institute of Economic Affairs.

Sloane, P.J. (1985) 'Discrimination in the Labour Market', in D. Carline *et al.*, *Labour Economics*, Harlow, UK: Longman.

Sloane, P.J. (ed.) (1997) 'The Economics of Sport: A Symposium', *Economic Affairs*, Vol. 17, No. 3 (September), pp. 2–41.

Sloane, P.J. (2002) 'The Regulation of Professional Team Sports', in C.P. Barros, M. Ibrahimo and S. Szymanski (eds), *Transatlantic Sport; The Comparative Economics of North American and European Sports*. Cheltenham, UK, and Northampton, MA: Edward Elgar.

Smart, R.A. and Goddard, J.A. (1991) 'The Determinants of Standing and Seated Football Attendances: Evidence from Three Scottish League Clubs', *Fraser of Allander Institute Quarterly Economic Commentary*, Vol. 16, No. 4 (June), pp. 61–4.

Smith, M. (1994) 'Fortunes of Football: Profit and Loss 1989–1993', *Scottish Business Insider*, August.

Sobel, L.S. (1977) *Professional Sports and the Law*. New York: Law-Arts.

Sommers, P.M. (ed.) (1992) *Diamonds Are Forever: The Business of Baseball*. Washington, DC: The Brookings Institution.

Sommers, P.M. and Quinton, N. (1982) 'Pay and Performance in Major League Baseball: The Case of the First Family of Free Agents', *Journal of Human Resources*, Vol. 17, No. 3, pp. 426–36.

Speight, A. and Thomas, D. (1994) 'Arbitration Decisions in the Transfer Market', *Aberystwyth Economic Research Papers*, No. 94–01 (April).

Speight, A. and Thomas, D. (1996) 'The Football League Appeals Committee: A Case Study in Arbitration', *Aberystwyth Economics Research Papers*, No. 96–14, p. 28.

Speight, A. and Thomas, D. (1997a) 'Football League Transfers: A Comparison of Negotiated Fees with Arbitration Settlements', *Applied Economics Letters*, Vol. 4, No. 1 (January), pp. 41–4.

Speight, A. and Thomas, D. (1997b) 'Arbitration Decision-Making in the Transfer Market: An Empirical Analysis', *Scottish Journal of Political Economy*, Vol. 44, No. 2 (May), pp. 198–215.

Spurr, S.S. (2000) 'The Baseball Draft: A Study of the Ability to Find Talent', *Journal of Sports Economics*, Vol. 1, No. 1 (February), pp. 66–85.

Spurr, S.J. and Barber, W. (1994) 'The Effect of Performance on a Worker's Career: Evidence from Minor League Baseball', *Industrial and Labor Relations Review*, Vol. 47, No. 4 (July), pp. 692–708.

Squires D. (1989), editor, *Unequal Partnerships: The Political Economy of Urban Redevelopment in Postwar America*, New Brunswick, New Jersey, Rutgers University Press.

Staudohar, P.D. (1989) *The Sports Industry and Collective Bargaining* (2nd edn). Ithaca, NY: Cornell University Press.

Staudohar, P.D. (1996) *Playing for Dollars: Labor Relations and the Sports Business.* Ithaca, NY: ILR Press.

Staudohar, P.D. and Mangan, J.D. (1991) *The Business of Professional Sports.* Urbana and Chicago, IL: University of Illinois Press.

Stewart, G. (1986) 'The Retain and Transfer System: An Alternative Approach', *Managerial Finance*, Vol. 12, pp. 25–9.

Stewart, K.G. *et al.* (1992) 'On Violence in Professional Team Sports as the Endogenous Result of Profit Maximisation', *Atlantic Economic Journal*, Vol. 20, No. 4 (December).

Stone, E.W. and Warren, R.S. Jr (1999) 'Customer Discrimination in Professional Basketball: Evidence from the Trading Card Market', *Applied Economics*, Vol. 31, No. 6 (June), pp. 679–86.

Stuart, J. (2000) 'Swinging a London Deal', *Street and Smith's Sports Business Journal*, (September 18–24), p. 47.

Suen, W. (1992) *Men, Money and Medals: An Econometric Analysis of the Olympic Games.* Hong Kong: University of Hong Kong, Department of Economics, September, p. 7.

Surdam, D.G. (2002) 'The American "Not so-Socialist" League in the Post-War Era: The Limitations of Gate Sharing in Reducing Revenue Disparity in Baseball', *Journal of Sports Economics*, Vol. 3, No. 3 (August), pp. 268–90.

Sutter, D. and Winkler, S. (2003) 'NCAA Scholarship Limits and Competitive Balance in College Football', *Journal of Sports Economics*, Vol. 4, No. 1 (February), pp. 3–18.

Swindell D. and Rosentraub, M.S. (1998) 'Who Benefits From the Presence of Professional Sports Teams? The Implication for Public Funding of Stadiums and Arenas', *Public Administration Review* Vol. 58, pp. 11–20.

Swindell, David and Rosentraub, Mark S. (2002) 'Negotiating Games: Cities, Sports, and the Winner's Curse', *Journal of Sport Management*, Vol. 16, No. 1 (January) pp. 18–35.

Swofford, James L. (1999) 'Arbitrage, Speculation, and Public Policy toward Ticket Scalping', *Public Finance Review*, Vol. 27, No. 5 (September), pp. 531–40.

Szymanski, S. (1997) 'Discrimination in the English Soccer Leagues: A Market Test', The Management School, Imperial College Discussion Paper (March), p. 30.

Szymanski, S. (2000) 'A Market Test for Discrimination in the English Professional Soccer Leagues', *Journal of Political Economy*, Vol. 108, No. 3 (June), pp. 590–603.

Szymanski, S. (2001) 'Income Inequality, Competitive Balance and Attractiveness of Team Sports: Some Evidence and a Natural Experiment from English Soccer', *Economic Journal*, Vol. III, No. 469 (February), pp. F4–F26.

Szymanski, S. (2001) 'The Economic Design of Sporting Contests: A Review', unpublished manuscript, Imperial College Management School, London, October.

Szymanski, S. and Hall, S. (2003) 'Making money out of Football; unpublished manuscript, The Business School, Imperial College, London.

Szymanski, S. and Kuypers, T. (1999) *Winners and Losers: The Business Strategy of Football*. London: Viking.

Szymanski, S. and Smith, R. (1997) 'The English Football Industry: Profit, Performance and Industrial Structure', *International Review of Applied Economics*, Vol. 11, No. 1, pp. 135–53.

Taboo, J.E. (2000) 'Why Black Athletes Dominate Sports and Why We are Afraid to Talk about It', *Public Affairs*, New York.

Taylor, B. and Trogden, J. (2002) 'Losing to Win: Tournament Incentives in the National Basketball Association', *Journal of Labor Economics*, Vol. 20, No. 1, pp. 23–41.

Tenorio, R. (2000) 'The Economics of Professional Boxing Contracts', *Journal of Sports Economics*, Vol. 1, No. 4 (November), pp. 363–84.

Thiel, S.E. (1993) 'Two Cheers for Touts', *Scottish Journal of Political Economy*, Vol. 40, No. 4 (November), pp. 447–55.

Thomas, D. (1996) 'Recent Developments in Sporting Labour Markets: Free Agency and New Slavery?', *Review of Policy Issues*, Vol. 2, No. 2, pp. 19–28.

Thomas, S.M. and Jolson, M.A. (1979) 'Components of the Demand for Major League Baseball, *University of Michigan Business Review*, Vol. 31, No. 3, pp. 1–6.

Topkins, J.H. (1949) 'Monopoly in Professional Sports', *Yale Law Journal*, Vol. 58, No. 5, pp. 691–712.

Trussell, P. (1976) 'Human Resource Accounting and the Football League', *Management Finance*, Vol. 2, No. 3, pp. 256–69.

Tucker III, Irvin B. and Amato, Louis (1993) 'Does Big Time Success in Football or Basketball Affect SAT Scores?', *Economics of Education Review*, Vol. 12, No. 2, pp. 177–81.

US Bureau of Economic Analysis, *Regional Multipliers: A User Handbook for the Regional Input-Output Modeling System (RIMSII)* Washington, DC: US Government Printing Office. Also available at: http://www.bea.gove/bea/regional/rims2/maintext.htm.

US House of Representatives (1966) *Professional Football League Merger*, Subcommittee Number 5 of the Committee of the Judiciary, 1966.

U.S. v. *Brown University et al.* (1992) 805 *Federal Supplement* 288, Sept. 2, 5 *Federal Reporter*, third series, 658 (3rd Circuit, 1993).

Utt, J. and Fort, R. (2002) 'Pitfalls to Measuring Competitive Balance with Gini Coefficients', *Journal of Sports Economics*, Vol. 3, No. 4 (November), pp. 367–73.

Vamplew, W. (1980) 'Playing for Pay: the Earnings of Professional Sportsmen in England 1870–1914', in R.L. Cashman and M. McKenna (eds), *Sport: Money, Morality and the Media*. Sydney: University of NSW Press.

Vamplew, W. (1982) 'The Economics of the Sports Industry', *Economic History Review*, Vol. 35, No. 4, pp. 549–67.

Vining, B.R. and Kerrigan, J.F. (1978) 'An Application of the Lexis Ratio to the Detection of Racial Quotas in Professional Sports: A Note', *American Economist*, Vol. 22, No. 2, pp. 71–5.

Von Allmen, P. (2001) 'Is the Reward System in NASCAR Efficient?', *Journal of Sports Economics*, Vol. 2, No. 1 (February) pp. 62–79.

Vrooman, J. (1995) 'A General Theory of Professional Sports Leagues', *Southern Economic Journal*, Vol. 61, No. 4 (April), pp. 971–90.

Vrooman, J. (1996) 'The Baseball Player's Labor Market Reconsidered', *Southern Economic Journal*, Vol. 63, No. 2 (October), pp. 339–60.

Vrooman, J. (1997) 'A Unified Theory of Capital and Labour Markets in Major League Baseball', *Southern Economic Journal*, Vol. 63, No. 3 (January), pp. 594–619.

Vrooman, J. (1998) 'Franchise Free Agency in Professional Sports Leagues', *Southern Economic Journal*, Vol. 64, No. 3 (July), pp. 191–210.

Vrooman, J. (2000) 'The Economics of American Sports Leagues', *Scottish Journal of Political Economy*, Vol. 47, No. 4 (September), pp. 364–98.

Walker, B. (1986) 'The Demand for Professional League Football and the Success of Football Teams: Some City Size Effects', *Urban Studies*, Vol. 23, pp. 209–20.

Walsh, W.D. (1992) 'The Entry Problem of Francophones in the National Hockey League: A Systematic Interpretation', *Canadian Public Policy*, Vol. XVIII, No. 4 (December), pp. 443–60.

Weiler, P.C. (2002) *Levelling the Playing Field; How the Law can Make Sport Better*. Cambridge, MA: Harvard University Press.

Weiner, J. (2000) *Stadium Games: 50 Years of Big League Greed and Bush Leagues Boondoggles*. Minneapolis: University of Minnesota Press.

Weistart, J.C. (1984) 'League Control of Market Opportunities: A Perspective on Competition and Co-operation in the Sports Industry', *Duke Law Journal*, Vol. 6, pp. 1013–70.

Welki, A. and Zlatoper, T. (1994) 'U.S. Professional Football; The Demand for Game-Day Attendance in 1991', *Managerial and Decision Economics*, Vol. 15, pp. 489–95.

Whitney, J.D. (1993) 'Bidding Till Bankrupt: Destructive Competition in Professional Team Sports', *Economic Inquiry*, Vol. XXXI, No. 1 (January), pp. 110–15.

Whitney, J.P. (1988) 'Winning Games Versus Winning Championships: The Economics of Fan Interest and Team Performance', *Economic Inquiry*, Vol. 26, No. 4, (October), pp. 703–24.

Wiedemann, Thomas (1992) *Emperors and Gladiators*. London and New York: Routledge.

Williams, Andrew T. (1994) 'Do Anti-Ticket Scalping Laws Make a Difference?' *Managerial and Decision Economics*, Vol. 15, pp. 503–9.

Williamson, O.E. (1963) 'Managerial Discretion and Business Behavior', *American Economic Review*, Vol. 53, pp. 1032–57.

Wilson, John (1994) *Playing by the Rules*. Detroit, MI: Wayne State University Press.

Wilson, P. and Sim, B. (1995) 'The Demand for Semi-Pro League Football on Malaysia 1989–91: A Panel Data Approach', *Applied Economics*, Vol. 27, pp. 131–8.

Wiseman, N.C. (1977) 'The Economics of Football', *Lloyds Bank Review*, Vol. 123, pp. 29–43.

Wittman, D. (1982) 'Efficient Rules in Highway Safety and Sports Activity', *American Economic Review*, Vol. 72, No. 1, pp. 78–90.

Wood, J. (1988) 'Pendulum Arbitration: A Modest Experiment', *Industrial Relations Journal*, Vol. 19, pp. 244–7.
Woodland, B.M. and Woodland, L.M. (2000) 'Testing Contrarian Strategies in the National Football League', *Journal of Sports Economics*, Vol. 1, No. 2 (May), pp. 187–93.
Woodland, L. and Woodland, B. (1994) Market Efficiency and the Favourite-Longshot Bias: The Baseball Betting Market, *Journal of Finance*, Vol. 49, pp. 269–79.
Woodland, L. and Woodland, B. (2001) 'Market Efficiency and Profitable Wagering in the National Hockey League; Can Betting Score in Longshots?', *Southern Economic Journal*, Vol. 67, pp. 983–95.
Wunderli, J (1995) 'Squeeze Play: the Game of Owners, Cities, Leagues and Congress', *Marquette Sport Law Review*, Vol. 5, No. 1, pp. 83–121.
Yilmaz, M.R., Chatterjee, S. and Habibullah, M. (2001) 'Improvement by Spreading the Wealth: The Case of Home Runs in Major League Baseball', *Journal of Sports Economics*, Vol. 2, No. 2 (May), pp. 181–93.
Zak, T.A., Huang, C.J. and Siegfried, J.J. (1979) 'Production Efficiency: The Case of Professional Basketball', *Journal of Business*, Vol. 52, No. 3, pp. 379–92.
Zech, C.E. (1981) 'An Empirical Estimation of a Production Function: The Case of Major League Baseball', *American Economist*, Vol. 25, No. 2, pp. 19–23.
Zhang, J.J. and Smith, S.W. (1997) 'Impact of Broadcasting on the Attendance at Professional Basketball Games', *Sports Marketing Quarterly*, Vol. 6, No. 1, pp. 23–9.
Zimbalist, A. (1992) *Baseball and Billions*. New York: Basic Books.
Zimbalist, A. (1999) *Unpaid Professionals: Commercialism and Conflict in Big Time College Sports*. Princeton, NJ: Princeton University Press.
Zimbalist, A.S. (2002) 'Competitive Balance in Sport Leagues; An Introduction', *Journal of Sport Economics*, Vol. 3, No. 2 (May), pp. 111–21.
Zimmerman, D. (1998) *Public Subsidy of Stadiums*, National Tax Association Forum, The Newsletter of the National Tax Association, December. Columbus, Ohio.
Zuber, R.A., Gandar, J.M. and Bowers, B.D. (1985) 'Beating the Spread: Testing the Efficiency of the Gambling Market for National Football League Games', *Journal of Political Economy*, Vol. 93, No. 4, pp. 800–6.

Index